The Negro Southern League

The Negro Southern League

A Baseball History, 1920–1951

William J. Plott

McFarland & Company, Inc., Publishers
Jefferson, North Carolina

LIBRARY OF CONGRESS CATALOGUING-IN-PUBLICATION DATA

The Negro southern league : a baseball history, 1920–1951 / William J. Plott.
p. cm.
Includes bibliographical references and index.

ISBN 978-0-7864-7544-5 (softcover : acid free paper) ∞
ISBN 978-1-4766-1739-8 (ebook)

1. Negro leagues—History.   2. Baseball—United States—History.   I. Title.
GV875.N35P56 2015   796.357'640973—dc23   2015008753

BRITISH LIBRARY CATALOGUING DATA ARE AVAILABLE

© 2015 William J. Plott. All rights reserved

*No part of this book may be reproduced or transmitted in any form
or by any means, electronic or mechanical, including photocopying
or recording, or by any information storage and retrieval system,
without permission in writing from the publisher.*

On the cover: The 1920 Montgomery
Grey Sox (courtesy James Hannon)

Printed in the United States of America

*McFarland & Company, Inc., Publishers
Box 611, Jefferson, North Carolina 28640*
www.mcfarlandpub.com

Table of Contents

Acknowledgments vi
Introduction 1

1 • 1920: The Beginning 7
2 • 1921: Expansion 24
3 • 1922: Regrouping 33
4 • 1923–25: Killed by Progress? 43
5 • 1926: Revival of the Negro Southern League 49
6 • 1927: Without Major Players 67
7 • 1928–30: A Tottering Revival 76
8 • 1931: Back Again 82
9 • 1932: Major League Status 91
10 • 1933: Putting It Back Together 105
11 • 1934: More New Faces 114
12 • 1935: Welcome Home, Black Barons 125
13 • 1936: The End of an Era 135
14 • 1937–44: The War and Waiting for the Future 142
15 • 1945: The League Returns 145
16 • 1946: Boom Times 156
17 • 1947: Cracks Appearing 167
18 • 1948: Changing Lineup 178
19 • 1949: The Hyphens Arrive 189
20 • 1950–51: The End 195

Appendix A: Champions, Playoffs, No Hit Games 201
Appendix B: Yearly Rosters 203
Chapter Notes 239
Bibliography 251
Index 257

Acknowledgments

There are scores of people who deserve thank-yous for assistance over the years. First up would have to be the late Lee Allen, historian at the National Baseball Hall of Fame and Museum, who assisted me with my first baseball project, a serious look at Ty Cobb's year with the Anniston Noblemen in the 1904 Tennessee-Alabama League. That work subsequently introduced me to two life-long friends and co-researchers, Ray Nemec and the late John Pardon. All three were founding members of the Society for American Baseball Research (SABR). I was among the very first non-founders to join in late 1971.

When Robert Peterson's *Only the Ball Was White* sparked the formation of SABR's Negro Leagues committee I was again among the first to sign up. The friendship and work with Larry Lester, Dick Clark, the late Jerry Malloy, John Holway, Jim Riley, Leslie Heaphy, Lyle Wilson, and others over the years helped shape and direct my research. Lester is owed still more thanks for his contribution of ten photos to this book, and for his help in identifying players in the James Hannon's picture of the Royal Poinciana Hotel team.

Larry Phillips, a SABR member in Cincinnati, answered a plea for help in locating results for games played by the Cincinnati Tigers. Alden Mead helped with Savannah, James B. Rasco with Little Rock, David Wade with Lexington, Charles Kaufman with a Negro Dixie Series between the Monroe Monarchs and Austin Black Senators, and Blake Sherry with Columbus Turf Club.

I was also fortunate to have employment situations in journalism and academia that allowed my research to often dovetail with my regular job. Admittedly, I probably occasionally took unfair advantage of that for the sake of research.

Many librarians, whose names sadly never got recorded properly in my notes, simplified much of the research with interlibrary loans of numerous newspapers on microfilm. In particular, librarians at the University of Montevallo's Carmichael Library and the Harrison Regional Library in Columbiana, Alabama, were more than accommodating over the years. At the latter, Kala Petric responded to dozens of interlibrary loan requests as I tried to finish the book.

Finally, my family played a significant role. I have been blessed with a wife, Nancy Wilstach, and four children, Charles, Mary, Maggie and Lillian, who have all tolerated my peculiar interests with their extensive excursions into dusty bound volumes, microfilm readers, travel to obscure places, and more recently, Internet search engines, in the hunt for arcane information.

Introduction

Although it started in 1920, just weeks after the founding of the Negro National League, the Negro Southern League never came close to achieving the status of the NNL. It operated until 1951, but there were stretches when it was shut down completely. Only in 1932, when the Depression wreaked havoc on many aspects of American life, was it accorded "major league" status, largely because it was the only circuit left standing.

Yet the Negro Southern League made a significant contribution to what is recognized as "major league" black baseball. The NSL sent a number of players on to that higher level, drawing them from cotton fields and steel mills alike. A number of players who got their start in the NSL also went on to play in Organized Baseball after Jackie Robinson broke the color barrier in 1948.

The two most recognizable names among the league's alumni are Leroy "Satchel" Paige and Willie Mays. Paige, the ageless pitcher with a bewildering array of pitches and charming aphorisms, began his professional career with the Chattanooga White Sox in 1926. Two decades later Mays would go to the Tennessee city to play his first pro ball with the Chattanooga Choo Choos. Both, of course, have been elected to the National Baseball Hall of Fame at Cooperstown, New York. Three other Hall of Fame members who wore NSL uniforms are Hilton Smith, Norman "Turkey" Stearnes, and George "Mule" Suttles.[1]

The Negro Southern League broke both gender and disability barriers. Although Toni Stone is rightly credited as being the first woman to have a *career* on a Negro League men's baseball team, she is erroneously cited as the first woman *to play* in the Negro leagues. In fact, at least four others preceded her in the NSL. The first was Georgia Mae Williams, a 5–6, 105-pound pitcher who started a game for Chattanooga against Little Rock in 1945. After striking out the first batter, she was replaced by one of the regular pitchers.[2] Three years later, the New Orleans club signed Fabiola Wilson and Gloria Dymond as "extra outfielders." Neither was really considered an athlete on par with Williams or, later, Toni Stone.

In addition to women players, the Negro Southern League pioneered the use of women coaches. In 1947 New Orleans Creoles owner and entrepreneur Allen Page put Lucille Bland, an athletically gifted cashier at his hotel, in uniform as third base coach. She held that role for a couple of years before being injured in an automobile accident. Although obviously hired as a drawing card, Bland was no joke on the diamond. One reporter noted that "She gives an active and fiery demonstration of her enthusiasm."[3] Bland herself said, "I'd get right in an umpire's face and let him have it."[4]

During World War II, with thousands of ball players serving in the military, the door was open for a lot of guys with physical limitations to play baseball, even in the major leagues. Pete Gray, who had lost his right arm as a child in Pennsylvania, played a few years in the minor leagues and then was signed by the St. Louis Browns in 1945, getting into 77 games.[5]

Way ahead of Gray in the NSL was Forest "One Wing" Maddox, who both pitched and played outfield for the better part of a decade with several NSL teams. A number of admiring descriptions of his ability will be found within the text.

This book, focusing more on the baseball than the sociology of the Negro leagues, was researched in many ways, but no resource was more valuable than the contemporary newspaper accounts of the players and the games. The author examined thousands of issues of more than one hundred newspapers from twenty states and the District of Columbia. It should be noted from the beginning that the Negro Southern League was considerably more difficult to research than the Negro National League or the Negro American League. Coverage in the smaller cities was more erratic and often even non-existent. In some years it is, even now, difficult to determine just who was actually in the league and who was possibly only an associate member or simply a barnstorming team that happened to play against most of the league members regularly.

How did this project originate? I daresay there are few Negro Leagues researchers of my generation who did not have the same seminal experience that I did in 1970, on opening the pages of Robert W. Peterson's *Only the Ball Was White* for the first time and discovering a whole new world. Not only that, but also a world that was waiting for further exploration and future discoveries.

In 1971 a number of these researchers, all plodding along independently at first, came together through the Society for American Baseball Research, forming the society's Negro Leagues Committee. This committee brought about an extraordinary sharing of information and encouragement, and as it grew, conferences became a part of the annual agenda. Thankfully at a conference in Harrisburg, Pennsylvania, in 1998, I was able to thank Bob Peterson for the profound influence his work had on my life.

Although I was an active member of the Negro Leagues Researchers and Authors Group that compiled many Negro Leagues records through a grant from the National Baseball Hall of Fame and Museum at Cooperstown, the greatest focus of my work was always black baseball in the South. To my knowledge no one else has done any serious research on the Negro Southern League. It was this minor league that gave early impetus to the Birmingham Black Barons, Nashville Elite Giants, Memphis Red Sox and several other teams that are now well known in black baseball lore.

The Negro Southern League gave a home to professional baseball in Southern cities that could not field teams at the Negro National League level. Birmingham and Nashville were charter cities in the league, followed a year later by Memphis. Over time teams would wear the livery of Atlanta, Chattanooga, Little Rock, Mobile, Montgomery, Raleigh and many other Southern cities. In those cities were players whose renown would hardly leave their expanded neighborhoods. Thousands of them played the game in even greater obscurity than did their counterparts in the "major league" Negro National League and later Negro American League. The Negro Southern League was minor league baseball, not unlike the white Southern Association, Three-I League, American Association, and dozens of others of white leagues of the time. That means that the number of players who went on to become major leaguers—in either a black or white context—was relatively small.

Yet for many fans of baseball history, league classification matters less than the game itself. Historians still marvel at Ike Boone's incredible performance for San Antonio in the Texas League in 1923 when he led the league in runs, hits, total bases, extra bases, doubles, triples, home runs, runs batted in, and batting average.[6] Equally astounding is Bob Riesener's pitching record with Alexandria in the 1957 Evangeline League. His final record was 20–0 with an earned run average of 2.16, more than a run better than the second place finisher.[7]

Because the reporting on games was so erratic, such seasonal totals are not available in the Negro Southern League. Some years the local white press gave substantial coverage to Negro League games, even to the extent of printing box scores; in other years, the local team was fortunate to get a paragraph and a line score after a game. No official statistics were ever issued by the league. Nevertheless, many examples of equally astounding individual effort in single games and doubleheaders will be shared in these pages.

When a sufficient number of box or line scores could be located, the author has compiled a measure of individual records for certain years. He has at times taken the same tack with standings. Although standings were frequently published during the season, it is rare to find a set that can be proven mathematically (i.e., the total number of wins for all teams is balanced by a similar total number of losses for all teams). When pennant winners were declared it was often based on narratives from reporters or partisan club officials rather than substantiated numbers. It was not unusual for the season to open with great fanfare, followed by two or three months of steady activity, then a withering away as revenues apparently failed to sustain the league. Some clubs would simply disappear from media notice while others spent more days barnstorming than playing the league schedule.

Many games were not reported at all, and others were reported a day or two late, with actual dates of the games uncertain. Sometimes different scores of the same game were reported in different newspapers

There was also a dearth of first and last names of players in the articles. Box scores were as likely to list a player by his given name or his nickname as by his surname. The rosters included in the appendices reflect cross-referencing from many sources to identify players. Names with question marks reflect a likely correct but unverified name.

In 1929, the Associated Negro Press syndicated an article by Raymond Drake, a baseball fan, who took Negro League owners to task for these very shortcomings. Calling "Negro baseball publicity" a joke, Drake said: "The proof of this statement is the fact that some weeks one does not hear from some of the clubs of the various leagues at all. When a certain club wins a game it is immediately sent to the newspapers, but when the same club drops a game—it never gets to the papers. And this happens in a city where organized baseball is supposed to be. Still other clubs have been known to go almost an entire season and fail to report the results of their games to league headquarters, making it impossible to keep any trace of their games with any degree of accuracy. Consequently, at the close of the season the league officials had to guess at the standing of the club in question. Nice publicity, this! Such business-like methods...."

"Another bad feature of baseball publicity is that where ball players are dropped from the roster of a club and no mention of it is made in print. The fact becomes known at the points where the player in question appears with some other club. In the meantime, the fans had been wondering where he had gone. The general public probably never knows what becomes of most of the ball players who leave one club for some other club. There are instances where a ball club has been changed almost completely overnight and no announcement made of it to the press."

Drake saw the publicity shortcoming as symptomatic of the owners' lack of respect for fans. He subsequently attributed waning attendance at Negro league games to that attitude.[8]

Those issues remained unresolved a dozen years later. Lucius "Melancholy" Jones, sports editor of the *Atlanta Daily World*, wrote this blistering indictment:

> Negro baseball is depressing to observe—particularly the professional brand among sepia performers.... Let us tell of the major shortcomings at one sitting. Among them these:
> (1) Absence of authentic box scores, game and attendance records.
> (2) Absence of college baseball, a natural "feeder" for the Negro leagues.
> (3) Total disrespect of player contracts and league canon and by-laws.
> (4) Excessive play of politics attendant in matters of the leagues.
> (5) Dishonesty of owners, managers, and higher officials.
> (6) Jumping of clubs by star players for "more virgin pay."
> (7) Laxity of enforcement of the rules regardless to who is affected.
> (8) Inadequate publicity, press cooperation, and general write up of games.[9]

Jones blasted Satchel Paige, arguably the black game's biggest star, as being the worst club jumper and rules-breaker of them all. By late July he had already played for four different teams, including one in each league.[10]

It should also be noted that contemporary newspapers reported on Negro League games in the context of their times. Occasionally there were stereotypical writings that today would be considered at the least politically incorrect, at the most outright racist. No effort has been made to clean up the terminology. It is what it is, a reflection of time and place, and, in no way, represents the feelings of the author. However, in defense of those writers who lived in a vastly different world from the one we share today, most of the reporting on individual baseball games was remarkably straightforward and frequently quite complimentary of the black athletes. It should also be noted that African American writers were not without fault in political incorrectness. For example, an *Atlanta Daily World* writer, commenting on a pitcher's ineptness, wrote that "he was wilder than Comache [sic] squaw with her first bottle of gin." Emory O. Jackson, writing in the *Birmingham World*, referred to third baseman Johnny Britton, as "the lemon-skinned third sacker."[11] Birmingham pitcher Leo Birdine was occasionally referred to as "Eight Rock." The derogatory term for "a very black Negro" came out of Harlem and apparently had some common usage in the 1920s.[12]

In 1941, a writer in the *Birmingham World*, probably Marion Jackson, referenced the Black Barons as "our dusky-skinned boys," "sooty-baseball," and "the tan-skinned Barons." All appellations that would not have been unexpected in the white press.[13] An equal opportunity denigrator, Jackson referred to the white Birmingham Barons a week later as "the milk-skinned Barons" and the Black Barons as "the tar-dipped horsehiders."[14] Today's political correctness notwithstanding, the author has made no effort to sanitize such writing.

The Negro Leaguers considered themselves first and foremost baseball players just like their white counterparts. On August 20, 1920, play was stopped for three minutes at black games, just as it was in white ballparks, in honor of Ray Chapman, the Cleveland Indians second baseman who died hours after being hit by a pitch on August 16.[15]

When Rainbow Division World War I veterans had come to Birmingham for their convention that July, the *Birmingham News* urged the former soldiers to go out to Rickwood Field for a double-header between the New Orleans Caulfield Ads and the Black Barons: "Don't think you will go out and see a gang of raw-boned negroes attempting to play a game of the national sport. They play it according to Hoyle."[16] The *Atlanta Constitution* even followed the customary practice of putting the local team in all capital letters in the standings—the same treatment accorded the white Atlanta Crackers.[17]

That is not to say that some black ball players were beyond putting on a show occasionally. Mathews Taylor, the Birmingham first baseman, "kept the fans in an uproar throughout the game with his funny one-handed work around the initial sack. He's a comedian worth seeing," reported the *News*. For the record, Taylor played errorless ball in the double-header, had two hits in seven at bats, one of them a triple.[18]

Of course, there was some blatant racism. A film company announced plans to shoot a comic movie at a New Orleans game. The film would feature both the game and New Orleans fans, particularly, "buxom cook ladies whose rooting for the Caulfields has been of considerable amusement for the white fans."[19] More poignant was a report from Atlanta in 1936: "Every colored fan will be glad to know that the management has responded to the request for an overhead roof under the left field bleachers. No longer may colored people approach the left field bleacher in fear of being spit upon by the men above."[20] The management of the white Atlanta Crackers appreciated the dollars brought into the ball park by black patrons enough to remove that indignity.

1

1920
The Beginning

Baseball is believed to have come to the South during the Civil War, largely through games played by Union soldiers during the war and during the occupation of the South in the Reconstruction years. As Southern whites embraced the pastime, blacks soon followed suit. The Southern League, formed by famous Atlanta newspaper editor Henry Grady and other white businessmen in 1885, was the first professional league in the South.[1] A year later an effort was made to establish a similar league of black teams. In Jacksonville, Florida, the Southern League of Colored Baseballists was established with clubs located in Jacksonville, New Orleans, Memphis, Atlanta and Savannah.[2]

The white league struggled for 15 years with a frequently changing lineup of clubs. Some seasons were completed, some were not, but a nucleus of interest and investment was established that resulted in the 1901 opening of the Southern Association, a circuit that would become a minor league mainstay for more than 60 years.

There was no parallel success story for black baseball. If the 1886 Southern League of Colored Baseballists enjoyed any success, it did not transfer to the operation of any other leagues, whether in the South or outside of it. There would be no more formal organization of black baseball teams until the near-simultaneous founding of the Negro National League and the Negro Southern League in 1920. There were, however, plenty of black baseball players. As early as 1879 a black player, William Edward White, had made an appearance in the major leagues, taking the field with the Providence Grays as a replacement for injured first baseman Joe Start. And two years before the formation of the Southern League of Colored Baseballists, in 1884, Moses Fleetwood Walker and his brother Welday famously played with Toledo, then in the major league American Association. Scores of other black players were on minor league teams throughout the latter part of the nineteenth century. George Stovey, a pitcher, set an International League record with 34 wins in 1887.[3] Most notable, perhaps, was John "Bud" Fowler, whose career ranged from 1878 through 1899. Fowler played for numerous teams, black and white, and managed some of them.[4] In 1896 Fowler managed the London Creole Giants, a team based in Muncie, Indiana. It was reported that the team would also "represent" Nashville, which would not have a team in the white Southern League that year. Fowler's team was a multi-talented outfit: "The boys are all musicians and each one plays a different instrument. They also have the finest quartette [*sic*] of singers in the South and they can give as fine a show as any minstrel people travelling." The team, expected to challenge the Page Fence Giants—organized the year before by Fowler, who also played for them in 1895—for the "Colored Championship," was expected to barnstorm throughout "the East and West and also in Canada."⁵

On February 13, 1920, a group of black baseball club owners and executives who had been meeting at the Paseo YMCA in Kansas City, Missouri, signed an important document. It was the constitution and charter of the Negro National League, the first network of black baseball teams that would have staying power. It brought to fruition a goal that Andrew "Rube" Foster, Frank Leland and other prominent black baseball men had sought for more than a decade. Participants in the up-and-coming league would be Foster's Chicago American Giants, the Indianapolis ABCs, the Chicago Giants, the Kansas City Monarchs, the St. Louis Giants, the Detroit Stars, the Dayton Marcos and the Cuban Stars.⁶

Less than a month later an equally momentous gathering was held in Atlanta, Georgia. "For the first time in the history of the national pastime the colored people are attempting organized baseball, and its success is largely assured by the number of representative men behind the movement," reported Louis R. Lautier in the *Atlanta Independent*.⁷ Inspired by the news out of Kansas City, Southern black businessmen had decided to launch a similar league in the South. Attending the organizational meeting in Atlanta were W. M. Brooks and Monroe D. Young of Knoxville; Mal Carter and Henry Brinson of Chattanooga; J.W. White and Marshall Garrett of Nashville; Dr. O. M. Thompson and J.R. Kennedy of Greenville, South Carolina; Frank M. Perdue and L. L. Barber of Birmingham; Henry Hannon of Montgomery; Dan Brown of Pensacola; Godfrey Williams of Jacksonville; Fred Caulfield of New Orleans; and W. J. Shaw of Atlanta.⁸

Three years later the Eastern Colored League was organized along the Atlantic seaboard and operated through 1928. The Negro National League lasted from 1920 to 1947.⁹ The Negro Southern League, which was generally considered a minor league, operated sporadically. The years were 1920–1923, 1926–1927, 1929, 1931–1936, and finally 1945–1951. It became the de facto major league in 1932 when the Negro National League failed to open and the East-West League limped through less than half a season before collapsing.¹⁰

Despite the attendance of representatives from several other cities, it was reported that the Negro Southern League franchises would be mostly in the white Southern Association cities. The black clubs would attempt to use the white ballparks, playing only on dates when the white teams were on the road. For some this worked out. In New Orleans, Fred Caulfield's team played at Heinemann Park, the home of the New Orleans Pelicans. In Birmingham, where the Black Barons, in some form or other, were already established tenants, games were played at Rickwood Field. The Atlanta Black Crackers played most of their games on the campus at Morris Brown College but occasionally had dates at Ponce de Leon Park, home of the white Crackers.

Everyone was aware of new dollars to be made. The white club and park owners saw an opportunity to fill seats when their teams were on the road. The black owners knew that white baseball fans would come watch their games, too, and made overtures to those fans. "The seating capacity is being greatly enlarged to accommodate white persons," the *Montgomery Advertiser* reported early in the season.¹¹ In Atlanta, it was likewise announced that "[s]pecial seats are being prepared for the white fans who attend."¹² Knoxville developed a particularly strong white following. At a critical game in June between frontrunners Montgomery and Knoxville, the attendance was reported at 1,100, "of which approximately 200 were white spectators."¹³ A few days later the attendance in Knoxville was reported at 1,000 with half of the fans white.¹⁴ On July 30, in a 3–2 win over Montgomery, "[a]bout 1,500 fans saw the game, the white sector overflowing the stand and lining the fence for the length of the field."¹⁵ In New Orleans, the Caulfield Ads not only played at Heinemann Field, the home of the white New Orleans Pelicans, but also posted the progress of the Pelicans games on the scoreboard during black games.¹⁶

Birmingham's owner-manager Frank Perdue was elected president of the league. The other officers included R.H. Tabor, Nashville, vice president; Prof. W.M. Brooks, Knoxville, secretary; and W.J. Shaw, Atlanta, treasurer. The franchise fee was set at $200 with a $25 assessment against each club for an expense fund to promote the league. Committees were appointed to draft a constitution and by-laws. A local sporting goods dealer appealed to the league to adopt the A.G. Spalding baseball and promised a trophy to the winning club.¹⁷ Interestingly, an important figure in the development of the league later that spring was C.I. Taylor, owner of the pre–World War I Birmingham Giants. Although Taylor had left the South some ten years earlier, he was "a deeply interested participant in the final arrangements, and his words of wisdom went a long ways towards encouraging options on franchises."¹⁸ In fact, Taylor still maintained contacts in Birmingham, often bringing his new team, the Indianapolis ABCs, to the city for spring training.¹⁹

When the season opened on April 29 the league was composed of eight clubs, six of them in Southern Association cities:

- Atlanta Black Crackers. The Atlanta club featured many of the same players who were on the independent Atlanta Cubs team the year before. A number of them were college students who played during the school year at Morehouse, Morris Brown, and Clark colleges and Atlanta University.²⁰
- Birmingham Black Barons. This team was formed from several others that played in the city's black industrial league, which drew from millworkers and miners. They played at storied Rickwood Field, today the oldest continuously used ballpark in the United States.
- Jacksonville Stars. An occasional member of the league. The Stars' one positively identified player is Willie Gisentaner, a left-handed pitcher who would play in the Negro Leagues for about 15 years.
- Knoxville Giants. The team played in Booker T. Washington Park, formerly known as Brewer's Park, which had been purchased by "a stock company of Knoxville Negroes" and "put in first class shape to accommodate the large number of white and [N]egro fans who are expected to attend."²¹ Among the players on the first Knoxville club were Ralph "Pete" Cleage, who enjoyed a long career in black baseball as a player and umpire, and Julian Bell, later the athletics director at Knoxville College.²² Knoxville also boasted two of Southern black baseball's more interesting pitchers in John "Steel Arm" Dickey and Forrest A. "One Wing" Maddox.

- Montgomery Grey Sox. Although C.I. Taylor may have started his Birmingham Giants earlier, this was the granddaddy of black baseball clubs in Alabama. The Grey Sox existed as far back as 1916. Henry Hannon, the 1920 manager, had also been manager of that team.[23] The 1920 games were played at Southside Park.
- Nashville White Sox. A year later this franchise would be renamed the Nashville Elite Giants, always a strong entry under owner Tom Wilson. Eventually Wilson would move the team to the Midwest and finally to Maryland, where it became the Baltimore Elite (pronounced EE-lite) Giants. The White Sox, and then the Elites, played at Sulphur Dell Park, primarily the home of the Nashville Vols white minor league team.
- New Orleans Caulfield Ads. Taking its name from owner-manager Fred Caulfield, the team played some seasons in the Negro Southern League and sometimes as an independent team. Sharing its spot and often its players in the NSL were two other New Orleans teams, the Crescent Stars and the Black Pelicans. In 1920 the Ads opened the season with a couple of veteran ballplayers, "Segula" Wilson and "Chief" Lewis. "Segula is a shineball pitcher," reported the *Knoxville Journal and Tribune*, "and the negro fans of New Orleans called him the 'Black Cicotte,' although Segula is not very black.... Lewis, the backstop, [is] one of the oldest and most experienced negro players in the south."[24]
- Pensacola Giants. Managed by Dan Brown, the Giants were in the NSL only two years, 1920 and 1926. As the semipro Pensacola Pepsi-Cola Giants, however, the team was widely known in the Florida Panhandle for a number of years. Games were played at Moro Castle Park.

For Opening Day, President Perdue announced that, like its white counterpart, the Negro Southern League would present trophies for the best attendance. The clubs were divided into two divisions for trophy competition. One was composed of Atlanta, Birmingham, Nashville, and New Orleans, the other of Jacksonville, Knoxville, Montgomery, and Pensacola.[25]

In Atlanta a campaign was launched to sell 3,000 tickets for the opening game against Jacksonville.[26] Although the attendance winners were not announced, crowds of 1,200 in Montgomery and "nearly 5,000" in Birmingham were reported.[27]

Opening Day was a community event in all of the participating cities. In Pensacola, the city's mayor threw out the first pitch. Owner A.J. Kerr introduced Fred Caulfield, owner-manager of the visiting New Orleans club, in pregame ceremonies. Kerr announced that the player hitting the first home run or collecting the most hits in the game would be awarded a wool sweater. R. Harris, the home club's left fielder, was the hands-down winner with a home run, triple, and two singles in four at-bats as the Giants won, 11–7.[28]

While promotions were nothing like the elaborate events staged today, extra efforts were made to pull in fans, particularly in Atlanta. The Black Crackers announced that "all wounded soldiers, white and colored," would be admitted free to one game.[29] Atlanta also had a children's day for both races, admitting free any child under 12 with an escort.[30] Before a Labor Day doubleheader, the management scheduled contests between

The 1920 New Orleans Caulfield Ads, a charter member of the NSL. Standing, from left: Loubie Fields, "Yab" Roberson, Louis Moffet, Fred Caulfield—manager, "Chief" Lewis, Winfield Welch, and Johnny George. Seated: George Collins, "Jumbo" Jackson, Phil Marquez, Mack Durant, Segula Wilson, Herman Roth, and Percy Wilson (courtesy Amistad Research Center, Tulane University in New Orleans).

the two teams, with players circling the bases against the clock, running the 100-yard dash, and throwing baseballs for distance. Prizes, respectively, were $5, a Stetson hat, and a silk shirt.[31]

At least three Opening Day games were played on April 29, as Atlanta beat Jacksonville, 5–3, at Ponce De Leon Park; Pensacola won, 11–7, at Moro Castle Park over New Orleans; and Knoxville defeated Nashville, 6–2, at Sulphur Dell. Birmingham and Montgomery opened the following day with the homestanding Grey Sox taking a 7–2 win before a Southside Park crowd of 1,200.

The Birmingham team was initially referred to as the All-Stars, a name that the local black weekly *Birmingham Reporter,* unlike the other papers covering the league, continued to use throughout the season. But the Black Barons were not the only team with an identity problem. When the New Orleans Caulfield Ads came to Birmingham to open the season there, one of the newspapers consistently referred to them as the New Orleans Browns.[32]

Aside from left fielder Harris's batting performance at Pensacola, the highlight of the first games was probably in Knoxville's road win at Nashville. The winning pitcher was John "Steel Arm" Dickey, who limited the White Sox to four hits. He would become the dominant pitcher throughout the NSL's first season.

After the first series was completed on Sunday afternoon, Pensacola was undefeated at 4–0; Knoxville and Montgomery had one loss apiece and stood at 2–1; Jacksonville and Atlanta split their series, each going 1–1; and Birmingham and Nashville, at 1–2, managed a win apiece. Only New Orleans, at 0–4, had failed to win during the first week.

The fact that not all teams had played the same number of games is reflective of the inconsistent reporting that plagued all Negro League baseball activity. It is not clear from the reporting whether Jacksonville and Atlanta had two games rained out or scheduled only two games. Similarly, the Sunday opening of the Birmingham-Montgomery series is unexplained. While the standings, compiled by the author from daily game reports, shows a balanced won-lost ratio, others in this narrative will not be neat or even consistent. Most standings published in newspapers did not include balanced won-lost columns, likely reflecting poor reporting of game results.

The second round of Opening Day games began on Monday, May 3, with some of the original road teams now enjoying a home opener.

Birmingham disappointed an estimated 5,000 fans by losing to winless New Orleans, 5–3. The next day, with first baseman Mathews Taylor getting four hits and Buford Meredith three, Birmingham won a slugfest, 12–11. "Chief" Lewis, a 45-year-old catcher and outfielder, hit a home run and a double for New Orleans. But the main attraction among the visitors was first baseman Percy Wilson, who was also sometimes referred to as Percy Segula. He was one of at least two players in the game referred to as one-handed fielders and batters. The description was not a lost limb but a style of play. Wilson, a switch-hitter, apparently held the bat with one hand whether hitting from the left or right side.[33]

John "Steel Arm" Dickey, the dominant pitcher in the Negro Southern League from 1920 to 1922, is shown here as a member of the 1920 Knoxville club (courtesy Beck Cultural Exchange Center, Knoxville).

There was no report on a doubleheader scheduled between the new clubs the following day. The pregame report had indicated that one of the Birmingham pitchers would be Forest "One Wing" Maddox, a pitcher-outfielder, who unlike Wilson, was indeed missing a limb, his left arm. Maddox showed up a few days later on the Atlanta roster and weeks later with Knoxville, joining John Dickey and William "Buddie" Force on a formidable pitching staff.

Both Dickey and Force would

throw no-hitters during the season. Dickey shut down Atlanta, 6–0, in the first game of a doubleheader on May 18. In July he won an odd 5–2 no-hitter against Winston-Salem in an exhibition game. Force won, 3–0, against Columbus, Ohio, in another exhibition game on July 10.

Knoxville won its home opener over Jacksonville, 8–4, with Dickey striking out eight batters. Jacksonville won on Tuesday. Montgomery, still playing at home, ended Pensacola's winning streak with 11–0 and 6–2 wins on Monday and Tuesday, respectively. There was no report on either date for Nashville and Atlanta, however, and after their series with New Orleans, Birmingham falls off the radar for 12 days, with its next reported game a rainout with Nashville on May 17. As previously noted, missing games were numerous. A check of each team's chronological results reveals stretches of as long as a week for which there is no accounting for the club's activity.

Knoxville's acquisition of "Wing" Maddox may have been the result of his work on the Cubs' first visit to the Tennessee city. Knoxville edged the Cubs, 4–3, in the first game, then pounded the visitors, 11–1, in the second. But the highlight of the second game, according to the *Knoxville Sentinel*, was the fielding of Maddox. The following day he was again outstanding, this time on the mound, where he outdueled Bud Force in a 1–0 game.[34] Before the month was out, Maddox was wearing a Knoxville uniform.

Montgomery, Knoxville, and Jacksonville played the best baseball the first three weeks of the season. Pensacola, after its 4–0 start, had plummeted in the standings. After three weeks Montgomery (10–2) had taken the lead, followed closely by Knoxville (11–4) and Jacksonville (10–7). New Orleans had risen to sixth place after its dismal start.[35]

The slight separation between Montgomery and Knoxville for first place was the story of the 1920 pennant race. Although other teams occasionally challenged, the Grey Sox and the Giants were obviously the best two teams, and their quest for the championship would go down to the final days of the season.

The next week only three games were reported for Montgomery while Knoxville was playing eight times. There was similar disparity among the other six clubs. But the new numbers showed Montgomery at 13–2 and Knoxville at 16–7. Birmingham, which had started slowly, was now one of the hotter clubs, jumping over Jacksonville into third place with a 13–7 record.[36]

Over the next three weeks Knoxville won 11 of 12 while Montgomery slumped, losing nine out of 20 games. Taking over first place, the Giants opened a three-game lead on the Grey Sox and the vastly improved Black Barons. No other clubs were over .500.[37]

While this was the basic scenario for standings over the course of the season, there were many exciting games and extraordinary individual and team performances.

Birmingham returned home on May 28 for a doubleheader with Pensacola, which they beat, 7–6, in the first game on the strength of eight stolen bases, including two each by Buford Meredith and John Kemp. Birmingham also took the second game, 2–1. The losses had to be especially disappointing for Pensacola, which two days earlier had shut out Nashville on both ends of a doubleheader. The Giants' Tally won, 4–0, in a three-hitter, followed by Rudolph's 1–0 one-hit game.[38]

In June the Negro Southern League may have seen two of the more remarkable

pitching performances of the year. On June 2, in Knoxville, Steel Arm Dickey beat Birmingham, 2–1, in a game that went 12 innings. Both Dickey, who struck out 10, and Birmingham's Gordon Zeigler pitched the entire game. Each gave up only seven hits, and Zeigler's single in the seventh inning tied the game for Birmingham.[39] There is uncertainty surrounding the game, however, as the accounts published in the Knoxville newspapers differ in important ways from the one just summarized, from the *Birmingham News*. Both the *Knoxville Journal* and the *Knoxville Sentinel* report Dickey beating Zeigler, 4–0, in a regular nine-inning game that same day.[40] Efforts to sort out the conflicting reports are fruitless. It is possible that the date of the game was reported incorrectly, but that would not explain why the Knoxville newspapers never mentioned the 12-inning game at all. It is possible that someone calling or telegraphing the result to Birmingham fabricated the pitching duel, but why do that if not claiming credit for a victory?

Knoxville swept the series, winning the second game, 8–4, on Forest Maddox's all-around play: "Maddox hit safely three times out of four chances. Two were Texas leaguers and one a long drive into center for two bags. His fielding was even better than his stick work. The climax of a series of good catches came in the ninth when Maddox sprinted to deep right and nabbed a long drive with a diving stab not ten feet distant from the fence. He throws with his glove hand without removing the glove and pegs unerringly to the base."[41] Such a move seems quite impossible. Knoxville player and manager Pete Cleage had a more plausible explanation in a June 28, 1978, interview with the *Knoxville Journal*. He said Maddox would catch a fly ball, flip the ball a foot or so in the air, sling his glove off, catch the dropping ball and make the throw.

Returning to the mound in the third game, the one-armed wonder pitched a two-hit shutout and "was elusive on the paths and sure with the stick." He drove in Knoxville's first run in the seventh with a single, then stole second base and came home on another hit.[42]

After another game near the end of the season, the *Birmingham News* reporter was effusive in his admiration of "Wing": "Maddox, the one-armed wonder, stood out as the star for the losers. He made a pretty catch in left, bagged one of the hits and swiped a base. Despite the handicap of one arm, Maddox managed to do what any other fielder can do. He is a Houdini when it comes to catching a ball and making his glove disappear."[43]

Assuming the account of the June 2 pitching duel between Zeigler and Dickey that reported the 12-inning game was the correct account, Zeigler surpassed Dickey's performance with one of his own a few days later back in Birmingham. As the Black Barons defeated Montgomery Grey Sox, 3–2, Zeigler outpitched future Black Baron Sam Streeter. Both pitchers went the distance in the 17-inning game. In front of some 3,500 fans Zeigler struck out 12, walked nine and gave up nine hits while Streeter struck out

Opposite: **The 1920 Montgomery Grey Sox. Standing: Hub McGavock—lf, Jimmy Moss—p, Patton—assistant manager, Pigler—vice president, John Staples—president, Charles "Two Sides" Wesley—2b, Bob McCormick—3b, George "Deacon" Myers—p, Mason—p. Seated: Poindexter Williams—c, Marion "Daddy" Cunningham—1b and captain, Preston—c, Sam Streeter—p, George "Tubby" Scales—rf, Herman "Rounder" Cunningham—ss, Clay Carpenter—cf (courtesy James Hannon, Montgomery, Alabama).**

12, walked two and gave up 12 hits. Birmingham won on an error, a walk and a pinch-hit single.[44] For this game, unlike the one on June 2, documentation still exists to confirm the details. The official scorer was longtime *Birmingham News* sports editor Zipp Newman, whose personal scorebook, now at the Alabama Department of Archives and History, was the source for the published box score.

Streeter, who would enjoy a 17-year career in the Negro Leagues, including stints with the Homestead Grays and Pittsburgh Crawfords, was a Birmingham area native. He had learned the game in the city's strong industrial league.[45] Earlier in the season in an exhibition game against the Chicago Black Sox, a barnstorming team, he had thrown 20 consecutive strikes.[46] Zeigler reportedly had another sensational outing the following month. On July 6 in Knoxville, he was involved in a 16-inning game, losing, 3–2. Both he and the opposing pitcher, Force, pitched all 16 innings. But here again, the *Knoxville Journal* and the *Knoxville Sentinel* reported quite a different outcome. According to the two Tennessee papers, Force beat Birmingham, 4–3, again in a nine-inning game, and Juanello Mirabel had come on in relief of Zeigler.[47]

While the Zeigler games are a mystery, there is little mystery about the prowess of John Dickey and the season he had in 1920. An early July series with Birmingham was significant in the close pennant race with Montgomery, and Dickey showed championship ability.

In a morning-afternoon Fourth of July doubleheader, Dickey beat Birmingham twice. He held the Black Barons to four hits in both the 3–2 morning game and the 5–3 afternoon game. They were his 19th and 20th consecutive wins.[48] Another of Knoxville's outstanding pitchers, Bun Moore, had a 15-game winning streak in June and July.[49]

In mid–June, Montgomery and Knoxville played another exciting series in Knoxville. Dickey beat the Grey Sox, 5–3, on June 17. It was Knoxville's 19th consecutive win, with 12 of the victories coming in league play and seven against semipro or independent teams. Montgomery ended the winning streak, 5–2, the next day in a game filled with squabbling but also some bizarre play. In the ninth inning, with the bases loaded and two out, a Montgomery batter hit a ball to the outfield with the following results: "The fielder was there waiting for it when it fell but instead of behaving like a perfectly $2.50 horsehide [sic] and falling in the Knoxville fielder's glove it dropped into a tree near the fence while three Alabama base runners romped home."[50] But there was more than blind luck at play; Montgomery was winning games on the strength of good pitching, with a staff led by the lefthander Streeter. The infield, too, was solid, with Charles "Two-Sides" Wesley at second base and the Cunningham family in the other positions.

Marion "Daddy" Cunningham was the patriarch of the ball-playing family. He often played first base and managed the team. His sons included Herman, or "Rounder," at shortstop and Johnnie at second base.[51]

The Grey Sox also had George "Tubby" Scales, who played both in the outfield and at third base. A native of Talladega, Alabama, Scales would enjoy a nearly 30-year career in the Negro Leagues, playing for the likes of the Homestead Grays, New York Lincoln Giants, New York Black Yankees, and Baltimore Elite Giants. He also managed several teams during his career.[52]

On July 27 the Grey Sox took a doubleheader from Atlanta, 3–0 and 7–1. In the first game Streeter pitched a no-hitter.[53] Atlanta had the dubious distinction of being the only team victimized by a no-hitter during the season—and it happened to the Black Crackers twice.

By the end of July, the Grey Sox had retaken first place, holding a three-and-a-half game lead over Knoxville. Although Atlanta, Birmingham, and New Orleans were now over .500, they were all at least 10 games behind Montgomery in the standings. The standings also reveal the apparent demise of Jacksonville, showing the Stars with from 18 to 28 fewer games played than the each of the other teams. The last reported results for Jacksonville came in a three-game series at Birmingham on June 28, 29, and 30.[54]

Dickey's phenomenal string of victories came to an end on July 29, perhaps appropriately at the hands of Montgomery, Knoxville's strongest rival. The visitors scored three runs in the first inning and added two more in the second, while Mason limited Knoxville to single runs in the first three innings. The *Journal and Tribune*, Dickey's constant champion throughout the season, took the pitcher to task over what it considered slack play:

Third baseman George "Tubby" Scales played for Montgomery Grey Sox first two league teams. Later he played with many Negro National League and Negro American League teams (courtesy NoirTech Research).

> It's tough on Dickey to have a perfectly good world's record stopped, but be it said that any man who play[s] the listless, don't care brand of ball exhibited by the Giant hurler yesterday deserves to lose.
>
> Dickey exhibited a wonderful grouch throughout the game after Mosley had allowed two runs in the first by booting fly balls in left field. He made little or no attempt to field his position. But the real offense came in the ninth when he committed the crowning crime of all baseball and failed to run out a hit ball.... He stood placidly at the plate, watching the fielder set himself for the catch. The fielder dropped it. It was then that Dickey decided to hoof it to the first, but his decision was too late. He was easily thrown out from deep center.
>
> Playing the game even at that late hour might have meant a victory. Earlier in the contest Maddox had lived on a similar error and scored. It was rank baseball, an injustice to the fans and to his club. No player ever attains that pinnacle of fame where he can

afford to fail to play the game. Dickey is a wonderful pitcher. He is without doubt the strongest twirler in the Negro Southern league and it is to be hoped that he will hereafter play the game to the finish and give fandom what it pays to see—a battle to the bitter end.[55]

The rivalry between Montgomery and Knoxville was intense and at times bitter. The Knoxville newspapers reported several times that Montgomery players had "beefed," or complained, over umpire decisions. In two games in Knoxville, the Montgomery club walked off the field in protest over umpiring decisions.[56] "This thing of leaving the field in protest to decisions has become the favorite outdoor sport of the Alabama leaguers. When they are not playing baseball they are protesting decisions and the strange part of it is that they get away with that sort of stuff in Knoxville," reported the *Journal and Tribune*.[57]

But umpiring, ever a point of contention in white as well as black minor league baseball, was the impetus for squabbles in other cities, too. On July 14 John Staples, president of the Montgomery club, umpired a game between his team and Pensacola because the visitors had "charged bad umpiring against them in the two previous games." Staples, possibly going overboard in trying to be evenhanded, threw Preston of the Grey Sox out of the game for complaining. "This has been a great obstacle in the atten-

The 1916 Montgomery Grey Sox, an independent team. Long-time Manager Henry Hannon is the only player identified. The spelling of the team's nickname was in fact "Gray Sox" in the early seasons, but it later gave way to "Grey Sox," which is how the team is now known (courtesy James Hannon).

dance at the park and the many fans who were present yesterday were strong in their belief that if all umpires would use their authority and get rid of the 'beefers' the teams would draw much bigger crowds," the *Advertiser* reported.[58] According to the *Atlanta Constitution*, a game there "was marred by the many arguments which were caused by the umpiring of Perkins, who had charge of the ground behind the plate."[59] The New Orleans Caulfield Ads claimed they were "up against home umpires" in the opening series in Pensacola.[60]

Sometimes managers faced disciplinary problems within their own ranks. The *Advertiser* reported that Henry Hannon, the Montgomery manager, benched two of his players "for trying to dictate to him."[61]

There were numerous roster changes on all of the teams as owners and managers sought to bolster faltering lineups throughout the season. Nashville used more than 35 players, including more than a dozen pitchers. The White Sox made at least one bad trade, sending one pitcher, Meyers, to Montgomery and selling another, Mason, to the Grey Sox. Mason became a stalwart in the Alabama city.

Gisentaner, the left-handed pitcher, started the season with Jacksonville. He later played with Atlanta, as did Jacksonville catcher O'Neil. Gisentaner was said to be a pitcher in the style of white major leaguer Mordecai "Three Finger" Brown. Because of a mangled pitching hand, Gisentaner threw with a three-finger delivery.[62] Another Jacksonville pitcher, Alonzo "Fluke" Mitchell, later joined Knoxville.

But no roster changes were more remarkable than those made by Birmingham in June. Frank Perdue, unhappy with the work of some of his players, signed five Cubans while reportedly on a road trip to Florida.[63] Where the five had been playing previously is unclear, although one report said they had been with the Cuban All-Stars out of Havana. There were a number of Cuban barnstorming teams throughout the 1920s and 1930s, including the Cuban Stars (East) and Cuban Stars (West). Regardless of the source of the players, box scores of Birmingham games were thereafter sprinkled with names such as Jimenez, Cardenas, Montalvo, Perez, and Rodriguez.

The Cubans didn't help much, and as the season neared its end Birmingham stayed around .500, finishing in fourth place. There were good outings along the way, however. Harry Salmon, Gordon Zeigler, and Conrado "Red" Rodriguez pitched consecutive shutouts against Nashville in late July. Salmon had three hits in his win.[64] Rodriguez, one of the Cuban players recently added to the roster, won both ends of a Labor Day doubleheader from Montgomery.[65] Centerfielder M. Rosella, a former Tuskegee Institute athlete, was cited for a great catch, made with his back to the ball, in a game at New Orleans.[66]

New Orleans played respectable ball at times. Oddly, the team not only opened on the road but played out of town the first three weeks of the season. When the Ads returned to New Orleans for a home opening on May 22, it was reported that they had played 17 games on the road, winning only five. Manager Caulfield claimed that "the team was crippled by the illness of three players and handicapped by 'home umpiring.'"[67]

Back home finally, they opened against Birmingham, dropping a 6–5, 10-inning decision to the Black Barons before "a fair-sized crowd." They lost the second game, too, but won the third and fourth for an even split in the first series at home.

On a later road trip, the New Orleans team witnessed something both strange and tragic. They were playing in Nashville when infielder Collins lashed a triple. A rooter in the bleachers reportedly stood up, yelled "Hoorah for New Orleans!" and then fell back into his seat, dead.[68]

New Orleans also experienced a bit of unusual media coverage. During a July series with Birmingham a film company decided the "darktime baseball games ... [made] good material for the comic movies." The company was to film both the game and the antics of the fans.[69] A later report explained: "The buxom cook ladies of color whose rooting for the Caulfields has been on considerable amusement for the white fans ... will have their inning on the movie screen before very long. Pictures are to be taken of them 'in action' during Sunday's doubleheader between the local negro team and the Birmingham Black Barons. It is to be regular Octavus Roy Cohen stuff."[70] Cohen was a popular white Birmingham-based writer who penned short stories and novels with African American characters who spoke in dialect and reflected many of the racial stereotypes of the time. Birmingham swept the Sunday twin bill. If the film crew was there, the local reporters found no occasion to mention its work the following day.

On at least one occasion that summer something unexpected seems also to have happened on the field. According to the *New Orleans Times-Picayune*, the Ads, in an 11–7 win over the Atlanta Black Crackers in June, hit seven doubles in the first inning, scoring an equal number of runs.[71] (The *Times-Picayune* report, it should be added, matches none of the game accounts published in the *Atlanta Constitution* for the three-game series.)[72] A more reliable success was the July 8 game at Heinemann Park when "Chief" Lewis, New Orleans' 45-year-old catcher, threw out seven base runners in a 7–1 win over the independent Baton Rouge team. Lewis threw out some attempting to steal and others were picked off. In the fourth inning the first three Baton Rouge batters reached first but none advanced to second. Lewis threw out two attempting to steal and pitcher Segula picked off the third one.[73]

When the Ads beat Birmingham, 1–0, in a late July game, the local press lauded the winning strategy: "The winning run was scored by Segula after he beat out a hit and made the circuit on Collins' sacrifice, Durand's Texas League and Wilson's bunt.... This shows that the negroes are playing smart baseball and using the squeeze successfully."[74] Incidentally, that Birmingham series also showed the groundskeeping skills of the Ads. It was reported that kerosene and straw would be burned "on the skinned places of the field" to dry out the turf from heavy rains.[75] In August in a game in Pensacola, Lewis Moffett struck out 15 batters in an 11-inning game.[76]

The Atlanta team was called the Cubs in preseason reports, but had become the Black Crackers by the time the season opened. Atlanta played in the middle of the pack most of the year, spending some time in third place. They came from behind to beat Jacksonville, 5–3, in the opener, "playing a sensational game before a large crowd" on the Morris Brown College campus.[77] Center fielder David Wingfield was a frequent hitting star for the Black Crackers. In an early season loss to Knoxville he had a double, triple, and three-run home run in three trips to the plate.[78] Later against Montgomery he had a single and a triple and was cited especially for his fielding: "One of his plays was a circus catch of a line drive to deep left and perfect peg to first, doubling a runner off that bag. The other play was a recovery of a hit to his garden, on which play he fell on his arm but cut the runner off at third. He was forced to retire from the game after this play."[79]

Nashville, although never a contender, had one of the future stars of the Negro Leagues.

He was Norman "Turkey" Stearnes, an outfielder whose 20-year career resulted in election to the National Baseball Hall of Fame in July 2000.[80] His formative years included seasons with the Montgomery Grey Sox and Memphis Red Sox before moving to higher levels.[81] Also, in early August, Nashville won two of three in Knoxville, becoming the first team to take a series from the Giants.[82] Jacksonville appears to have pretty much foundered in midsummer, which might explain the migration of Gisentaner and other players to other NSL teams. The final standings show the team playing only 44 games, losing 26 of them. A rare highlight for the Stars came in a losing effort in Birmingham near the end of June. Although the Giants lost the 10-inning game, 4–3, pitcher Harris struck out nine Birmingham batters and held the home team to just five hits. At the plate, he had two hits, both of them triples.[83]

All NSL teams playing on August 20 participated in a national expression of honor for Ray Chapman, the Cleveland shortstop who died after being hit by a pitch. While there have been several minor league players killed in similar circumstances, Chapman remains the only major leaguer to suffer that fate. "In the eighth inning play was held up for three minutes in honor of Ray Chapman ... whose funeral was held Friday afternoon," reported a Montgomery newspaper.[84]

Norman "Turkey" Stearnes started with the Nashville White Sox in the NSL in 1920. He later played with the Montgomery Grey Sox and Memphis Red Sox before going to greater fame with the Detroit Stars, Kansas City Monarchs and Chicago American Giants. He was elected to the Hall of Fame in 2000 (National Baseball Hall of Fame in Cooperstown, New York).

The pennant race all season was a battle between Montgomery and Knoxville. It was permeated with squabbling over each team's correct won-lost record and whether or not certain forfeits were included. One set of standings showed Knoxville clearly the pennant winner.

Knoxville	55	21	.724
Montgomery	47	39	.547
Atlanta	45	39	.536
Birmingham	43	39	.524
New Orleans	43	39	.524
Nashville	40	40	.500
Jacksonville	18	26	.409[85]
	291	243	

There was no explanation for the absence of Pensacola in the standings, which were also published a few days later in *The Chicago Defender*.[86] Apparently, it was just a dropped line of type because Pensacola was reflected in standings published in the (Montgomery) *Alabama Journal*. Fred Caulfield, the New Orleans manager, told the *Journal* that Knoxville was going to have to forfeit several games. He did not explain why, however.[87] The paper subsequently published the following standings:

Montgomery	48	40	.545
Knoxville	34	30	.531
New Orleans	44	39	.530
Birmingham	43	39	.524
Atlanta	45	44	.505
Nashville	40	40	.500
Pensacola	40	43	.482
Jacksonville	18	26	.407
	312	301	

While there is a reasonable similarity for wins and losses for each in the two sets of standings, there is no way to explain the huge disparity of Knoxville's record being 55–21 in the *Journal and Tribune* on September 6 and being 34–30 in the *Chicago Defender* on September 11. Neither set of standings is mathematically provable.

On August 30, as Montgomery arrived in Knoxville for a three-game series, the *Knoxville Journal and Tribune* reported that two clubs were in a battle for first place. However, "The league is so jumbled and accurate reports are so difficult to obtain that it cannot be said which team is leading at present, although it is known that that the clubs are not separated by a wide margin."[88]

The following day it was reported that Knoxville and Montgomery would play an additional 13-game series to settle the uncertainty. The games were to be divided among four cities, Knoxville, Montgomery, Birmingham, and Chattanooga. The winner of this unusual playoff format would then play the winner of the Negro National League "in a world's championship series."[89]

Knoxville swept the three-game series to close the regular season. Dickey threw a shutout in the third game. The 13-game series never materialized. The *Journal and Tribune* published the September 6 standings proclaiming the Giants as Negro Southern League champions. A representative of the club was said to heading to Chicago to arrange the championship series with the Chicago American Giants.[90]

Club official Monroe D. Young sent "telegraphic advices" to the *Journal and Tribune* to inform that the series with Chicago would begin September 21 with games being played in Birmingham, New Orleans, Chattanooga, and Knoxville.

The major league club swamped the Giants, taking all three games. Chicago then went on to play Montgomery and Birmingham for two games each. The American Giants won all of those games, also. The day after Chicago won the second Montgomery game the *Knoxville Sentinel* reported that League President Perdue declared that Montgomery had won the pennant, apparently drawing the previously-mentioned forfeits into the picture. Statistically, the individual leaders are just as difficult to identify. No batting and pitching records were published. Some 70 box scores have been located for the season. They were dispersed with as few as six for one team to more than 30 for another. Only a dozen games were found for Knoxville and Montgomery, the league's two best teams. Those factors considered, it would not be fair to proclaim a batting champion for the Negro Southern League's opening season. Based on available data, the leading hitters were:

Player, Team	G	AB	H	BA
Pete Cleage, Knoxville	11	49	15	.306
Chief Lewis, New Orleans	33	125	38	.304
Percy Wilson, New Orleans	37	130	38	.292
Harris, Pensacola	33	129	48	.292
Talley, Pensacola	28	105	30	.286
John Kemp, Birmingham	28	102	29	.284
Smith, Knoxville	11	47	13	.277

Although Pete Cleage hit .306, his numbers come from only 11 games. Most notable is "Chief" Lewis' .304 batting average. Lewis, reported to be 45 years old, played right field but also caught a number of games.

Adding line scores to the 70 box scores, it is possible to come up with pitching records that are a little more comprehensive. The following matrix shows the leaders:

Pitcher, Team	G	GS	CG	Won	Lost	Tied	Pct.	ShO
Dickey, Knoxville	26	21	21	17	6	0	.739	5
Force, Knoxville	26	22	21	17	10	1	.630	3
Streeter, Montgomery	27	24	20	15	10	0	.600	1
Rodriguez, Birmingham	16	14	14	12	3	0	.800	4
S. Wilson, New Orleans	19	16	15	11	4	1	.577	2

If Dickey's win total seems erroneous, given his 25-game winning streak, it should be noted that a number of games in the streak were victories over independent teams.

Newspapers reporting on his remarkable success rarely distinguished league games from barnstorming games against semipro opponents like Winston-Salem and Asheville.

Although the NSL season ended around Labor Day, several teams continued to play exhibition games well into the fall. Montgomery's extended season ended on Oct. 3 with a 5–2 loss to the touring Cuban Stars. The Cubans scored three in the top of the ninth to win the game with most of the runs coming on errors, a circumstance that seriously annoyed the Grey Sox. "After two men had been retired catcher Williams threw the ball into center field in an attempt to catch [the] runner at second. At this juncture Pitcher Mason walked out of the box discourage[d] over the support he was receiving. Meyer went and pitched one ball, the batter popping to short."[91]

Despite the loss of one team in mid-season, the 1920 Negro Southern League was a successful enterprise. There was an exciting pennant race and respectable attendance in most cities. More than 20 players in the fledgling league would go on to play in the Negro "major leagues." Indeed, among the various Negro minor leagues, the NSL was the one consistently providing players who moved up.

Among the more notables from the 1920 season are infielders Charles "Two Sides" Wesley and Johnny "Jesse" Edwards, outfielder Stearnes, pitchers Juanelo Mirable and Streeter, and catchers Poindexter Williams and Bobby Roth.[92]

2

1921
Expansion

Although which team had won the 1920 pennant had been disputed bitterly by Knoxville and Montgomery supporters, it nevertheless had been an exciting championship race. Birmingham, New Orleans and Pensacola had shown off some capable, exciting players, even if they did not seriously challenge the leaders for the title.

Undaunted by the apparent failure of the Jacksonville franchise, the Negro Southern League sent 10 teams to the field for the 1921 campaign. Several familiar teams were back, but there were also newcomers. Returning clubs were the Birmingham Black Barons, Knoxville Giants, Montgomery Grey Sox, and New Orleans Caulfield Ads. Nashville was back, but not with a team called the White Sox. Instead the city was represented by the Elite Giants, a team that would become well known over the next two or three decades. The White Sox, under General Manager Marshall Garrett, were being organized as a barnstorming team.[1]

Also debuting were the Memphis Red Sox, another club that would become nationally known. Other new franchises went to the Bessemer, Alabama, Stars; Chattanooga Tigers, Gadsden, Alabama, Giants; and Mobile Braves.

Among the missing were the Atlanta Black Crackers, Jacksonville Stars and Pensacola Giants. Jacksonville and Pensacola would return occasionally to the NSL ranks but could not be considered regular members of the peripatetic league. Atlanta, would also return to the league, and that would be very quickly in 1921.

The Black Crackers, resurfacing as the Atlanta Cubs, had moved over to a brand new circuit, the Negro Southeastern League. The new league, organized in Atlanta under President C. H. McCarthy, set a fourteen-player, $1,500 per month salary team roster limit and an ambitious 126-game schedule at its organizational meeting.[2] Others in the mostly Georgia league included the Albany Giants, Macon White Sox, and Thomasville Giants as well as teams in Moultrie and Savannah. The lone non–Georgia entry was the Montgomery White Sox, managed by Henry Hannon, a long-time fixture with the city's Grey Sox.[3] Interestingly, in addition to two black professional teams in separate leagues, Montgomery also had an independent team called the Black Sox. The manager was Ernest Douglass, a "blind man who has been selling newspapers in front of the post office."[4]

The Memphis Red Sox, making their league debut, were owned by two dentist brothers, Dr. J. B. Martin and Dr. B. B. Martin. Both had extensive additional business interests in Memphis. J. B. built a ballpark for the Red Sox and erected a hotel next door.[5] Both the Martin family and the Red Sox would be prominent fixtures in black baseball into the early 1950s. The Red Sox would play in the Negro National League and the Negro American League as well as spending several years in the Negro Southern League.

At the organizational meeting Frank Perdue of Birmingham was again elected president. Other officers were R. H. Tabor of Nashville, vice president; Professor W. M. Brooks of Knoxville, secretary; and W. J. Shaw, of Atlanta, treasurer.

The season opened early with five games scheduled on April 21 with the home teams winning each opener: New Orleans 6, Mobile 1; Montgomery 2, Birmingham 1; Memphis 5, Nashville 2; Knoxville 5, Chattanooga 4; and Bessemer 3, Gadsden 2.

In taking the first two games from the new Mobile club, New Orleans unveiled a pair of outstanding hitters. Second baseman "Baby" Bryant was three for four in the opener and four for four in the second game. Left fielder Harrison had only one hit in the first game but he was five-for-five in the second.[6]

The second series began on April 25 and again the home teams were largely successful with four victories. New Orleans and Mobile battled to a tie. The results: Birmingham 8, Montgomery 1; Nashville 5, Memphis 4; Gadsden 4, Chattanooga 3; Knoxville 4, Bessemer 3; and Mobile 8, New Orleans 8.

Nashville marked its home opener with a festive occasion. A parade, brass band and first pitch by community notable Blain Boyd were part of the pregame agenda. The parade was headed by the club's directors, followed by automobiles carrying the two ball teams. A special section was set aside for white patrons.[7]

Despite a slow start—losing two and tying one at Montgomery—the Black Barons quickly became contenders for the pennant. They opened at home against the defending champions. Montgomery scored first on a pair of singles and an error. It was the visitors' only run. John "Steel Arm" Dickey completely controlled the rest of the game, yielding only four hits the rest of the way, winning, 8–1, and striking out four. Will Holt was the hitting star with three doubles and a single in five at bats. The *Birmingham News* reported that "he came within a hair's breadth of beating the throw on a grounder on his last appearance at the plate."

Forest "Wing" Maddox, the one-armed pitcher-outfielder, started in left field and had two hits in four at bats. It was his only appearance with Birmingham at Rickwood Field that year. By late May he was reported to be with Knoxville. Buford "Geechie" Meredith handled six chances without an error at second base. Montgomery had stars in the field, also. Future Hall of Famer Norman "Turkey" Stearnes made "two nice throws to the plate" while Marion "Dad" Cunningham was the pivot man on two double plays that ended at home plate.[8]

Birmingham swept the series. The Black Barons won the second game, 7–1, behind the five-hit pitching of Rudolph, a right-hander who is almost certainly Rudolph Ash. He had played with Pensacola in 1920 and always appears as Rudolph in the box scores and line scores. First name identification of that sort was not uncommon in the Negro Leagues game reports. He was listed as Rudolph in every box score the previous season. He had a shutout until the ninth inning. Bob McCormick at shortstop handled nine of 10 chances perfectly. A highlight for fans was a squabble between Black Barons left fielder Smith and Grey Sox third baseman George Scales. "It took two umpires and four players to keep the belligerents off each other and both were ejected from the battle.

Geecher Meredeth [sic] ... and M. Cunningham ... were both spiked during the course of the game, but neither seriously enough to stop playing."[9]

Although there was not a single shutout on opening day, the 1921 NSL season would be another highlighted by outstanding pitching. No one repeated Dickey's 25-game winning streak or the number of extra-inning games by Gordon Zeigler, but there was something equally remarkable. NSL pitchers threw no fewer than 10 no-hit games in 1921. Eight of these gems were in league play and two others by New Orleans hurlers were in exhibition games.

The first no-hitter was thrown by George "Deacon" Meyers of Montgomery against Knoxville. Most of the outs were in the infield while Grey Sox batters pounded visiting pitchers for 18 runs.[10] Just a week later Nesbitt of Nashville pitched one against Chattanooga in the first game of a double-header.[11]

The new Nashville club, the Elite Giants, under the ownership of Thomas T. Wilson, would become a fixture in both Negro Southern League and Negro National League play into the 1930s. Wilson, "a prominent sportsman, businessman and numbers [a daily lottery, then illegal although highly popular] banker in Nashville," organized the Elite Giants for the 1921 season and would be a major figure in various Negro leagues until his death in 1947. The Nashville club would eventually move to Cleveland; Columbus, Ohio; and Washington, D.C. before finally settling in Baltimore.[12]

Manager Garrett of the Nashville White Sox announced in the *Chicago Defender* that he was accepting engagements for the coming season. The team had been renamed the Nashville Pythian Giants and each member would be a "tried and true" member of the fraternal organization. The projected lineup featured mostly of the players from the 1920 NSL team, notably George Meyers, Eddie Noel, Leroy Stratton, Amos Allison, and Clay Carpenter. Most of them would eventually be with the Elite Giants.[13]

New Orleans, for reasons known only to the NSL schedule makers, opened at home, but then embarked on a 21-day road trip that carried the Ads to Mobile, Birmingham, Nashville, Bessemer, Birmingham again, Tuscaloosa for two exhibition games, and finally Montgomery. The Ads were equal to the arduous task, however. When they returned to New Orleans to host Montgomery on May 19, they were in the thick of the young pennant race with a record of 11–6. Percy Wilson, considered by many to be the best first baseman in the league, had 19 hits on the trip. They included one home run, five triples, three doubles and 10 singles. A 17-year-old rookie pitcher named B. Platt had been equally sensational. Including the opening home series he had a record of five wins and one loss with three of his triumphs being shutouts.[14] He picked up his sixth win, 5–2, in the first game against Montgomery.[15]

No other city probably entertained its fans as well as the Crescent City. New Orleans being New Orleans, there was always music around: "The jazz band was a big attraction at the park and as one fan remarked, 'The band alone is worth the time to come out to see the game.' The jazz band received its share of the applause during the contest."[16] When Montgomery came to town in July, it was during an important series for the white Pelicans against the Atlanta Crackers in Atlanta. "The details of the Atlanta-New Orleans game will be called out by a strong-voiced man through a megaphone," announced the *New Orleans Times-Picayune*."[17]

After breaking even with Montgomery, Birmingham, and Nashville, the Ads left town again on a trip that stretched from June 6 until July 1. It was later reported that they had won 14 of 20 games on that trip.[18] The season was less than a month old when league officials announced a major lineup change. Gadsden, although playing at around a .500 pace, was struggling financially. On May 13, it was reported that the team had surrendered its franchise after playing only a dozen or so games. President John Staples of the Grey Sox announced in Montgomery that the franchise would be awarded to the Atlanta Black Crackers, who had jumped over from the new Negro Southeastern League.[19]

Gadsden, under business manager John Tyler, had held spring training at Pratt City near Birmingham. The team had exhibition games scheduled in March with Rube Foster's Chicago American Giants and with the Birmingham Black Barons. Although it lost the Birmingham game, 3–1, pitcher Pickens was said to have outpitched Barons star Harry Salmon, losing because of poor support.[20] The Giants opened the season on the road, losing two of three at Bessemer. The home opener on April 25 was with Chattanooga. The game was preceded by a parade featuring a brass band and the two ball clubs.[21] Gadsden won the opener, 4–3, and the second in the series, 9–2, giving the team a 3–2 start. But that bright start did not foreshadow the team's short future. The dozen known Gadsden players included two pitching brothers named "Durand." They are almost certainly Eli and John Juran of Birmingham. They would also pitch for Knoxville and for Birmingham before the 1921 season was over.

Completely dominating the Negro Southeastern League, the Atlanta Black Crackers were primed for a move up. By mid–May their NSEL record was 12–1.[22] The Black Crackers made their NSL debut on May 19 with a 2–1, 11-inning win at Chattanooga. Pitcher Ben Harris held the Tigers to just two hits.

Montgomery was the strongest team the first few weeks. Standings in mid–May showed the Grey Sox at 18–7, with a game and a half lead over second-place Birmingham (16–8). Chattanooga (11–9) was third, four and a half games back, and New Orleans was 11–10. The other six teams were all under .500. Knoxville was reported to have won only three games in 21 starts. The standings, however, were obviously out of kilter, likely because of unreported games. They showed 93 total wins and 122 total losses for the 10 teams in the league.

By early June, the Grey Sox (28–8) had extended their lead to four games over Birmingham (22–10). New Orleans (17–11) and Bessemer (18–17) were the only other clubs over .500. Knoxville, although still in last place, appeared to be improving. Its record was now 9–19. Atlanta was not listed in the standings, which still showed the defunct Gadsden team in ninth place with only 14 games played.[23]

Although no standings accompanied the article, the *Chicago Defender* in mid–July reported that New Orleans had moved into first place with a three-game lead over an unidentified second place team. There was no indication if the reference was to the first or second half of the season.[24]

As would often be the pattern for the Negro Leagues, the heaviest league schedule was played during the first half of the season, which ended around July 4. Much of the second half was spent barnstorming and playing independent teams rather than league opponents. After hosting Chattanooga over the July Fourth holiday period, the New Orleans club then played a series of successful games with teams from McComb, Mississippi, and Bogalusa, Baton Rouge, and McDonough, Louisiana. The *Times-Picayune* then proclaimed Fred Caulfield's team to be Louisiana state champions and southern champions by virtue of their NSL play. Next up was a series with the independent New Orleans Black Sox for the city championship.[25] However, New Orleans played no league games after a late July series with Montgomery. Birmingham played no more league games after August 7. Only a handful of Memphis scores were found for June, July and August. Nashville was the only team playing a consistent schedule against other league teams in July and August.

By the time the second half got underway the league was apparently down to eight teams. Bessemer, which had been a respectable team at times, played no more games after June 23, when they lost an 11–10 slugfest at Mobile. The Mobile team's future was limited, also. After losing a July Fourth double-header at Birmingham, then three straight to Montgomery at home, the Braves disappeared. Neither Bessemer nor Mobile appeared in the final published standings in September.

Knoxville, still chapped over the disputed flag of 1920, was regularly referred to as "last year's pennant winners" by the local press.[26] After breaking even the first couple of weeks of the season, Manager Brooks made wholesale personnel changes in order "to secure the best ball players available." As the team returned home for a series with New Orleans in early May, he announced that he had signed three new pitchers, two infielders, and an outfielder. Team President Chris Contax reportedly made a trip through the South and East where he signed "several other players."[27] When the Gadsden club folded in May, Knoxville quickly grabbed a pair of infielders.[28] None of this seemed to help, though, as the club was in last place with a 9–19 record on June 11.

In late May when the Atlanta Black Crackers came to town for a set, the Giants were using a drastically shuffled lineup. Atlanta pounded the Giants, 12–0, and the local newspaper attributed the high score to Knoxville errors: "Poor fielding by the locals aided the visitors materially in scoring their runs. Cleage is playing shortstop for Knoxville until Manager Brooks can get a new one, and Juran, a pitcher who was forced to play center field because of a lack of other men, made several costly errors. These, coupled with the inability of Sampson to field bunts, allowed several Crackers to cross the plate who should never have scored."[29] There was no explanation for the absence of the previous shortstop. Pete Cleage normally played first base.

Sampson, described as a "giant" from Corbin Hill, Alabama, may have had trouble with bunts, but he provided a major lift on the mound. On May 29 Knoxville won, 5–4, at Memphis with Sampson throwing a two-hitter and striking out 16 Red Sox batters. Norman, now playing shortstop, handled eight chances flawlessly, and Cleage, Miller and McIntyre all hit triples to spark the offense.[30]

McIntyre, the regular second baseman, was also a power hitter. On June 24, he reportedly hit his ninth home run of the season in an exhibition win over the Knoxville Independents.[31] Sampson, whose hometown was likely the mining community of Carbon Hill, Alabama, pitched a no-hitter on June 22, but lost the game to Atlanta, 2–1. No other details of the game were published in the Knoxville papers.[32]

One-armed Forest "Wing" Maddox was back with Knoxville in early June. Playing center field in a game at Chattanooga, "his old-time bunting brought many squalls from the fans."[33] On June 21, Maddox preserved a 3–2 win over Atlanta in center field with "a perfect throw to the plate cutting off the tying run."[34] There is no indication that Maddox pitched for Knoxville, although there were several weeks of no results being reported.

Birmingham's run with John Dickey was short-lived. He was scheduled to open a series with Atlanta on June 6 at Rickwood Field in Birmingham. Instead, he next faced the Black Crackers on June 9 in Atlanta, this time as a member of the Montgomery pitching staff. Dickey beat the Black Crackers, 8–5, in his Grey Sox debut.[35]

Chattanooga's plunge from third to eighth place in June was not the club's only problem. Catcher Andrew Morris was arrested before a game in June on an old charge of public profanity. He had been given "a workhouse sentence" but escaped before serving his time. The authorities caught up with him just before a game with Knoxville.[36] Like many other league teams, the Tigers did a lot of barnstorming during the second half. Over a stretch of four weeks in July and August the team was continuously away, playing league games at Memphis and Nashville and barnstorming games in Arkansas. The team "has been away from the city so long that most folks thought it was disbanded," reported the *Chattanooga Daily Times*.[37]

There had already been a previous belief that the team had folded. In mid–July the Tigers were scheduled to return home from a 10-day road trip to host a series with Nashville. The Tigers did not show up, forcing the Elite Giants to play a local semipro team in a pickup game. It was noted that on the road trip the *Times* had received telegraphic dispatches on the first couple of games, then nothing at all, leading to speculation of the team's demise.

Forest "Wing" Maddox, whose left arm was lost near the elbow, was one of the most popular players in the NSL in the 1920s. He was a pitcher-outfielder with several different teams (courtesy Collection of Robert Reeves).

A few days later Manager A. W. Bishop sent a telegram to the paper, dispelling the rumor. "It was known that the negro leaguers had already had some rough sailing financially, and it was feared that their absence meant that they were crawling the crossties or riding the rods toward Chattanooga individually. Such, however, is not the case and the Tigers, it seems are very much alive as an organization," reported the paper.[38] Despite the erratic schedule the team claimed it was still in the Negro Southern League and was home for a series with Atlanta. There was no report on the Atlanta games. A series with Knoxville was played the following week.

The Montgomery club's strength was reflected clearly in an early June game against Mobile when Mason bested Dickey in a 1–0 battle. Mason, who struck out six, gave up three hits while Dickey held the Grey Sox to just two hits. A hit and an error produced the winning run in the eighth inning.[39] No further identification has been found for Mason other than the epithet "Big," which was used frequently with his name.

Montgomery, billed as NSL champions by the *Chicago Defender*, went to Chicago in September for a Sunday afternoon game with Rube Foster's American Giants. Oscar W. Adams, who rarely mentioned sports in his "What Negroes Are Doing" column in the *Birmingham News*, wrote that it was the first time a black team from the South had ever played in Chicago.[40] After the Grey Sox had added Dickey to their pitching rotation, manager John Staples said he and Mason gave his team a strong mound presence. He released the following lineup for the series: Cardenas and Charleston, catchers; M. Cunningham, 1b; J. Cunningham, 2b; H. Cunningham, ss; Russell, 3b; Stearnes, rf; Barker, cf; McGavock, lf; Sallee and Parker, additional pitchers; and McCarver, utility.[41]

Some 14,000 fans turned out to see the Grey Sox and the American Giants at Schorling's Park in Chicago on Sunday, September 11. Dickey went up against Dave Brown in a classic pitching duel. The home team won, 1–0, on a throwing error in the bottom of the ninth. Columnist Frank Young said it was a grand spectacle: "...baseball is a funny game. The unexpected makes it and the unexpected happened. No alibis. Good game. Dickey's pitching wonderful. Hard game to lose and just as sweet to win. Come again, boys from Dixie—you've won lots of friends here."[42]

The championship billing by the *Defender* notwithstanding, the Grey Sox returned South the following week to face the Nashville Elite Giants in a championship playoff although there was no split season and even though Montgomery had a better regular season record (60–41 compared to Nashville's 41–30 by the author's tabulation of league game results).[43]

In late August the *Montgomery Advertiser* reported that the Grey Sox had won the pennant for the second year in a row, compiling a record of 80 wins, 32 losses and three ties.[44] Of course, those numbers do not match any set of published standings or the author's tabulation. A few days later, the paper reported that Montgomery had won the championship by taking the last series before Labor Day and was now en route to St. Louis and Chicago. It would play a five-game series with Nashville afterward.[45] There was no mention of this being a championship series.

Standings published on September 14, the day before the playoff series was to begin, showed Nashville with a three and a half game lead over Montgomery. There are two odd things about the standings. First, Nashville's percentage is listed as .615, but the 72–46 record works out to .667. Second, the standings are balanced with 473 total wins and total losses. There is no accounting for the games played with Bessemer and Gadsden, both of which failed to complete the season. The standings:

Team	Won	Lost	Pct.
Nashville	72	46	.615
Montgomery	69	50	.580
New Orleans	66	50	.569
Birmingham	61	56	.521
Atlanta	61	57	.517
Memphis	52	69	.430
Chattanooga	49	66	.426
Knoxville	43	79	.353[46]
	473	473	

The credibility for the standings is highly questionable. Most clubs are shown as having played almost twice as many league games as actual results reflect. In order to account for say, Birmingham's 117 games or New Orleans 116 games, the above standings would have to include many barnstorming games.

The entire five-game series was played in Nashville with decisive results for the home team. The series opened on September 15 at Athletic Park. Daltie Cooper threw a four-hitter as Nashville edged out "Slim" Sallee and the Grey Sox, 2–1. Another one-run game followed the next day. This time "Kid" Billings outdueled Dickey, 3–2.

After a rainout on September 17, the third game was played with "Big" Mason going against Lawrence "Cannonball" Graves. Nashville made it three straight with a 2–0 shutout. Montgomery had only three hits. Games four and five were a doubleheader. Eddie Noel pitched Nashville to a 3–1 victory in the first game. Montgomery finally won a game, taking the six-inning nightcap, 4–1, behind Dickey.

President Frank Perdue subsequently awarded the championship trophy to the Elite Giants.[47]

In the fall extended series, the New Orleans Caulfield Ads won five out of eight from the Texas All-Stars.[48]

Another series of interest was played in August when Montgomery hosted the Thomasville, Georgia, Giants, reported to be champions of the Negro Southeastern League. Thomasville won the first game, 6–3, behind a pitcher named Williams. Both Dickey and Mason pitched for Montgomery. Two days later, Meyers and Sallee pitched Montgomery to a 3–2 win.[49] If any other games were played, they were not reported. The *Daily Times-Enterprise*, the Thomasville newspaper, had no coverage of the Giants after mid–July.

The number of box scores and line scores available for 1921 Negro Southern League season were proportionally fewer than those found for 1920. For example, 80 box scores and 135 line scores were found for the eight clubs in 1920. For 1921 there were 75 box scores and 145 line scores, but for 10 clubs. In fact, no box scores or line scores were found for the Gadsden team. Consequently, representative statistics were impossible to compile except for four teams—Birmingham, Montgomery, Nashville, and New Orleans. The combined box scores and line scores for those four teams covered about 60 games.

There is a little more information available on the New Orleans club, but it must be presented with a footnote. In late September the *Times-Picayune* published individual batting and pitching records for the Caulfield Ads. The figures were from 115 games, of which the Ads were reported to have won 83 and lost only 32. The final league standings published on September 14 had shown the Ads with having played 116 games, winning 66 wins and losing 50.

It was even more difficult to determine individual statistical leaders in 1921 than it had been for 1920. The dispersal of box scores for 1921 was Birmingham (36), Nashville (29), New Orleans (27), Montgomery (21), Atlanta (16), Bessemer (10), Knoxville (7), Mobile (7), Chattanooga (5), Memphis (3), and Gadsden (0). With that kind of data base, it seemed hardly fair to compare the .370 batting average of Hill of Mobile, for whom only seven games were available, with the .307 batting average of Griffin of Nashville, who appeared in at least 28 games.

Only four teams—Birmingham, Montgomery, Nashville and New Orleans—had enough available box scores to make a reasonable determination of season-long hitting prowess. Using those parameters, the league's top hitter was Birmingham outfielder Will Holt with a batting average of .387. He was closely followed by New Orleans' venerable catcher-outfielder "Chief" Lewis with .381. First baseman Gray of Birmingham (.338) and infielder Griffin of Nashville (.307) also hit over .300. Gray led in stolen bases with 21 while Holt, whose season ended with a broken leg in June, had 14.

The leading pitcher was "Frenchy" Gibson of Nashville with a 15–6 record. His teammate Daltie Cooper was 14–8. Montgomery had five pitchers with double figures wins: Slim Sallee, 15–4; Eddie Noel, 12–3; "Big" Mason, 12–8; George Meyers, 11–6; and John Dickey, 11–5. B. Platt, the 17-year-old phenomenon, was 11–4 and Lewis Moffett 10–9 for New Orleans.

Dickey, the 1920 Knoxville sensation, played for three different teams in 1921. His combined record with Birmingham, Mobile, and Montgomery, where he finished the season, was 15–10. Sam Streeter pitched for both Atlanta and Mobile, compiling a 9–3 record.

The strikeout artists were Cooper (53 in 92 innings), Platt (35 in 63 innings) and Harry Salmon of Birmingham (34 in 62 innings).

Of the 10 no-hitters thrown by NSL pitchers in 1921, Cooper of Nashville pitched two no-hitters, both in league competition. Owens of New Orleans had one in league play and one in an exhibition game. The list:

1921 No-Hitters

May 8, Meyers, Montgomery vs. Knoxville, 18–0
May 10, 2nd game, Sallee, Montgomery vs. Knoxville, 7 innings, 6–0
May 14, 1st game, Nesbitt, Nashville vs. Chattanooga, 7 innings, 3–0
June 15, Owens, New Orleans vs. Chattanooga, 4–0
June 16, Cooper, Nashville vs. Montgomery, 1–0
June 22, Sampson, Knoxville vs. Atlanta, 1–2
June 26, Cooper, Nashville vs. Montgomery, 4–0
July 26, J. Juran, Birmingham vs. Atlanta, 4–0
Aug. 3, Owens, New Orleans vs. Baton Rouge, 5–0, exhibition
Aug. 19, Moffett, New Orleans vs. Corpus Christi, 8–0, exhibition

3

1922
Regrouping

Having started the 1921 season with 10 teams, replacing one of them the first month, and finishing the year with eight clubs, the Negro Southern League had mixed success in its second year of operation. There would be similar lineup shifts in 1922.

Seven of the clubs that finished the previous season returned: Birmingham, Chattanooga, Knoxville, Memphis, Montgomery, Nashville, and New Orleans. Gone were Atlanta, Bessemer, Gadsden, and Mobile. The surprise loss was Atlanta, replaced by the Louisville Stars. One team would be lost over the course of the season. Fred Caulfield's Ads dropped out by early June, but were ably replaced by the New Orleans Crescent Stars.

Newspaper coverage of the league was not as extensive as in previous years. Conflicting reports had both Frank Perdue of Birmingham and J. W. Miller of Memphis serving as president. No others officers were identified. Near the end of May the *Birmingham News* published a set of standings with the following notation: "It is hoped now that the standing ... can be given out regularly. Permanent headquarters have been established and a secretary has been established to look after the averages, standings, etc."[1] The article did not identify the location of the headquarters or the secretary.

Opening day was Monday, May 1, with each team said to have a 125-game league schedule. Opening day managers were listed by the *Chicago Defender* as Fred Caulfield, New Orleans; J. T. Staples, Montgomery; Pete Cleage, Knoxville; Robert Bridgeforth, Chattanooga; P. Perdue, Birmingham; J. Miller, Memphis; T. Wilson, Nashville; and E. Arnold, Louisville.[2]

The Chicago writer actually presented a mixture of club officials, owners, and managers. Bridgeforth, Wilson, and Staples were owners. The men in the dugout were Frank Perdue, Birmingham; J. A. Newton, Chattanooga; Cleage, Knoxville; Arnold, Louisville; Chick Cummings, Memphis; Henry Hannon, Montgomery; Leroy Stratton, Nashville; and Caulfield, New Orleans. Frank Perdue was again the league president and the "P. Perdue" listed as manager was obviously a typographical error.

Only one game has been located for opening day. Memphis won a 12-inning game at Birmingham. The same teams were rained out on Tuesday. On Wednesday, May 3, Birmingham went to Memphis for the Red Sox' home opener. Other games scheduled that day were Knoxville at Chattanooga, New Orleans at Montgomery, and Louisville at Nashville. That was the first date for games involving the six clubs besides Memphis and Birmingham. It has not been determined if those teams had earlier openings or if other games were simply not reported. Knoxville's 2–1 win at Chattanooga on May 3 was reported as an opening game. "Parson" Miller beat John "Steel Arm" Dickey in a contest shortened to five innings by rain.[3]

The new Louisville team made its debut in Nashville, where it was handed a 14–1 trouncing. Catcher Andrew Morris hit a home run over the right field wall. Infielder Leroy Stratton had a triple and three other players hit doubles as Nashville got 16 hits off of two Louisville pitchers. Eddie Noel held the visitors to just three safeties. Morris's home run was said to be "one of the longest ... ever hit" at Sulphur Dell.[4]

Although the series was plagued by rain on two days, four games were finally played with Nashville winning them all. The second win was another three-hit pitching masterpiece by Noel. Nashville then stretched its winning streak to six games by taking the first two in a series with Birmingham. The Black Barons finally stopped the Elite Giants with a "husky" right-hander named Young.

Louisville's troubles continued the second week of the season. Although Riley beat Knoxville, 3–1, on May 10, the following day saw the Stars fall, 1–0, as Ray pitched a no-hitter.[5]

At Nashville on May 16, left-hander Carl Glass beat the Elite Giants, 4–1, holding the home team to five hits. There was no report on his total strikeouts, but it was noted that he struck out the first five batters in the game.[6]

Nashville, holding onto its small lead, went into New Orleans on May 20–24 for an important five-game series with the Caulfield Ads. Nashville won three of the five games, including the one that had local fans buzzing. The Sunday afternoon game drew an estimated 3,000 spectators to Heinemann Park. They saw an exciting pitching battle between Eddie Noel and B. Platt, the youthful New Orleans pitcher who had been a sensation in 1921. Platt struck out six of the first nine batters he faced, but Noel got the win when Nashville scored the game's only run in the top of the ninth.[7]

Nashville also left New Orleans with a commodity besides victories. Owner Tom Wilson bought shortstop "Hooty" Phillips and pitcher Ralph "Square" Moore outright from Caulfield. They were scheduled to join the Elite Giants in Memphis the first week in June.[8] The sale may have been transacted because Fred Caulfield knew he would soon go in another direction. The Ads hosted the Memphis Red Sox in a series after Nashville. It was the team's last league encounters. The Ads began playing independent baseball and the New Orleans Negro Southern League franchise was taken over by the New Orleans Crescent Stars. The Crescent Stars Athletic Club had been reported in early May as playing in the Southwestern Colored League, but there were no other references to that league.[9]

From the beginning of the 1922 season there were several teams battling for the lead in the NSL. Early standings are filled with discrepancies. For example, Memphis was reported with a 15–7 record on May 22 and less than a week later with a 12–6 record. By early June it was clear that five teams were serious contenders for the pennant. Knoxville, returning to its 1920 form, surged to an early lead. Close behind were Nashville, Memphis, Montgomery, and Birmingham. The other three teams—Chattanooga, New Orleans, and Louisville—had faded by that point and never recovered.

Standings published on June 12 showed Knoxville (21–8) slightly ahead of Memphis (22–9). Other teams over .500 and within striking distance were Nashville (18–10), Montgomery (12–8), and Birmingham (13–11). Chattanooga, New Orleans, and Louisville had winning percentages below .400.[10]

Knoxville, which had fought Montgomery to the end for the 1920 pennant and then dropped to last place in 1921, had Dickey back on the mound. Two other pitchers, who also doubled as outfielders, were Forest "Wing" Maddox and Harry "Fish" Salmon. Manager Ralph "Pete" Cleage was a versatile athlete who could play wherever needed.

Cleage, who was to have one year in the Negro National League, played and managed into the 1930s. He also became an NNL umpire for a while.[11] He also provides another of the eyewitness descriptions of "Wing" Maddox: "He would catch a fly ball, throw it up a foot or two in the air and sling his glove off, then catch the ball again as it came back down and throw it back into the infield. He had an awfully strong arm. I've seen him cut down a lot of runners at home plate."[12]

The management of the Memphis club is a puzzle. In an advance story on the opening game a Birmingham sportswriter listed the manager as Chick Cummings.[13] Other reports identified him as J. Miller. The latter appears to have more credibility as Miller was the identification in the *Commercial-Appeal*.[14]

The Red Sox launched their season auspiciously by winning a 12-inning game in Birmingham by 2–1. It was an extraordinary pitching duel between two lefthanders, Eli Juran of Birmingham and Glass of Memphis. Juran allowed Memphis eight hits, striking out 12 and walking three, a sensational performance. However, it paled in comparison to that of Glass, who held Birmingham to just five hits and one walk while striking out an incredible 22 batters.[15]

Although never identified with a first name during the season, the author has determined that the Memphis pitcher is almost certainly Carl Glass. A left-hander whose career spanned nearly two decades, Glass was born in Lexington, Kentucky, in 1898. In 1920 he was a United States Army private stationed at the Fort Huachuca, an Army post in southern Arizona, and is believed to have played at least one game with the 25th Infantry team in St. Louis.[16] Starting in 1913 Fort Huachuca was the home of the 10th Calvary Regiment, better known as the Buffalo Soldiers. Many black soldiers were trained and stationed there during World War II. Black baseball historian Jim Riley says Glass's career began in 1923 with the Memphis Red Sox, but based on additional evidence, it seems likely now that he started pitching with Memphis as early as 1921.[17]

After a second game rainout in Birmingham, the two teams moved to Memphis for a home opener. The Red Sox continued their early winning streak with a 4–0 shutout, then made it three in a row before the Black Barons finally got their first win.[18]

Nashville was one of the best teams in the league from the beginning. After opening with four straight wins over the new Louisville franchise, the Elite Giants hosted Birmingham and extended their winning streak to six before finally losing a game. The fielding of outfielders Will Holt and George "Jew Baby" Bennett drew early praise from sportswriters. "They pulled down a number of drives labeled for extra base hits," reported the *Nashville Tennessean*.

Owner Tom Wilson had bolstered an already strong pitching staff with the purchase of "Square" Moore from New Orleans early in the season. He also picked up Young, a right-hander from Birmingham. It had been Young, with five-hit pitching, who had handed the Elite Giants their first loss of the season.

Montgomery's team again had the Cunningham nucleus with brothers Johnnie at second base and Herman at shortstop. Marion "Daddy" Cunningham was at first base.

Outfielder Norman "Turkey" Stearnes was back, as was catcher John "Red" Charleston. Pitchers included "Big" Mason, one of the strong starters of 1921 and Lewis Moffett, who was with New Orleans the previous year.

Catcher Charleston, who would play for at least 10 years, was known for a strong arm, perhaps too strong: "Charleston caught a beautiful game for the Sox Saturday, but he seems a little hard on his pitchers, in that he cares but little how hard he returns the ball. Seemingly, he forgets the hurler has nothing but a thin glove," wrote a local sportswriter.[19]

By August, Marion Cunningham was reported to be "in charge of the team" as it went into a series with Augusta, champion of the Negro Southeastern League. Coverage was sparse, but Montgomery won the opening game, 4–3, in 11 innings on August 19. There was no report on a double-header scheduled the following day.[20]

Birmingham had an infield nucleus returning with Buford "Geechie" Meredith at second base and Bob McCormick at third base. "Black Babe Ruth" Tubbs in right field was also back. He "is known throughout Southern colored baseball … a wicked stick wielder."[21] The description of Tubbs added that his home run prowess the year before had been a feature for the Birmingham team. However, in fact, in 11 box scores for 1921 Tubbs had 13 hits in 45 at bats. The only extra base hit was a double. McCormick hit the only home run recorded for Birmingham in 36 team box scores.

A newcomer at first base was George McAllister, a Birmingham industrial leaguer. He and three other players, pitcher Tom Watson, catcher A. Watson, and infielder Miles, all appear to have been picked up from the 1921 Bessemer team. A new outfielder, George "Mule" Suttles, usually listed as Sellers in game reports, would prove to be a future Hall of Famer. Among the pitchers were brothers Johnny and Eli Juran. Like Suttles, they were subject to much incorrect identification, often listed as Durand. As both were pitchers, it is sometimes impossible to determine who pitched a particular game due to the lack of a first names in newspaper accounts.

After the two-game home opener series Birmingham spent the next two weeks on the road, playing at Memphis, Nashville, and Louisville. The team, playing about .500 baseball, returned home on May 15 for a series with New Orleans. The home fans had to be disappointed as New Orleans scored seven runs in one inning and won, 14–9. "The outfield at Rickwood Tuesday is full of dents from the number of balls that landed there in Monday's contest," reported the *Birmingham News*, adding that there were 33 hits in the game. Although errors were also numerous, the local fans were treated to some excellent work by Suttles and one of the Juran brothers, who was playing first base:

"The fielding feature of the afternoon was one-handed catch by Sellers [sic] in deep left field in the sixth. He sprinted towards the fence and snagged the ball while on the run. When he came in he was peppered with a deluge of coins from the stands and realized quite a nifty amount from the dusky fans, it taking about ten minutes for him to collect the offering. Jurand [sic] made three nice catches of fouls, going over to the first base bleachers on each occasion and taking the ball off the stands."[22]

Nashville had a lot of good players who turned in fine performances throughout the season. When the Elite Giants swept a double-header from Birmingham on June 11, winning 8–1 and 7–1, manager Leroy Stratton had six hits for 10 total bases in the two games. Newly-acquired shortstop "Hooty" Phillips was cited for his base running.[23]

On June 18 Noel shut out Montgomery, 10–0, holding the visitors to just three hits. The visitors were hitless until two were out in the seventh inning. Noel stuck out 10 during the game.[24]

Montgomery went to Nashville in mid–June for an important series between frontrunners. Young, the Birmingham acquisition, pitched a shutout in the opener, beating the Grey Sox, 7–0. He struck out 12.[25] Nashville scored four in the seventh to win the second game, 8–7. With Noel again pitching brilliantly, they won the third contest, 10–0. Noel struck out 10 and scattered three Montgomery hits as the Elite Giants swept the series.[26]

The Chattanooga Tigers opened under the leadership of J. A. Newton, the man who had led the Nashville Elite Giants to the championship the year before. Club President Robert Bridgeforth is possibly the father of William "Soo" Bridgeforth, who would be a Negro leagues owner and official in the 1950s.[27] The Tigers roster included Hub McGavock, who had played with both Montgomery and Nashville. Two other former Montgomery players, Jim Hall and "Parson" Miller, were among the pitchers. Behind the plate was Andrew Morris, apparently free from his previous problems with the law. He spent part of the season with Nashville.[28]

The team opened at home with Knoxville, losing two out of three games. The Tigers never seemed to rebound from that. By the end of June they were in seventh place. An effort to build a fan base may have been hampered by scheduling difficulties. At least two home series were played in Nashville, 130 miles away, because the local Andrews Field was being used by the white Chattanooga Lookouts. There were also other problems, financial and managerial:

"Chattanooga Tigers, the negro Southern league club, are not playing at Andrews field this week as per schedule. Efforts to ascertain yesterday just what has happened to the organization were futile. It was stated that Chattanooga Lookouts Manager Strang Nicklin has barred the negro team from Andrews field pending payment for use of the same, and [a] decision as to just who has the right to run the club.

"The Tigers so manipulated the use of Andrews field Sunday with the two Appalachian league teams that they seemed to clean up sufficient coin to tide them along for awhile. But it is understood that Nashville interests, which are running the club, sent in a new business manager, and that there was disagreement as to who really had the right to operate the venture.

"The Tigers announced a game with the Birmingham Grey Sox [sic] Monday afternoon and since that time have not been around newspaper offices with any information as to their club."[29]

There was no report of a game with Birmingham for that date and later in the week the Chattanooga team was in Montgomery.

The newspaper article is quite confusing. It seems highly unlikely that the Tigers had control of the field's use. Also, there were no Appalachian League (white Class D ball) teams anywhere close to Chattanooga. Results from the Sunday game show a 1–0 loss by Chattanooga to an independent Asheville club.

In July the *Times* reported that the team was now under the management of Andrew Morris. They were to return to the city the next afternoon to begin a four-game series with Louisville. The series would conclude with a July Fourth doubleheader.[30] Because the white Chattanooga Lookouts were already scheduled for a home series that week, the Tigers were forced to move the Louisville games to Nashville.[31]

At the same time the games were being moved to Nashville, pitcher Jim Hall sued the team for back salary. Hall said he was owed $219 in wages by Thomas Wilson, the man who was also reported to own the Nashville and Louisville clubs. Wilson denied ownership, saying the Chattanooga club was owned "by a Negro living in Nashville." Magistrate Pete Lawrence named attorney S. R. Roddy as receiver, giving him $500 in July Fourth gate receipts to hold until the matter was settled.[32]

The fans who attended the first game at Sulphur Dell saw a spectacular contest. Chattanooga and Louisville battled to a 7–7 tie over 14 innings. The game was called "when it was too dark to play." Hogan pitched the entire game for Louisville, giving up only seven hits but walking nine. He struck out 12. Miller started for Chattanooga but was replaced by Nesbitt after five innings.[33]

Nashville fans saw another great extra-inning game later in the month when the Elite Giants played to a 13-inning 4–4 tie against Knoxville. Again, it was called because of darkness. Lighted fields would not become available until the 1930s. The starting pitchers, "Parson" Miller for Nashville and Rogers for Knoxville, each pitched nine innings. Young finished the game for Nashville while Knoxville turned to "Wing" Maddox for the final four innings.[34]

The second Chattanooga-Louisville game in Nashville was a 9–2 walkover for the Stars. Hogan scattered eight hits, but four of them were by Hub McGavock, who had a triple, double, and two singles in four at-bats for Chattanooga. McGavock's hitting show was likely the last hurrah for the Tigers. Although a doubleheader was scheduled for July 8, there was no report on it or any other Chattanooga games that season.

On May 22, Montgomery started a series in Birmingham. The opener was another exciting pitching duel with Johnny Juran winning an 11-inning game, 4–3. Catcher Watson's single with two on provided the winning margin. Sloppy fielding kept Birmingham from winning the game in regulation. The visitors were cited for outstanding base running and fielding. First baseman Marion Cunningham made several nice catches, had three hits in five at-bats, and "gave the game most of its spice." Cunningham, and other Montgomery players, argued frequently about the umpiring. At one time, the home plate umpire threatened to quit rather than put up with the abuse.[35]

By late June, Memphis had replaced Knoxville atop standings published in Memphis. However, Memphis is shown with a record of 28–19 and an obviously incorrect percentage of .737. With a 28–19 record, the correct percentage is .596. That would actually put Nashville (23–14, .622) in first place, Knoxville (22–14, .611) in second, and Memphis in third. The standings had the usual imbalance between total wins and total losses, as well as inexplicable differences in the number of games played. Memphis for example, was shown with having played 47 games while Montgomery had played only 29 games. Louisville was in last place with a dismal record of only six wins in 30 games.[36]

The puzzling figures fly in the face of assurances from league officials that professionalism would hold forth in the league's numbers in 1922. "The writer was in conversation with the secretary of the Negro Southern League a day or so ago and local followers of colored baseball will be glad to know that a strong effort is being made to keep an official standing of the Negro Southern League, and also an attempt is being made to publish regular batting, fielding, and pitching averages. This information should strengthen largely the interest in the league, and with permanent headquarters being established it should not be long before the above mentioned dope will be forthcoming," reported the *Birmingham News*.[37]

Despite Memphis' supposed domination the first few weeks, there were enough contenders for the lead that most series were important.

After nearly a month on the road, Birmingham returned home for games with Montgomery. With Johnny Juran pitching a five-hitter, the Black Barons won the opener by a lopsided 13–1 score. The Montgomery club, normally noted for good fielding, committed eight errors in the loss.[38]

Birmingham took three straight from Montgomery and reportedly had a 12-game winning streak going into its next series with Nashville. According to the *Birmingham News*, the Elite Giants were now in first place. If Birmingham won the series, it was reported, the Black Barons would take over the top spot.[39]

The 12-game winning streak cannot be substantiated, and Nashville made it irrelevant. The Elite Giants won all three games at Rickwood Field. The first game "was a thriller from the start to the thrilling finish and kept the colored fans on their toes throughout the nine innings of real baseball," reported the *News*. Birmingham fell behind, then fought back before falling, 7–6.[40]

The second game, scheduled for Tuesday, June 27, was rained out, setting up a double-header on Wednesday. Nashville won the opener, 4–1, scoring three runs in the top of the 12th inning. With two men on base, shortstop Philips hit a line drive to center field. Mitchell "made a desperate stab" at the ball but it got past him, allowing all three to score. The Elites took a five-inning second game, 5–3.[41]

Nashville and Knoxville battled into the poorly reported second half of the season, setting up an important series in late July.

Knoxville went into Nashville trailing the Elite Giants by just a few games in the standings. The visitors won the opener, 7–2, behind the pitching of Sampson. The second game was the 13-inning 4–4 tie. The third game went to the Elite Giants by forfeit. Third baseman Miles of Knoxville was blamed for the ruckus that resulted in the forfeit. Trailing 2–0, Nashville loaded the bases with just one out. Miles was said to have started an argument after each play. Maddox, Rogers, McCrary, and Hamilton also fueled the unpleasantness. When the Knoxville team left the field in protest, Umpire Rubber declared the forfeit.[42] Standings published in the newspaper that day showed Nashville with a three-game lead:

Nashville	47	24	.662
Knoxville	44	27	.620
Memphis	42	27	.609
New Orleans	39	30	.565
Louisville	37	32	.536
Chattanooga	35	34	.607
Montgomery	29	38	.433
Birmingham	29	41	.414
	302	253	

There was a wide margin of discrepancy between the total number of games won (302) and the number of games lost (253) by the eight teams.[43]

The following day the Elite Giants extended their lead by beating Knoxville twice. Sampson and Warren gave up 14 hits and Knoxville fielders committed six errors as Nashville won the first game, 12–8. In winning the seven inning nightcap 9–1, "Parson" Miller shut down the visitors on three hits. He struck out eight.[44]

The battle for the pennant resumed in Nashville a few days later when Knoxville returned for another series. The visitors cut into the margin with a 6–4 win in the opener. Nashville came back to take the next two games, winning 10–7 and 9–3. In the latter, Eddie Noel pitched a three-hitter and Leroy Stratton hit two doubles for the winners.[45]

The July 30 standings above were the last located, likely because the league blew up around the middle of the month. Birmingham and Montgomery disappeared from newspaper accounts after playing a July Fourth double-header. Louisville and Chattanooga's final games were apparently the July 6–7 encounters in Nashville. Memphis continued to play isolated series with league teams but was playing more games with teams such as the St. Louis Stars and Chicago American Giants, members of the major Negro National League, which Memphis was to join in 1923. New Orleans played a few league games, but most games were with local independent teams or on barnstorming trips to such far-flung locations as Selma, Alabama. Only Nashville and Knoxville appeared to have remained basically intact as viable NSL teams, playing each other the first week in August.

Following the Knoxville series, the Elite Giants left the city and did not return until September 3. There was no report on where the team was travelling and who it was playing during those absent weeks. Indeed, except for the Nashville-Knoxville series and one between Memphis and New Orleans later in the month, no league activity was located for the entire month of August.

Maddox, although playing with the independent Asheville, North Carolina, Giants, continued to wow Negro Southern League fans occasionally when the Giants played non-league games against NSL teams. His fielding was cited in a report on a game at Chattanooga in June. His work was even more notable because of the environment: "Andrews Field was in bad condition, really unfit for play, and the performance was badly slowed up," reported the *Chattanooga Times*.[46]

But later that month, the one-armed wonder was playing for Knoxville. A *Memphis Commercial-Appeal* sportswriter was exuberant in his report on Maddox's play: "The feature of the game was the fielding and batting of Madox [sic], the one-armed left fielder for Knoxville. He secured three of the four hits made by his team. He made a line drive over second, a single to right. He opened the ninth by beating out a perfect bunt. He stole second and went to third on an infield out. Madox had home stolen by a wide a margin, when the batter hit the ball and grounded out to retire the side. Madox went over into center field along the slope of the hill and speared a long fly—of course he speared it one-handed."[47]

In mid–August New Orleans Crescent Stars official W. C. Marine made a visit to Chicago to finalize plans for a Midwestern barnstorming tour to start with the St. Louis Stars on August 20. Marine's business partners in New Orleans were said to be Walter Cohen and C. C. Dejoie, president of the Unity Insurance Company. The *Chicago Defender* seemed to be favorably impressed with Marine and his associates: "The company operates a fine park, owned and controlled by them, but the patronage in that city is not what it should be. The public has not rallied to the support of the venture as it should. A talk with Mr. Marine leads us to believe that the city of New Orleans could be second to Chicago in baseball. His efforts to bring the patronage above the gambler type is succeeding although slowly."[48]

A few weeks later, Marine was among several men listed as the main proponents of a new Negro Southern League to be formed sometime in the fall.[49]

Once again a diminished number of box scores make meaningful individual statistics all but impossible to ascertain. As the number of boxes declined from 1920 to 1921, there was an even greater drop from 1921 to 1922. The 1922 dispersal was Memphis (16), Nashville (9), New Orleans Ads (9), Louisville (6), Knoxville (5), New Orleans Crescent Stars (5), Montgomery (2), Birmingham (1), and Chattanooga (0).

Memphis, with 16 total box scores, offers the best glimpse at the top players. Infielder William Griffin batted .378 in 13 games, while catcher Eppie Hampton hit .357 in as many games. Outfielder Carpenter batted .347 in 16 games. He had five extra base hits and five stolen bases.

It is difficult to determine just when the league folded. The final published standings on July 30 showed Nashville with a three-game lead over Knoxville. Memphis, which had run away with the lead most of the season, was in third place, four games back. Birmingham was in eighth place with a 29–41 record. To further complicate matters, the *Memphis Commercial-Appeal* in August referred to the Red Sox as "winners of the Negro Southern League pennant."[50]

The *Commercial-Appeal* further reported that the Red Sox would soon take on Dallas in a seven-game series to determine "the negro championship of the south."[51] One game with the Texans was reported with the Red Sox winning, 6–2, at Dallas on September 9.

Although the league disbanded, several of the teams continued to play independent ball into the fall, barnstorming in the East and the Midwest. The Montgomery Grey Sox arranged a series of games with the Augusta, Georgia team, called champions of the Southeastern Negro League.[52] Nashville and Memphis also continued travelling and playing well into September.

In September, reporting on plans for a new Southern league for 1923, the *Defender* said the 1922 league blew up "partly through mismanagement and lack of baseball experience." While it would be difficult to argue against mismanagement the lack of experience is peculiar. The 1922 season was the third in a row for several of the owners and managers. The *Defender* said the new league was being organized out of New Orleans and "The following businessmen have been interested in the venture, besides W. C. Marine and the present heads of the Crescent Stars of New Orleans: R. A. Lewis of Barnett & Lewis, undertakers of Memphis, ten. [sic]; Cashier Roddy of the Solvent Savings Bank of Memphis, Attorney J. Ernest Floyd and A.G. Reeves of the same city."

Likely members of the proposed new league were New Orleans, Memphis, Little Rock, Birmingham, Nashville, Selma "and two other cities yet to be decided on."

"The young enterprising business men of the Race in these cities will be approach [sic] with the ideal of making this league one of the strongest that has ever been formed. It will meet with the approval of the majority of the fans throughout the country."[53]

An intriguing footnote to the 1922 season is the game of June 11, the third in a four-game series between Birmingham and Nashville. Birmingham's starting pitcher in the 8–1 loss was a player identified only as Moss.[54] It seems likely that it was the final NSL appearance of Jimmy Moss, who had played compiled a 9–8 record with Montgomery in 1920. In 1921 Moss was 2–3 with Atlanta and 4–4 with Bessemer. He was also reported to have been with Knoxville, although no games were found to verify that.

The fascination with the game is trying to determine if Jimmy Moss was Jim Hugh Moss, who was executed for murder in Atlanta in 1927. Jim Hugh Moss had played briefly with Chicago teams in 1918 and 1919. The newspaper stories about his death in the electric chair indicated he had been a professional baseball player. Internet blogger Gary Ashwill, posting a biography of Moss in 2012, strongly suggested that the Chicago and NSL players were one and the same.[55]

On August 5, 1927, Moss, 21-year-old Clifford Thompson, and Thompson's 22-year-old wife Eula were transporting whiskey from their home near Etowah, Tennessee. They ran out of gas in Chatsworth, Georgia, near the store owned by Coleman Osborne. An after-hours attempt to purchase gas resulted in the shooting death of Osborne. Moss and the Thompsons were subsequently arrested and charged with murder. The two men were executed a year later and Eula Thompson was sent to prison.[56] Ashwill quotes an *Atlanta Constitution* story in which Moss is reported to be talking baseball just minutes before he was strapped into the electric chair.[57]

4

1923–25
Killed by Progress?

Again undaunted by the previous year's second half collapse, the Negro Southern League's backers spent the winter making plans for the 1923 season. That planning culminated in Birmingham with a league meeting on April 2. The meeting attracted representatives from "nearly every club in the South." Officers elected included J. T. Suttles of Memphis, president; Joe Rush of Birmingham, treasurer; and W. C. Marine of New Orleans, secretary. "Every President of a Club expressed enthusiasm and guaranteed the League that the best possible men have been drafted and none of them were ashamed of their teams and could present them in any section of the country and expect good baseball playing," wrote Oscar Adams in his "Sunday Negro" news column in the *Birmingham News*. A schedule committee meeting was set for April 17.[1]

Adams wrote that Birmingham owner Joe Rush had a good lineup of veteran players who would open spring training in Birmingham, then go on the road for a couple of weeks of exhibition games before opening the regular season with Memphis.

In addition to Birmingham and Memphis, the league was expected to be comprised of Chattanooga, Mobile, Nashville, and New Orleans, with two additional clubs to be added before the season opened.[2] The actual lineup for the 1923 season is difficult to pin down. Birmingham, Memphis, Nashville, and New Orleans were definitely members. No results were found for clubs in either Chattanooga or Mobile. There was a reference to Pensacola as a possible member and, indeed, at least one series was played between a Pensacola club and Birmingham. However, a check of the *Pensacola Journal* indicated only occasional weekend games between the Pensacola Colored Giants and visiting teams from Mobile and Montgomery. There was no mention of the NSL. Curiously absent were the Montgomery Grey Sox, a founding member and strong contender in years past.[3]

However, as the season progressed no new teams joined the league. In fact, the circuit may have opened with just four viable teams. Schedules were supplemented by games with such independent teams as the Atlanta Black Crackers, Pensacola Stars, Arkansas Travelers, and the 24th Infantry Regiment team from Fort Benning, Georgia. Interestingly, when Pensacola and Fort Benning went to Birmingham in June, they were referred to as "newcomers to the Negro Southern League."[4] That was probably a generic reference by the sportswriter, especially regarding Fort Benning. It would be highly unlikely that a military team could be cut loose for the rigors of a professional schedule for a period of several months.

No published standings were found for 1923, leaving the lineup of teams even murkier. The author, using Birmingham, Memphis, Nashville, and New Orleans as the only members, compiled the following first half standings:

Birmingham	24	8	.750
Memphis	15	16	.488
New Orleans	5	13	.278
Nashville	0	7	.000
	44	44	

It bears noting that of Memphis' 16 losses, 14 of them were to the powerful Birmingham club.

If filling a league lineup was already difficult, league leaders had to be stunned in July when the two most stable clubs, Birmingham and Memphis, jumped the NSL and applied for membership in the black major league, the Negro National League. That transition killed the season's second half, leaving Nashville and New Orleans with no league foes except each other. Additionally, no games between the two cities were located for either the season's first half or for whatever stab might have been made at a second half.

Opening Day was set for Monday, April 30. In the only game located, Birmingham beat Memphis, 4–0. Johnny Juran pitched a seven-hitter before a crowd reported at 8,500. The following day the Black Barons walloped the Red Sox 16–4.[5]

On May 18, Memphis opened a home series with Birmingham at its new Lewis Athletic Park, "one of the most modern negro amusement parks in the country." The facility, located at the intersection of South Lauderdale and Iowa, was built at a cost of about $10,000. In addition to the baseball venue, it contained tennis courts, croquet grounds, and a playground with other amenities expected to be added in the future. R. S. Lewis was listed as president of the park. Dedicatory activities included T. H. Hayes throwing out the first pitch to club official J. B. Martin.[6]

While Memphis fans celebrated the opening of the park, they were likely disappointed in the Red Sox. Birmingham swept the three-game series. Two of the games were shutouts. Despite those results, the Red Sox were second only to Birmingham in the 1923 NSL. Both started the season impressively, sweeping series after series from the other clubs. Indeed, it seemed at times as if the only teams who could best Birmingham and Memphis when they crossed bats were each other. And Birmingham won most of those encounters. By early July they totally dominated the league and were ready for an extraordinary, seldom seen move—leaving the NSL and joining the Negro National League in mid-season. It was the beginning of the black major league experience for both the Black Barons and Memphis.

Memphis had gotten a boost in June when Manager Walls signed catcher Larry Brown and pitcher Ralph "Squire" Moore away from Indianapolis. He also picked up C. B. "Bob" McCormick from Birmingham.[7] McCormick would only play briefly with the Red Sox, but Brown and Moore were mainstays for the rest of the season. Indeed, Brown would become one of the Memphis team's most familiar players for years to come. Although he played for other clubs at times, his career with Memphis as catcher and manager stretched to 1947.[8] Moore, also called "Square" and "Bun," was one of the original Red Sox in 1921 and played parts of several other seasons with the club.[9]

On July 2 against the Arkansas Travelers from Hot Springs, Willie Foster threw a no-hitter as Memphis won, 7–0. Foster, the half brother of Negro Leagues pioneer Rube

Foster, struck out 14 Arkansas batters.[10] Two years later he would throw a no-hitter for Birmingham against the Detroit Stars, but most of his best years were spent with his half brother's Chicago American Giants. Willie eventually joined Rube in the National Baseball Hall of Fame.

Birmingham's lineup included several players who would have notable careers in black baseball. The best of the lot was George "Mule" Suttles, called "Sellers" in most game accounts. A power-hitter who used a 50-ounce bat, Suttles was also inducted into the Hall of Fame, in 2006.[11] Poindexter Williams was the Birmingham manager, but missed most of the season after suffering a broken leg. Charles "Two Sides" Wesley and Buford "Geechie" Meredith were back in the infield and right-hander Harry "Fish" Salmon was back on the mound. Two other pitchers were the Juran brothers, left-hander Eli and right-hander Johnny. Like Suttles, they were rarely correctly identified. Game accounts and box scores frequently listed them as Durant and Durand. When newspaper stories made an effort at identification through the use of an initial and last name, it often resulted in more confusion. Johnny's nickname was "Bubber," occasionally leading to "B. Juran" in a box score or line score. Over several seasons the brothers were variously identified in game accounts as B. Durand, E. Durand, E. Durant, Jimmy Durant, M. Durant, B. Juran, D. Juran, Eli Juran, and Johnny Juran.

Birmingham owner Rush, who had taken over from Frank Perdue, predicted a stellar season for his ball club. It was not just rash, spring training optimism. Birmingham dominated the league in a manner that was hard to believe. From the 4–0 shutout of Memphis on opening day until the end of the first half in July, the Black Barons were in control.

In May they had a 12-game winning streak. Even more remarkable was the streak within the streak. From May 18 through May 26 the Black Barons won seven straight shutout games, producing a skein of 68 consecutive scoreless innings. It would likely have reached eight straight games, 72 innings, except for what the local media called a poor decision by an umpire. In the sixth inning of a game with Atlanta the umpire called a hotly disputed balk on Salmon, allowing a run to cross the plate. Birmingham won the game 11–1.[12]

According to the *Birmingham News,* the 68 innings were 14 innings shy of the world record established by Portland of the Pacific Coast League in 1913. Interestingly, the writer made no distinction between records held by white or black teams; it was just baseball.[13]

The games in the streak:
May 18, Birmingham 6, Memphis 0, at Memphis
May 19, Birmingham 6, Memphis 0, at Memphis
May 20, Birmingham 2, Memphis 0, at Memphis
May 21, Birmingham 16, Nashville 0, at Birmingham
May 22, Birmingham 5, Nashville 0, at Birmingham
May 23, Birmingham 3, Nashville 0, at Birmingham
May 25, @Birmingham 6, Atlanta 0
May 26, @Birmingham 11, Atlanta 1

The Atlanta pitcher in the May 26 game was "Wing" Maddox, the one-armed player who made his first appearance in Birmingham with the Atlanta Cubs in 1919. He pitched a creditable game against Birmingham, trailing by only 3–1 up to the point of the disputed balk call. The umpire's ruling, according to the *News*, so infuriated the Black Barons that they exploded for a seven-run seventh inning.

Maddox, who rarely spent an entire season with one team, was wearing a Birmingham uniform when the team returned home for a series with New Orleans in June. This time, playing center field, he was the catalyst for a 9–3 Birmingham win: "Maddox, the one-armed wonder of the locals, hit three times in four trips to the plate, getting a base on balls in his fifth appearance. Also handled two putouts in center with ease. This lad is really a wonder, both at bat and afield, his bunting exhibition being fine Wednesday." Maddox also stole a base in the game.[14]

By mid–May Birmingham was reported to have a record of 16–2. Some of the games were possibly against non-league teams, but it was clear that the team was dominant. Of 12 documented series from Opening Day through mid–July, Birmingham won nine and tied three. The ties were all against Memphis, which also lost three series to Birmingham. Memphis, which won all three series played against New Orleans and Nashville, was easily in second place.

Rain caused the cancellation of a number of games during the season, including a whole series in Memphis. The *New Orleans Times-Picayune* reported in May that just an hour before the Caulfield Ads were to board a train for Memphis Fred Caulfield received word that weather conditions in the Bluff City were so bad, it was best for the team not to leave New Orleans.

When the two clubs finally met in New Orleans a few weeks later, the Ads won the opener, 12–11. It was a game marked by 30 total hits and 16 stolen bases. Ads center fielder Roussell and his teammates Durand and Harris each had three hits, as did Russell and Ellis of the Red Sox. The local press, though, suggested that New Orleans was lucky to pull out the victory, given the work of its catcher: "The loose play of Catcher Nelson was really the direct reason of so many runs being scored. The Memphis players almost stole Nelson's uniform off his back." The Red Sox had 10 stolen bases, including three by third baseman Russell. Garrett Norman and "Red" Charleston each had two steals.[15] The Durand mentioned above was an infielder by this name, not a misidentified Juran brother from Birmingham.

As the first half wound down toward the traditional July Fourth finish, negotiations were apparently going on behind the scenes. On July 24, Joe Rush of Birmingham and J. T. Settles of Memphis went to Chicago for a meeting with officials of the Negro National League. The two Negro Southern League clubs petitioned the NNL for membership. They were accepted and a tentative schedule had Toledo and Milwaukee as the first clubs heading south. A news report from Chicago suggested that the acceptance of the two Southern clubs was not without a codicil: "According to present plans the Birmingham and Memphis teams will be taken into the Negro National only on condition that attendance at Birmingham and Memphis warrant the long jump of present teams in the league."[16]

The Negro National League had started the season with the Chicago American Giants, Cuban Stars, Detroit Stars, Indianapolis ABCs, Kansas City Monarchs, Milwaukee Bears, Toledo Tigers, and St. Louis Stars. Birmingham and Memphis played several games against NNL teams, but do not appear in the published standings, leading to the likelihood they were "associate members" of the league. The National League often had associate teams, which in return for promising not to raid league teams' rosters for players gained that protection themselves, in addition to the opportunity to play potentially lucrative games against league opponents. Black baseball historian John Holway provides rosters and statistics for Birmingham and Memphis, but does not recognize them as viable league members. Certainly neither team played enough games to qualify for pennant contention. League leader Kansas City is credited with a final record of 57–33. Two other black baseball historians, Dick Clark and Larry Lester credited Birmingham with a record of 15–23 and Memphis with 13–6.[17] Holway has Memphis at 17–8, but lists no record for Birmingham.[18]

Neither team played as well in the major league as it had in the NSL, but they were not bad additions to the NNL, either. Birmingham made its National League debut in Birmingham on July 19, playing a 4–4 tie with the Milwaukee Bears. After three games in Birmingham the Bears went to Memphis for a series, then returned to Birmingham for three more games. One game was rained out in each city. When Milwaukee departed it was with a record of 2–2–1 against Birmingham and 1–1 against Memphis.

The Bears were followed south by the Toledo Tigers, who played the two southern teams in a similar rotation. Toledo won the Birmingham series, 2–1, then dropped four straight to Memphis. The St. Louis Stars split six games with Birmingham, each winning and losing two games with two ties, while falling to Memphis three out of four games. Thus, Birmingham held its own with its first three NNL foes while Memphis won two out of three series.

Birmingham's nemesis would prove to be the league champion Chicago American Giants. Rube Foster's team won two and tied one in Birmingham in August. They ended Birmingham's season in late September with a four-game sweep. The Black Barons also lost series to the Cuban Stars and the Kansas City Monarchs in September.

As for the NSL, there appears to have been no second-half season. If there had been only four teams playing regularly, the loss of Birmingham and Memphis left only two. That number also was halved before July was over. Fred Caulfield, disappointed by attendance, disbanded his New Orleans team. Most of the better players were playing for the Cohen Stars and the New Orleans Giants, local independent teams, by later in the summer.

Ironically, Caulfield's disappointment was directed largely at the black community, saying that far more whites than blacks were attending the Ads' games. "I cannot see why we do not get better support," he complained to a New Orleans sports writer. "During that last two years I have dropped a small fortune in colored baseball in New Orleans and it is indeed discouraging."[19]

The Nashville Elite Giants survived as an independent team for several more weeks. When an Evansville team, scheduled to play at Memphis in late August, was unable to make the trip, the Elite Giants were drafted to fill the dates. Two games were played, with Memphis winning both, 6–0. A third game was canceled because of "weakened condition" of the Nashville club.[20]

The Black Barons had been dazzling in the Negro Southern League, completely dominating all opponents. With the almost certain demise of the league in July, it seems safe to award that 1923 pennant to Birmingham.

As the overwhelmingly dominant team in the league, Birmingham also dominated the individual statistics that could be compiled from 43 box scores with the following distribution: Memphis 34, Birmingham 30, New Orleans 15, and Nashville 7. Although box scores were available for games with Atlanta and Pensacola, they were not included because of the uncertainty of their league membership.

Two Birmingham players had their career best NSL seasons in the few short weeks of the first half schedule. Second baseman Charles "Two Sides" Wesley batted .424 in 31 games. His slugging percentage was .612. Shortstop Buford "Geechie" Meredith batted .362 in 32 games with a slugging percentage of .596. First baseman George McAllister batted .306, catcher Poindexter Williams .333, and pitchers Gordon Zeigler and Harry Salmon .421 and .326, respectively. Future Hall of Famer Suttles batted .286 and had only one home run, an off year for what would be the standard most of his career.

For Memphis the leading hitters were infielders T. Russell (.325) and Ellis (.312). Catcher "Red" Charleston hit .348 in a part-time role. New Orleans outfielder Harris and second baseman Durand batted .460 and .431, respectively, but only a dozen games were available for their team, fewer than half the number for Birmingham and Memphis players.

All pitching honors belonged to Birmingham's Harry Salmon, with a 7–2 record. He led in games started with nine, and in complete games with seven. He had two shutouts while teammate Johnny Juran had three.

When Birmingham faced the stronger competition of the Negro National League teams, batting and pitching records dropped significantly. For example, Wesley fell from .424 to .279 and Meredith from .362 to .288. Salmon's NNL pitching record was 5–3, but included three shutouts. Johnny Juran dropped to 1–3 with no shutouts.

With the Birmingham Black Barons and Memphis Red Sox playing in the Negro National League as full-fledged members, there was really nobody left to provide the backbone for a Negro Southern league during the 1924 and 1925 baseball seasons. Former NSL members that played independent ball during those two years were the Atlanta Black Crackers, Chattanooga Black Lookouts, Nashville Elite Giants, and the New Orleans Caulfield Ads.

Birmingham and Memphis enjoyed only marginal success as full-time members of the Negro National League in those two years. They each finished both seasons in the second division of the standings. Although neither wound up in last place, it was also true that neither completed a season above .500.

The one really bright spot was the work of Suttles for Birmingham. According to John Holway's detailed research, the big first baseman led the league in batting (.428) in 1925. He also finished fourth in home runs behind Charles Blackwell with 15 and Edgar Wesley and Turkey Stearnes with 18 each.[21]

There was also an economic factor involved with Memphis and Birmingham playing in the NNL. The two teams' travel to Chicago, Kansas City, and St. Louis was more time consuming and more expensive than trips to Atlanta, Chattanooga, or Nashville. There were indications that Midwestern teams shared similar concerns about their trips to the South. By mutual agreement of all parties, Birmingham and Memphis pulled out of the Negro National League before the 1926 season.

While losing major league status was not a proud moment for either city, the fans were likely ready for an environment in which their teams could be more competitive. That situation came about with the rebirth of the Negro Southern League in 1926.

5

1926
Revival of the Negro Southern League

The Associated Negro Press reported that when news of the withdrawal of Birmingham and Memphis from the Negro National League became known, "the interest of southern baseball fans in the two cities was so aroused that R. S. Lewis, owner of the Memphis Red Sox, sought a conference with leading business and professional men ... looking towards the formation of a Southern League."[1]

At a meeting in Memphis attended by Dr. J. B. Martin, B.M. Roddy, T. J. Johnson, and others, only two days was needed to for the organization of the league. Officers were elected and a first-half schedule drawn up for a season to open on May 1.[2]

The smoothness of that finalization of league plans was due, in part, to a preliminary meeting in January held in Birmingham at the Pythian Temple. At that meeting each prospective member put up a $500 franchise fee and $70 "for promotional purposes." In another financial matters it was determined that five percent of gross gate receipts at each game would go to the central organization. League officers selected at the meeting were Joe Rush, Birmingham, president; Henry Hannon, Montgomery, vice president; A. G. Montgomery, Albany, Georgia, secretary.[3]

The initial officers were, perhaps, selected for organizational purposes only. When the season began Bert M. Roddy, owner of the Solvent Savings Bank of Memphis, was listed as president, and R. T. Jackson of Birmingham was secretary-treasurer. Oscar W. Adams, who had defended Joe Rush at the heated Elks Lodge meeting, was named to the board of directors. Adams was publisher of the *Birmingham Reporter*, the local black newspaper, and president of the Colored Citizens' League. He also wrote a weekly "What Negroes Are Doing" column in the Sunday *Birmingham News*, the daily white newspaper. His son, Oscar W. Adams, Jr., would later become the first black to serve on the Alabama Supreme Court.[4]

But the resurrection of the Negro Southern League was far from a totally smooth transaction. In fact, a dispute over ownership of the Birmingham club threatened to derail the league's revival. Joe Rush, owner of the Black Barons for the past three years, was in the forefront of the new NSL. In early March it was rumored that the team was owned by Rube Foster of Chicago, not Rush, and that Foster was sending his man Sam Crawford to run the operation and secure Rickwood Field for a Negro National League franchise.

At a somewhat heated meeting at the Jones Valley Elks Lodge in Birmingham Crawford, Quincy. J. Gilmore of Kansas City, and W. N. Kritzky of Birmingham spoke to the NNL's interest. Kritzky, whose name had been spelled incorrectly in the newspaper report of the meeting, was a white man who announced that he taken over the operation of the Black Barons and that Sam Crawford would be his field manager. Adams, a Birmingham club director, spoke forcefully against that proposal, saying Joe Rush deserved better treatment for his work for the Birmingham community.[5]

Shortly after this rancorous gathering at the Elks lodge, Roddy, the president of the NSL, came to Birmingham to personally negotiate a contract for Rickwood Field. He emerged from meetings with Billy West, general manager of the Birmingham Barons, and Kritzky with an agreement for the Black Barons, through the NSL, to use the field when the white club was away. Kritzky relinquished all previous claims to the facility and said further negotiations with Rube Foster had been canceled.[6] Still, the meetings in Birmingham and Memphis laid the foundation for the new league. In addition to Rush and Roddy, other prominent blacks involved in the reorganization of the league included R. S. Lewis, prominent undertaker and owner of the Memphis Red Sox; Fred Caulfield of the New Orleans club; H. J. Bailey of the Montgomery Grey Sox; George S. Stewart, Atlanta business man and owner of the Black Crackers; J. S. Montgomery of the Albany, Georgia, Giants; and C. M. Carter of the Chattanooga Giants.[7]

The 1926 season would prove to be one of the most successful in the league's history. Most of the eight teams finished the season, although the Atlanta club was placed in receivership and eventually declared bankruptcy. Montgomery apparently folded in early August after a disastrous series in Memphis that included a 22–3 loss. Standings were published frequently in a number of newspapers during the first half. Not nearly as many were published during the second half, but that was offset by those carried each week in the *Memphis Commercial-Appeal*. This offered a rare glimpse at accurate second-half standings when league play was customarily curtailed by barnstorming road trips.

A Nashville writer, obviously expecting to be entertained by "Negro antics" at a Sulphur Dell game, found a bit of that but also something more: "Witnessing our first Elite Giant Negro Southern League game, we were pleasantly surprised at the class of baseball the darktown stars are showing. Nashville senegambian heroes walloped the Montgomery entry rather handily by a 10 to 4 margin, but displayed baseball worthy of real Southern League competition. Negroes are naturally comedians and carry quite a bit of that to the diamond with them, but take the pennant race much more seriously than might be expected…. The game abounded in sparkling catches, fleet base-running, and heavy slugging by the Elite Giants."[8] The writer, Joe Hatcher, was so impressed with the caliber of baseball he had seen that he appended the box score of the game to his article. It was one of the few for a Negro Leagues game ever published in the Nashville papers.

In all, 154 box scores were located for the season, offering one of the best opportunities for compiling individual player statistics in the history of the league. Indeed, the *Commercial-Appeal* even ran a set of individual batting averages, presumably released by the league office, in mid–June. This is the only such offering ever located for the NSL in any season.

"The first four weeks' play in the Southern League has shown two things: first, that the fans in this section want organized baseball, and, second, … the pennant race is going to be tight," reported the *Commercial-Appeal* in early June, adding that attendance

5. 1926: Revival of the Negro Southern League

had been good in all league cities to that point.[9] Both observations proved generally true as the season progressed.

There were eight teams in the new league, seven of them familiar names and one newcomer:

- Albany, Georgia, Giants. The manager of the new club was big Bill Gatewood, a durable pitcher who would play with more than a dozen clubs over a 24-year career. Usually referred to as "Big Bill," he is credited with bestowing the nickname "Cool Papa" on Hall of Famer James Bell.[10] Most of the Giant players were listed only by last name. Two exceptions were Peter Washington and Jim Jeffries. Washington, a fast outfielder, played about a dozen years, mostly with Eastern teams. Jeffries was a durable pitcher, whose career started in 1913 and continued into the early 1930s, much of it with the Indianapolis ABCs.[11]
- Atlanta Black Crackers. The manager was W. J. Johnson, the "heavy hitting catcher of this year's Morris Brown team." He was said to be an experienced ball player in Eastern and Western leagues. It was not clear why he was on the Morris Brown College team, unless he was the team's coach.[12] The Atlanta team counted on local players from Atlanta University, Morris Brown College, and Morehouse College to bolster its roster. Catcher "Nish" Williams, infielders "Suggarty" Murden and Charlie Hawkins, and first baseman Ted Gilliam were all familiar players in Atlanta.
- Birmingham Black Barons. The new Birmingham manager was Clarence Smith, a veteran outfielder who started with Columbus Buckeyes in 1921 and played with the Detroit Stars for several years. This was one of Birmingham's best teams. Two key players for Birmingham would be catcher Poindexter Williams and pitcher Robert Poindexter, a pair of names tailor-made for confusion in the reporting of those times.
- Chattanooga Black Lookouts. William Lowe, a versatile infielder who spent most of his career with the Memphis Red Sox, was the manager. One of his top players was a young, lanky right-handed pitcher named Leroy "Satchel" Paige. He would not dominate the league the first year the way his

A legend even before his Negro major league career, Leroy "Satchel" Paige made his professional debut with the Chattanooga Black Lookouts in 1926 (courtesy Faye Davis and the Birmingham Public Library Archives).

legend suggests, but he did show plenty of talent and, early on, he was captivating the fans. In late July, a *Chattanooga Daily Times* writer referenced a semipro pitcher who had thrown a no-hitter, striking out 17. The writer called the pitcher "a rival to Satchell [*sic*]."

- Memphis Red Sox. Managed by Charles "Two-Sides" Wesley, the Red Sox would challenge Birmingham for supremacy in 1926. Among his best players would be left-handed pitchers Carl Glass and Hulan Stamps, outfielder C. "Pinky" Ward, and catcher Larry Brown, a late season addition.
- Montgomery Grey Sox. Managed by veteran Henry Hannon, this Grey Sox team would struggle, never approaching the kind of play that dominated the league in the early 1920s. "Dad" Cunningham played shortstop and Forest "Wing" Maddox was with the team later, taking over as manager in mid-summer. Montgomery's troubles included a car wreck en route from Memphis to Chattanooga in August.
- Nashville Elite Giants. Owner Tom Wilson signed Leroy Stratton, a stalwart on the strong 1923 Birmingham team, as the manager. Eddie Noel anchored his pitching staff and William McNeil was a capable outfielder.
- New Orleans Black Pelicans. This team, filling the spot in the league in which the Caulfield Ads had been in previous years, was managed by Eddie Caulfield, according to one report. The *New Orleans Times-Picayune*, however, indicated that the manager was Fred Caulfield. The star position player was outfielder Roy "Red" Parnell, who had come from the Houston Black Buffaloes and whose career spanned nearly 20 years. In July, Parnell was reported to have hit 25 home runs. If so, that likely included barnstorming games, because his league total was six in 50 New Orleans games for which box scores were located.

Outfielder Roy "Red" Parnell was one of the all-time great hitters in the NSL, playing with Birmingham, Monroe, New Orleans and Nashville. In 1926 with New Orleans he hit .381 with nine triples (courtesy of NoirTech Research).

5. 1926: Revival of the Negro Southern League

Grey Sox manager Henry Hannon had been involved in high-level black baseball for years by the time he signed on to manage Montgomery. In this circa 1920 photograph Royal Ponciana Hotel club, he stands second from the right in the back row. In addition to Hannon, the team included players Robinson (1), James H. Smith (2), H. Brown (4), George Wright (5), Johnson (6), Sam Anderson (7), Charles Earle (8), Bradley (9), and Charles Winston (10). Child is unidentified (courtesy James Hannon).

The schedule drawn up by the league officials for the first half was something of an anomaly. A matrix published in the *Pittsburgh Courier* showed 190 league games, but the distribution ranged from a low of 43 games for Chattanooga to a high of 54 games for Memphis. Likewise, the distribution of home and away games showed a great disparity:

Team	Home	Away	Total
Albany	27	18	45
Atlanta	16	31	47
Birmingham	17	24	41
Chattanooga	19	24	43
Memphis	43	11	54
Montgomery	38	13	51
Nashville	20	31	51
New Orleans	10	38	48
	190	190[13]	

There was also an inconsistency in schedule dates that appears to parallel the uneven number of games per team. While most dates saw all eight teams in action, there are others when two or four teams are noticeably unaccounted for. Those dates are blanks on the schedule matrix.

Since all of the teams were playing in cities with white professional clubs, it seems likely that NSL scheduling took a back seat to the white Southern Association teams' schedules and also possibly to amateur events such as city league games. The Association lineup for 1926 included Atlanta, Birmingham, Chattanooga, Little Rock, Memphis, Mobile, Nashville, and New Orleans. Albany and Montgomery were in the Class B Southeastern League with Columbus, Jacksonville, Savannah, and St. Augustine.[14]

Memphis had its own facility, Lewis Park. Consequently, that venue could be available almost any time it was needed. The Montgomery Grey Sox at times played at Cramton Bowl there, and also on the Alabama State campus and at other local parks. This made them less dependent on white teams for a playing field.

Opening Day was Saturday, May 1, with all eight teams playing. The newcomer, Albany, played at Montgomery, swamping the Grey Sox, 19–5, before a large crowd. The locals had lined up the Rev. S. Davis, pastor of the First Baptist Church, and Dr. L. D. Workman, respectively, to throw and receive the ceremonial first pitch. Albany apparently filled several train cars with fans who wanted to see their team's first game, even if it was on the road: "...the little town of Albany, rich in pomp and loyalty, declared a holiday for Monday so the whole city, including the thousands who came in on excursions, might go to the park and give Gatewood their backing," wrote league President Roddy in the *Chicago Defender*.[15] In the other three opening games the home teams all won. Memphis beat New Orleans, 7–6, Chattanooga beat Birmingham, 5–4, and Nashville shut out Atlanta, 5–0.

About 50 fans from Birmingham were expected to take a train to Chattanooga for that opener. When the Black Barons returned to Birmingham for their home opener on May 10, "colored business men are asked to give half-holiday and white concerns are requested to let their employees off for a few hours."[16]

The Birmingham club had lined up the Industrial High School band for musical entertainment, Presiding Bishop Benjamin. G. Shaw of the A.M.E. Zion Church was invited to throw out the first pitch to a local minister with the appropriate name of Dr. J. W. Goodgame. Civic and business organizations pledged to attend the game as groups. P. D. Davis, president of the Civic Association, said he would give a new Stetson hat to the first Birmingham player hitting a home run.[17] Rain shortened the 5–1 Birmingham win over Memphis to five innings and cut down on the expected crowd.[18]

In Memphis, "many thousands were present before the game was called." One report estimated the crowd at 15,000.[19] In one of the most exciting openers, the Red Sox broke a 6–6 tie in the bottom of the 12th inning to edge New Orleans, 7–6.[20]

Although the weather was threatening, a large crowd "from all walks of life and from every section of the city" turned out at Spiller Park in Atlanta for the Black Crackers' opener with Nashville. Benjamin J. Davis, editor of the *Atlanta Independent* newspaper, threw the first pitch to President Roddy, who drilled it down the third base line "for a fair hit amid the cheers of the anxious throng." Also present was Mal Carter, owner of the Chattanooga Black Lookouts.[21]

Forbes, a Morehouse College ace, struck out the first two batters he faced. Then Cotton, from Morris Brown, led off for Atlanta and brought the crowd to its feet with drive that appeared certain to leave the park. However, "the ball was hit into the territory of one of the greatest outfielders in colored baseball—Carpenter, who made the chance easy, and with a sweep of his hand caught the ball as it floated over his head, but the crowd continued to yell for it was one of the most beautiful catches that has been seen in Spiller's Park in many a day."

Atlanta gave Forbes a run in the bottom of the fourth but he couldn't hold the lead. Nashville scored three runs in each of the fifth, seventh, and ninth innings to win the game, 9–2. Eddie Noel limited Atlanta to six hits and first baseman Ellis hit a home run for the Elite Giants.[22]

Despite the disappointing opening day start, Montgomery management was determined to make getting to the game easy for the fans. The team chartered a number of automobiles "to meet the street cars and convey the fans from there to the ball grounds free of charge."[23] Women were frequently admitted free. The street car stop nearest the ball park was Pickett Springs, once a popular resort where the community of Chisholm is today.[24]

After a week of play, the new Albany club was off to a highly successful start, having won all five of its games, including a 15-run outburst two days after opening day. Memphis (4–2) was second. Chattanooga, Nashville, New Orleans, and Birmingham were bunched in the middle of the standings, all hovering around .500. Atlanta (1–5) and Montgomery (0–5) were off to horrendous starts.[25]

Albany, Birmingham, New Orleans, and Memphis quickly established themselves as the better teams. Atlanta, after a poor start, put a winning streak together and reached .500. But that was a short-lived success and the Black Crackers were soon in the second division for the remainder of the season.

New Orleans' early success was notable because the Black Pelicans played their first 12 games on the road, winning nine of them. They returned to New Orleans on May 21 to host Chattanooga. Outfielder Parnell was reported to have hit five home runs, including two in one game at Montgomery, during the first three weeks of the season.

Chattanooga won the game, 4–1, behind the six-hit pitching of Satchel Paige and six errors by New Orleans fielders. Paige struck out six. But that was as good as Chattanooga would be in the Crescent City. The Black Pelicans won the next four games in the series to remain in the thick of the pennant race.

By mid–June Birmingham (16–6) had taken over first place with a one-game lead over Albany (15–7). New Orleans (13–10) was the only other club over .500. Paige notwithstanding, Chattanooga at 7–13 was tied with Montgomery for last place.[26]

That same week, a Memphis paper carried the only individual statistics ever found for the NSL. The release consisted of batting averages for all players hitting over .300. "Pinky" Ward of Memphis and "Red" Parnell of New Orleans were listed as tied for the lead. Unfortunately, none of the batting averages match the hits and times at bat when the standard batting average formula is applied. For example, both Ward (30 hits, 70 at-bats) and Parnell (28 hits, 60 at-bats) are reported at .420. However, a quick use of a calculator shows those averages should be .429 and .467, respectively. Indeed, none of the batting averages match the hits and at-bats in the published figures.[27]

Although no other individual averages were found, toward the end of June it was reported that Parnell was leading the league in home runs with 22.[28] This figure, if accurate, would have to include games played against semipro and other non-league teams. In box scores for 50 New Orleans games, 38 in which Parnell played, his home run total is only six. Parnell missed several games in August, possibly with an injury. The local press noted his absence from the lineup, but did not explain why.[29]

While only the one set of league individual batting averages has ever been located, such figures were provided occasionally for local teams. When Atlanta returned home for a series with Chattanooga in late June, it was reported that Cotton led the team in batting with a .303 average. He had collected 27 hits in 89 at bats over 24 games. The earnest effort of 1926 league officials to provide the kinds of numbers that drive baseball fans' enthusiasm was frustrated at every turn. Following is a succession of notations, presumably from President Roddy, about the lack of cooperation from the teams:

"Southern league scores are not being sent in properly. Games should be mailed, score by innings, hits and errors, including batteries of both clubs, by special delivery night of game and not held until you have finished the series.

"The success of the league depends upon the interest the public has in the league and this interest is not aroused by the printing of stale games, but up-to-the-minute matter."[30]

"We have sent the Southern league owners score sheets so we could give you the score by innings, but they refuse to send the scores in as per instructions. If you are interested in the league you might help by getting behind the owners in your home town. We can't take an airplane and come down there and get the scores."[31] "Birmingham, Albany, New Orleans, Chattanooga, Montgomery and Atlanta haven't got men who can keep score by innings—a thing any 10-year-old boy can do—then add the batteries, place a special delivery stamp on letter after game and mail it to us. We believe if they had such men the fans in the Southern league would not go without scores week after week. Not our fault, folks—get after your home town club. Memphis is doing fine, but the others need some red pepper."[32]

Then, in August as the Red Sox were in the thick of the pennant race, there was apparently a lapse in the Bluff City: "Memphis reports come in four and five games at a time. There are no dates on the reports, and we, of course, are not mind readers or we would be sitting in an office with a palmist's sign hung on the outside, making an easy living. It is hard to get Memphis and some of the owners of the Southern league clubs to mail in their games special delivery the night of the game or the morning after. They hold them until four or five games have been played and then shoot them in without a date or days when the games have been played. The result is they hit the waste basket. Repeated requests to L.C. Sharp, R. C. Lewis, and those connected with the Memphis club have gone unheeded."[33]

On the field, the players were not as negligent in their duties. In a Memphis doubleheader "Steel Arm" Tyler threw a two-hitter on June 27 to beat New Orleans, 1–0, in the second game. In the opener, which New Orleans won, 9–6, Roy Parnell hit a three-run homer off Tyler, who was pitching in relief. The homer was said to be Parnell's 23rd of the season.[34]

On Monday, June 27, Birmingham and Albany, in a virtual tie for first place, opened a series in Albany. Only two games were played and Albany was dominant in both. Big

Bill Gatewood threw a no-hitter in the first contest, although three Birmingham batters reached first base, two on errors and one when the catcher missed a third strike.[35]

When the first-half season ended during the first week in July, John Montgomery, a local backer of the team, told the *Albany Herald* that the local Giants had won the first half pennant. Montgomery said that while Birmingham was winning four out of five at Memphis (actually three out of four), Albany had claimed four forfeits over New Orleans, which had failed to show up for the final first half series.[36] New Orleans also owed Albany $250 for failing to show up. In addition, he also claimed two forfeits over Birmingham when the Black Barons refused to play an unscheduled doubleheader on July 1. League officials apparently denied Albany's claims, thus giving the first half flag to Birmingham.[37]

When Roddy offered no explanation for the denial, the rumor mill in Albany provided one: "There is a strong rumor going the rounds that the officers of the league could not afford to let Albany win the first half of the league race because the city is too small, and that the league would lose money, playing the fall series between winner of the first half and the winner of the second half."[38]

At a June 23–24 meeting in Montgomery, league officials drew up a second-half schedule and also adopted by-laws and a constitution similar to that employed by the white Southern Association.[39]

As the season's second half got under way it was reported that each owner proclaimed his team was certain to win the second-half pennant. "Due to the fact that there were 8 claimants, President Bert M. Roddy ruled that in order to settle the question the pennant would have to be won on the diamond and not in the meeting. So they are off," reported the *Pittsburgh Courier*.[40]

New Orleans continued to play well in the second half, sweeping a series from Memphis and then one from Montgomery. The struggling Grey Sox were now being managed by "Wing" Maddox, who continued to astound fans everywhere he played. "Maddox is one of the curiosities of the diamond. Minus his left arm, which is cut off just below the shoulder, Maddox gets around in the outfield and at bat, in fine fashion. When chasing flies, he makes his catch with one hand, slips the glove under his stump, and heaves the ball into infield. His agility is amazing," reported a New Orleans writer.[41] His pitching repertoire was said to include "a fine collection of curves and his speed and control, considering the lack of balance caused by his handicap, is remarkable."[42] A Birmingham writer described Maddox as "the most sensational and scientific baseball player in negro baseball circles."[43]

But Maddox was ever the traveler. On August 7, he "brought the fans up" in Chattanooga when he hit a triple for the Atlanta club. Chattanooga won the game, 8–7, but that series saw Maddox in every game with the Black Crackers. Montgomery apparently disbanded after a series with Memphis a few days earlier.

After a week's play in the second half the New Orleans Black Pelicans were 6–0, followed by Chattanooga at 4–1 and Birmingham at 3–2. Next up for them was a series at Birmingham. The *Birmingham News* was effusive on the strength of the New Orleans club: "The Ads [sic] will bring some of the best players in the league.... Parnell, who patrols one of the outer gardens for Caulfield's crew, is the leading hitter of the league and also the leader in home runs. He has 25 four-base clouts to his credit, nine more than Sammy West, home run king of the Southern Association. Jemison is another hard-hitting outfielder with the Ads. Lourant is one of Caulfield's star hurlers and will likely open against the Black Barons Monday. Willis, another of the Ads staff of hurlers, has the best record in negro baseball. He has not lost a single game this season and will likely work the game against the Smithies Tuesday. The Ads keystone combination is one of the best in the league. Collins and Alexander [are] working together like parts of a well oiled machine."[44]

Another outstanding New Orleans player was Roussell, an outfielder whose first name is unknown. He was noted during the season for his strong throwing arm. In a series at Atlanta in late July, Roussell attempted to beat the world's record for a distance throw. He hurled the baseball 391 feet and seven inches, far short of the reported world record of 426 feet, nine and one-half inches. It was said that a previous throw by Roussell two days earlier had come closer to the world mark.[45]

But despite the assertion of the *News,* Jim Willis was far from having an undefeated pitching record. Indeed, he was the losing pitcher in the club's very first game of the season in Memphis. Still Willis, often called "Smokey," was a formidable moundsman. Based on the author's compilations, he finished the 1926 season with a 17–9 record. He would later play with Birmingham and a number of other clubs. He was most noted for several successful years with the Nashville Elite Giants.[46] The outfielder Jemison is a puzzle, because no player with that name was referenced in a box score or game report. It is possibly the first name of another player.

Birmingham, although trailing in the new standings for the second half, was still a strong ball club and added several new players. The big signee was Robert Poindexter, a right-handed curve and spitball pitcher who had been with the team in 1924–25 in the Negro National League. Poindexter was obtained from the Chicago American Giants. John Lilly, an Alabama outfielder, and Daniels, a player from Texas, were also added.

Manager Smith said the addition of Poindexter to a staff that included Harry Salmon and Leo Birdine gave his team a good mound corps. One writer said Salmon and Birdine were capable of pitching for the white Barons and lauded the caliber of play the black team was exhibiting: "The baseball played by the negro Southern League teams at Rickwood this year has been very good, and they deserve a better support than they have been getting. The white fans of the city, as a whole, are not aware of the class of baseball being exhibited by the negro teams at the 'Wood.... Monday will be a good time to go and take your first look at the Ebony Barons."[47]

New Orleans increased its lead with a 4–1 win in the first game on July 19. Parnell, with two hits and two stolen bases, paced the offensive attack and "Collins' fielding around base was spectacular and uncanny." Poindexter gave up only six hits, but Birmingham committed five errors behind him, accounting for the visitors' runs.[48]

Salmon and Birdine pitched Birmingham to wins in the next two games. Parnell continued his strong hitting, getting two doubles in one game and two singles in the other.

Still, after two weeks of play, the Crescent City team was 9–3 with a half-game lead over Chattanooga (9–4). Birmingham (7–6) was the only other team over .500. Nashville and Atlanta were tied for last place with 3–10 records.[49]

5. 1926: Revival of the Negro Southern League

The second half was barely two weeks old when it was reported that the Atlanta club, struggling all year with poor attendance, had been "put in the hands of the receivers." One black sports writer predicted that the dissolution of the club was likely:

> Experience has taught us that no concern, even though it is a going concern, can survive a contest in the courts of Atlanta. It will end with the courts having all and you left the balance. We understand that the receiver is a white man, who cares as much about a Negro baseball game as a cat does about a dog, and when they went off on a trip he did not even go.... We blame Negroes for not being able to do anything without calling in a white man whose duty it is to get what money there is in it.[50]

The paper later reported that receivership was the incorrect action and an injustice to Atlanta club's investors. It was noted that capital investment totaled $493 while expenditures were approximately $1,800. Thus, the legal action should have been bankruptcy.[51]

By early August it was reported that catcher Vinicius "Nish" Williams, pitcher Joe Daniels, and infielder "Suggarty" Murden had quit the foundering team.[52] When the Birmingham Black Barons came to town in late August their opponent was an all-star team comprised of local city leaguers and former Black Crackers.[53]

Late in the season, both the *Atlanta Journal* and the *Atlanta Constitution* were referring to the local NSL team as the Cubs rather than the Black Crackers. There was no explanation for the change. Nor was this change in nomenclature observed by the black *Atlanta Independent*.

By mid–August Memphis, New Orleans, and Albany were locked in a three-way battle for first place. The Black Pelicans went to Memphis for a three-game series that propelled the home team into the lead. After a 9–9 tie on Friday night, they were rained out on Saturday. Memphis then took a Sunday double-header, 5–1 and 1–0, to take the lead.

William Tyler struck out six and held the Black Pelicans to eight hits in the opener. J. C. McHaskell and Bob Miller each had three hits for the Red Sox. In the five-inning nightcap, Augustus outdueled Willis. "Pinky" Ward had a triple for the winners.[54]

Birmingham, the first half winner, had dropped to fourth place, followed by Chattanooga and Nashville. Atlanta and Montgomery continued to struggle.[55]

On August 19, New Orleans returned home for a series with Albany. The Black Pels and Memphis were said to be tied for first with 17–5 records.[56] That number was obviously incorrect, but the Black Pelicans swept the four-game series, pushing Albany out of contention. The sweep kept New Orleans close behind Memphis, which solidified its lead with a four-game sweep of Chattanooga.

Following the second-half tradition of barnstorming tours, both Birmingham and Memphis made forays into the Midwest to play the Negro National League's St. Louis Stars. Birmingham managed to win one of four while Memphis lost all four games to the Stars. On the Midwestern trip, Birmingham also played a series of games with Nashville at St. Louis.

Albany took an extensive road trip in July and August, starting at Fort Benning in Columbus, Georgia. The trip would include NSL games but also off-day games in Evansville, Chicago, and Detroit. "The Giants' fame has gone before them as the fastest negro team ever in the South, and the management is thronged with requests from teams in the East and Northwest for open dates," reported the local newspaper.[57]

Interestingly, the Giants were said to be playing the role of good-will ambassador for their Georgia city on the extensive road trip. Club management announced that they would advertise the City of Albany in their travels, taking along promotional pamphlets for distribution. The team's uniforms would have not only "Albany" on the front but also "World's Pecan Center" on the back. The white Southeastern League team had started its season with the nickname of "Pecans." Predictably, media and fans quickly replaced that with "Nuts" as the season progressed.

The team issued an appeal for support as it prepared its departure: "In contemplation of the road trip, the management is appealing to the loyal fans, both white and colored, to rally to the support of the club by turning out in full force for the final games here on Tuesday, Wednesday and Thursday.

"There is heavy expense to be met before the club hits the roads and the management finds it necessary to make this urgent appeal to all those who believe in progressive Albany."[58]

There was no report on response to the appeal. The Atlanta club failed to make it to Albany for the first game on Tuesday because of tire troubles and bad weather. It appears likely that the entire series was rained out.[59]

Montgomery and Atlanta, as in the first half, spent most of the second at or near the bottom of the standings.

Montgomery's troubles continued on the field, but the team was also plagued by outside forces. On July 30 the Grey Sox had to forfeit a game at Memphis because they couldn't field a team: "...the Alabamians were unable to place a team on the field for yesterday's game. An automobile bearing over a half of the Montgomery team broke down near Tupelo, Miss., yesterday and only four of the team members reached Memphis yesterday afternoon in an advance car."[60]

It only got worse. After the team was finally assembled for the series, the Red Sox took four straight games by scores of 6–2, 7–1, 22–3, and 9–3. Although Montgomery pitchers only gave up five bases on balls, they were pummeled for 57 hits in the four games.

When they left Memphis the Montgomerians were headed to Chattanooga to open a series on August 6. They never made it because "somewhere on the way their automobile was wrecked."[61] That was apparently the end of the season for the Grey Sox. No further results were found after the Memphis series.

Atlanta, although with a roster of popular local players, was obviously a mediocre team with poor support at home. But Dr. A. D. Jones, writing in the *Atlanta Independent*, lauded the quality of baseball being played by the Black Crackers and appealed to the "race conscience" of the local citizenry:

> They are playing for the entertainment of the Colored people of Atlanta, the majority of the players are school boys. Now these boys cannot play baseball without money, and the manager of the Black Crackers cannot hire them unless the games are patronized. Now it is up to the Colored people of Atlanta to patronize these games. It is known that the white games at Spillers Field, you are compelled to go way over beyond left field. So far, in fact, from the batter that you need a telescope to see him.
>
> Yet under these conditions you go out there in droves, to see no better baseball than the Black Crackers are giving you. I am appealing to your race conscience to come to these games and show the players that you are willing to patronize good clean baseball.

Jones added that, in his experience at the ball park, the spectators had behaved, presenting a setting where a man could take his wife or daughter without being "made to feel ashamed."[62]

A few weeks later, Davis, the *Independent*'s editor, once again noting sometimes sparse attendance at the games, chided the black community for not supporting the Atlanta team:

> We cannot see why Colored Atlanta does not patronize our own games, which are indeed interesting and clean. They are permitted to sit in the grandstand and boxes where they can see the game right off the bat. And why they persist in going out there when the white Crackers play and are forced way down behind the left field where they can hardly see the batter in preference to the way they sit in our games, we cannot understand. We are almost forced to say the Negro likes to be Jim-Crowed. We see nothing else. Now lets [sic] come out and give the Black Crackers a good crowd and we promised you they will have a ball club that will hold its own with any in the league.[63]

The segregation for baseball games was not only carried out on the field, but at the ticket window as well. The *Atlanta Constitution* announced that tickets for an upcoming Black Crackers game could be purchased at 41 West Mitchell and at the business of Milton & Yost at the corner of Auburn and Butler streets. "The 41 West Mitchell office is for the white people and the Auburn avenue office for the colored," the paper reported.[64]

In an effort to boost flagging attendance, the Atlanta club announced reduced prices for a Ladies Day game with Memphis. The price was 50 cents for the grandstand and 35 cents for the bleachers.[65]

Despite the financial problems, the team held on for most of the season, playing games into late August.

Nashville, another second division club most of the season, occasionally showed flashes of respectability on the field. The Elite Giants, along with Montgomery, may have shared in the origin of one the more entertaining stories of the Negro Leagues.

As the season neared its close Nashville picked up catcher Westmoreland from the defunct Montgomery Grey Sox. In a Labor Day weekend series with Chattanooga, he was said to have lived up to his reputation. Supposedly written on his chest protector was, "Thou Shall Not Steal."[66] It should be noted that a similar story has been told about other catchers, most notably Ted "Double Duty" Radcliffe. It was credited, also, to Bill Perkins, one of Satchel Paige's favorite catchers.[67]

Although the slogan was never specifically attributed to him, it became the title of a book on Bill "Ready" Cash, a strong catcher of the 1940s. Writer Gene Elston relates a story told by Joe Durham, a Chicago American Giants outfielder: "[He] used to tell of a story about a catcher (no name mentioned) who used to wear a sign saying, 'Thou shall Not Steal.' When a runner would try to steal on him, the catcher would come up throwing and yelling, 'The speed cop'll get you.' Durham added, and he was usually right. True or false, it's a great story!"[68]

Since both Perkins' and Radcliffe's careers began about the same time as Westmoreland's, the originator of the slogan is open to speculation. The *Tennessean* comment on Westmoreland's slogan corroborates an earlier reference to it when Montgomery was in Nashville for a series in June.[69]

Albany's dwindling pennant hopes were put to rest in Birmingham in late August. Birmingham won a nail-biter 4–3 when Reuben Jones singled in the winning run in the 12th inning. Both Robert Poindexter and Albany's McDonald pitched the entire game. Leo Birdine shutout the Giants, 11–0, on a two-hitter in the second game. Harry Salmon then pitched a no-hitter, winning the third game, 8–0. "Fish" struck out seven and walked two as Birmingham got revenge for the no-hitter thrown against them by Bill Gatewood in June. Curtis Harris beat the luckless McDonald, 6–1, in the fourth game. Then, Poindexter made it a sweep with a 1–0 one-hitter in the fifth game.[70]

Memphis returned home in early September for a final regular season series with Albany. Standings on the Sunday before Labor Day showed the Red Sox with a three-game lead over New Orleans:

Memphis	27	7
New Orleans	24	10
Birmingham	18	11
Albany	17	17
Chattanooga	16	19
Nashville	15	21
Montgomery	11	23
Atlanta	7	27[71]
	135	135

Memphis won all five games, including a Labor Day doubleheader, to lock up the second half pennant. Rejoining the team for the upcoming playoffs with Birmingham was catcher Larry Brown, who had been playing with the Detroit Stars earlier in the season.[72]

The Red Sox also picked up Bill Drake, an experienced pitcher who had won 10 games in 1925 with the Kansas City Monarchs. In 1926 he was 7–6 with the Indianapolis ABCs.[73] He left the ABCs in mid–August and joined the Red Sox.

Drake had a good curve ball and good control, but he was also known for using a number of trick pitches.[74] One of the nicknames hung on him in 1926 was "Emery," derived from the illegal use of a piece of sandpaper to scuff up the ball.

Of course, Memphis already had a formidable pitcher in William "Steel Arm" Tyler, who had joined the club in June after starting the season with the Chicago American Giants. According to a report out of the league office he had won 14 of 16 games during the second half.[75] Those numbers are not substantiated by game reports.

Birmingham also reportedly strengthened for the playoffs. Outfielder Jones, who had also been with the ABCs, was signed and this quickly paid off.[76] After Birmingham took three out of four from New Orleans over the Labor Day weekend, it was reported that Jones was batting .468 in 10 home games since joining the team.[77] Equally important in the playoffs was the acquisition of left-hander Jim Jeffries from Albany. He would be the dominant player in the post-season.

As the playoffs neared, it was reported that the winner would play a "Dixie series" with the Dallas club. The winner of that series would be "in position to play off the world's series with the Negro National Baseball League. It will mean much for the negroes of the South, and put the Southern League indelibly on the map."[78] Neither of those events materialized, but the NSL postseason was itself a well-played series that drew large crowds to the Birmingham and Memphis ball parks.

Memphis got a scheduling break. The series stretched over three weeks, beginning with three games at Memphis, followed by three in Birmingham, and then returning to Memphis for the final four games.

The series would hang on pitching when it was all over, with six of the 10 games being shutouts. Of the other four games, two ended in 2–2 ties and two were won by Birmingham, which scored nine runs in each. A third tie, scoreless, was one of the six shutouts.

The playoffs opened in Memphis on September 11. For 12 long innings Harry Salmon and two Memphis pitchers mowed down batter after batter. Salmon gave up 10 hits and struck out 10. Tyler gave up eight hits and struck out nine in nine innings. He was relieved by Nat Trammell, who surrendered one hit and struck out three. The score was 2–2 when the game was called because of darkness.[79]

Birmingham Manager Clarence Smith sent Leo Birdine to the mound for Game Number Two. He gave up 11 hits and walked two, but kept them scattered. Birmingham batters bunched hits in the fourth and sixth innings, scoring four times in each. "Geechie" Meredith had a double and a triple.[80]

Newcomer Jeffries pitched masterfully in Game Three. Holding Memphis to just seven hits, Jeffries shut out the home team. "Emery" Drake limited Birmingham to only three hits, but the Black Barons managed in the seventh to send catcher Poindexter Williams across the plate with the game's only run.[81]

After a week's break, the series moved to Birmingham where the opener on September 20 was rained out. The following day Drake was the hard luck loser in another 1–0 game. Although Memphis outhit Birmingham six to four, the Black Barons used one of their hits to decisive advantage. With two out in the ninth, manager Smith hit a single to center field, scoring George McAllister, who had walked and advanced to third on a couple of put outs. Robert Poindexter was the winning pitcher. He struck out seven and walked none. Drake struck out four and walked one and that was his downfall. The walk to McAllister sparked a delay over Drake's alleged use of the illegal emery ball pitch. Earlier in the game, the umpires had "searched Drake's clothing for the sand paper and after the search Drake allowed his third baseman and shortstop to doctor the ball," reported the *Memphis Commercial-Appeal*. When Smith protested again in the ninth, a new ball was put into play and the Birmingham manager hit it into center field to win the game.[82]

With three wins recorded, Birmingham fans were primed for their team to take the next two games and bring a great season to its conclusion. Once again the celebration would be delayed by a tie. Game Five was called by darkness after nine innings. Tyler was just two outs from victory when Birmingham put together an infield hit, a single to center, and a sacrifice fly by Joe Mitchell to tie the game. With Poindexter Williams coming to bat with the potential winning run at second, Manager Charley Wesley opted for an intentional pass to the big catcher. The strategy worked. Tyler struck out Webb Oden to end the inning and the umpires declared it a draw.[83]

In Game Six Birmingham pulled within a single win of taking the flag. With left-hander Jeffries outpitching Willis, Birmingham won the last game at Rickwood Field, 2–0. Singles by Mitchell, Owens and Oden gave Birmingham a 1–0 lead in the fifth. Reuben Jones made it 2–0 with a home run over the right field fence in the sixth. Jeffries, pitching his second shutout in the series, scattered six Memphis hits and struck out three. Rickwood Field was scheduled for a high school football game the next day, thus forcing the series back to Memphis.[84]

Birmingham's hopes of a quick end to the series were dashed by the weather and a tough Memphis team. Wet grounds and cold weather pushed Game Seven to Sunday afternoon. The result was the third tie in the series. This time it was Birdine and Drake dueling for 11 innings. Again Memphis outhit Birmingham, eight to four, but neither team could score a run.[85]

After seven games, Memphis was still without a win. Logically, with only three games to go and Birmingham already with four wins and three ties, the 10-game series should have been declared settled. However, that was not the case. The remaining three games were approached as if the matter was still to be decided.

Games Eight and Nine on Monday and Tuesday kept Birmingham's celebration on hold. In Game Eight Willis threw a two-hitter, striking out 10 Black Barons as the Red Sox won their first game in the series, 2–0. Robert Poindexter lost a five-hit game. In Game Nine the Red Sox used first inning hits to score a quick run. Nat Trammell, a 24th Infantry Regiment pitcher who had joined Memphis after his discharge in mid–August, beat Birmingham, 1–0, for the sixth shutout in the series. Harry Salmon was the losing pitcher. Memphis had now won two in a row.[86]

Game Ten was scheduled at Lewis Park on Wednesday, September 29. Birmingham, thwarted for four straight days, quickly put this one out of reach. The Black Barons scored four in the first and added another in the second. By the time Memphis got a run in the bottom of the fourth, the score was 8–0. Jeffries won his third game of the series, 9–3. Poindexter Williams had two hits, one of them a triple, and Clarence Smith had his fourth three-hit game in the series He also scored four times and stole a base.[87]

Despite the problems of the Atlanta and Montgomery clubs, the exciting playoff between Birmingham and Memphis concluded a highly successful season for the Negro Southern League, perhaps its best.

To be sure, there were the obligatory protests of umpiring and rowdy behavior, usually by players rather than fans. A writer in the *Atlanta Independent* noted that the Albany was "inclined to fussing and arguing with the umpire."[88]

Manager William Lowe pulled the Chattanooga team off the field in Atlanta in June, perhaps with good cause. Trailing 4–2 in the ninth, the Black Crackers loaded the bases, then saw the next batters go out on a popup and a strikeout. "As a last desperate maneuver, Captain Clay, of the Black Crackers, ordered the hit and run. Left Fielder Williams shot a skipper to short and legged it to first. The play was not even close but [base umpire] motioned him safe, and the tying winnings were across." After an appeal to umpire in chief, Lowe got the call reversed and "bedlam broke loose." Chattanooga won the game.[89]

Later in the season, Lowe saw the New Orleans skipper pull his team off the field in Chattanooga. There the two umpires differed on a fly ball call and neither would back down. When New Orleans refused to continue play the head umpire took out his watch, allowed a certain amount of time to pass and declared that the Black Pelicans had forfeited the game. Management reported that rain checks for the game would be honored during the upcoming series with Montgomery. The local newspaper alleged

5. 1926: Revival of the Negro Southern League

that "squawking and squabbling on the field ... has marred every game play by the negro Southern league at Andrews field."[90]

An entirely different picture was painted in Nashville: "The games are run off with less squabbling than Dixie [white Southern Association] battles and the umpire is king. Greene sent Anderson from the game on his first appearance at the plate and thereafter argument subsided."[91]

But when the quality of umpiring came into question in a Saturday afternoon doubleheader in Albany, the outcome was extraordinary. "At the end of the first game the white fans attending took up a collection to put Umpire Jones behind the plate to look 'em over. The umpires working before him had not been giving the satisfactory service Jones puts out. Following this move on the part of the hundreds of white fans attending, the president of the league announced that travelling umpires will be employed by the colored Southern League as is the case with all other good baseball loops."[92]

No confirmation of the president's action was noted in other publications.

But player highlights during the season were numerous and memorable. They included no-hit pitching by Salmon and Gatewood. One-hitters were thrown by Daniels of Atlanta, Robert Poindexter of Birmingham, and Rowe and Benjamin of New Orleans. Satchel Paige also appears to have pitched a one-hitter against Atlanta on July 15, but vagueness of the game report makes it difficult to confirm.

Salmon and Stamps of Memphis had double-digit strikeout performances with 13 and 11, respectively.

In an era when pitchers were expected to complete what they started, not be bailed out by a bullpen, a number of them had complete games of 10 or more innings:

- 12 innings, Salmon and Poindexter, Birmingham.
- 11.2 innings, McDonald, Albany.
- 11 innings, Birdine, Poindexter and Salmon, Birmingham; Tyler, Memphis; and White, Nashville.
- 10.2 innings, Bissant, New Orleans.
- 10.1 innings, Redding, Albany; and Tyler, Memphis.
- 10 innings, Canty, Atlanta; Birdine and Poindexter, Birmingham; Noel and White, Nashville; Elllis, Nashville and Benjamin, New Orleans; and Paige, Chattanooga, twice.

Each of the partial inning games (11.2, 11.2, etc.) was a walk-off loss for the designated pitcher except for the game of July 10. In that game both Tyler and Benjamin entered the game in the first inning as relief pitchers. Tyler subsequently lost after pitching 10.1 innings and Benjamin won after pitching 11.1 innings.

One of the best overall efforts was given by New Orleans' "Red" Parnell on June 10 in the first game of a doubleheader. The outfielder took the mound and held Birmingham to five hits while striking out three and walking three in a 7–4 win. At bat in the number three spot in the batting order, he got a single and a home run in four at-bats. He hit "one of the longest home runs of the year when he parked the ball over the centerfield fence just to the right of Chero-Cola board." Birmingham won the second game behind Harry Salmon's relief pitching but Parnell had two more hits, a double and triple in three at-bats.[93]

On July 5, right fielder Ross of Albany hit two home runs as Albany beat Atlanta, 12–1. "One clout was of such terrific force that it struck a home outside the right field fence and bounded back into the playing field. It was a terrific wallop."[94]

Several players were sold or traded to other league teams during the season. One of the most notable was Saul Davis, an infielder whose career spanned more than 10 years. On July 13, at shortstop, Davis played his last game as a Birmingham Black Baron, going hitless in a 6–3 win over Memphis. After the game he was sold to Memphis, thus switching uniforms for the second game of the series at Rickwood Field. Birmingham may have regretted the sale: "Davis starred against his [former] teammates. He got three hits, three runs and stole three bases. Davis knotted the score in the fourth by stealing home. In the sixth and eighth he started rallies with clean singles and each time stole second."[95]

There were many outstanding fielding plays duly noted in game accounts around the league. One fielding performance that might be called a low light, though, came on Aug. 3 at New Orleans. The Black Pelicans pounded Albany, 21–4, picking up 19 hits, nine of them for extra bases. Collins and Robinson hit home runs. But Albany infielders contributed to the damage also. Shortstop Gaithers committed six errors in 14 chances that day while third baseman Johnson committed three errors in five chances. Catcher Charleston and leftfielder Davis each contributed a fielding miscue.

6

1927
Without Major Players

The extraordinary success of the 1926 season would not be mirrored in 1927. Two of the league's strongest franchises, Birmingham and Memphis, were once again in the Negro National League.

Returning were only the Atlanta Black Crackers, Nashville Elite Giants, and the Chattanooga Black Lookouts, the new name for the team that played the year before as the White Sox. Also gone were the Albany Giants, Montgomery Grey Sox, and New Orleans Black Pelicans. The league was formed with five new teams, untested in league play, to fill the vacancies.

Early reports indicated the 1927 newcomers would be the Decatur, Alabama, Royal Giants; Evansville, Indiana, Reichert Giants; Hopkinsville, Kentucky, Athletics; Jackson, Tennessee, Cubs; and Memphis Giants. By early June a set of standings in the *Chicago Defender* showed Bessemer, Alabama, as a participant. There was no mention of the Decatur team in standings published in May or June.

The inclusion of Evansville in the Negro *Southern* League seems odd, but it was not the only time Midwestern teams helped fill the lineup. Evansville returned in 1929. In 1932, when the NSL was the only real survivor of a Depression-year slump, the Chicago American Giants, Indianapolis ABCs, and Columbus, Ohio, Turf Stars were league members. In 1934 and 1936 the Cincinnati Tigers were NSL members.

The Evansville team was apparently sponsored by the Louis Reichert construction company. The white Reichert family supported a wide range of local civic activities. In 1942, when Manson L. Reichert, Louis' son, ran for mayor of Evansville, he was endorsed by the *Evansville Argus*, a black newspaper, as "a friend to the Negro."[1]

Chattanooga, with a new nickname and new manager, Pete Cleage, had one significant returning player. Back with a year of professional ball under his belt was pitcher Leroy "Satchel" Paige. His service would be limited, though. When a July 9 exhibition game with Birmingham of the Negro National rolled around, Satchel was on the field in the livery of the Black Barons. Satchel had reached the big time.[2]

The difficulties that had dogged the Atlanta team in 1926 had not been forgotten by a writer for the *Atlanta Independent*. In early March, the writer seemed uncertain as to whether or not there would be a Black Crackers team in 1927. Just in case the team was formed, the following warning was issued to prospective players, particularly those who played for one of the local college teams: "...be careful as to how you sign up, because judging from the past the paper you sign is no more than a scrap of paper. Before you go into any agreement with the management at least see the color of their money, because it is hardly fair for the school boy who must go to school with the money he earns in the summer, to get a job that lasts about four weeks and then it is all over, and perhaps he does not receive the money that has been due him for past services. Boys, it is much better to seek other employment in more fertile fields [sic] if you have nothing to do but play baseball for the sake of playing it, then we refer you to the City League which is destined to be a faction in athletics of Atlanta, or go to the tobacco farms, or any place other than professional baseball."[3]

Later in the spring, as the likelihood of a Black Crackers team emerged, the *Independent* once again was the voice of caution: "We notice that in all of the write-ups we do not know who is heading the Black Crackers. Now we want to know who are the leaders in the movement. In other words, who is president, vice president and secretary? At this time last year we knew who the officers were. Now we would like for them to come out in the open and let us have the names. Of course, we need not say that you can't have a baseball club where the public is supposed to patronize and keep the officers of said club a secret."[4]

When opening day rolled around, the *Independent* had seemingly upped its support. There was a brief report on the Chattanooga series and an interview with W. R. Abrahams, owner of the Black Lookouts. Abrahams said the league would operate "on as conservative a basis as possible." He said the NSL schedule had been arranged to allow a break between league games so other contests could be played to boost revenues. He also promised that the official scores of the league games would be sent to the newspaper each week.[5]

For reason unclear, there were lapses in the *Independent*'s coverage of the Atlanta team. In early June there was a cryptic reference to a dispute between the league president and the local club. The league official appeared to have threatened to take the franchise away from the Atlanta club. The *Independent* sports writer was livid over the threat. His response, in a rambling, barely coherent sentence structure, included: "... when our boys went to Memphis, played three games, and did not have any crowd and, of course, the gate receipts were not up to the standard and when we demand a guarantee, why there was 'nobody home.' And the president claims that he is either unable or unwilling to force Memphis to pay the guarantee. Now we don' [sic] know anything about the baseball laws in the league, but we do know from the standpoint of right that it is that it is absolutely unfair and unsportsmanlike to attempt to do anything with the Cracker management until that guarantee of Memphis is paid." The writer went on to suggest that the Black Crackers would be better off leaving the league and playing the many baseball teams "in Georgia and near-by-cities."[6] Whether it was a consequence of the dispute, the writer's suggestion, or a general collapse of the Atlanta club, the Black Cracker season appears to have been over by mid–June.

On June 14, Chattanooga went into Atlanta for a series only to find the Black Crackers had apparently disbanded. The Black Lookouts were hooked up with the Atlanta All-Stars, "a collection of the best colored players in the city, under the management of W. J. Shaw."[7] There was no report on the game's outcome, nor information regarding additional games between the two teams.

Opening day coverage was erratic throughout the league. Evansville played at Jackson as the two new clubs made their debut. There was no coverage in the Tennessee city's newspaper, but the *Evansville Courier* reported that Austin pitched the Giants to a 5–3 win.[8] The following day they battled to an 8–8 tie in 10 innings. Jackson finally gave its fans a win in the third game, 2–1. The Jackson pitcher is unknown but Austin was again on the mound for Evansville because "Terry does not appear to be in condition." Still, it was noted that Terry hit a triple when he pinch-hit later in the game.[9] There was no report on the fourth game of the series.

Although Chattanooga and Atlanta played on May 2, the first game found for the Memphis Cubs was on Saturday, May 14. Atlanta was scheduled to open a four-game set with Memphis at Lewis Park. The park's owners, the Memphis Red Sox, were in St. Louis for a Negro National League series. It was reported that the Cubs would use the facility when the Red Sox were on the road.[10]

Unfortunately, the Cubs opener was postponed when it was learned that the field had been "previously let for a field meet." On Sunday the Cubs won, 13–3. There were few details, but Pryor held the visitors to four hits, striking out 13 and walking three. Shortstop Haley had three hits and five other Memphis players had two apiece.[11]

Atlanta came back to take the next game on Monday, 2–1, although pitcher W. Parker gave up nine hits. Haley again starred for Memphis with two hits in four at-bats.[12]

The *Commercial-Appeal* covered both games, printing box scores of each. The paper reported that the Cubs would return to Lewis Park the following Saturday (May 21) to face the Jackson club.[13] However, there was no report on the Jackson series and no further mention of the Cubs the remainder of the summer.

Evansville had its home opener on Sunday, May 8, against the same Jackson club with whom it had opened the season. A "big parade through the downtown section" was scheduled before the game. Again, there was no report on the game, but two days later it was noted that Jackson had won. The Reichert Giants won the second and third games in the series, 8–4 and 9–4, respectively. In the latter Harris, Mitchell, McNeal, and English each had two hits.[14]

One of the Jackson players in the games at Evansville was a catcher named Radcliffe. Later, a player of the same surname pitched for Jackson. There is a reasonable assumption for this player being Ted "Double Duty" Radcliffe,

Theodore Radcliffe, nicknamed "Double Duty" after sportswriter Damon Runyon saw him catch Satchel Paige in the first game of a doubleheader, then pitch the second game. Radcliffe's career spanned parts of four decades (courtesy NoirTech Research).

whose career spanned three decades. Legendary for his ability to catch one game of a double-header, then pitch the other, Radcliffe was born in Mobile, Alabama, in 1902. His early career was spent with a semipro team called the Illinois Giants. He also had a short stint with the Detroit Stars in 1926 before joining that team as a starter in 1928.[15]

Although the "Double Duty" nickname was soon applied to any player who both caught and pitched, much as "Babe Ruth" became a nickname for anyone who could hit home runs regularly, it was Radcliffe who first had it. The moniker was hung on him by the great New York sportswriter Damon Runyon after watching Radcliffe work both ends of a double-header.[16]

Radcliffe, in a biography written by Kyle P. McNary, said he played with the Illinois Giants from 1920 to 1926. "A few times I took off and played for other teams when they called for me," he told McNary. He does not mention the Jackson club, but he does claim to have played with Chattanooga occasionally the previous year and related the following story:

> I remember in 1926 Satchel was pitching with the Chattanooga Black Lookouts and the kid they had catching him was missing every other pitch. Very few catchers could catch that man when he was young. It was like catching a bullet. Satchel told his manager, "Get me someone who can catch me." Manager said, "Like Who?" He said, "Get Ted Radcliffe." So they called me up and I caught him a few games and then met back up with the Illinois Giants in Wisconsin.[17]

There is no confirmation of the story. Chattanooga used at least three different catchers in 1926. Radcliffe was not among them in the 47 box scores and 21 line scores located for the Chattanooga club. In 1927 Radcliffe was playing with the Gilkerson Union Giants barnstorming team. That time frame and the barnstorming schedule would make it possible for him to have been also with Jackson in 1927.

Nashville's home opener was also scheduled for May 14, although the Elite Giants had already played at least one series on the road against Chattanooga. At Sulphur Dell, the Elite Giants defeated the Jackson Tigers, 9–1, in the first game, then swept the next three 10–0, 4–3, and 12–8.[18] The sweep of Jackson set up an important series with the Evansville Reichert Giants, reported to be in first place. Nashville won the opener, 5–4, on Saturday and appeared to have taken the second game on Sunday. However, the winning margin came "on a play over which there was a long argument." Officials for the Elite Giants, yielding to Reichert Manager Baker's protest, agreed to call the game a 1–1 tie and play a doubleheader on Monday.[19]

Evansville won both games of the doubleheader, then made it three in a row on Tuesday. If the Reichert Giants had come into town in first place, they no doubt left in an even better position.[20]

Nashville's tailspin continued on Wednesday when the Elite Giants lost a double-header to Chattanooga. Satchel Paige won a four-hitter, 5–2, and a pitcher named Frederick followed with a 2–1 win. The games extended Nashville's losing streak to five in a row.[21]

The team improved over the next few weeks, though. The *Nashville Banner* reported that the club had won 12 out of 14 games on a 15-day road trip. There is confirmation of series taken from Jackson and Atlanta during that time span.

Three sets of standings were published in the *Chicago Defender* in May and June.

All of them showed Chattanooga the dominant team. After the first week of the season the Black Lookouts were 5–3. Tied for second with 2–2 records were Atlanta, Jackson, and Evansville. Nashville and Memphis brought up the rear.[22]

Although the standings were accompanied by an article summarizing the first week of the season, there was no explanation for the disparity in the number of games played or for the omission of Hopkinsville and Decatur or Bessemer.

The next set of standings on June 4 again showed Chattanooga was clearly the best team, although there was a growing disparity in the number of games played by each team. The disparity may be explained by just poor reporting of games from the individual clubs. The new figures had Chattanooga (12–6) two and a half games ahead of Evansville (7–6) the only other team over .500. Nashville (7–8) was third. Hopkinsville and Bessemer were included this time, but with the unlikely records of two wins and two losses.[23]

Regardless of the *Defender*'s standings, the *Evansville Courier* continued to report the local team as being the league leader. When Evansville and Hopkinsville played two of their games at Vincennes, Indiana, near mid–June, the Reichert Giants were again said to be leading the league.[24]

On June 18 Nashville returned home for a series with the Bessemer Grey Sox. It is not really clear if Bessemer was now a member of the league. The Elite Giants had defeated the Alabama team at least once on the two-week road trip. Going into the home stand the Elite Giants' record was reported to be 18–9 and Bessemer's 9–9.[25] Nashville was said to be leading the league by two and a half games with Evansville and Chattanooga tied for second.[26]

The Elite Giants took four straight from Bessemer on June 18, 19 and 20 and were said to be leading the Negro Southern League "by a good margin."[27] In one game, which Nashville won, 10–0, the highlight was the team's fielding, particularly the work of Leroy Stratton. He had an unassisted double play and started another one. Nashville also had a triple play in the game.[28]

Again, the ongoing news reports of Evansville and Nashville front running notwithstanding, the final set of standings published in the *Chicago Defender* once again had Chattanooga ahead of the pack in late June. Missing from the standings is Memphis. The Cubs, who were shown to have played only four games in the June 4 standings, possibly folded or became an independent team in mid–May. Their last reported games were played about that time with Atlanta. A series scheduled for June 18–22 in Evansville was cancelled. The final published standings:

Team	Won	Lost	Pct.
Chattanooga	22	8	.733
Nashville	18	9	.667
Evansville	12	8	.600
Bessemer	4	5	.444
Hopkinsville	4	5	.444
Jackson	8	18	.308
Atlanta	4	12	.250
	72	65[29]	

For once the leaders in the standings seem to match the news stories as the Reichert Giants prepared to open a home series with Chattanooga.[30]

A Sunday doubleheader was split on June 26 with Evansville winning the first game, 6–5, and Chattanooga the second by 3–2. The Evansville pitcher in the last game was reported to be Forest "Wing" Maddox, who "pulled out of many tight spots and pitched good ball." Maddox was expected to play in the outfield on Monday.[31] It seems likely that Maddox was actually the pitcher for Chattanooga, not Evansville. The report on the Monday game referred to "Frederick, the one armed wonder," with Chattanooga. However, Frederick was a totally different Chattanooga pitcher. No other report throughout the season suggested that Maddox was with the Evansville club.[32]

On July 6, Nashville returned home for two games with Hopkinsville. The Elite Giants were reported to have a game and a half lead over Chattanooga. Consequently, just one win from Hopkinsville would give them the first half pennant.

The Thursday night game was rained out, forcing a doubleheader on Friday. It was perhaps rained out also, as there was no report in the Nashville papers.

Similarly, no reports were located for Chattanooga's results for the same dates. Newspapers in Chattanooga and Nashville said the teams from their respective cities were first half champions.[33] In fact, the Chattanooga paper declared its local team the winner even before the Nashville-Hopkinsville series came up. There is no clear resolution to this debate except to note that late in the season Nashville seemed to be recognized as the first-half winner.

In late July, the Evansville team got publicity from an unwanted source. Catcher Adolph Spratt, 25, and business manager Robert Murray, 52, got in an argument as players went to the club house to collect their salaries. The specifics of their quarrel were not reported, but as other players attempted to intervene Murray fired a pistol, the bullet striking the toes of Spratt's right foot. Murray was charged with shooting with intent. Spratt was taken to his home where the wound was treated. There was no further report on Murray's legal situation, but in mid–August Spratt was reported to be still "nursing an injured foot."[34]

On August 10 Nashville returned from a road trip for a four-game series with Hopkinsville. The Elite Giants were reported to be in second place with Hopkinsville third. Evansville was the leader.[35] The Hopkinsville team was said to have won 12 games in a row and "has been playing some flashy ball for the past two weeks."[36]

The series was the last one for which any league results were located. The Elite Giants won the opener, 8–2. A Sunday double header was split and a Monday game ended in a 9–9 tie. With no results available for Evansville, it is impossible to ascertain a second half winner.

But then, at least one newspaper indicated that there had essentially been no second half of the season. On August 7, in an advance story about a Hopkinsville-Evansville game that afternoon, the *Evansville Courier* said: "Both are former members of the Southern Colored league which went to pieces in July." The teams were reported to have split 10 games during the season.

There were other signs of the league's foundering. A Sunday, August 14, game in Chattanooga featured Knoxville and the Chattanooga All-Stars. The All-Stars were said to be the former Black Lookouts. Apparently, the team held together to scrounge up a few dollars in the Sunday game. The All-Stars were managed by Cleage, and Maddox was scheduled to pitch. Knoxville was reported to have won 19 out of 27 games "played in their league this summer."[37]

Evansville, which had played many exhibition games with Tri-State (Indiana, Illinois, Kentucky) semipro and town teams between NSL games, continued that schedule after the league's demise. One frequent opponent was the Evansville Eagles, one of a number of apparently white teams the Reichert Giants played with some regularity.

In August the black Evansville team played a two-game series with the East St. Louis Giants, a barnstorming team that traced its history to the early 1900s. Founder Charles A. Mills, a black bank messenger and baseball fan, had persuaded Conrad Kuebler, a white man who owned a ball park, to invest in the Giants. With some outstanding ball players like shortstop Joe Hewitt, pitchers Bill Drake, and Bill Gatewood, and outfielders Jimmie Lyons and Charles Blackwell, the Giants competed well with other Midwestern teams. In 1920 they were one of the founding members of the Negro National League. In 1922 the franchise was sold and changed to the St. Louis Stars, a dominant NNL team for the next 10 years. Mills later organized a new independent team using the old Giants name. The team was reported to have barnstormed from the mid to late 1920s.[38] The Reichert Giants played three consecutive weekend series with the St. Louis team in August. In the first series, St. Louis won a Saturday game, 6–3, and lost on Sunday, 5–4, in St. Louis. "While paying due respects to the St. Louis Giants, the local Giants believe they would have won both games if they had not played without any sleep the night before," reported the *Courier*; "The local squad had car and tire trouble and arrived just in time to play."[39] Later articles suggest that the games in St. Louis were played against the East St. Louis Giants and the two series in Evansville were played with a completely different team called the St. Louis Giants. While that is questionable, the outcome of the series was two out of three for St. Louis in the first and the same number for Evansville in the next series.

A much more intriguing series was the one the Reichert Giants played in September against "the Three-Eye League All Stars." The Three-I League (Illinois, Indiana, Iowa), which operated from 1901 to 1961, was the nation's oldest Class B minor league and a major force in Organized Baseball. Hall of Fame members who came through the circuit included Lou Boudreau, Mordecai Brown, Hank Greenberg, Carl Hubbell, and Burleigh Grimes.[40]

The team that faced Evansville in the postseason was an amalgam of current players and alumni. The nucleus of the team was Charley Fulton, Jimmy Conley, and Red Heskett, three former members of the Evansville Three-I team, who had spent the past season with Elmira, New York, in the New York-Pennsylvania League.

The games were set for five consecutive Sunday afternoons at Bosse Field in Evansville. Behind the pitching of Charley Fulton, the All-Stars beat the Giants, 5–1, in the first game. The All-Stars won the first game, 5–1, behind Fulton. He held the Giants to six hits and struck out five. All-Star third baseman Sylvester Simon scored from third on a balk after rattling pitcher Finner with feints toward the plate.[41]

Strengthening for the second game, the Giants added St. Louis Stars pitcher Ted Trent and shortstop Willie Wells, and Birmingham Black Barons right fielder James Gurley.[42] A week later, the All-Stars announced that Detroit Tigers infielder Jack Warner, a local boy, would play with the All-Stars.[43]

But that first win was as good as it would get for the white team. The Reichert Giants dominated the remainder of the series. The Giants won the second game, 8–3. Trent, the recruit from the St. Louis Stars, limited the All-Stars to six hits and he struck out nine. Simon hit a solo home run in the second, but the Giants had already jumped out to a 3–0 lead in the first inning. The All-Stars committed seven errors behind their pitcher, Babe Heitzman.[44]

Game Three was a pitching duel between Fulton and Hensley, a right-hander added to the Giants roster for the postseason. A fluke double by catcher English and a fluke home run by left fielder Cornelius gave the Giants the two runs they needed for the 2–1 victory, according to the newspaper report on the game.[45]

Even the presence of Warner could not save the All-Stars from the pitching of Hensley in Game Four. He held the whites to five hits as the Reichert Giants won again by a 2–1 score. Warner had a single in four at-bats against Hensley.[46]

Although the black team had clinched the series the week before, Game Five was played on October 16. The game "came near ending in a riot," according to the *Courier*. The paper reported that the Reichert Giants, "protesting against ball and strike decisions of Umpire Lockyear," left the field in the eighth inning. The All-Stars had the bases loaded and none out when the Giants walked off the field. Manager Baker's decision was reportedly sanctioned by Manson Reichert, the son of founder Louis Reichert.[47]

A lot of fans "let out a big howl" and charged the Giants with poor sportsmanship. There were others who said the black team had indeed received "the worst of the breaks in officiating."[48]

A second series, this one three games, was scheduled to begin on October 16. The *Courier* reported that the All-Stars "feel sure that the colored boys are in for a sound thumping today. Losing three out of four of the first series didn't set well with Simon, Warner and company."[49] However that series never materialized.

The collapse of the league during the second half did not prevent officials from putting together a post-season playoff series, however. From July 10 through August 12 only one result was a located, a Nashville win over Evansville. That would explain why Nashville, the generally declared first half winner, played the Dallas Black Sox in a Negro Dixie Series in late August and early September. As the series was under way the *Nashville Tennessean* reported that the NSL second half was still ongoing, but that Nashville was so far ahead of second place Evansville that the Elite Giants were going ahead with the playoffs.[50] At any rate, the series was set with the first two games being played in Dallas and the remainder in Nashville.

En route to Dallas, Nashville played at least one series of barnstorming. The Elite Giants beat the Shreveport Sports, 9–5, then tied the same team, 5–5, in a second game.[51]

The Dixie Series was an annual postseason matchup between the champions of the white Southern Association and the Texas League. It started in 1920 with Fort Worth, Texas, opposing Little Rock, Arkansas, and continued through 1957.[52] Given the other parallels of white and black baseball in the South, it was logical that a similar competition between black leagues would be called the Negro Dixie Series.

The Negro Dixie Series opened in Dallas on Saturday, August 27, with the home team winning, 3–2. It was reported to be the Black Sox's 30th consecutive victory.

Nashville won, 3–1, on Sunday, ending Dallas's winning streak and sending the series to Nashville for Games Three and Four on Sunday and Monday, September 4–5. According to the *Nashville Banner*, if the Elite Giants split those two games, "a deciding tilt will be played here Tuesday."[53] Nashville won on both Sunday and Monday, which would seem to end the series. However, a full seven-game series was played. Dallas won Game Five. Nashville won Game Six, the decider, and also Game Seven.

Not even the Nashville papers could agree on the playoff results. On Thursday, September 8, the *Tennessean* reported that Dallas would be at Sulphur Dell for Saturday and Sunday games. Nashville was said to lead the series four games to two with another game having ended in a tie. That would suggest that the series was already decided, but the newspaper said Nashville needed one win to take the series. At the same time, games reported in the *Banner* had Nashville leading three games to one.

Dallas won the September 10 Saturday game, 2–1, prompting the *Tennesseean* to report a that if Dallas won the first game of the Sunday doubleheader, then the series would be tied at four games apiece with the nightcap deciding the champion. The winning margin on Saturday came on an error by Mack, the Nashville first baseman. It was the only error of the game, dashing a "masterful" pitching performance by William Spearman. Patterson, the Dallas hurler, gave up only five hits.[54] Regardless of the muddled playoff standings, Nashville made them moot by sweeping the Sunday games. Outfielder William Anderson's home run in the bottom of the ninth gave the Elite Giants a 5–4 victory and the championship in the opener. In the meaningless second game, Jack Ridley hit a home run as Nashville won it, also, 5–2. The fielding of Leroy Stratton was again a feature of both Sunday games.[55]

A versatile ball player, Stratton's career stretched from 1920 into the early 1930s. He played for both the Birmingham Black Barons and the Chicago American Giants but was best known for his work with the Elite Giants.[56] In 1923, when he was with the short-lived Milwaukee Bears team, he was "said to be the best looking infielder among the colored leaguers."[57] He was also a manager occasionally.

7

1928–30
A Tottering Revival

In 1928 Birmingham and Memphis again remained in the Negro National League, leaving no real nucleus for a Negro Southern League. Cities such as Hopkinsville, Jackson, Bessemer, and Evansville that had filled the void the year before no longer had teams in the league. The first three mentioned above apparently had little fan support in 1927. Evansville had good local support, but probably found the long travel jumps to Atlanta, Chattanooga, and Nashville expensive.

Consequently, Atlanta, Chattanooga, Evansville, and Nashville all played independent ball during the 1928 season. The Black Lookouts and Elite Giants played a series in Nashville in June.[1] Evansville had exhibition games scheduled with Memphis in the spring.[2] The Atlanta Black Crackers were reorganized as the Atlanta Grey Sox.[3] Many of the 1927 players were on the team when it played a series with the 24th Infantry team from Fort Benning.[4] The team played a varied schedule well into the fall.[5]

The Memphis Red Sox underwent an ownership change during the offseason. The club was sold to a corporation of businessmen headed by C. B. King, an official with the National Benefit Life Insurance Company. M. B. Burnett was listed as secretary-treasurer. Other stockholders were J. C. Walker, A. M. McCullough, S. W. Qualls, and W. C. Cole. Judge William C. Hueston and R. T. Jackson, president and vice president, respectively, of the Negro National League, reportedly spent four days in Memphis "directing formation of the corporation."[6]

The revival of the Negro Southern League in 1929 was reflective of apparent flush times for black baseball in general. The Negro National League launched its 10th season with a lineup that included the St. Louis Stars, Kansas City Monarchs, Detroit Stars, Chicago American Giants, Cuban Stars (West), Birmingham Black Barons, and Memphis Red Sox. Also listed were the Nashville Elite Giants, but that proved to be only partially true.[7]

Over on the Eastern Seaboard, where the Eastern Colored League had operated from 1923 to 1928, a new league was formed. The American Negro League featured the Baltimore Black Sox, Lincoln Giants, Homestead Grays, Hilldale, Bacharach Giants, and Cuban Stars (East). Each team except the Homestead Grays had appeared in at least one ECL season before that league went out of business in mid–1928.[8]

Also operating in 1929 was a black Texas-Oklahoma-Louisiana League. Members included Dallas, Fort Worth, Houston, Oklahoma City, San Antonio, Shreveport, Tulsa, and Wichita Falls. Dallas attracted attention with pitcher Horace Cole, who was said

7. 1928–30: A Tottering Revival

to "pitch equally well with either hand, and is never quite sure himself until game time, which wing he will use."[9]

And down south, the new NSL was resurrected at a meeting in Nashville.

The lineup included the Atlanta Grey Sox, Chattanooga Black Cats, Evansville Reichert Giants, Louisville Black Caps (Cats), New Orleans Black Pelicans, and Nashville Elite Giants. R. T. Jackson, vice president of the Negro National League and president of the Birmingham Black Barons, attended the meet to help with reorganization.

Opening Day was set for May 18 and a committee was appointed to draft a new constitution, fix salary and player limits, and draw up a schedule.[10]

The fact that the league meeting was in Nashville was a prelude to confusion over just where the Nashville team stood that year. The *Nashville Tennessean* frequently referred to the local team as being in the NSL. There was no mention of the fact that the team was also an associate member of the Negro National League. The confusion was further reflected in the writer's reference to Memphis being an NSL member when the Red Sox were actually a full-fledged member of the NNL.[11] The *Nashville Banner*, on the other hand, usually just referenced the Elite Giants as the "local Negro team" with no league affiliation mentioned.[12] However, when the Louisville Black Caps came to town for a series in June, the paper identified both as NSL teams.[13] In late July, the *Banner* put the Elite Giants in the NNL, which suggested it had a full membership rather than an associate position.[14]

Finally, the only definitive clarification came from the *Chicago Defender*. As the Nashville club headed into the Windy City for a five-game series, the club was described as "members of the Southern league and associate members of the National league.... These are not league games, but will keep the American Giants in trim for the 15 remaining games of the season."[15] That would explain the large number of games the Nashville club played with teams from both leagues. Nashville is not listed in any 1929 NNL standings as it played its games with those clubs as an associate member.

If Nashville was serving two masters, New Orleans was apparently serving none. Despite being listed as one of the league members, no result was ever found for a game involving the New Orleans team. Thus, it would appear the league operated with five teams including Nashville, which played as many games against NNL teams as it did against NSL teams.

Opening Day was very late compared to other years, official games not beginning until May 19. Evansville opened at home against Chattanooga in one of the "longest games ever played at Bosse Field." Gigo of Chattanooga and John Finner of Evansville each pitched 17 innings before the game was finally decided in Evansville's favor, 3–2. Finner scored the winning run after taking base on a single, advancing on a double by Pritchett and coming home on Miller's single. Although the stamina of the pitchers was remarkable, it was the fielding that drew the most postgame attention. "Pritchett, McNeil, Miller and Scott all turned in some brilliant fielding work," reported the local paper. Scott handled 27 chances at first base without an error. Chattanooga first baseman Gurley recorded 22 putouts without an error. Pritchett and McNeil both made shoestring catches for Evansville, and Chattanooga shortstop Murdon was applauded for "his fast and brilliant work."[16]

The following day's game required 10 innings for completion, with Chattanooga scoring a 6–4 win. The Black Cats scored twice after two were out in the 10th. Pritchett, Gurley, and Murdon again were cited for their fielding.[17]

On May 6 Atlanta opened a home exhibition series with the Sunshine Babies out of St. Petersburg, Florida. T. F. Fortson's team was reported to have won 35 out of 45 games played as an independent team in 1928.

The team's NSL opener was set for May 18 against Louisville. R. J. Spiller, owner of the white Southern Association Atlanta Crackers club, announced that he would present an attendance cup to the NSL team pulling the biggest crowd on opening day. The Grey Sox would occupy Spiller Field when the Crackers were on the road.[18] The series was canceled when an automobile accident prevented the Louisville team from reaching Atlanta.

Atlanta fans got their first look at their team in league play later in the week against Evansville. The Grey Sox, behind the four-hit pitching of "Lefty" Williams, took the first game of the series, 2–1. Williams not only pitched a fine game, but drove in both Atlanta runs with a single in the fifth inning.[19]

Two days later Williams pitched a six-hitter as Atlanta won, 9–2, taking two out of three from Evansville. The wins reportedly put the Grey Sox in a tie with Chattanooga for the league lead.[20] This was one of the few media references to a league leader throughout the season.

Nashville, enjoying its status as an associate member of the major league NNL, spent the NSL opening day hosting the Kansas City Monarchs. The big league club swamped the Elite Giants, 8–2, on Sunday and then 10–1 on Monday.[21] Nashville apparently went on the road afterward, losing at least one series in Detroit. The team returned to Nashville on June 2 for its first NSL games with Evansville. The first game was rained out and Evansville won the second, 8–6.[22]

Nashville fared much better the following weekend on a visit to Evansville. In Indiana, the Elite Giants won a Sunday double-header, then beat the home team, 18–4, on Monday. Jim Willis pitched a five-hitter to win the first Sunday game, 3–2, in 12 innings. Henry "Red" Wright won the five-inning second game, 5–1. Evansville batters got 13 hits off of William "Sug" Cornelius in the Monday game, but could only score four runs. With "Black Bottom" Buford, Charles Blackwell, William Bobo and Cornelius each getting three hits, the Elite Giants made their 17 hits off of Smiley pay dividends. Smiley added to his troubles by walking four batters, hitting another and throwing three wild pitches.[23] Nashville first baseman Bobo had a double and a home run. To make matters worse for the home team, Evansville catcher English was knocked out when accidentally hit by a bat in the first inning. After 10 minutes or so he returned to the game.[24]

Nashville third baseman Buford is an intriguing figure. This very capable infielder first surfaced with the Nashville Cubs in 1927. Although his career spanned 10 or more years with stops in Birmingham, Cleveland, Detroit, and Louisville, also, he was never identified with his given first name. At first glance, Buford's nickname appears to be a racial epithet, but the author has determined that it could also be of geographical origin.

A section of Detroit, largely inhabited by an African American population, was long known as Black Bottom. The name came from French settlers who applied it because of the fertile, dark soil, not the population.[25] There is a similar neighborhood

7. 1928–30: A Tottering Revival

in Philadelphia, again populated largely by blacks. The name here is one of social strata. Wealthy and middle class residents lived at the "top" of the city while the lower classes, including most blacks, lived at the "bottom."[26] The mystery of Black Bottom Buford's name is not solved, but the author has presented additional possibilities.

There was no report on a scheduled fourth game in the series.

Although the *Chicago Defender* published a first-half schedule that showed games scheduled for practically every day of the week, the sparse results found suggested that league games were played almost exclusively on Sunday and Monday, with the rest of the week devoted to barnstorming and exhibition games. The *Defender*, which also published a schedule for the Texas-Oklahoma-Louisiana League, published no standings for either circuit. There was some reportage, even a few box scores, on games in the NSL.

Altogether, scores were found for 27 NSL games in 1929. Standings based on those results are:

Team	Won	Lost	Pct.
Nashville	9	3	.750
Evansville	7	6	.538
Atlanta	3	3	.500
Louisville	4	7	.364
Chattanooga	4	8	.333
New Orleans	0	0	.000

Nashville, with such players as infielders Buford and Leroy Stratton, catcher "Red" Charleston, and pitchers Eddie Noel and Willis, was obviously the better team among the five. Evansville was not up to the standard it had shown in 1927, but was still a good team.

The Atlanta Grey Sox, as with the Black Crackers, relied heavily on local college players to fill its roster. First baseman John McFarland and catcher Nish Williams were familiar names. Louisville, which, remarkably, received no coverage at all in the *Louisville Courier-Journal*, was managed by Jim Morris, a former Nashville catcher. First names could not be ascertained for any of the Louisville players.

Chattanooga, although a mediocre team in 1929, was nonetheless intriguing. The Black Cats, at various times, had five Henderson brothers in their lineup.[27] On May 11, Chattanooga defeated the Florida Cuban Giants, 11–9. "The hitting of two Hendersons and the pitching of another Henderson was the feature of the game."[28] Chattanooga also had a regular Ladies Day to boost attendance.[29]

It seems unlikely that a second-half schedule was ever drawn up, given the irregularity of play in the first half. The standings compiled by the writer above are through games of July 30. No league contests appear to have been played after that date. Given those results, we can award the pennant, such as it was, to Nashville.

During what would have been the second half, Evansville played more and more games with its tri-state rivals and with barnstorming teams. The Reichert Giants were swamped by the Oklahoma Indians, a team managed by L. Jaynes, reported to be a former major leaguer. However, no "Jaynes" appears in any major league reference in print or online.

Evansville hosted the Chicago American Giants of the NNL for a three game series.

The local team beat the Chicago club, 8–7 and 8–3. Afterward Manager Charles Baker announced that he was canceling the third game due to poor attendance.[30]

But despite the success against the NNL team, this was not an Evansville team of the caliber of some past nines. Later in the fall exhibition season the Reichert Giants lost games to Indiana town teams such as the Huntingburg Athletics and Tell City.[31]

The dismal lack of success in 1929 showed the continued weakness of the Negro Southern League without its two strongest franchises, Birmingham and Memphis. With both of them still playing in the Negro National League, there was little left to build on after the 1929 collapse. Joining those two clubs in the NNL in 1930 were the Nashville Elite Giants, now a full member, and the Louisville White Sox, apparently a reorganization of the previous year's Black Caps.

For the rest of the South, the 1930 season saw independent play only. Among the familiar names were the Atlanta Grey Sox, Chattanooga Black Lookouts, and Montgomery Grey Sox. The New Orleans Black Pelicans apparently had found a new home in the Texas-Louisiana League. Although an article in the *Chicago Defender* referenced a "Colored Southern league," it is clear that there was no organized circuit in 1930.[32]

The Atlanta Grey Sox, under owner T. F. Fortson and business manager S. M. Humphrey, were organized later and opened play in June with the 24th Infantry Regiment team out of Fort Benning in Columbus, Georgia.[33]

The opener was a big event in Atlanta's black community. Among the dignitaries expected to attend were Thomas T. Wilson, Nashville Elite Giants owner; R. T. Jackson, president of the Birmingham Black Barons; H. Strawbridge, secretary of the Birmingham team; Fred Caulfield, president of the New Orleans Black Pelicans; Dr. E. E. Nesbit, president of Memphis Red Sox; and John Dixon, owner of Louisville Black Caps.

William Dirskell, president of local Business league, was to throw out first pitch. Mayor Isaac N. Ragsdale and other city officials had also been invited.[34]

The 24th Infantry Regiment was one of the original six Buffalo Soldier units formed in 1869. The regiment saw service in the American West, Cuba, and the Philippines during the Spanish-American War and the Mexican border skirmish with Pancho Villa from 1916 to 1919. In 1917 the regiment was involved in a race riot in Houston that resulted in the deaths of several soldiers and civilians. In subsequent courts martial proceedings 14 soldiers were executed and 41 given life sentences for their roles in the riot.[35]

The unit eventually was assigned to Fort Benning, where during the 1920s and 1930s, its athletic teams played throughout the Southeast against college, town, semipro, and professional teams. Several players went on to play in the Negro Southern League and Negro National League. Among them were outfielder Fendall Williams, pitcher Columbus Vance, and first baseman-pitcher Nat Trammell.

Most notable, though, was pitcher-outfielder Terris McDuffie, who joined the Birmingham Black Barons in 1930 after a six-year stint in the military and played professionally into the 1950s. In 1941, probably his best year, he was 27–5 with the Homestead Grays and was the winning pitcher in the East-West All-Star game.[36]

When the Fort Benning team came to town for a series in cities such as Birmingham and Memphis, the local media covered the games with the same diligence as they did league games.

7. 1928–30: A Tottering Revival

In addition to the New Orleans club, the 1930 Texas-Louisiana League was comprised of Dallas, Houston, Port Arthur, San Antonio, and Waco. Standings were published several times in the *Chicago Defender*. The following chart is from the July 12, 1930, edition:

Team	G	W	L	Pct.
Houston	42	30	12	.715
San Antonio	24	16	8	.665
New Orleans	42	26	16	.619
Port Arthur	21	10	11	.480
Waco	20	8	12	.400
Dallas	14	4	10	.290

8

1931
Back Again

After a four-year run in the Negro National League, Birmingham and Memphis returned home to help reorganize the Negro Southern League. Joining them was the Nashville Elite Giants club after two years in the NNL.

With that nucleus, the new league was formed. The departure of Birmingham and Memphis from the NNL was not completely a decision by those ball clubs. At a meeting in Chicago in January 1931 there was widespread talk that those two franchises might be transferred to other cities. Indianapolis and Louisville were most often mentioned. Called a move to make the league "more compact," the action once again reflected the travel costs for all clubs, with the league stretching from Michigan to Alabama.[1]

The league meeting opened on a somber note with tribute being paid to Rube Foster. The father of the NNL had died December 9, 1930, in a mental hospital in Kankakee, Illinois. He had been hospitalized in 1926 when an apparent mental illness intensified. He never left the institution once he was committed.[2]

With the Southern cities gone, the NNL was now comprised of the Chicago American Giants, Cleveland Cubs, Detroit Stars, Indianapolis ABCs, Louisville White Sox, and St. Louis Stars. Cleveland replaced the Kansas City Monarchs, now an independent team. The other five had been in the nine-team league in 1930.[3]

When the Louisville team began its spring training in March, the manager was Poindexter Williams, the former Birmingham Black Barons catcher. Williams was succeeding another former Birmingham player, Charles "Two Sides" Wesley.[4]

The new NSL was organized in Montgomery, Alabama, in early March. Joining the three former NNL members were Chattanooga, Montgomery, and New Orleans. Atlanta was listed as an associate member. A first-half schedule for a split season was approved with an opening date set for April 24. Each club was limited to 13 players, including the manager. Birmingham owner R. T. Jackson was elected president of the league. Other officers included Dr. R.B. Jackson, Nashville, vice president; Joe Vaughn, Chattanooga, secretary; and Thomas T. Wilson, Nashville, treasurer.[5]

By the time spring training was under way, New Orleans was no longer in the picture. The Black Pelicans were in the Texas-Louisiana league. The eight-team league was comprised of Monroe, New Orleans, and Shreveport, Louisiana, and Dallas, Galveston, Houston, Longview, and San Antonio, Texas.[6] The TLL would provide a playoff opponent for the NSL at the end of the season. New Orleans' spot in the NSL was filled by the Knoxville Giants.[7] During the second half, the league would expand to eight clubs with the addition of the Atlanta Panthers and the Little Rock Black Travelers or Grays, depending on which newspaper article was read.

Veteran catcher Larry Brown was named manager of the Memphis team while infielder Buford "Geechie" Meredith was in Birmingham, "Daddy" Cunningham in Montgomery, Leroy Stratton in Nashville, and James Edwards in Chattanooga. The new Knoxville club was "under the management of J. A. Nance and W. M. Jenkins." It was not clear if one of them was also the field manager.[8]

Brown, who had been with the New York Lincoln Giants in 1930, was brought back to Memphis by Dr. B. M. Martin, president of the club. There was no mention of Brown's salary but he was said to be "one of the highest paid men in negro circles" while he was with the New York club.[9]

Montgomery, fielding a black professional team for the first time in "several years," was host to Birmingham in its opener. The game was played at College Hill Park, a new facility near the Alabama State Teachers College campus. Harper C. Trenholm, president of the school, was to throw out the first pitch.[10] Although the new park had seating for approximately 1,000, an estimated 2,000 fans turned out at College Hill Park to see the Grey Sox win, 6–3. Wheeler Hardy, a pitcher from Alcorn State College, struck out 12 in outdueling Harry "Fish" Salmon of Birmingham.[11] Birmingham won the second game of the series, 12–1. After a rainout the teams split two games played at Rowell Field in Selma, Alabama.

In other openers Nashville defeated Memphis 3–1 at Sulphur Dell and Chattanooga beat Knoxville 5–3 at Engel Stadium. Details were sparse on the Nashville game, but Jim Willis was the winning pitcher. In Chattanooga a crowd of 1,000 turned out to see Jim Jeffries outpitch Tuggle Dawson. Left fielder Clarke hit a home run for the home team.[12]

Nashville won all three games in the series, then went to Memphis for four games. Beginning with a 20–6 win on May 9, the Red Sox swept their first series at home.

At Chattanooga Mrs. C. C. Looney was slated to throw out the first pitch. "Misses Cox and Barnes will present the managers of the rival teams with flowers," and the Keith Simmons Company of Nashville offered "a handsome loving cup" to the team with the best opening day attendance in the league.[13]

The Black Lookouts then went to Montgomery, where they won the first game of the series, 6–1. The second game was an 11-inning, 13–13 tie. Chattanooga used only two pitchers while Montgomery put in four. Among the four Grey Sox hurlers was Robert Veale, Sr., who would become the father of a future major league pitcher. Veale had mixed success in the league. The following day he threw a 4–0 shutout against Chattanooga, but a few days later in Memphis he lost, 8—6. The Red Sox collected 15 hits off of the righthander.[14]

Left-hander Murray Gillespie of Memphis picked up two wins in one day as the Red Sox hosted Chattanooga on May 31. Gillespie won the first game, 2–1, limiting the visitors to four hits and striking out 11 batters. In the second game he came on in relief of "Sug" Cornelius in the fifth inning. The Black Lookouts had taken a 4–3 lead that inning. Gillespie held them scoreless the rest of the way and got the victory when Memphis scored two in last inning to win, 5–4.[15]

Nashville and Memphis were the frontrunners early on. When Chattanooga used a seven-run fourth inning to beat the Elite Giants at Sulphur Dell on June 8, it was said to have broken an 11-game winning streak.[16] Although Nashville had lost a pair of games in Chicago, the Elite Giants had won at least 10 consecutive games against NSL opponents during the first month of the season. Memphis followed its sweep of Nashville with one against Montgomery, then split a series with Birmingham.

Standings in mid–June showed Nashville (14–6) one game ahead of Memphis (13–7). Chattanooga, even at 12–12, was the only other club over .500. Birmingham and Montgomery were in the middle of the pack with Knoxville (5–21) in last place.[17]

Birmingham was in that middle ground most of the season despite having one of the league's best pitchers in Salmon. Another good pitcher was Walter Calhoun, who would also play with both Chattanooga and Montgomery in 1931. But with Birmingham, Calhoun hit his peak with an 11–0 no-hitter against Ft. Benning.[18] Outfielder Hank Anderson wowed everyone with a June 1 hit in an 8–7 loss to Montgomery: "Hank Anderson hit a home run for the books in the third when he crashed a drive into right center for 431 feet, the ball bouncing over the concrete wall. It was the first time in the history of the park for a ball to bounce over the right center wall. Under the new rule Anderson's 431-foot drive was only a two-bagger—but the boys were playing under the old rule Monday."[19]

On June 17 Montgomery was scheduled to play a barnstorming Indiana team in the first Negro night game at Cramton Bowl. When the Indiana team canceled its appearance, Birmingham stepped in as a substitute. There was no report on the historic game.[20]

By mid–July Henry Hannon was reported to be manager of Montgomery.[21]

Under his leadership the team improved some during the second half, at one point taking eight out of 10 games.[22]

As the two leaders fought it out down the stretch, Nashville pulled out the first half pennant, according to standings published in the *Nashville Banner* and the *Pittsburgh Courier*. Like many NSL standings, though, the numbers were marked with discrepancies. Nashville was shown in first with a 22–11 record and winning percentage .667. Memphis, playing nine more games, was shown at 26–16 with a percentage of .664. If the wins and losses are correct, the Memphis percentage was actually .619. Birmingham (20–19) had climbed above .500 while Knoxville (11–19) remained in the cellar.[23]

And as in some other seasons, there was disagreement over the accuracy of the standings and who was the league leader. On July 3 Memphis manager Larry Brown announced that Memphis was actually in first place with a three-game lead. He said his club needed only one win over Birmingham on the Fourth of July to win the first half.[24]

Birmingham won both games on the holiday, but lost two the following day. Brown's figures must have been incorrect in this case, because Nashville was awarded the first-half flag and there was no further protest from Memphis.

However, the disagreement did resurface at the end of the season. Nashville, the recognized NSL champion, played in a Negro Dixie Series with the Monroe Monarchs, champions of the Texas-Louisiana League. The series paralleled the white Dixie Series held annually between the Southern Association and Texas League teams. A few days after the Negro Dixie Series ended Memphis and Montgomery held a Negro Southern League playoff. More on this series is at the end of the chapter.

8. 1931: Back Again

Although the results do not confirm it, a Chattanooga newspaper reported that the Black Lookouts were contenders during the final week of the first half. As the Elite Giants went into Chattanooga for a July 4 doubleheader, the *Chattanooga Daily Times* reported that Nashville was 24–16 while Chattanooga was 23–17, a game back. There was no mention of Memphis.

Accurate or not, the case for Chattanooga was nullified when the two games were split. The Black Lookouts played brilliantly to win the first game, 2–1. Pitcher Claude Rhodes controlled the game behind great fielding. Outfielder Henry Henderson had eight putouts during the game. Nashville won the nightcap, 4–2.[25]

There were not many highlights for Knoxville's return to the NSL. One of them came on May 30 when Dawson threw a no-hitter against Montgomery, but lost the game 1–0. "A crazy bounding ball thru short allowed the Gray [*sic*] Sox to score."[26] It was the first of four no-hitters thrown in the league in 1931.

On June 21, the *News-Sentinel* reported that J. T. Holland of Cleveland, Tennessee, had taken over the Knoxville club. It fared little better under the new leadership.

Although black ball clubs frequently played games in neutral cities, one of those pairings in June set the stage for a second-half change in the league. On June 3, Memphis won a doubleheader from Birmingham in Little Rock. Later in the month, the Red Sox won Friday and Saturday games in the same city. It is unclear why the games were played in Arkansas, but it is certain that the Little Rock Black Travelers, an independent team, was enjoying a highly successful season. By early July the team had reportedly recorded 24 wins against just two losses.[27]

Little Rock officials were petitioning Negro Southern League leaders to expand the NSL for the second half season, taking in the Black Travelers and an Atlanta club.[28] If they used the Birmingham-Memphis games to showcase black baseball in general, the effort was likely successful. Seating was provided for white patrons and the games were well played. Memphis won the first game, 5–4, but Birmingham catcher Tommy Dukes was the star of the game: "Duke [*sic*] ... turned a sensational catch in the first inning. Lewis tipped a short fly along the third base line and Duke dived full length, caught the ball, turned a complete flip, but retained the ball for a putout."[29] The games apparently had been heavily promoted in Memphis, with the Missouri Pacific Railroad running an excursion to Little Rock. The cost of the fare was three dollars for a round trip.[30]

Oddly, most of reports on the Little Rock club indicated that it had acquired the New Orleans franchise. However, New Orleans was not in the NSL at all.

Another curiosity is the nickname of the Little Rock club. Referred to as the Black Travelers throughout the independent season, when the club made its home debut against Nashville on July 17 it was called the Grays.[31] Since there were further reports on Black Travelers playing independent teams in July and August, it appears there were two separate black teams in Little Rock, the Grays in the NSL and the Black Travelers as an independent team. Game reports suggest some players suited up for both teams. In late August there were reports of the two teams playing against each other.[32]

Finally, to add a little more confusion to the situation, when the Little Rock team went to Memphis for a series in late July the Memphis newspaper referred to the visitors as the "Gray Travelers." Regardless of the name, the series belonged to Memphis. Not only did the Red Sox win all four games, but one of them was a no-hitter by Homer "Goose" Curry, beginning a long Negro League career. The right-hander struck out nine.[33]

Curry duplicated his no-hit feat in September, beating Birmingham, 6–1, in a seven-inning game. Birmingham's run was the result of an error in the third inning.[34]

The Little Rock club played decent baseball at times during its NSL run. In early August the Black Travelers (or Grays) were reported to have won 14 out of their last 15 contests. They were en route to Monroe, Louisiana, to play a doubleheader with the Monroe Monarchs.[35] There, the bubble was burst. The games were one-sided affairs with Monroe winning, 14–6 and 10–1.[36]

Nashville won the Negro Southern League opener in Little Rock, which apparently was delayed until July 18, 10–9. A doubleheader was scheduled for Sunday. Pitching one game for Little Rock would be former Memphis pitcher Murray Gillespie. The left-hander had been sensational in the games against Birmingham in June, striking out 16 in one game and 10 in another.[37] The games were possibly rained out, as there was no report in the *Arkansas Gazette* the following day. There were also no additional reports of either the Grays or the Black Travelers playing other NSL teams.

As in previous seasons, there were many more barnstorming games and fewer league games during the second half of the season.

Chattanooga had road trips that carried the Black Lookouts to Cleveland, Indianapolis, and Louisville in July. In August they had a trip scheduled that would take them to Detroit, Battle Creek, and Pontiac, Michigan.[38]

During the second half Nashville and Memphis continued to do well while Birmingham improved. Birmingham catcher Dukes continued to impress with his "spectacular catches."[39] The Black Barons went into Nashville for an important single game in early August. Nashville, hoping to take both halves of the season, brought in Pete Cleage, the respected Chattanooga manager-first baseman, to umpire the contest. The two teams had split four games earlier and the deciding match was expected to draw a large crowd, including many white patrons.[40]

For such a highly anticipated game, the result was obviously disappointing. Nashville won, 13–8, in a contest that "featured about everything but good baseball," read one report. The writer added: "There was Slim Henderson, Elite left

Ralph "Pete" Cleage, longtime Knoxville Giants player and manager. Photograph is from 1920 (courtesy Beck Cultural Exchange Center).

fielder, who must be seven feet tall if he is an inch. Slim had a terrible time keeping off his own dogs. He got his number twenties tangled three or four times during the game, each time taking a full length sprawl over the landscape.

"Charleston, Nashville catcher, was another who chipped in with his share of the fun. He persisted in molesting the alien hitters until removed from the game after Birmingham base runners had pilfered six bags in one inning.

"Birdine, Baron pitcher, refused to take the game seriously He grinned tooth-filled grins throughout the tilt."[41]

However the following day, in an unusual bylined piece, *Nashville Banner* sports writer Tom Anderson served up a heavy plate of praise for the Elite Giants: "Civic pride is one reason explanatory of the Giants' extraordinary combative spirit on the diamond, seven of the eleven men on the roster being natives of the city. The others are unsullied sons of Dixie, one hailing from Memphis, one from Chattanooga, one from Birmingham, and the other from Lexington, Ky."[42]

Anderson continued to make fun of Slim Henderson and "Red" Charleston, but also showed grudging respect for the catcher:

"One of his pet stunts is to playfully touch the bat with his mitt, thus impeding its swing. Another is to call them for the umpire. Still another is to confuse the opposition:

"He is catching. There is a man on first and one down. The batter hits a fly.

"'Run Boy, there's two gone!' yells Charley."

Although acknowledging that some of his information might not be "entirely exact," Anderson presented positive profiles of the playing ability of the entire team. One interesting note was the mention of first baseman Granville Lyons, a 20-year-old local boy. Lyons was filling the position formerly held by Willie Bobo, who had died earlier that year in San Diego. Bobo was playing in a California winter league when he and two teammates crossed the border into Mexico in search of alcohol. Bobo apparently drank a significant quantity of wood alcohol and died the next day. He was 27.[43]

At least one member of the white press had similar appreciation for the caliber of baseball being played by the Chattanooga team. "They really play the game. Don't let anyone tell you they don't shoot that ball around. They clout the pellet lustily, field amazingly. Their pitchers had the Magic City brown warriors in the hollow of their hand," he wrote in the *Chattanooga Daily Times*.[44]

The Henderson brothers, first baseman Henry and third baseman Leonard, were praised for both their fielding and hitting. Shortstop William Lowe, pitcher Claude Rhodes, and catcher Andrew Drake also drew acclaim, Drake for his base stealing.

"Atlanta fans are still talking about the way the local darkies beat the Black Panthers in a colorful night game there last week," the writer continued. "Born ball players, they call the Black Lookouts. Chattanooga's high-class ball field impressed Atlanta considerably, but that was just another ball game to local players. They are fielding demons all the time, it seems."[45] Memphis could provide additional entertainment not available in league rival cities. When the barnstorming Cuban House of David came to Lewis Park in August, fans not only saw baseball but had music between innings from the band of W.C. Handy, the Father of the Blues.[46]

In late August Nashville owner Tom Wilson announced he was bringing his

National League Cleveland Cubs team to town for a five-game series. The games would feature a number of players who had performed in both the NSL and the NNL during the season.

Two of the games were canceled because Sulphur Dell was not available. Another problem was encountered when one of the buses carrying the Cleveland team broke down en route, forcing the Cubs to play "with a makeshift combination." With no box scores available for the Sunday doubleheader, it is impossible to assess the rosters. Nashville won the opener, 13–3. Cleveland took the nightcap, 2–1, with Jim Willis, who had spent time with both clubs, which had the same ownership, back in a Cubs uniform.[47] There was no report on the third game of the series.

At the end of the regular season the Negro Southern League once again provided playoffs that seemed to bear little resemblance to what the preceding months might have dictated.

There were two postseason series in 1931. The first one—Nashville's dominant play not withstanding—matched the alleged first and second-half winners Memphis and Montgomery, respectively. The winner of this series was to play Monroe, champions of the Negro Texas-Louisiana League in a Negro Dixie Series.[48]

The series opened in Montgomery on Saturday, September 12, with Montgomery winning the first game, 5–0. A new pitcher named White held the Red Sox to five hits while Curry gave up seven in taking the loss. Center fielder McNeal hit a home run for the winners.[49] Memphis won the next two games, 7–6 and 4–2. The winning pitcher for the 7–6 game appears to by Harry Salmon, picked up for the postseason. Batteries for the third game were not published.

The series then moved to Memphis for a single game on Saturday, September 19, and a doubleheader on Sunday, September 20. There was no report on the Saturday game, which apparently was won by Montgomery. On Sunday the Red Sox won the opener, 5–4. Montgomery came back to take the six-inning nightcap by the same score. The second game was called after six innings because of darkness.[50]

A seventh game scheduled for Monday, Sept. 21, which would have decided the champion, was canceled. There was no explanation for the cancellation, thus bringing another Negro Southern League season to a close with questions unanswered after the bats and gloves were put away.[51]

It is unclear if the failure of the playoff to produce a legitimate champion was the overriding factor, or if it was just another example of fuzzy organization in black baseball, but Nashville, the champion by all earlier accounts, resurfaced for the Negro Dixie Series feature against Monroe. Newspaper reports made no reference to the Memphis-Montgomery series.

Nashville had had home field advantage and made good use of it, winning the opening game, 1–0, in 13 innings at Wilson Park. Righthander Willis outdueled Monroe's Bob Sloan in the Sunday, August 30, contest. Willis gave up only two hits while Sloan surrendered nine.[52] According to the *Pittsburgh Courier,* Nashville was represented by "the entire team of Cleveland playing under the name of the Elite Giants." Tom Wilson, who owned both clubs, reportedly sent the Cleveland club down for the championship series.[53] There was indeed a lot of overlapping during the regular season between the two clubs. Richard Cannon, Comer Cox, Jesse Edwards, Willis and Henry

Wright were among a number of players who were on both rosters during the season.[54] Willis started the season in Nashville, went up to Cleveland for a while, and apparently returned to Nashville at least briefly in July.[55] As the Dixie Series neared, it was reported that "Willis and several other present members of the Cleveland Cubs will be returned to Nashville for the seven-game sets of games."[56]

After a day off, the second game saw Nashville win a night game, 10–1. Dempsey Miller held the Monarchs to six hits and Leroy Stratton hit a home run. "Unaccustomed to playing night games, the Monarchs errors were attributed to the glare of lights," reported the *Monroe World*, adding that six Cleveland Cubs were in the Nashville lineup.[57] A third game, scheduled the next day, was rained out.

The series then moved to Monroe. If having the home field had been an advantage for Nashville in the first two games, it was even more so for Monroe the rest of the series. Back at their Casino Park the Monarchs took four out of five games from the Elite Giants. Projected to start in the first game for Monroe was Robert "Black Diamond" Pipkin, who was said to have been with Indianapolis during the regular season, although he does not appear on that team's roster. Actually, he was with Cleveland.[58]

Monroe quickly set the tone for the final games. The Monarchs collected 21 hits off of Cannon and Wright, pounding out a 19–10 win the first game. There was no box score published and the game story gave no details on the hitting performances in that 29-run, 34-hit contest. "Smut" Alexander started for Monroe and was relieved by Bob Sloan. Pipkin did not appear.[59]

Willis, whose 13-inning performance had given Nashville the first win in the series, was beaten, 5–3, in the fourth game, giving up 11 hits. Willie Markham, with relief help from Sloan, was the winning pitcher. Outfielder Zollie Wright drove in four of the Monroe runs and "Red" Parnell, recently obtained from Houston, hit a triple and two singles in four at-bats. Shortstop Leroy Morney was the fielding star as Monroe evened the series at two games each.[60]

But, despite two losses in a row, Nashville still had a good team. In Game Five the Elite Giants regained the series lead with a 5–2 win at Casino Park. Clifford Bell pitched Nashville to a three-to-two edge in the series. The Nashville win presented two problems to the Monarchs. First, they were only a game from elimination in the series. Second, they were scheduled to leave town on the following evening for an extensive Mexican road trip.

A doubleheader was scheduled for Wednesday, September 9. If Nashville won the first game, the series was over. If the Monroe won the first game, the second game would be played to settle the championship, still allowing the Monarchs time to make their train connection for Mexico.[61]

The Monarchs won both games. They came from behind, 2–0, to win the first game 4–2 as Willie B. Burnham scattered 10 Nashville hits. John Markham would have had a shutout in the 6–1 second game except for a throwing error. As the Monroe players packed their bags for the Latin trip, the Monarchs claimed an even bigger accolade than the Negro Dixie Series title: "As a result of the victory over the Giants, the Monarchs are now laying claim to the negro national championship as the Nashville team is composed chiefly of players recruited from the Cleveland team, which tied the St. Louis Stars for the National league title."[62] This was not a totally indisputable claim, but historian John Holway says St. Louis was the "declared champion."[63] On September 10, the victorious Monarchs left the city for their three-month exhibition tour of Mexico. Although the second half of the season disintegrated, almost according to form in the NSL, there was enough of a pennant race to call the season a success, especially with the Negro Dixie Series.

The number of box scores available for individual performance recognition were: Memphis 43, Birmingham 22, Nashville 16, Chattanooga 9, Montgomery 9, Knoxville 8, and Little Rock, 4. Although first baseman Manning of Montgomery batted .441 and Jerry Benjamin of Knoxville .379, those figures came from totals of eight and seven games, respectively. The only fair measurements would be from three teams with at least double digit box scores. Given those parameters, the top hitters and the number of games played were:

Murray Gillespie, Memphis, 22 games, .419
George McAllister, Birmingham, 22 games, .388
Larry Brown, Memphis, 39 games, .374
Claude Johnson, Nashville, 10 games, .370
Homer Curry, Memphis, 37 games, .369
Clarence Threakill, Nashville, 10 games, .351.

Home runs were scarce but stolen bases were plentiful during the season. Outfielder Purvis of Memphis had 15 steals in 37 games while teammates Curry and Elvin Powell had 13 and 12 respectively.

The top pitcher was Harry "Baby" Cunningham of Memphis with a 12–2 record. Nelson of Montgomery was 9–6 and Harry Salmon of Birmingham, 6–4. The strikeout leader was Gillespie with 122 in 120.1 innings. Next was "Sug" Cornelius of Memphis with 59 in 126 innings.

9

1932
Major League Status

The year of 1932 was, by one measure, the Negro Southern League's greatest year. The league has been accorded Negro major league status by baseball historians because it survived while all others fell by the wayside during the worst of the Great Depression.

On the other hand, there has never been a more confusing season for the NSL, or for black league baseball in general. More than a dozen teams were part of the league over the course of the season.

Overall in 1932, Negro League baseball hit probably the lowest point it would know in the pre-integration years before Jackie Robinson's major league debut. The Negro National League, which had started organized league black baseball in 1920, did not operate. The Eastern Colored League, which had operated without a break from 1923 to 1928, was defunct and its successor, the American Negro League, ended after a single season in 1929. Taking their place was a new East-West League, an amalgam of teams from the Midwest and the Atlantic coast. It lasted about half the season with 10 different teams from Baltimore to Detroit being members at various times.[1]

Out of these Depression-era financial difficulties emerged the Negro Southern League, but it was not the NSL of the past. It was, in fact, a hybrid of teams from three different Negro leagues. The Society for American Baseball Research book on the Negro Leagues lists 11 cities fielding teams at various times during the season: Atlanta, Birmingham, Chicago, Cleveland, Indianapolis, Little Rock, Louisville, Memphis, Monroe, Montgomery, and Nashville.[2] Historian John Holway lists seven teams: Chicago, Indianapolis, Louisville, Memphis, Monroe, Montgomery, and Nashville.[3]

Another source also reports possible second half franchise shifts involving Alcoa, Tennessee; Columbus, Ohio; and Lexington, Kentucky. Alcoa was said to be taking over Knoxville's spot, Columbus replacing Atlanta, and Lexington replacing Birmingham. Quite confusing, as Knoxville was not in the league during the first half.[4]

However, yet another newspaper threw a fourth team into the picture. The *Knoxville News-Sentinel* reported that the Knoxville Giants, which had been playing independent ball, were being reorganized and had been "assured of Southern league play." This followed a dispute between Manager J. A. Nance and Floyd Holland, who had reportedly taken over the team. Nance said his Knoxville Giants would be in the league and the other team, Holland's Knoxville Giants, would not be.[5] If Knoxville joined the league, the addition of Alcoa, Columbus, and Lexington as replacements raised the number of participating cities for the season to 15.

Primarily using contemporary newspaper accounts, the author will attempt to report chronologically the organization of the league at the beginning of the season and the widely reported franchise shifts that occurred during the season. All teams that were or may have been members are included in the roster appendix.

Owners met in Nashville in March to formulate plans for the new season. An official league ball, from the well-known Worth sporting goods line, was adopted and required for all league games included in the standings. Again, there would be a split season, followed by a championship series. A report in the *Pittsburgh Courier* did not identify the full league lineup, but did welcome newcomers "Gus Greenlea [sic] and his Pittsburgh Crawfords, Jim Taylor's Indianapolis A.B.C.s, John Dixon's Louisville Black Caps and S. M. Terrell's Cleveland Cubs."[6]

Representing the Negro National League were the Chicago American Giants, the Cubs, the ABCs, and the Black Caps, a reconfiguration of the Louisville White Sox. Representing the Negro Southern League were the Atlanta Black Crackers, Birmingham Black Barons, Little Rock Black Travelers, Memphis Red Sox, Montgomery Grey Sox, and Nashville Elite Giants. Coming over from the Negro Louisiana-Texas League were Fred Stovall's Monroe, Louisiana, Monarchs, the 1931 pennant-winning team that had swamped the Elite Giants in the "Negro Dixie Series."[7]

A report out of Pittsburgh said Gus Greenlee would be in Louisville on March 10 for an NSL meeting, where it would be determined if Pittsburgh would be a regular member or an associate member.[8]

By mid–March the league lineup appeared to have settled on 10 teams, with Cleveland and the Pittsburgh Crawfords being associate members.[9]

The Louisville meeting was a tense affair with tough membership discussions: "Chief among the problems and issues discussed were the fates of Louisville, which city did not choose to enter league baseball, and the attempt of Monroe, La., to force its way into the body over the protest of the other teams. Argument against Monroe was that its location made travel from the other cities too much of a financial burden," wrote Richard Downs in the *Atlanta Daily World*.[10]

Meanwhile Chicago, which had been leaning toward an associate membership, decided to become a regular member. Afterward, franchises were awarded to 10 cities: Atlanta, Birming-

Pitcher Andy Porter started the 1932 season with Louisville, then moved to Nashville Elite Giants, remaining with that team for more than a decade (courtesy NoirTech Research).

ham, Chicago, Indianapolis, Little Rock, Louisville, Memphis, Montgomery, Monroe, and Nashville, and associate memberships to Pittsburgh and Cleveland.[11] The schedule released after the meeting showed all 12 teams playing each other in an organized home and away format.

In addition to the Cleveland Cubs in the NSL, there was the Cleveland Stars team in the East-West League.[12] The Chicago team, which had been started by the great Rube Foster in 1910, had a new owner, Robert A. Cole. He changed the name of the team to Cole's American Giants.[13] However, few newspapers ever referred to it as anything but the Chicago American Giants throughout the season.

The first set of published standings on May 20 listed the 10 teams from the March 20 projected lineup. The associates Pittsburgh and Cleveland, the games for which would not have counted in the standings, were not mentioned. By June there were only nine teams listed, with Atlanta missing.[14] The final first half standings carried only seven clubs, with Birmingham and Little Rock now among the missing.[15]

The first reported second-half standings in late July listed Chicago, Indianapolis, Louisville, Memphis, Monroe, Montgomery, and Nashville.[16] A week later a new set of standings had added Columbus to the lineup.[17]

Birmingham, which would not even last the entire first half, was managed by catcher Poindexter Williams. He had managed the team in 1928, but his 1932 role was likely the direct result of an off-season death. Veteran infielder Buford "Geechie" Meredith, the 1931 manager, had been killed in a mining accident in January.[18]

The spring training camp included first baseman George McAllister, outfielder Jim West and utility man Martin Oliver. Pitchers were Alonzo Boone, Harry Salmon and Ernest "Spoon" Carter.[19] Signed to replace the popular Meredith in the infield was Milt Laurent, who had played for several New Orleans teams. Another newcomer was Lenon Henderson, one of several brothers who played with the Chattanooga teams over the years.

But Meredith's death foreshadowed what became the worst season in Black Barons history. The team played decent ball, hovering just over .500 most of the season. Unfortunately, its season lasted barely a month. Like several other clubs, it was plagued by bad weather early in the season. In early June, the Louisville Black Caps had reportedly been strengthened by the addition of six new players from Birmingham, a sign the Black Barons had folded.[20]

Monroe opened on the road with series at Little Rock and Memphis. The Monarchs had been impressive in winning exhibition series from Chicago and the Houston Black Buffaloes. Enthusiastic fans were offered the opportunity to take a special bus to Little Rock for the opening series.[21] Monroe would return home to face the Cleveland Cubs. Owner Stovall had bolstered his team with acquisition of pitchers Murray Gillespie and Elbert Williams, also first baseman Chuffy Alexander, and outfielder Roy "Red" Parnell from Houston. For the home opener, a parade was scheduled to start at noon at the black high school with a prize for the best decorated car or float. Opening ceremonies also included two bands and a community glee club performance. Seats were set aside for white fans at Casino Park.[22]

The opening game on May 6 was a huge success. A large crowd saw the Monarchs pull out a 4–3 win in 12 innings. Andrew "Pullman" Porter of the Cubs and Dick

Matthews of the Monarchs each went the distance, giving up seven and eight hits, respectively.[23] The next day, Monroe made it two in a row with a 5–2 win behind the four-hit pitching of the versatile Parnell.[24] On Sunday, it was a clean sweep with Barney Morris throwing a no-hitter in the seven-inning second game. Morris won, 4–0, striking out six. Williams also pitched a one-hit 6–0 shutout in the first game, striking out eight.[25]

After mashing Rayville, Louisiana, 27–3, in an exhibition game, Monroe returned to league play with a four-game sweep of Little Rock. The Monarchs outscored the Grays, 20–7, in the four games. Their league record was reported to be 11–2 after the sweep.

With a nine-game winning streak on the line, Monroe found the visiting Birmingham Black Barons a more challenging opponent. Birmingham won the opener at Casino Park, 5–1. Alonzo Boone set the home team down on six hits, not giving up the lone run until the last inning. Monroe won the Sunday double-header, but both games were hard-fought. Matthews got two runs of support in the bottom of the eighth inning to win the opener, 2–1. Williams pitched a seven inning one-hitter in the nightcap. "Only heads-up baseball caused the Monarchs to retain their top position in the league," reported the local press.[26]

Nashville opened at home against the Pittsburgh Crawfords. Although the Crawfords and the Cleveland Cubs had been referred to as associate members in previous reports, the *Nashville Tennesseean* said "twelve of the leading negro baseball clubs open their diamonds campaigns this afternoon...."[27] That, of course, suggests they were full-fledged members of the league. Nashville's opening festivities also included a parade and a ceremonial first pitch by Police Chief Lon Foster to Fire Commissioner Luther Lutton. Nashville manager Joe Hewitt was given a floral wreath and the home team beat the visitors by 8–2.[28]

Memphis started its parade in front of the Red Sox park. Robert R. Church, Jr., a prestigious local African American leader, was selected to throw out the first pitch with club owner Tom Hayes receiving.[29] Birmingham spoiled the occasion with a 7–3 win.

Indianapolis, a founding team of the Negro National League, but mostly playing independently since 1926 before joining the NSL this season, was managed by "Candy Jim" Taylor. As the ABCs neared their home opener, the local press reported that the league was made up of eight cities. In addition to Indianapolis, they were Atlanta, Birmingham, Chicago, Louisville, Memphis, Montgomery, and Nashville. There was no mention of Monroe and Louisville, no mention of the two associate members, Pittsburgh and Cleveland.[30]

The ABCs opened in Chicago on April 23, defeating Cole's team, 2–1. Their home opener a week later was against Nashville in Perry Stadium. As usual it was scheduled while the white Indianapolis Indians of the American Association were away. The ABCs won their first league home game, 4–3.[31]

A couple of weeks later they lost first baseman Willie Lee Scott for a time. Struck in the mouth by a thrown ball, Scott had two teeth knocked out and his mouth badly lacerated in the first game of a double-header with Pittsburgh. "The A.B.C.s seemed to fold up for a while after Scott was injured, but they braced up and made a real contest out of the nightcap," reported the *Indianapolis News*.[32]

The Louisville Black Caps were managed by Jim Brown, a former Chicago American Giants pitcher. Interestingly, the *Louisville Courier-Journal*, perhaps ahead of its time, identified the Black Caps as the city's "entry in the Afro-American Southern League."[33] The team started off poorly, but improved with the addition of as many as eight former Birmingham players when the Black Barons foundered.

In Atlanta, the white Junior Chamber of Commerce was sponsoring an effort to put 20,000 fans in the stands for the Atlanta Crackers' opening day, thus assuring the white team an attendance trophy. This led a black Atlanta writer to ask, "What shall the Negro do in this effort? Shall we help the city to win? Or shall we stay away and sulk because of real or imaginary grievances?"[34] Over the years there had been complaints about the treatment of black fans at the white team's games. The black writer suggested that some of those concerns had been addressed:

> There are already some forces at work that will be of benefit to us as a race which may be news to some of us. For instance, a colored man will take up your tickets and let you into the turnstiles, colored boys will sell you cold drinks, sandwiches and cushions; and the curtain will be let down to keep the sun or rain off of you while you are enjoying the game. And all of these things are only the beginning of the improvements of the many things that the management is contemplating making if the colored people will only show their appreciation.[35]

That was to say, black fans should forget past indignities and spend their money supporting the white Southern Association team.

For the Black Crackers opener on May 2, a crowd of 5,000 was sought, according to sports writer Lucius "Melancholy" Jones.[36] The crowd was not noted in the subsequent game account, but Atlanta upended Montgomery, 3–2, at Ponce de Leon Park. The Grey Sox had taken three from Atlanta in their home park the previous week.[37] The following day, Montgomery won, 12–1, as catcher Paul Hardy went four-for-four at the plate and scored four runs. That gave Hardy a perfect six hits in six at-bats in the two games.[38]

Atlanta finished the series with a double-header sweep, winning 6–2 and 10–7. It was not reported how Hardy fared in those two games. The Black Crackers then went on the road to Knoxville and Indianapolis. In keeping with the general confusion over the NSL's make-up, the *Atlanta Daily World* reported that Knoxville was a member of the league.[39]

There was also controversy early on. The *Pittsburgh Courier* reported on June 4 that the Memphis club might be dropped from the league for playing men who were not eligible. The Atlanta club, which had take three out of four from Montgomery in early May, was declared winless because they had not used official league balls in those games.[40]

In mid–June, Montgomery went into Monroe for a four-game series and lost them all. The Monarchs won the opener, 3–0, with Parnell not only pitching a six-hit shutout but also collecting three hits. In the Sunday double header Williams pitched a scoreless ninth inning to save the first game, then went the distance to win the second game. Parnell pitched another complete game on Monday.[41]

As the season neared the July 4 weekend and the end of the first half, it remained a tight race between Chicago and Monroe. The American Giants were scheduled to play at Louisville while the Monarchs were at home against the Memphis Red Sox.

While those series would decide the first-half championship, the local Monroe press made it clear that the Monarchs were fighting more than the Red Sox: "Monroe has won more games and lost less than Chicago but in order to give the Chicago team the break it was ruled to throw out some of the games Chicago lost."[42] Monroe won the Saturday opener, 6–5, in 11 innings. Pitcher Morris singled in the winning running for the home team. After giving up three runs in the first inning, he had kept Memphis' remaining hits scattered. A Sunday double-header was limited to one seven-inning game because of wet weather. Monroe won the shortened game, 5–3. The Monarchs then won the Independence Day double-header, 5–1 and 8–2, to take "undisputed possession of the first half," the *Monroe Morning World* reported.[43]

Two sets of final first-half standings contained varying numbers, but both showed Monroe ahead:

Monroe Morning World				*Atlanta Daily World*			
Team	Won	Lost	Pct	Team	Won	Lost	Pct.
Monroe	33	7	.825	Monroe	31	7	.816
Chicago	28	9	.756	Chicago	31	8	.795
Nashville	24	13	.646	Nashville	24	13	.646
Montgomery	22	17	.564	Montgomery	22	17	.564
Memphis	22	19	.537	Memphis	22	22	.500
Louisville	12	15	.444	Louisville	13	17	.433
Indianapolis	14	19	.444	Indianapolis	14	19	.444[44]

At the league meeting in Nashville in early July, plans were made for the second half of the season: "Following a general check up of the first half, regardless of the cry of depression and other hard luck stories, President Jackson extended congratulations to the unit of baseball moguls which numbered and represented 26 cities. A high degree of enthusiasm and interest was shown throughout the two days in Nashville."[45]

It is difficult to reconcile President R. B. Jackson's enthusiasm with the next paragraph of the newspaper story, which related: "The case of run away players, incompetent umpires, games played with unofficial balls and general moral of manager, captain and even sub was dealt a hard blow from the president's decisions." Jackson had booted from the league Murray Gillespie, "Dim'" Miller, and Joe Wiggins. In another personnel matter, he awarded Jim West, a former Birmingham player, to Memphis. There was no detailed explanation of the need for these actions.

And then there were the announced franchises changes: Atlanta to Columbus, Birmingham to Lexington, and Little Rock to Kansas City. Associate memberships were awarded to Knoxville and Alcoa, Tennessee.[46]

The opening games for the second half were:

- July 9–10, Nashville at Indianapolis
- July 9–11, Montgomery at Louisville
- July 9–12, Kansas City at Chicago
- July 9–11, Monroe at Memphis
- July 7, Knoxville at Alcoa.

That schedule would suggest that the Kansas City Monarchs had been added to league for the second half. The obvious question would be: What about Columbus and Lexington, and do Knoxville and Alcoa games count in the standings? When Alcoa beat

Montgomery, 3–2, around July 14, it was reported that Alcoa was a new member of "the Southern league." Other games in the series were rained out.[47]

Alcoa, frequently misspelled as Alcoe, was a Knoxville suburb that drew its name from the Alcoa Aluminum Company plant located in the town. Previously known as North Maryville, the town's name was formally changed to Alcoa in 1919.[48] The company had sponsored baseball teams as far back as 1917.[49] A 1920 company publication contained photographs of both white and black baseball teams. The white team had been admitted to the Knoxville City League and played other industrial sponsored teams in the amateur league.[50]

Lexington's first foray into the NSL was through the Hard Hitters, a team that had been around for several years, but had never played in an organized professional league. In mid–July a local newspaper reported that the team was in Knoxville for a series and would return home July 22 for a series with the Nashville Elite Giants. The article said the Hard Hitters had been admitted to the NSL. The other members of the league were said to be Chicago, Columbus, Louisville, Memphis, Monroe, and Nashville. There was no reference to Knoxville and Alcoa as league members.[51]

Lexington, in its league debut at Stivers Field, was shut out by Nashville, 4–0.[52] On July 30 the Hard Hitters were shut out again, this time by Alcoa, 2–0. James Carr of the Aluminum Sluggers limited the Lexington team to six hits. The *Lexington Leader* reported that the shutout extended Lexington's scoreless streak to 34 innings. "Since joining the Negro Southern League, the Hitters have found the going tough and have been unable, so far, to cross the fourth base against league teams."[53] Defining the scoreless string is difficult because Lexington had scored 15 runs in splitting two games at Alcoa on July 19–20. Then again, results of some games were likely never reported.

Finally, the Hard Hitters came to life, winning a doubleheader from Alcoa on Sunday, July 31, and a single game the following day.[54] Later in the month they beat Columbus three straight.[55]

That franchise shifts were imminent in the second half was made clear in late June by the squabble between black baseball promoters in Knoxville. J.A. Nance announced that he was reorganizing the Knoxville Giants in preparation for play in the NSL. Floyd Holland had reportedly taken control of Nance's team and renamed it Holland's Knoxville Giants. Nance said Holland's team was in no way connected with the NSL. Nance said the players on Holland's teams were players that would have been released anyway. Both men had apparently obtained attorneys and filed legal actions against each other.[56] As the summer progressed the Knoxville newspapers sometimes referred to the team as Holland's Knoxville Giants and sometimes as just the Knoxville Giants with no mention of either Holland or Nance. The author has made no effort to distinguish between the two claimants in adding Knoxville results to the league record.

The *Knoxville Journal* reported on July 2 that the Knoxville Giants—under J. A. Nance—were given a place in the Negro Southern League at a recent meeting of the association in Nashville. The team would open the league season in a home stand against the Louisville Red Sox.[57] That would be followed by a series at Lexington, then return home to face the same team.[58] Whether the Louisville Red Sox were the same as the original Louisville Red Caps is not clear.

Knoxville made its NSL debut, the *Journal* reported, with a 9–8 win over the

Louisville team. In August when the Knoxville and Alcoa teams played, local newspapers continued to report that both were members of the Negro Southern League.[59]

Black fans in Knoxville may have been primed to once again have a league team of their own. In June, a Knoxville newspaper had reported that the management of the white Knoxville Smokies was disappointed in the support being given the team by black fans. This apparently stemmed from "a little joke" between Chattanooga owner Joe Engel and Secretary Allen of the Smokies. One can assume that there were racial overtones to the joke that disturbed black fans in Knoxville. "The Knoxville club wants the support of the colored fans as much as any others. If the owners had not wanted them they would not have built the grandstand for them. It is the best colored grandstand in the Southern League," pleaded W.N. Smithson, vice president of the Smokies.[60]

The Columbus Turf Club team was announced as a new league member in early July. The Ohio team was to play its first league game on Saturday, July 16, at Neil Park, the home of the city's white American Association team. A Sunday doubleheader and single game on Monday were to follow.[61] It was reported that the Turf Club, sometimes called the Turf Stars, was bringing "colored professional baseball to Columbus" for the first time in 10 years.[62] The cost of admission was 35 cents and 50 cents for the weekend games, with ladies being admitted free, and 25 cents for Monday.

There was no report on the Saturday game, but the two teams split the Sunday doubleheader, Nashville winning the opener, 11–0, and Columbus the nightcap, 6–1.[63]

Second-half play had only gone on about two weeks when there was a startling announcement out of Nashville that changed the first-half finish of the teams. League President R. B. Jackson declared that Chicago, not Monroe, had won the first half. Jackson's explanation: "Ending the first-half of the split season around July 4, we were faced with a very complex decision, that is, a statement in regards to which team really attained the highest percentage of the close of the first half," the statement read, then digressed into a discourse on how well all of the clubs had played and how well they had represented the league. The narrative then continued with, "Cole's American Giants are winners for the first-half, this team played and won more games, presenting the best attraction qualities, and above all, their individual respect for league affiliation is unsurpassed." Jackson said there had been no release of official final standings and seemed to attribute Monroe's claim to "some few sports writers [who] have overzealously accepted reports of games won and averaged a percentage for publication."

It is interesting to note that Jackson's telegram did not include the still-unreleased final standings.[64]

Sports writer Al Monroe wrote about the dispute in the *Chicago Defender* under the headline: "Who Won the First Half!? You Tell Us." Monroe wrote that President Jackson had based his decision on Chicago having a record of 34–7 compared to Monroe's 33–7. But it was not that easy. "One game played in Louisville between the club of that city and Chicago which the latter lost was given to the Giants because nonleague balls were used. Then, too, Chicago was allowed the two games won from Louisville in Chicago near the close of the season. Dave Malarcher asked permission to play the games, which had been postponed because of rain."

Then, the Monroe team arrived with letters and telegrams that purported to prove that two games lost to Memphis had been played under protest because of the use of nonleague balls. "This the president did not deny, but admitted that he had received no official protest in writing that such had been the case. A telegram from D. Martin of Memphis, however, gave some credit to Monroe's cause when it stated that the prexy had admitted receiving the protest, but told league officials at the last meeting that they had been misplaced."[65]

Jackson, possibly succumbing to pressure from Midwestern interests unhappy over the long travel jump to Monroe, apparently chose to ignore Monroe's protest case, thus awarding the first half pennant to Chicago.

It will be seen that the substance of Jackson's ruling was both ignored in Louisiana and embraced in Chicago during the postseason. While Chicago and Nashville, the clear second half winner, played a fall championship series, Monroe also played a similar series against a different champion.

The second-half schedule followed the projected pattern for a few weeks, then deteriorated rapidly into the usual second-half smorgasbord of league and barnstorming games. Monroe, after a road trip to Chicago, Louisville, and Memphis, returned home to entertain the Red Sox at Casino Park the last weekend in July. Although this was a league series, the pregame story reported that "The Monarchs have been granted permission to play any teams they desire in the second half and the fans of Monroe will see the Monarchs in action with teams of others leagues until the play-off."[66]

In late July the Little Rock club, although apparently no longer in the league, continued to operate. Now managed by Reuben Jones, it went to Mexico City to play a seven-game series with the Azetecas there.[67]

On July 24, as Pittsburgh and Indianapolis split a double-header at Perry Field in Indianapolis, future Hall of Famer Josh Gibson recorded a bit of history: "Gibson, giant catcher of the Crawfords, hit the longest home run ever made in the park Sunday when he blasted the ball over the right field wall, more than 400 feet."[68]

In August it was reported that the second-half schedule had been suspended "because of the heavy expenses incurred by transporting teams." However, the teams were to be kept together "for special games in order to keep baseball going in their respective cities." The Montgomery Grey Sox, reportedly in third place in the league, would play a series at home with the Birmingham All-Stars under the new arrangement.[69]

Standings published on July 23 showed a seven-team league:

Team	Won	Lost	Pct.
Chicago	4	1	.800
Memphis	6	2	.750
Indianapolis	3	2	.600
Louisville	4	3	.571
Nashville	1	2	.333
Monroe	2	6	.250
Montgomery	1	4	.200[70]
	21	20	

Missing from the standings were all four of the new second-half clubs. Yet, games played among Knoxville, Alcoa, and Lexington were regularly reported in Knoxville newspapers to be Negro Southern League games.

Standings published a week later included Columbus, which was reported to be winless in seven league games. The standings also showed dramatically different records for several teams. Nashville was now presented as undefeated in seven games and Indianapolis, 3–2 on July 23, was now 1–4:

Team	Won	Lost	Pct.
Nashville	7	0	1.000
Chicago	7	1	.875
Memphis	6	2	.750
Louisville	5	3	.625
Monroe	2	7	.222
Indianapolis	1	4	.200
Montgomery	1	5	.177
Columbus	0	7	.000[71]
	39	29	

That same weekend, a story in the *Atlanta Daily World* reported that the Louisville Black Caps had disbanded. A few days earlier Louisville Manager Brown had put together a pickup team called the NSL All-Stars to provide Monroe with opposition when the Monarchs arrived in Louisville. The All-Stars and Monarchs split a double-header.[72]

On July 31 the Black Caps reportedly lost a doubleheader with Columbus. But the following day it was the NSL All-Stars in a losing effort against Columbus.[73]

In early August the *Chicago Defender* reported that the NSL season was in danger of not being completed: "Although nothing has been received from the offices of Dr. R. B. Jackson, president of the Southern baseball league, rumor coming from that section still persists that the second half of the pennant race may not be completed. Monroe, La., has had no league games for the past several weeks and Montgomery, Atlanta and Alcoa have already folded up," the paper reported.[74]

Actually, Monroe had just completed a five-game series with Memphis, but it was true that no results for the other teams had been reported since July.

The same edition carried a piece out of Monroe, saying the Monarchs were looking for a major postseason series with Chicago or some team from the East. The article was also adamant about Monroe's claim to the first-half title: "The people in this section kept up with the Monarchs and the records of all the teams in the Southern league, and know the games actually won and lost in the first half, and no news item from any papers in the country could make them believe that Monroe did not win the first half."[75]

On August 20, a Columbus newspaper reported that the Turf Club team was looking for opponents for later in the month "because Knoxville and Memphis have dropped out of the Southern Association Colored league," leaving the team without games.[76]

The last set of published standings appeared in the *Defender* on August 13. Nashville, Chicago, and Memphis were still the top three teams:

Team	Won	Lost	Pct.
Nashville	11	0	1.000
Chicago	8	1	.888
Memphis	11	5	.688
Louisville	7	5	.583
Monroe	5	9	.357
Columbus	2	10	.167
Montgomery	1	5	.166
Indianapolis	1	12	.077[77]
	46	47	

Knoxville, Alcoa, and Lexington again were omitted from the standings although their games had been billed as league contests. Knoxville and Alcoa, just a few miles apart, played a five-game series in September for "the East Tennessee championship." Knoxville won the series three games to two.[78]

In late August an announcement, curiously out of Birmingham, reported that the NSL regular season would end on September 3, followed by "the Dixie Series, which will feature the two Leading Teams connected with Southern League Cole's America Giants and Tom Wilson's Elite Giants of Nashville, Tenn." There was also a reference to upcoming "World Championship Games" to be played against the Pittsburgh Crawfords, New York Black Yankees, or Homestead Grays.[79]

The series was to begin in Chicago, then move to Nashville in a peculiar every-other-week format. An assortment of prizes would be awarded to fans and the games would be on the radio. "The series will be broadcast play-by-play, the National and Columbia broadcasting systems will begin the distribution of the scheduled series Aug. 25, at 8 p.m.," reported the *Chicago Defender*.[80]

Meanwhile in Louisiana, the Monroe Monarchs were already involved in a Louisiana state championship series with the New Orleans Black Pelicans, Alexandria Lincoln Giants, and Algiers Giants. All of the games were not reported. Among those that were, Monroe won two of three from New Orleans, lost two of three with Alexandria and won a single game from Algiers. On August 19, as the team prepared to head to Texas for the Negro Dixie Series, it was reported that they had won five out of seven from the New Orleans team to take the Louisiana championship.[81]

Both postseason series, the one involving Chicago and Nashville and one with Monroe, were billed as the Negro Dixie Series. It was an odd identification for the Chicago-Nashville series, because the Negro Dixie Series was patterned after the white series in which the Southern Association and Texas League champions met in a Dixie Series each year. That scenario better fit Monroe's series with the Austin Black Senators, champions of the Negro Texas League.

Also, as it would turn out, neither Chicago nor Nashville played again after their series. However, Monroe went on to play a series with the Pittsburgh Crawfords.

The Monroe-Austin series opened in Texas on Saturday, August 20. Barney Morris limited Austin to three hits and struck out eight as Monroe won the first game, 5–2. The game was shortened to seven innings because of rain.[82] Although the Monarchs outhit the Black Senators 8–5, Austin won the second game, 3–2. Monroe took a two games to one lead in the series with a 5–4 win on Monday, August 22.

Hopes for a quick windup at Casino Park were dashed when Austin won the first game in Monroe, 4–2. A young pitcher named Hilton Smith gave up 11 hits, but only one earned run to tie the series at two games apiece.[83] The game was said to be Smith's 13th consecutive win.[84] Monroe came from behind to win the fifth game, 3–2. Trailing 2–0, the Monarchs scored twice in the eighth inning, then pushed across the winning run in the ninth. Williams, who had come on in relief of Morris in the ninth, singled home the winning run.[85] The following day the Monarchs won their second consecutive Negro Dixie Series. Williams shut out the visitors, 10–0, giving up only three hits and striking out five. Porter Dallas and Bob Saunders each had three hits.[86]

The team immediately began preparations for the trip north to meet the Pittsburgh

Crawfords in what Monroe newspapers called the Negro World Series. Indeed, the *Atlanta Daily World* also referred to it as Negro World Series.[87]

As that series began on Saturday, September 3, the other Dixie Series between Nashville and Chicago began the same day in Chicago. In both series, the teams from the Deep South were beaten by their northern foes.

The Crawfords defeated Monroe, 7–3, in the first game of their series. Monroe came back on Sunday to win, 2–1, in 10 innings. Zollie Wright drove in Leroy Morney with a single for the winning margin. Williams, who had come on in relief of Morris in the last three innings, shut down the Crawfords in the bottom of the 10th inning.

In a morning-afternoon Labor Day doubleheader Pittsburgh won a pair of lopsided games, 7–2 and 9–2. With either a two-games-to-one or a three-games-to-one lead, the series was moved to Monroe.[88] According to the *Monroe World*, one of the Labor Day games in Pittsburgh was "an exhibition contest, with the gate receipts going to charity." Thus, it was now stated that the champion only needed to win four games.[89]

A right-hander out of Texas, Hilton Smith started his NSL career with the Monroe Monarchs, then played for New Orleans teams before going on to a long career with the Kansas City Monarchs. He is one of five NSL players in the Hall of Fame (National Baseball Hall of Fame in Cooperstown, New York).

Fred Stovall had strengthened his club for the series by signing the star pitcher of the Austin Black Senators. Hilton Smith was said to have participated in 30 games, losing none of them for Austin.[90] While the perfect record is questionable, he did, indeed, win both games he pitched against Monroe in the Negro Dixie Series. Smith would go on to become one of black baseball's best pitchers. He spent several years as a teammate with Satchel Paige on great Kansas City Monarch teams, although in this series Paige was an opponent as a pitcher for the Crawfords.[91] Smith was elected to the Hall of Fame in 2001.

The opening game in Monroe on Saturday, September 10, was one of the best of the series, although without a conclusion. Monroe jumped out to a 1–0 lead, only to see the powerful Crawfords coming back behind the hitting of Oscar Charleston and Josh Gibson. Each had two hits, with one of Charleston's being a triple and one of Gibson's a home run. Entering the bottom of the ninth inning, Pittsburgh held a 6–2 lead. The Monarchs scored four runs to tie the game, at which point it was called because of darkness. Each team had used three pitchers.

On Sunday Gibson and Charleston were held to single hits in five at-bats, but other Crawfords more than took up the slack. Led by Ted Page with three hits, the visitors pounded the Monarchs, 11–4, with a 13-hit attack. Satchel Paige, pitching in relief for the second day in a row, gave up two runs and three hits in four innings. Shortstop Morney had four hits for Monroe as leadoff batter. The Crawfords wrapped up the championship on Monday, winning 9–6. The Monroe newspapers carried only a single paragraph to report the game's outcome.

With the series over, the Monarchs embarked on along barnstorming tour that was expected to keep the players employed until mid–October.[92]

In Chicago, Nashville scored five times in the ninth inning to win the opening game, 6–5. It was poorly reported in both cities, but the Elites apparently used three walks, two singles, and a Chicago error to score five runs in the ninth inning and win the game. Reports gave no details of how the rally transpired.

A Sunday double-header saw each taking one game. Nashville won the opener, 3–2, with Jim Willis outdueling William Powell in a 15-inning contest. Both pitchers went the distance. Again newspaper coverage was sparse, offering few details on the extraordinary contest. Nashville won the nightcap, 5–3.

The series was also played in a peculiar manner, apparently not resuming for two weeks. When it did resume in Nashville, the *Atlanta Daily World* identified it as "the Southern League Championship Series." On Sunday, September 18, Chicago won Game No. Four by a score of 10–5 at Sulphur Dell. Robert Cole's American Giants racked up 11 hits, five of them home runs off the usually dependable Willis. Norman "Turkey" Stearnes and Walter "Steel Arm" Davis had two circuit blows each. The other belonged to outfielder William "Nat" Rogers. Bill Foster, half-brother of the late Rube Foster, kept the Elite Giants at bay.[93]

The next two games were a mid-week doubleheader played at Nashville on Wednesday, September 21. Sam Bankhead was the winning pitcher and Melvin Powell the loser as the home team took the first game, 5–4. The championship seemed almost certainly Nashville's late in the second game. The Elite Giants led, 2–0, going into the sixth inning. But Chicago bats came to life. Sparked by Stearnes' home run over the right field wall at Sulphur Dell, the Chicago club won, 5–2, and tied the series at three games apiece.[94]

Again, there was an odd delay in the schedule. The seventh game was not played until Sunday, October 2, at Nashville. There were no home runs this time, but Stearnes had a triple among his four hits and Davis and pitcher Foster also had triples. Chicago won, 9–2, outhitting Nashville 12 to 8. Foster was the winning pitcher, striking out nine and scattering eight Nashville hits.[95] After the game Robert Cole was presented a silver loving cup and the championship pennant. Each Chicago player was give a gold baseball and the Nashville players silver baseballs. Tom Wilson, the Nashville owner, was also given a silver cup and "was applauded immensely by the crowd."[96]

In summary, the Negro Southern League was the last league standing in that troublesome Depression year. Monroe in the first half had proven the mettle of southern clubs against northern competition. In the end, though, when the playoffs came around the southern teams fell woefully short.

Given the usual disparity in box scores for each team, certain judgments have to be made about individual leaders. In this instance, the author, drawing from the averages compiled by the Hall of Fame–sanctioned Negro Leagues Researchers and Authors Group project, has used 100 at-bats as a cutoff point. That being said, the batting leader was unquestionably Monroe's Roy Parnell. In 41 games he had 58 hits in 151 at-bats for a .384 batting average. A distant second with a .336 average in 30 games was Joe Scott of Indianapolis.

Parnell led the league in not only average and hits but also in runs scored (40), doubles (10), triples (10), total bases (88), and runs batted in (23). It should be noted that many box scores of the period did not include RBIs. The home run leader was Walter Davis of Chicago with five and the stolen base leader was J. Thomas of Indianapolis with 14.

The pitching leaders, based on total wins, were Monroe's Dick Matthews (9–3) and Barney Morris (9–4). Bill Foster and Malvin Powell of Chicago were 8–2 and 7–0, respectively, and Elbert Williams of Monroe (7–5).

Although Holway lists Graham Williams as the pitcher above, the author is persuaded by his own research that the pitcher is Elbert Williams. The author further believes Graham Williams's role with the club was insignificant.

10

1933
Putting It Back Together

After the wildly dysfunctional league structure of 1932, owners were ready for a return to pre–Depression stability. They would not find that at the level they would have liked, but there was some semblance of the old normalcy again.

The year 1933 was something of a rebirth for black baseball after 1932's disorderly season. Although leagues had merged to find a path to survival, numerous clubs folded as the Depression sapped resources. At one doubleheader in Atlanta, a sports writer had noted that it was played "before a crowd of 500, almost 400 of which witnessed the game from the outside of the park," presumably unable afford or unwilling to spend the price of admission.[1] Lagging attendance would be a common theme throughout the season.

The 1933 season saw the return of the Negro National League to join the Negro Southern League. Gone was the East-West League, which had not even made it through its first season in 1932. The NNL was revived with a mix of Midwestern, Southern, and Eastern teams. Representing the Midwest contingent were Cole's American Giants, arguably the 1932 Negro Southern League champion, the Columbus Blue Birds, and the Detroit Stars. From the South were the Nashville Elite Giants. From the East were the Baltimore Black Sox, Homestead Grays, and Pittsburgh Crawfords.[2] For Nashville, it was the beginning of an odyssey that would carry the club to Columbus, Ohio, in 1935, to Washington, D.C., in 1936, and finally to a permanent home in Baltimore in 1938. Never again would the Elite Giants play in the NSL.[3] The lineup of previously-strong franchises looked good on paper. Again, that proved to be flawed at the gate. There had been off-season rumors that Tom Wilson might move his Elite Giants to Detroit.[4] As the season began a fire destroyed the American Giants' home park, forcing the team to move temporarily to Indianapolis, where they played at Perry Park, the facility used by the white Indianapolis Indians and the barnstorming Indianapolis ABCs.[5]

Detroit did get the Indianapolis franchise, which relocated in mid–May. Baltimore was voted a franchise at the same league meeting approving the transfer.[6] But that didn't solve the NNL's problems. The Columbus Blue Birds dropped out of the league in August, replaced by the Cleveland Giants, a new team pulled together by Bingo DeMoss, former star with the Chicago American Giants.[7]

The Negro Southern League was back as well. Its projected lineup included entries from such familiar cities as Little Rock, Memphis, Monroe, Montgomery, and New Orleans. There were also newcomers from Jackson, Mississippi; Shreveport, Louisiana;

Alexandria, Louisiana; and Algiers, a suburb of New Orleans. Missing were the Birmingham Black Barons and Montgomery Grey Sox. The Grey Sox, however, would return as a replacement team before the season was out. For Birmingham, the 1933 season would be one of only three years from 1920 to 1963 without a team called the Black Barons. The others were 1934 and 1939.

There was a new league president, Dr. J. B. Martin of Memphis. Martin and his brother B. B. Martin were Memphis dentists and businessmen. They were longtime owners of the Memphis Red Sox. When they built Martin Park on Crump Boulevard, the Red Sox became one of the few teams in the Negro leagues with their own ballpark.[8]

The final organizational meeting was held in New Orleans in late February and Louisiana teams claimed five of the eight franchises. The lineup would include the New Orleans Crescent Stars, Monroe Monarchs, Shreveport Cubs, Alexandria Giants, and Algiers Giants. The other three teams were the Jackson Black Senators, Little Rock Stars, and Memphis Red Sox. A schedule was drawn up with April 14 set as Opening Day with Little Rock at Monroe, Algiers at New Orleans, Memphis at Jackson, and Shreveport at Alexandria.[9] The owners had also resolved the sticky problem of player ownership that had caused problems the year before. It was determined that "all players finishing the season with a member of the Negro Southern League for 1932 are still the property of those teams and cannot be used by any other member ... without an outright release, sale or transfer in some agreeable manner."[10]

They also decided to continue as the Negro Southern League although Dixie League had been a working name during early planning.

Nashville, of course, had moved to the Negro National League. Both Montgomery and Birmingham fielded independent teams in 1933 that played schedules filled with Negro Southern League members. Indeed, Montgomery's team was the familiar Grey Sox. Birmingham's team was usually referred to as the Monarchs. As noted above, Montgomery would figure in the NSL during the second half of the season.

Although mentioned briefly in one pre-season article about possible NSL members, no Birmingham team ever appeared in league standings.[11] In early May the Montgomery Grey Sox hosted the Monarchs, whose roster included a number of names familiar to Birmingham fans. The Birmingham team returned to Montgomery for another series in late June. They were called Monarchs in pregame stories, but Foxes in an article explaining that the previous day's game had been rained out.[12]

On May 27, 1933, the *Birmingham Reporter* reported that the Memphis Red Sox of the Negro Southern league would be in the city the next day, Sunday, to play the Monarchs. The newspaper said the Monarchs would present a "stronger lineup over previous weeks and a good brand of baseball is expected." The team was said to have signed Harry Barnes, Bozo Jackson, Walter Cooley, Joe Turner, and the Frazier brothers from Montgomery. After the single game with Memphis, the Birmingham team was going to Atlanta for two games and then would return to Birmingham on Thursday for Ladies Day with an as-yet-unannounced opponent. These games would not be played at storied Rickwood Field, but rather at the city's Fair Park.[13]

There was no game on Sunday afternoon. The following week, the newspaper reported that "Baseball is at a low ebb. No one to back teams, hence no playing. Results, fans are suffering for the want of some place to go. What kind of management is this that it will advertise a game and then when it is called off never say a word."[14]

But a Birmingham team, various nicknames notwithstanding, continued to play into August.

Shreveport, making its first venture in NSL play, treated local fans to a quality exhibition schedule. Management brought in the Pittsburgh Crawfords for a three-game series, although there was no report on the outcome. Coverage was very sparse in the *Shreveport Times*, usually just the score of the game and an announcement for the next game. Seating was provided for whites, and "ladies' day" was a regular attendance booster.[15]

When the Cubs took a five-game series from Alexandria near the end of May, each score was reported. Again, there were no details on the games themselves, but it was also reported that Shreveport had replaced Memphis as the league leader.[16]

In early June Shreveport was said to be in a three-way tie for first with Memphis and Algiers. The Cubs had been strengthened by the acquisition of eight players from the Monroe club.[17]

Monroe, the strongest team in the league the previous two seasons, also had big promotional plans for its April 14 home opener at 4 p.m. against Little Rock. Ceremonies would start with a parade at the "colored high school, going through town." A prize would be given for the best float. Local merchants donated more than 50 prizes for festivities that would begin at 2:30 p.m. A coop of chickens was to be turned loose with the birds belonging to whoever could catch them. Then, an airplane would drop "the first ball to be used in the game with money attached to it." Boys under 12 would be permitted to scramble after the ball. The grand prize give-away was a diamond ring.[18] And for further interest, a three-inning game between girls' teams from Little Rock and Monroe would be played before the NSL game.[19]

Opening Day was postponed twice by rain before the two clubs were able to hold a doubleheader on Sunday, April 16. Monroe won both games and "The chicken chase was the center of attraction before the game and brought the fans to their feet in excitement." Monroe played errorless ball in the 2–1 and 6–0 wins with shortstop Hickman handling 12 chances perfectly.[20] Elsie Deselles was the lucky winner of the diamond ring.[21]

Little Rock also brought in the Crawfords on April 2 during its exhibition season. They spotted the Easterners a 3–0 lead in the first two innings, then came back to treat the home crowd to a 6–3 win in the opener. Pitcher F. Sims not only shut down the visitors after the first two innings, but also hit a grand slam home run during the home team's rally.[22]

The home opener was with Monroe and a festive occasion was planned, beginning with a parade. Four "outstanding members of the Citizen Congress Association" were selected to participate in first pitch ceremonies. They were E. S. Hubble, pitcher; G. H. Evans, catcher; Dan Dubisson, batter; and Scipio A. Jones, umpire.

The Stars also, had some promotions worthy of legendary Chattanooga Lookouts owner Joe Engel and the American League's Bill Veeck. For the opener five dollars in nickels was to be dropped from an airplane for a fan scramble. Then, 50 loaves of bread were to be dropped "in a special contest for women." Finally, five baseballs were to be tossed on the field. The boy or girl under 12 retrieving the most and returning them to Dubisson would receive 50 cents.[23]

All of these spectacular events were delayed a day when the opening game was rained out. While the Stars rallied with a four-run ninth inning to win the delayed opener, 4–3, there was no report on which activities had been carried over and how they were received by the fans.[24]

The Jackson Bear Cats were scheduled to open their NSL season the weekend of April 14–16 with the Memphis Red Sox.[25]

Later there were reports of Little Rock coming to play on April 29, Memphis on May 18, and Shreveport on May 28.

Although the *Jackson Clarion-Ledger* did not provide any coverage of actual games or even much information on team personnel, it did provide some interesting information on front office management.

On April 23, shortly before the NSL season began, the newspaper reported that Negroes had assumed control of the team, suggesting that whites had held that power previously. "The negro lovers of baseball have been clamoring since the organization of professional negro baseball at Jackson for a management of negroes from top to bottom. They claim that under the leadership of their own people, the management can and will get 100 per cent support."

Thus, a group of black businessmen formed the Jackson Colored Baseball Association with the following officers: Dr. R. L. Johnson, president; J. W. Wilson, vice president; Frank Ralton, secretary; and Clarence Winters, treasurer.

"The psychology of all athletic endeavor is helped by a united front for the contestants who represent a school, a town or a state, so let the fans get ready for the game between the Memphis Red Sox and the Jackson team April 26 at League park. An overflow crowd of the negro fans is expected."[26]

The response of the local fans was not reported, nor was the outcome of the game.

Indeed, it's difficult to even determine if the game was played. Subsequent schedule results show Memphis at Monroe on April 27, at home against Nashville on April 29, and at Alexandria on April 30. Such a hodge-podge of travel seems very unlikely for a league as cash-strapped as the NSL was most of the time.

The next mention of the team in the Jackson paper was on Sunday, May 28. It was reported that Jackson would play Shreveport at Bailey Avenue Park on Tuesday. A barbecue was among the festivities planned for the team, which had just returned from a road trip to England, Arkansas, and Little Rock. Several new players had been signed and President Johnson offered this admonition for support: "We wish to assure the fans that it will be impossible for Jackson to continue in the Negro Southern League unless we get a better attendance from the fans. We are herewith pleading to the fans both white and colored to help us stay in the circuit as it means much for the city of Jackson to be associated with progressive cities and towns of the south in the great national pastime."[27] Jackson's problems continued away from home, also. The Black Senators, as they were called in this instance, were scheduled to be in Memphis for a pre–Fourth of July series. The team had a highway accident about 50 miles out of Jackson and was forced to return home. Several players were injured, though none seriously.[28]

On May 3, Monroe won an 11-inning battle with Memphis. Elbert Williams went the distance to get the win, giving up only seven hits and striking out seven. Maxwell's double with the bases load brought in the winning run. The hard-luck loser for Memphis was Son Harvey, who gave up only five this and struck out 11.[29]

Memphis won a mid–May doubleheader from Birmingham, 5–3 and 5–0. The Birmingham team was identified as the Black Barons and the games were said to be Negro Southern League games.[30] Since Birmingham appeared in no published league standings, it must be assumed that the independent team (the Monarchs or Foxes) was called Black Barons by the press because of past affiliations.

On May 21, Monroe showed its old form by taking a doubleheader from Shreveport. Both games were shutouts. Barney Morris won the opener, 9–0, holding the Cubs to four hits and striking out six. In the seven-inning nightcap, Williams got the win, a six-hitter.[31] Williams, referred to as a former Cuban House of David pitcher, seems likely to have been Elbert Williams,

In late May the Crescent Stars returned from a road trip in which they were reported to have won 10 out of 11 games. They had now won 17 of 18, including a 14-game winning streak that put them in first place, followed by Memphis.[32]

By early June, Memphis and New Orleans were the clear leaders in the pennant race. Standings published on June 10 in the two leading black newspapers, however, showed apparent franchise changes among the weaker clubs:

From the *Chicago Defender*:

	W	L	Pct.
Memphis	36	8	.763
New Orleans	20	14	.615
Algiers	18	14	.533
Little Rock	16	15	.512
Jackson	11	18	.386
Alexandria	10	19	.279
Montgomery	1	4	.200
	102	91	

From the *Pittsburgh Courier*:

	W	L	Pct.
Memphis	26	8	.765
New Orleans	20	13	.615
Algiers	18	14	.593
Shreveport	17	13	.533
Little Rock	16	15	.512
Jackson	11	18	.380
Alexandria	10	19	.279
Montgomery	1	4	.200
	119	104	

Not only are the won-lost numbers not balanced but several percentages are also incorrect.

The Chicago version suggests immediately that Montgomery had replaced Shreveport, but the Pittsburgh version shows Montgomery replacing Monroe. Formal documentation for the franchise shift did not come until the league meeting on July 5, when it was announced that Montgomery would replace Monroe for the second half. The above standings show that the change obviously occurred late in the first half. Standings in August list a six-team league, including Montgomery. Gone, along with Monroe, are

Jackson, Little Rock, and Shreveport.³³ Monroe, in fact, jettisoned NSL play in late May for a more lucrative set of engagements in the Midwest. After completing a three-game home series with Shreveport the Monarchs were said to be leaving "for the Negro National League and three week's play in Chicago at the World['s] Fair."³⁴

Shortly afterward, the league office announced that Monroe had dropped out of the league. President Martin was credited with quickly securing Montgomery to fill Monroe's spot and keep the league operating smoothly. Although the details are extremely vague, it appears that several Monroe players joined the Shreveport club before the Monarchs set off for the Midwestern trip. Immediately after the second game, Monroe embarked on another lengthy second-half road trip of the sort that had become familiar to many Negro Southern League teams. It was stated that "the best players of the Monroe team have now joined in with Shreveport, and it seems now that all teams will have to contend with the Shreveport nine for the pennant." There was also vagueness regarding a ruling Martin had made concerning games played with New Orleans prior to Monroe's withdrawal.³⁵

Although challenged by New Orleans, Memphis was plainly the best team in the league. In early June the Red Sox secured Monroe Manager Frank Johnson to run the team on the field. Homer "Goose" Curry, the manager when the season opened, was still with the club, pitching and playing a number of other positions when necessary. Curry was reported to be the club's stolen base leader when Johnson took over. The pitching staff included Marlin "Spoon" Carter, "Hooks" Johnson, and a right-hander named Peterson, said to be from Fairfield, Alabama. First baseman Jim Mason was hitting well and the infield sparkled with McAllister, Matthew "Lick" Carlisle, Lewis and Jim Ford.³⁶

At league meeting in Memphis on July 5, the Red Sox were declared first half winners, not that the standings left little doubt about the team's dominance. It was also formally announced at the meeting that William Brown's Montgomery club was replacing Monroe for the second half. The second half schedule concluded on Sunday, August 20. League games were played Friday through Sunday with open dates for each team during the final weeks.³⁷

In late June the *Memphis Commercial Appeal* reported that the Red Sox had been declared first-half winners at a meeting of the club owners. Memphis was said to have won 32 and lost 20 during the first half.³⁸ Other accounts listed the record as 32–10.³⁹

The last published standings for the first half showed Memphis running away from the pack:

Team	P	W	L	Pct.
Memphis	42	32	10	.761
Algiers	41	23	19	.560
New Orleans	43	24	19	.558
Shreveport	36	19	17	.527
Little Rock	39	20	19	.513
Alexandria	39	18	21	.461
Montgomery	9	4	5	.445
Jackson	33	13	20	.303
	282	153	130⁴⁰	

On the weekend of July 7–9 Memphis filled its open dates with an interleague series with the Nashville Elite Giants. Nashville won the Saturday game, 6–4, then took the first game on Sunday by 7–4. Memphis, behind the no-hit pitching of Harvey, won the second game on Sunday, 1–0. The game went six innings. The pitcher laid down a perfect bunt to bring the winning run across the plate in the last inning.[41]

New Orleans and Montgomery played an unusual doubleheader at Montgomery on July 14. The Crescent Stars won the first game, 11–8. It was played in the afternoon at College Hill Park. Montgomery won the nightcap, 7–1, and it was literally a nightcap, played under the lights at Cramton Bowl.[42]

Yet another franchise shift was reported in mid–July. Returning home from a road trip into Alabama, Little Rock was scheduled to play a game with a team called the Boosters at Pine Bluff, Arkansas. "The game will serve as a test of the Boosters' fitness to fill the vacancy in the league caused by the withdrawal of the Jackson club," according to the *Arkansas Gazette*. There was no report on the outcome of the game, but a week later the Pine Bluff team, "which recently joined the league in the place of the Jackson (Miss.) nine, was at Little Rock for a series."[43] Little Rock swept the series, winning a single game on Saturday and a doubleheader on Sunday.[44]

No further results were found for Pine Bluff, and Little Rock continued to field a team into August, although it is impossible to place the club in or out of the league by that time.

Generally, second-half play included a lot of barnstorming trips played around a handful of league games. Only one set of standings was found for the second half. They offer the work of six teams, making no mention of Pine Bluff. The slim figures showed Memphis leading the league with a 3–0 record, followed by Algiers (5–4) and New Orleans (6–5). Montgomery and Alexandria were each 3–3 and Little Rock was 3–4. Those numbers total an unbalanced 23 wins and 19 losses for the league.[45]

In late August, the Crescent Stars took three straight from the crosstown independent Black Pelicans. The team, laying claim to the NSL title, was apparently scheduled to play the Houston Black Buffaloes of the Negro Texas League in a Negro Dixie Series. "If they come through with that series o.k., they feel that there will be nothing to keep them from playing in the Negro World Series with winners of the Negro National League," a newspaper reported.[46] In early September New Orleans began the best-of-seven series with Houston. The series was billed as one to determine which club would play the Nashville Elite Giants in the Negro Dixie Series.[47] There was no explanation for why these two teams were playing for that right. Previously the Negro Dixie Series had always been between a Negro Southern League champion and Negro Texas League champion. Regardless, the Crescent Stars swept Houston, winning the first four games, all of which were played in New Orleans.[48] On September 9 the *Nashville Banner* reported that the Elite Giants would open a Negro Dixie Series that day with the Crescent Stars. The Stars won the NSL championship and the Elite Giants won the second half of the Negro National League. Three games were to be played in New Orleans, starting that day, then move to Nashville.[49]

At the same time, the *Arkansas Gazette* reported that the Little Rock Stars and Memphis Red Sox would begin a playoff for the Negro Southern League championship on Sunday, September 11 at Crump Park in Memphis. The story said Memphis had won the first half and Little Rock the second half of the NSL season. The seven-game series would determine the championship.[50] Lineups for both team were given in a pregame story about tomorrow's game. There was no report in the next day's paper. At any rate, in New Orleans the series with Nashville was called the Negro Dixie Series, with the winner to go on to play in the Negro World Series. But there was no explanation of where an opponent would come from since there were only two leagues. Additional seats were added at Crescent Park "to accommodate the large crowd expected to attend. Reserve seats for white fans at all games."[51]

New Orleans won the first game, 6–5. Smith pitched for the Crescent Stars while Nashville used Jim Willis and Percy Miller. It is not clear if the New Orleans pitcher was Hilton Smith or Morris Smith, both of whom were with the team during the season.

Game Two was another one-run game with Williams outdueling Willie Gisentaner 3–2. Williams gave up only two hits, but lost his shutout because of New Orleans errors.[52] Williams is likely Elbert Williams who had apparently been picked up from Shreveport, which had gotten him from Monroe when the Monarchs left the league. With Morris pitching a shutout, New Orleans won the third game, 8–0, on its home field.

The following Sunday the Crescent Stars wrapped up the Negro Dixie Series by taking the second game of a double-header, 2–1, at Nashville. The Elite Giants had won the opener, 8–2.

With the win the New Orleans club was said to be facing Chicago in the Negro World Series. Just why New Orleans would play Nashville, another Negro National League member, in the Negro Dixie Series, then play the NNL's Chicago club in the Negro World Series is another of those Negro Leagues organizational anomalies. John Holway writes that Nashville won a first-half playoff with the Pittsburgh Crawfords, then lost a second-half playoff with the same team.[53] Yet the Crawfords were never mentioned in the postseason picture. There will never likely be a satisfactory explanation.

The *Times-Picayune* of New Orleans referred to the Crescent Stars-American Giants games of September and October as the Negro World Series.[54] When the American Giants won the final game of the series, they were referred to as the "world's champions."[55]

Nevertheless, the Negro World Series began on Sunday, September 24, in New Orleans.[56] Again, there was no explanation for the World Series proclamation if Chicago had won the first half of the NNL and Nashville the second half without a playoff to determine an overall champion.

Three thousand additional seats were added at Crescent Park to accommodate the large crowd expected for the series.[57] The opening game was scheduled for Saturday, September 23.

Williams set the American Giants down in order to start the game, and there it ended. Rain forced the game to be called after just half an inning. New Orleans Manager Roy Parnell announced that Williams would also be the starter on Sunday. Chicago would counter with Bill Foster, reportedly 38–4 during the 1933 regular season.[58]

Chicago blasted Williams and Barney Morris, 6–0, with Turkey Stearnes hitting two home runs. Foster only allowed three hits by the Crescent Stars.[59]

The American Giants made it two in a row on Monday, tripping the Crescent Stars, 6–1. Mule Suttles, the former NSL slugger, hit a grand slam home run for Chicago.[60]

Game Three was scheduled for Saturday, September 30, at Heinemann Park, the home of the white New Orleans Pelicans of the Southern Association. This was expected to boost the Crescent Stars chances of a comeback, because Chicago had supposedly taken advantage of "pop-fly home runs" of the shorter fences in Crescent Park.[61]

Things did improve for the home team. The Crescent Stars won a 4–3 decision after 12 innings in the first game of a doubleheader. Williams came on in relief in the second inning with Chicago ahead, 3–1. He held the visitors scoreless the rest of the way. Sias' triple brought Parnell home with the winning run.[62]

Chicago took a five-inning second game, 3–0, to give the American Giants a three games to one lead in the series. Apparently the series was never intended to be more than five games. Newspapers reported that the Monday would be the final game of the series. Chicago won, 6–3. It was reported that Crescent Stars, jubilant over having played in the Negro World Series, were looking to bring the Pittsburgh Crawfords, "Eastern champions," to New Orleans for an eight-game series.[63]

The Negro National League did not do any better economically than the NSL when it was all over in 1933. Only three teams—Pittsburgh, Chicago, and Nashville—completed all scheduled games, according to an article by league Secretary John Clark in the *Pittsburgh Courier*.[64]

With only two teams with a significant number of box scores—Memphis, 19, and Monroe, 12—it is difficult to project batting leaders. Lick Carlisle with 23 hits in 63 at-bats had an average of .338 for Memphis. That was in 19 games. Infielder Maxwell of Monroe was 15 for 42, .357.

Bill Howard of Little Rock (7–4) was the top winner among pitchers, followed by Son Harvey of Memphis (6–2). No other pitcher won more than four games.

11

1934
More New Faces

The league was back for the 1934 season, but again things were quite different. Of the five Louisiana teams that had made up such a large segment of the 1933 league, only the Monroe Monarchs returned. And as in 1933, their participation would again be brief. The New Orleans Crescent Stars, among the strongest teams the previous year, were listed only as an associate member of the circuit.

Other familiar cities were represented by different entities. In lieu of the Black Crackers, Atlanta was represented by the Atlanta Athletics. The Black Barons were still missing and in their stead were the Birmingham Giants. Louisville's entry was simply called the Caps. Once again the Midwest contributed an NSL team, this time the Cincinnati Tigers. Only the Memphis Red Sox carried on in their traditional livery.

Although all of the clubs played heavy schedules in April and well into May, the formal opening of the league season did not happen until May 20.

A series of organizational meetings was held, the first one in Memphis on February 4. Another one near the end of the month drew representatives from Birmingham, Knoxville, Memphis, Monroe, and Nashville. Telegrams of interests had been received from Cincinnati, Louisville, and Montgomery. Officers were reported to be Dr. J.B. Martin, president, and L.S. N. Cobb, secretary. Those two positions were the only ones ever identified.[1] Soon afterward Atlanta expressed interest in an associate rather than a regular membership. The Atlanta club was to be managed by W. L. Joseph, former business manager of the Chattanooga Black Lookouts.[2]

The first meeting in Memphis, described curiously as "the largest gathering of Southern League Moguls" ever, was held at the Martin Building on Florida Street, the office of League President Dr. J. B. Martin. Participants included J. L. Wilkinson, Kansas City; Al Monroe, sports editor of the *Chicago Defender*; William Brown, Montgomery; Thomas T. Wilson, Nashville; C. M. Carter, Chattanooga; J.A. Nance, Knoxville; Frank Johnson and C. Jackson, Monroe; W. H. Lanoy, A. Crump and William Young, Little Rock; Drs. W. S. Martin, A. B. Martin, and B. B Martin, Memphis, all brothers of the league president. Wilkinson, owner of the Kansas City Monarchs, a charter member of the first Negro National League, now playing independently, was said to be considering a membership application. The consensus, though, was that "a better circuit should be formed to include a shorter mileage, larger population, and salary base to enable each team to finish with a little cash."[3]

Subsequent meetings were held at the Page Hotel in New Orleans and the Nashville YMCA as owners, anticipating improving business conditions, pulled the league together.⁴ Addressing the Nashville meeting was William "Gus" Greenlee, president of the current Negro National League, who talked about possible cooperative arrangements with teams from his league. Team representatives included Johnson of Monroe; Nance of Knoxville; Frank Perdue and Ludie Key, Birmingham; B. B. and A.B. Martin of Memphis; and Wilson, Vernon Green, Fred D. McCrary and Jim Taylor, Nashville. Telegrams of interest were received from officials in Louisville, Montgomery, and Cincinnati.⁵

Yet another organizational meeting was held in Memphis on the weekend of March 30–31. Owners present were A. F. Scott, Louisville; Keys and Perdue, Birmingham; Johnson and C. W. Nail, Monroe; J. B. and W. S. Martin, Memphis; W. L. Joseph, Atlanta; and T. T. Wilson, Cincinnati. James Taylor, catcher [Bill] Perkins of Cleveland last year, and Homer Curry of Memphis were also present. Thomas T. Wilson, president of the Negro National League, was an observer.⁶

Expected to be present, but missing were representatives from Chattanooga, Knoxville, Little Rock, Montgomery, and New Orleans. However, Fred Caulfield of New Orleans had sent in an application for an associate membership, which was accepted. Officers were again said to be Dr. J. B. Martin of Memphis, president, and L.S.N. Cobb of Birmingham, secretary. Martin appointed a schedule committee and asked Thomas Wilson to serve on it to coordinate games with the NNL.⁷

It was reported finally that the league lineup would be the Atlanta Athletics, Birmingham Giants, Cincinnati Tigers, Louisville Black Sox, Memphis Red Sox, and Monroe Monarchs with New Orleans Crescent Stars as an associate member. It was also noted that the Chicago American Giants, Cleveland Stars, Nashville Elite Giants, and Pittsburgh Crawfords of the Negro National League would be "guests of the Southern league cities for spring training."⁸ The Cleveland NNL club was actually the Red Sox. No reports were found for a team named Stars. President Martin, determined to prevent club jumping by players and player-raiding by northern clubs, announced that he had affiliated the NSL with the major league NN League. National League President Greenlee, owner of the Pittsburgh Crawfords, told Martin he would not seek three players who had tried out with his team the previous spring, but who Martin claimed were NSL property.⁹

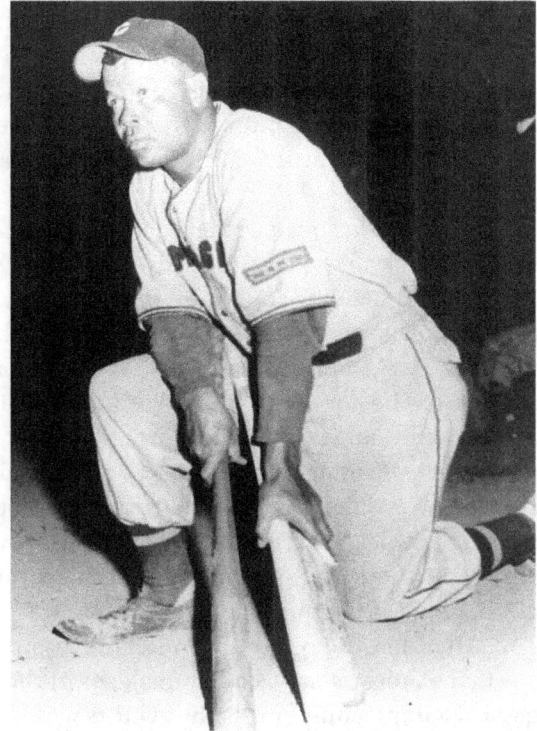

Catcher Lloyd "Pepper" Bassett was noted for occasionally catching in a rocking chair. His long career began with the New Orleans Crescent Stars in 1934 (courtesy NoirTech Research).

The application from Fred Caulfield of New Orleans, which had already been accepted, was not mentioned in these later reports. Yet, Caulfield did have a team that played independent ball in New Orleans in 1934. Meanwhile, the New Orleans Crescent Stars, champions in 1933, opened spring training under Manager Roy "Red" Parnell. Returning players included Milt Laurent, "Big Train" Parker, Zollie Wright, Moocha Harris and "Nunny" Beverly.[10] And although the Crescent Stars had not been mentioned as anything more than an associate member in other reports, the *Louisiana Weekly* continued to make references to the team fighting "to retain the Dixie pennant."[11]

Enthusiasm in Atlanta and Birmingham was boosted by the fact that both cities had repealed blue laws that had previously prohibited Sunday baseball.[12]

In Atlanta, as manager C. E. Jackson and general manager W. L. Joseph were signing both new players and local favorites like first baseman James "Red" Moore, a considerable effort was under way to organize the black community on behalf of the white Atlanta Crackers.[13] John Parks, "veteran baseball fan and sports authority and proprietor of the Blue Front Baseball Headquarters on Auburn avenue," began a drive to put 3,000 black fans in the stands for the Crackers' opener. The campaign was said to be in appreciation of the current administration's overtures to improve facilities available for black fans at Ponce de Leon Park. In currying the black support, the Crackers ran a three-column advertisement in the *Daily World*.[14]

Although official league games appear to have started on May 22, Atlanta's weekend series with Birmingham on May 3–5, was billed as opening day in the Gate City. The Negro Chamber of Commerce was pushing to have 5,000 fans in the stands for the first game. Mayor James L. Key was out of the city so his secretary, Luke Arnold, was selected to throw out the first pitch. Mrs. Dora Moore was to receive the pitch, with Col. A.T. Walden swinging at it.[15] Walden was an Atlanta University graduate and prominent attorney.[16]

Daily World sportswriter Lucius "Melancholy" Jones' exuberant welcoming of NSL baseball back to Atlanta proved to be somewhat futile. The crowd was estimated at 1,000 rather than the sought-after 5,000 fans. Game time was set for 3 o'clock, but neither team was on time. The Birmingham club did not arrive until five minutes before the hour. Five Atlanta players, "just in from a long Florida trip," did not reach the ballpark until 3:30. The home club was forced to reach into the stands and draft John McFarland, Muff Moffitt, and a few other former players to field a team. The game finally started at 4 o'clock. Birmingham had run up a 7–1 lead before the remainder of Atlanta's players showed up. "When they did, matters were not helped any as this tired and travel worn bunch of athletes were no match for the Barons." The visitors won the game, 15–2.[17] Note that the Birmingham team, perhaps out of habit, was still called the "Barons" although its real name was the Giants.

After an off day the second game was played at the Morris Brown College field. Herman Andrews, now called manager of the Birmingham club, hit two doubles and a game-winning home run as the visitors won, 6–5. The home run, in the top of the ninth inning, was said to have traveled some 400 feet. Matt Carlisle also hit a home run for Birmingham, which had compiled 21 runs and 30 hits in the two games.[18] Birmingham won the third game, 8–0, behind the three-hit pitching of Glover. Again Birmingham bats boomed with 13 hits. The team's total for the three games was 29 runs and 43 hits.

Birmingham was under the ownership of former owner-manager Frank Perdue and Ludie Keys. The *Birmingham News* referred to the ball club as the "Birmingham Giants, alias the Black Barons." The field manager changed at the beginning of the season. The *Atlanta Daily World* reported in March that the team was working out under "the watchful eye of Manager [Bill] Perkins," assisted by the veteran catcher Poindexter Williams.[19] By early May, however, the *Daily World* listed Herman Andrews as manager.[20] Perkins, at first available due to his early-season holdout from the Pittsburgh Crawfords, agreed to terms with his previous team and returned there for 1934. Birmingham media never referenced a field manager throughout the season.

There was a promising start for the Giants. Although the first two games were rained out, an estimated 3,000 turned out for an exhibition game with Cleveland at Rickwood Field in mid–May.[21] In late May it was reported the team was "playing to more fans this season than at any time since 1929, and there is always a space in the grandstand reserved for white patrons."[22]

The Giants split a pair with Cleveland, then took two out of three from the Kansas City Monarchs. A pitcher named Walter Glover was showing up as the team's best moundsman, shutting out Cleveland, then holding the Monarchs to six hits in a 5–2 win.[23] Glover, although identified as Walter by Birmingham newspapers, was actually Tom Glover, who had a long career in black baseball.[24]

Opening Day for league play was on Sunday, May 20, with Memphis the opposition. Birmingham continued to show fine form, winning both games of a doubleheader. Glover won the first game, 5–4, giving up only five hits and striking out seven. Bill Jones won the five-inning nightcap, 10–4. Andrews had three hits, including a triple and a home run, in the second game.[25] The teams then played in Montgomery the next two days, where Birmingham apparently won both games. The fifth game of the series at Rickwood was another Birmingham victory. Center fielder Jerry Benjamin, who had five hits in the game, scored the winning run in the 11th inning on a single by Harvey Peterson.[26]

The next series was in Memphis, where the Red Sox won three of four. When Birmingham returned home to face the Atlanta Athletics, it was without pitcher Glover, who had joined the Cleveland club in the Negro National League.

Standings published in the *Daily World* in early June showed a great disparity in games played, ranging from three games played by Monroe to 13 played by Birmingham. Cincinnati was shown as not having played any league games at all in the first two weeks of the season. Monroe was said to be in first place with a 3–0 record. Birmingham was second at 9–4.[27]

On June 8–9 Birmingham played a pair of games in Cincinnati, then returned home to host the Atlanta Athletics.[28] It was the last mention of the Giants that season. There was no report on the scheduled games with Atlanta and no further acknowledgement of the team's existence.

In an effort to bolster his team in mid–May, Cincinnati manager Jim Glass announced the signing of several new players. One was Milton "Mighty Blood" Smith, a 29-year-old switch-hitting catcher from St. Louis. He was said to have played for the St. Louis Stars and also a Jackson, Tennessee, team. Other new players were right-handed pitcher Joe Henderson, shortstop Carl Green, and first baseman Tuker Smith.[29]

The Louisville Caps opened their season at home against the Kansas City Monarchs in a non-league game. Police Court Judge John B. Brachey was to throw out the first pitch. Other opening day festivities include a flag-raising ceremony and music by the Booker T. Washington Community Center Band.

Caps manager Joe Hewitt announced that he would start left-hander Willie Gisentaner against the Monarchs' "Bullet" Rogan.[30]

The Caps seems like an odd name. There was in the city at the same time an independent team called the Louisville Red Caps under the helm of Charles Newton.

In late May the Atlanta Athletics went to Louisville for a four-game series. Louisville won the Saturday opener by 14–5. "The Atlanta boys said a 500-mile journey by automobiles here tired them so they couldn't play very well" in the Saturday game and promised a better showing in Sunday's double-header.[31] The Athletics must not have gotten enough rest because Louisville won both games, 11–5 and 2–0. The Caps made it a sweep on Monday with a 4–1 win as Richard Cannon threw a four-hitter.[32]

The mysterious New Orleans Crescent Stars—mysterious in the uncertainty of their even being in the league—opened on April 21 with Birmingham, which the local press still believed to be the Black Barons. It was to be a festive occasion in honor of manager Parnell, who was given a car in appreciation of his services to the team. "Miss Zona known as the best lady rooter in the Crescent City, will present a beautiful bouquet from the car," reported the *Louisiana Weekly*.[33] The Crescent Stars made Parnell's day memorable with an 8–1 win, and took three out of the four games over the weekend.[34]

As Monroe played exhibition games with the Pittsburgh Crawfords and Memphis Red Sox, the local papers made no mention of the Monarchs being in any league. Yet Monroe appeared in standings published several times during the season.

Indeed, they were in the last standings located. Published in late June, those figures included only four teams in the league—Birmingham, Louisville, Memphis, and Monroe. Missing with no explanation were Atlanta and Cincinnati:

Standings[35]

Birmingham	6	6	.500
Memphis	8	8	.500
Louisville	5	5	.500
Monroe	6	7	.461
	25	26	

When President Martin called a league meeting for Sunday, June 24, to review and conclude first half business, only those four teams were mentioned as being in the league for the second half.[36] Yet, the *Louisiana Weekly* continued to promote the Crescent Stars as a member of the league. In fact, the Stars were credited with "winning the first half" of the season."[37] League officials, either seeing the world through rose-colored glasses or putting an unbelievable positive spin on disaster, called the first half "the best season so far that has ever happened in this part of the Dixie lands, due mostly to the advertisement by news papers and the working agreement between the National League heads and the president of the Southern." The Pollyanna picture continued: "These things will always work for the uplift and growth of baseball among our group as long as such men make up their minds to look after the welfare of each other.

"Large crowds have turned out as never before to witness the appearance of the players in this section and will continue. The team winning the pennant will be able to take on the club from the National League.

"President Martin is planning to make this one of the biggest affairs that has ever come to this part of the country."[38]

The statement ignored the demise of two league members, just weeks after the season began. That demise would prove a bigger predictor of the second half than Martin's quixotic mid-season report. For example, there was no further mention of the Memphis team in the *Commercial Appeal* after the June 23–24 games with Louisville. It was later learned that the Red Sox had spent some two months in the Midwest.[39]

At the league meeting in Memphis, there were mixed reports from attendees. Charles Walker of Birmingham said the city "had been very well pleased with the team" so far. A. F. Scott of Louisville said he would use all means to give the city a winner "and all the other owners desire to do all in their power to help the situation in Louisville, especially since the statement came out that they were quitting the league." Dr. B. B. Martin of Memphis "gave a short talk on the deportment of players and said this season had gained much with the working agreement between the leagues." Fred Caulfield of New Orleans said his city was ready for "full membership for the second half." There was no mention of the Cincinnati Tigers or the Atlanta Athletics.[40]

Things were far from perfect in Monroe, also. The team that had been a big drawing card in 1932 and 1933 appeared to have lost some of its support. A game with New Orleans was cancelled "because of poor attendance at Monroe, which no one can account for."[41]

There was also the question of just who won the first half. At the league meeting, "it was decided that Monroe which had failed to play some games was not entitled to as many games as the standing was given."[42] Following are three sets of standings from the *Chicago Defender* in consecutive issues. Discrepancies from week to week are evi-

---

BASEBALL!!
AUSTIN, TEXAS, BLACK SENATORS
—vs.—
CRESCENT STARS

CRESCENT PARK—NEW ORLEANS AND DORGENOIS STS.
SATURDAY, SUNDAY, MONDAY, TUESDAY and WEDNESDAY
JUNE 30, JULY 1, 2, 3 and 4

Saturday, Monday and Tuesday games called at 4 o'clock;
Sunday and Wednesday Games (doubleheaders) called at 1:45
Saturday, kiddies free—Monday and Tuesday, ladies free.

ADMISSION . . . . . ADULTS, 35c; CHILDREN, 10c
Chuffie Alexander is managing the Texas Senators

Newspaper advertisement for a 1934 game between the Austin Black Senators and the New Orleans Crescent Stars, who were then an NSL associate member. From *Louisiana Weekly*.

dent: Following is the report for each team, with its reported won-lost record, respectively for the dates of June 16, June 23, and June 30: Monroe, 5–2, 7–6, 6–7; Memphis, 5–5, 7–7, 8–8; Birmingham, 5–6, 5–5, 6–6; Louisville, 2–4, 4–8, 5–5.

Curiously, three weeks later the *Defender* carried an article out of New Orleans that proclaimed the Crescent Stars as first half "Southern title" champions. This proclamation appeared to be based on nothing more than the fact that the Stars had taken three out of four from Monroe. The possibility that New Orleans was only an associate member appeared irrelevant to the title claim and plans for a postseason playoff with the second half champion.[43]

The Louisiana club had played a first-half schedule that made the associate role more likely. Although opening with Birmingham and later playing series with Monroe, the Crescent Stars played a majority of their games with non-league teams from various cities. Among them were series with the Houston, Austin, and Dallas teams of the Negro Texas League. An interesting opponent of the Stars was the Caulfield Ads, the current representation of one of the Negro Southern League's charter members. Fred Caulfield's team was the dominant club in "Uptown" New Orleans while the Crescent Stars represented "down-town."[44]

George "Mule" Suttles, a great power hitter who also could hit for average. He started with the Birmingham Black Barons in 1923 and played with various teams through 1944. Elected to the Hall of Fame in 2006 (National Baseball Hall of Fame in Cooperstown, New York).

Did Fred Caulfield's baseball team join the NSL during the second half? There was nothing in most league-city newspapers to indicate such had happened, but once again the *Louisiana Weekly* clouded the situation. In its July 28 edition the paper reported that "The Caulfield Ads will meet the strong Birmingham Black Barons ... in the only Negro Southern leagues games to be played here over the weekend." Business manager J. L. Patterson said his team would "make a strong bid for the second half ... they are planning to make Birmingham their first victims."[45]

The Ads split two games with Birmingham, winning a Wednesday encounter, 7–2, and losing, 6–4, on Sunday afternoon. The game reports do not specify if they were NSL contests.[46]

But the Crescent Stars, who had won a Sunday doubleheader in July from Birmingham (still being called the Black Barons) were still being championed as the cream of the league. The Stars were said to have "a clean slate" thus far into the second half and had not lost a series played in the first half.[47] Yet, after the Birmingham games, the Stars headed to the East and Midwest and would not play in New Orleans again until September.

In early July the *Monroe World* reported that the Monarchs, returning home after six weeks on the road, would play the Texas All-Stars at Casino Park. Following a July 4 doubleheader the Monarchs would begin an extensive Midwestern tour. All of this suggests that, standings notwithstanding, Monroe may not have been in the NSL in 1934 or maintained a membership that was quite peripatetic.[48]

In the same vein, the New Orleans Crescent Stars began a road trip on July 22 that would have the team on the road until September 1.[49]

In early July there were reports of an all-star game being organized to feature teams from the Negro National League and the Negro Southern League. Birmingham, Atlanta, New Orleans, Memphis, Louisville, and Knoxville were all expressing interest in hosting such games.[50] Dr. B. B. Martin of Memphis threw out a possible NSL lineup:

Outfielders—Zollie Wright and Parnell of New Orleans, Jerry Benjamin of Birmingham.
Infielders—Carlyle, Birmingham; Dortch, New Orleans; Mayweather and Brown, Monroe; Smith, Memphis.
Battery—Harvey, Memphis; Gisentanner, Louisville; Else, Monroe.
Utility—Laurant, New Orleans.
Coach—Frank Johnson, Monroe.
Manager—Joe Hewitt, Louisville.

As all-star talk went on, the league itself pretty much collapsed. In addition to Monroe's western swing, the Memphis Red Sox also hit the road: "Those Memphis Red Sox, who deserted the Southern League several weeks ago to barnstorm though Northwestern states, are doing better than breaking even, local officials would have you know. The Reddies are knocking homeruns, drawing big crowds and are even making attractive money."[51] States on the Memphis club's travels included Iowa, Nebraska, and North Dakota.

New Orleans and Monroe were headed to Texas, and Louisville to Detroit. Birmingham was supposed to be hosting Atlanta, which was now out of the league.[52] A week later, it was reported that Birmingham had returned home after a long trip through the Northeast. Monroe, Memphis, Louisville, and New Orleans were all said to be doing well. Amidst all of this travel, President Martin announced Joe Hewitt of Louisville would be the Negro Southern League All-Stars manager with Frank Johnson of Monroe as assistant.[53]

As time passed in July and August, fewer and fewer games were reported and the impending all-star game became the overriding focus of all newspaper coverage. League Secretary L. S. N. Cobb, writing in the *Defender*'s July 21 edition, suggested that the all-star teams might play games in several different cities. He also announced the names of players that been qualified by an NSL committee and "placed in the hands of Manager Joe." Also selected were two umpires from the Southern league, Greenie Walls of Memphis and Professor William Moore of Birmingham.[54]

League play and coverage of the Negro National League took a back seat in late summer to the promotion of the East-West Game at Comiskey Park in Chicago. In just two years, this all-star contest had become a major black sports and social event. Huge crowds turned out for the game and everybody wanted to be there: "Dr. W. S. Martin, Supt. Of Collins Chapel Hospital and owner of the Red Sox Baseball Park; W.S. Hart, president of the Hart Undertaking Parlor; John C. Claybrook, a wealthy farmer of Claybrook, Ark.; Dr. B. B. Martin, business manager of the Memphis Red Sox; L. S. N. Cobb, secretary of the Southern League; Benjamin Olive, director and stockholder, Universal Life; Dr. J. B. Martin, president of the Southern League and his wife will make the trip along with many others.... President J. B. Martin and wife will take an airplane from Memphis direct to the park."[55]

The popularity of the East-West Game no doubt helped generate a similar interest in a North-South game being proposed between the NSL and the NNL. The *Pittsburgh Courier* reported in early August that "The Southern League fans are red hot over the coming series between the National League All-Stars and the Southern. Letters have come in asking who would manage the team from the northern states."[56]

Details were hammered out for the series of games. The first game was scheduled for Rickwood Field in Birmingham on September 23, followed by games in New Orleans, Memphis, Louisville, and Nashville.[57] The players for the two teams would be "named by the *Chicago Defender* and other newspapers just as was done for the East-West game." That balloting process was a vote by fans tabulated and published by the newspapers. Later, in the same article the all-star series was listed as four games, with Louisville not in the picture.[58] On September 15, a list of eligible players for the Southern team was released from Nashville. The team was to come from the four surviving NSL clubs and the Nashville Elite Giants. The eligible players were:

Birmingham—McAllister, 1b; Carlisle, 2b; Jackson, ss; Cowan, 3b; Cooper, rf; Benjamin, cf; Peterson, lf; Hardy, c; Oliver, c; Vance, p; Nash, p; Jones, p.
New Orleans—Laurant, 1b; Collins, 2b; Miller, ss; Sias, 3b; Z. Wright, rf; Pipkins, cf; Dallas, lf; Labott, c; Matthews, p; Beverly, p; Marcum, p.
Memphis—Nunley, 1b; Sanders, 2b; Longley, ss; Carter, 3b; Mason, rf; Curry, cf; Gilliard, lf; Smith, c; Hampton, c; B. Brown, p; Howard, p; Ligon, p.
Nashville—West, 1b; Hughes, 2b; Bankhead, ss; Snow, 3b; Parnell, lf; Parker, rf; Wright, cf; Dukes, c; Williams, c; Willis, p; Miller, p; Porter, p.
Monroe—Meriwether, 1b; Henry, 2b; Brown, ss; Jones, 3b; Griffin, lf; Johnson, rf; Sims, cf; Else, c; C. Smith, c; Cranson, p; Morris, p; Williams, p.[59]

However, the format and venues for the North-South games seemed to be ever changing. The September 23 game in Birmingham ceased to be mentioned. Finally, it appeared that the series would begin in Nashville on Sunday, October 7. There would be three games, all played in that city. The lineups as listed in the Courier, with Nashville players being on the North rather than the South team, were:

North
Mule Suttles, Chicago, 1b
Sammy Hughes, Nashville, 2b
Willie Wells, Chicago, ss
Felton Snow, Nashville, 3b

Cool Papa Bell, Kansas City cf
Turkey Stearnes, Kansas City, rf
Vick [Vic] Harris, Pittsburgh Crawford[s], lf
[Satchel] "Speedball" Paige, Pittsburgh Crawfords, p
Luis Tiant, House of David, p
Jim Willis, Nashville, p
Andy Porter, Nashville, p
Tommy Dukes, Nashville, c
Josh Gibson, Pittsburgh Crawfords, c

South
Eldridge Mayweather, Monroe, 1b
Matthew Carlisle, Birmingham 2b
Wayman Longley, Memphis, ss
Robert Smith, Memphis, 3b
Jerry Benjamin, Birmingham or Homer Curry, Memphis, rf
Jim Mason, Memphis, lf
Griffin, Monroe, p
Herman Howard, Memphis, p
Columbus Vance, Birmingham, p
Floyd Kranson, Monroe, p
Harry Else, c[60]

The fans at Sulphur Dell got their money's worth in the first game of the doubleheader on Sunday. Stearnes hit a home run with two out in the 12th inning to give the NNL a 2–1 victory in the first game. The North then wrapped up the series with an 8–1 win in the nightcap. The third game was scheduled for Monday night.[61]

But all of the per-game hype notwithstanding, the coverage was extremely poor. The *Nashville Banner*, which had championed the series, gave the Sunday doubleheader just one paragraph, seven lines of type on Monday morning. Stearnes' home run was the only play mentioned for the two games. If the Monday night game was played, there was no report on its outcome on Tuesday.

While the second-half season obviously disintegrated rapidly, it is interesting to note that both Memphis and

Sam Bankhead was one of five brothers who played in the Negro leagues. An infielder, primarily second base and shortstop, he began his career with Birmingham in 1931 and played for Negro Southern League teams Nashville and Louisville (courtesy NoirTech Research).

Monroe not only continued playing, but excelled on a broader front. Both clubs participated in "the 14th annual baseball tournament in Council Bluffs, Iowa." The *Defender* reported that there were three black teams playing in the mixed race event—the Red Sox, Monroe Monarchs, and Sioux City Ghosts. All three played deep into the tournament. The Sioux City Ghosts team is a curiosity because it was primarily a softball team. Started in the in the Iowa city in 1925 as a boys club, the team evolved into a barnstorming outfit that crossed the country throughout the 1930s and up until 1956.[62] In 1934 the team apparently had little trouble making the transition from softball to baseball to participate in the Council Bluffs tournament. It defeated Monroe, 7–4, to advance to the semifinals against Memphis. The Red Sox won that encounter, 7–3, on Labor Day behind the pitching of "Suit Case" Mason. Memphis, managed by Reuben Jones, appeared to have the championship in hand, leading the white, bewhiskered House of David team, 3–0, after eight innings. The bearded wonders, though, scored six runs in the top of the ninth inning to win the championship game, 6–3.[63]

Although this was the original House of David team, not the split-off City of David or one of the numerous imitation House of David teams that barnstormed around the country, the most famous players of 1934 did not appear in the Iowa game. Female Olympian Babe Didrikson Zaharias, Satchel Paige, and his catcher Bill Perkins all played with the 1934 team at times. Statistical superlatives are difficult to determine for the 1934 season, with only 56 box scores and 22 line scores located. Birmingham (16) and Memphis (17) were the only teams with box scores in double digits, thus providing some idea of individual accomplishment. Birmingham's leading hitters were Jerry Benjamin, on the verge of becoming a longtime Negro National League regular, at .400 in 60 at-bats, followed by Matthew Jackson with .323 in 65 at-bats. For Memphis the leaders were Reuben Jones, .346 in 26 at-bats and Luther Gilliard, .315 in 54 at-bats. Intriguing players with extremely sparse numbers to work with were Herman Andrews of Birmingham, "Wu Fang" Ward of Cincinnati, and Griffin of Monroe. Andrews hit .692 in four games, Ward .478 in seven games, and Griffin .470 in four games.

The top pitcher was Mutt Jones of Birmingham, 4–1, and William Howard of Memphis, 4–2–1. Based on available information there were no no-hit games in 1934 and no pitcher had more than one shutout game.

12

1935
Welcome Home, Black Barons

The disappointing collapse of the league in 1934 notwithstanding, black baseball men in the South were back for another try at a viable Negro Southern League in 1935.

Meeting at the Martin Building in Memphis on April 7, representatives cobbled out another six-team league. Cities represented at the meeting included Atlanta; Birmingham; Cincinnati; Claybrook, Arkansas;, Louisville; Memphis; Monroe; and New Orleans. Business accomplished included selecting an official league ball, a slate of umpires, and an expectation of inter-league games being played with Negro National League teams. There would also be a championship series at the end of the year.[1]

League officers were elected. They included President J. B. Martin, Memphis; First Vice President Milton H. Grey, Birmingham; Second Vice President W. B. Baker, Atlanta; Secretary L.S.N. Cobb, Memphis; Treasurer W. S. Martin, Memphis; Corresponding Secretary B. T. Harvey, Atlanta; and Schedule Committee Chairman, B. B. Martin, Memphis.[2]

The formal league lineup contained old and new teams. Back under its familiar name were the Birmingham Black Barons after two years as Monarchs, Foxes, and Giants. Also resuming its old name was the Atlanta team, once again called the Black Crackers. Debuting were the Claybrook Tigers, representing an Arkansas sawmill community about twenty miles west of Memphis. The sawmill was located on a 1,700-acre plantation owned, remarkably for the time, by John C. Claybrook, a black businessman. He built Claybrook Park, which had a capacity of 2,000–3,000 and stocked his team with a number of outstanding players.[3]

Claybrook's spring training was planned in Texas and Mexico.[4] The Tigers would prove to be formidable in their first NSL season.

On April 21, the *Atlanta Daily World* reported that the league membership consisted of Atlanta, Birmingham, Chattanooga, Memphis, Montgomery and New Orleans. The Monroe Monarchs were playing as an independent team this year.

As the season progressed, though, it seemed likely that both Montgomery and New Orleans also were independent clubs rather than actual league members, even though both played many games against league teams. When the Grey Sox played games against Atlanta, Birmingham, and other NSL teams, there was no reference to league membership in the Montgomery newspapers. No field manager was identified, just William M. Brown, an owner and club official for several years. In late July the team had reportedly been reorganized and was looking for road opponents.[5] When Montgomery played a series with Birmingham in late August, it was reported that the team

125

The 1935 Claybrook Tigers, Back row, from left, Charlie Henderson, Alfred Saylor, Dan Wilson, Bill "Wing" Ball, Logan "Eggie" Hensley, and John "The Brute" Lyles. Middle row, Theolic Smith, Walter Calhoun, Roosevelt "Bill" Tate, Jessie Askew, unidentified player. Front row, "Handful" Davis, Bill Adams, Emmett Wilson (courtesy John Haddock).

had a record of 28–11 compared with Birmingham's 43–16.[6] Chattanooga and New Orleans may have been in a similar not-actually-in-the-league situation as fewer than five games were located for either club throughout the season.

The New Orleans team was owned by Allen Page, a hotel man, who had built Crescent Park as a home for his team. He brought in Sandy Thompson, a veteran Negro Leaguer, to manage the club. But, as in the case of Montgomery, there eventually arose a question of whether or not New Orleans was in the NSL. In early March Page chaired a committee looking at forming a Tri-State League composed of teams from various Louisiana and Mississippi municipalities, plus Mobile, Alabama.[7] In June, it was reported that the Black Pelicans had won a Tri-State League doubleheader from the Louisiana Stars club. The league was said to be composed of teams from Mobile; Pensacola, Florida; Laurel and Newton, Mississippi; Ferriday, Clinton, and New Orleans, Louisiana; and the Louisiana Stars of Donaldsonville.[8]

Perhaps a bigger clue about the Black Pelicans' status was a story in early March, announcing the hiring of Thompson as manager. The article further related that Page's Crescent Park would be "open to the National and Southern League teams for their training and also for exhibition games." There was no suggestion in the article that the Black Pelicans were in any league. When the Birmingham Black Barons appeared in New Orleans for a Sunday doubleheader on May 5, they were identified as "a Southern

League member" while no such designation was afforded the New Orleans club. And there was no reference to league membership at all in coverage of New Orleans' sweep of that doubleheader or at any other time the remainder of the season. In fact, the Black Pelicans were on an extensive barnstorming tour of Alabama, Georgia, and Florida throughout much of July, playing teams in cities like Mobile and Columbus, Georgia. They returned to New Orleans for a few days and were said to be leaving on another long road trip. That was the last reference to the team in 1935.

Interestingly, two former NSL members from New Orleans resurfaced in the summer of 1935. Both the Crescent Stars and the Algiers Giants were "reorganized" and played independent ball for a few weeks.

As the teams began spring training, the Memphis Red Sox initiated an interesting concept in getting the players to camp. Manager Reuben Jones took the Red Sox team bus on a swing through Texas, picking up prospects Pete McQueen of Fort Worth, R. C. Kenney and Claude Johnson of Dallas, and Marlin Carter of San Antonio. The bus then looped through Arkansas to gather up Red Langley, Edgar Jackson, Beauford Nunley, Robert Liggons, and others. Meanwhile owner Dr. W. S. Martin had "a crew of carpenters at work putting the finishing touches on the latest conveniences in seating, screening, and loud speakers for the enjoyment and comfort of the fans."[9]

In both Atlanta and Birmingham there was a celebration of the return of the familiar team names Black Crackers and Black Barons.

The Atlanta Athletics were gone and the Black Crackers back after a two-year absence. The new manager would be Sammy "Runt" Thompson, "short but stocky young second baseman who was voted the best keystoner in the Negro Southern League by Dixie sports writers in 1931 when he performed for the championship Memphis Red Sox." Thompson had played with Little Rock in 1932, then went to Sioux City, Iowa, for two years as playing manager of the Van Dyke Colored House of David, touring the Pacific Coast and Canada.[10] The team began its spring training at the Booker T. Washington High School field in Atlanta.[11] Earl Mann, general manager of the white Atlanta Crackers, reportedly had shown "unusual interest in the doings of the team and is entirely hopeful of a successful season here with colored patrons swarming to Spillers to see the local plays some grand ball."[12]

When the opening game was announced at Rickwood Field in Birmingham, it was reported to be between the Atlanta Black Crackers and "the new Black Barons of Birmingham."[13] Along with the familiar nickname there was a familiar face in charge. Although one newspaper reported the manager as pitcher Robert Poindexter, it was actually veteran catcher Poindexter Williams at the helm. Owner Gus Allen promised "to give the fans more for their money this season than ever before." Top players included first baseman George McAllister and pitcher Jeff Posey. A peculiar name was the second baseman identified as "Good Black."[14] One can assume that Good Black was Sylvester Owens, who appeared in the box score of the first game at second base. An interesting name was W. H. Mays, the left fielder. Mays would become the father to one of the greatest players of all-time, the legendary Willie Mays.

Opening day festivities in Birmingham included a first pitch ceremony with AME Zion Bishop B. G. Shaw and a preliminary game between Stockham and Acipco, two of the industrial league teams that had sent so many players to the Black Barons and other teams over the years. Atlanta scored three runs in the ninth inning to win the game, 3–2. Norman Cross limited the home team to five hits and struck out seven.[15] The following day Birmingham won by the same score.[16]

Although Birmingham went through all of the opening day trappings for the Atlanta games, those games were reported to be part of Atlanta's exhibition season. The *Atlanta Daily World* indicated the Black Crackers would play their opening day games with Memphis on May 4–5.[17]

A new name among the Atlanta club's officials was B. T. Harvey. Burwell Towns Harvey was the long time coach, athletic director, and science professor at Morehouse College.[18] He frequently umpired Negro Southern League games in the Atlanta area. In an era when eligibility was of small concern among historic black colleges and universities, numerous Atlanta Black Crackers players were also students or recent graduates from local schools such as Morehouse, Morris Brown, and Clark. The following year, 1936, the Atlanta team had no fewer than seven Morris Brown men on the roster.[19]

The May 15 opening date set by the league did not seem to fit what happened around the league.[20] When Atlanta visited Birmingham on Monday, April 29, it was called the season opener. On Saturday, May 4 Memphis announced that it would open its season against the Atlanta Black Crackers that day at Martin Stadium. The game was rained out as was a doubleheader on Sunday.

The two teams finally played on Tuesday, May 7, in Atlanta with Atlanta winning, 7–6. Pitcher Cross of Atlanta gave up 10 hits and walked four batters, but he struck out 10 and managed to keep the Memphis base runners somewhat contained. After Atlanta had scored four in the eighth to take the lead, Cross got the leadoff batter in the ninth on a ground out and struck out the last two to preserve the win. Memphis used five pitchers, who yielded only seven hits, but the home team made them count.[21]

Memphis finally had an opening day at Martin's Park on Sunday, May 12, taking a doubleheader from Birmingham. The festivities include a first pitch from "Miss Freddie Perkins, smiling young lady from Booker T. Washington High School." Sam Qualls, a local undertaker, was the recipient of her toss.[22]

The Atlanta opener had been heavily promoted by the *Atlanta Daily World* and its sports editor, Ric Roberts: "Remember, mates, this is May 7. Today the Negro Southern League returns to the strangest city this side of Zanzibar, Atlanta. If you have a date for four o'clock this afternoon, forget it. Cancel it. Why this is opening Day. Why, for land sakes, the rest of those Crackers have done in anticipation of this day. This is the return of the national pastime in Atlanta."[23]

Festivities include a parade, pregame track and golf exhibitions, "Miss Atlanta" Barbara Schell, new uniforms, and "a grand ball club ... something which Atlanta has not had since the present college generation was way down in the fifth grade."[24]

The Red Sox got even the next day with a 7–2 win. Pitcher Bill Howard, who had been driven from the mound in the second inning of the opener, started again. He held Atlanta to just four hits but was "wilder than a Comache [*sic*] squaw with her first bottle of gin," wrote Ric Roberts. Howard walked 10, but only two of Atlanta's 14 base runners were able to score.[25] Roberts, often a colorful writer, had become the first sports editor of the *Daily World* while a sophomore at Clark College in Atlanta. Later he worked at the *Pittsburgh Courier, Norfolk Journal and Guide,* and *Baltimore Afro-American.* Eventually he left the newspaper business and became public relations director at Howard University in Washington, D.C.[26]

Reporting on a 4–3 win over Birmingham a couple of weeks later, Roberts offered this comment after Birmingham had taken a 3–2 lead in the sixth: "The barons were one run to the good and, with Nash mowing our boys down with ease, were as fresh as a peddler with one foot in the door." The 10-inning game lasted three hours and 10 minutes and ended only after Atlanta players got hungry, Roberts reported: "...until Donald began smelling steaks frying in a beanery on Ponce de Leon nearby and Smith got an odor of pork chops wafting from some grill, the two teams had been composed of nine guys named Alphonse and nine others known as Gaston."[27]

Although only playing at around a .500 pace, the Atlanta club was performing before an appreciative audience. Black fans were obviously glad to have league ball back in the community and the Black Crackers showed flashes of good talent occasionally. They lost a tightly-played game to Birmingham at Ponce de Leon Park on June 2 before a crowd of 3,500, of which an estimated 1,000 were whites. Earl Mann, general manager of the Atlanta Crackers, was ecstatic over the crowd: "Why, you played to far more fans than Little Rock or Knoxville are able to draw when they play the white Crackers here. We pledge you these grounds any day you have games billed and hope you can come out on Sunday dates when our team is out of town."[28]

But Mann took a different tack in August when attendance fell off. The Black Crackers were told the park was no longer available. Ric Roberts wrote that black fans "hardly made it interesting for the office out there to realize regular expenses—it does cost money to run a ball yard." There was also speculation that the white team needed to get the field in shape for an upcoming Dixie Series. Roberts did not score the white owners for their action, but expressed regret that the Black Crackers would not have an opportunity to close their season before a large Labor Day crowd.[29]

The Claybrook Tigers, who had done their spring training in Texas and Mexico, did not schedule a league opening until June 2. As they returned to Arkansas in late May the Tigers were reported to have played six games in Mexico and 18 in the United States, getting ready for the season. Their record in Mexico was three wins, a loss, and two ties. In the U.S. they had won 16 of 18, losing only to the Chicago American Giants, twice.[30]

Although the team had a good mix of veterans and young players, the one who attracted lots of attention early on was "One-Arm" Ball, an outfielder reminiscent of the popular "Wing" Maddox. In the second game of a doubleheader win over Memphis he "made two sensational catches ... the last coming in the seventh when he went to the back fence to snag Longley's long drive."[31] In September Ball had two doubles in a game against the Memphis Red Sox.[32]

Birmingham returned home on May 19 for series with Memphis. According to the *Birmingham News*, the team "was away to one of the greatest seasons of colored baseball in the Birmingham district." They reported that the team was back from a successful road trip.[33] However, results indicate that while Birmingham won two out of three in Atlanta, they lost three straight at Memphis. The Red Sox made it five in a row over the Black Barons with a 14–4 and 6–3 doubleheader sweep. A second baseman named Canada had five hits in the first game and one in the second to pace the Memphis offense. The series was to be continued the next two days in Anniston and Gadsden, Alabama.[34]

But the report on the doubleheader was the last mention of the Black Barons in the *News* that season. The *Daily World* did report that Birmingham had won a 5–4 game from Atlanta on June 2 and would play again on June 3, but that game was rained out. That was the final mention of the Birmingham team in any newspaper until late August when the Black Barons played Montgomery. In the box score for that game shortstop Owens is the only recognizable name from the box scores at the start of the season in the spring. It is impossible to determine if this is the same Black Barons team or a reorganized group just using the name.

Although no standings were located, there was evidently a viable pennant race under way. The *Memphis Commercial-Appeal* reported that Memphis had won the first half title by virtue of a doubleheader sweep of Claybrook on Sunday, June 30. Utility man Jim Ford, playing second base in the first game, drove in five runs, scored three times, and stole three bases in Memphis' 9–3 win. He had three singles in four at bats.[35] Both teams apparently opened their second half schedules with July 4 doubleheaders. Memphis hosted Chattanooga with a boxing match to open the day's celebration. Claybrook was at home against the Cuban Stars.[36]

The following standings below are compiled from scores located through June 30. They include only games played among the five teams listed since it appears Monroe, Montgomery, and New Orleans were not full-fledged league members by the time the season started:

Outfielder Oscar "Heavy" Johnson played in the Negro National League for several years but ended his career with the 1931 Memphis Red Sox of the Negro Southern League (courtesy NoirTech Research).

Memphis	12	4	.750
Chattanooga	1	1	.500
Atlanta	4	7	.364
Birmingham	3	6	.333
Claybrook	2	4	.333
	22	22	

For the second half, there is even less information to work with. Memphis opened with a doubleheader sweep of Chattanooga, 20–6 and 12–6, on July 4. Chattanooga won two from Atlanta on July 21 by scores of 2–1 and 2–0. No other league matchups were found in July and August. By mid–August

Memphis was in the nation's heartland, playing in the national semipro baseball tournament in Wichita, Kansas. When they returned home at the end of the month it was to open a seven-game series with Claybrook for the championship. It is unclear if this was a second-half championship or an overall league championship, since no Claybrook league games could be located for the second half. Games were scheduled in Memphis on Sunday, September 1, and the next day, Labor Day. The series would then move to Claybrook for four games.[37]

Claybrook won the Sunday doubleheader, 6–2 and 3–2, but Memphis came back on Labor Day to win 7–6. The Memphis victory came on a six-run rally in the bottom of the ninth inning. Although the box score was printed in the *Commercial-Appeal*, there were no details on the spectacular rally.[38]

The following Sunday, September 8, the two teams played a doubleheader at Claybrook. The Red Sox swamped the Tigers, 11–4, in the first game. Claybrook won, 2–1, in the five-inning second game. The *Commercial-Appeal* report said the two teams were tied at three games each in the championship series, but no record was found of Memphis' other win.

The final game of the series was scheduled for Sunday, September 16, at Claybrook, but it was actually played at Martin's Park in Memphis. Theolic "Fireball" Smith, who would begin a long Negro League big league career the next season, struck out eight in pitching the Tigers to a 5–2 triumph.[39]

Although the regular season had ended in shambles, the Memphis-Claybrook series did provide the Negro Southern League with a rare uncontested champion.

There was no mention of a post-season series with the Negro National League champion. However, the Monroe Monarchs scheduled a Louisiana-Arkansas Negro championship series with the Crossett, Arkansas, Athletics in September. The Monarchs were reported to have won 68 games while losing just 18 over the course of the 1935 season. There was no reference to Negro Southern League play.[40]

There was also a profusion of all-star games at the end of the season.

The first game surfaced in September, but not even an all-star game could be announced without confusion: "For the past three years Southern cities have been asking for this game. Critics argue that stars which form the backbone of the National body have been drafted from Southern Colleges and semi-pros teams. These players perform throughout in the East or North of their home and the homefolk are denied an opportunity to see them."[41] Curiously, the "three years" statement ignores the 1934 all-star games. Negro Southern League President J. B. Martin and Negro National League President William "Gus" Greenlee were said to be the architects for a series of games to pit a "North" team from the Negro National League against a "South" team from the NSL and independent teams from the region. Martin and Greenlee would select the teams with help from the managers. Also, the black press was expected to have some role in the selection and/or promotion of the games. The first contest was to be in Memphis on September 29.[42] The North manager would be the great Oscar Charleston of the Pittsburgh Crawfords. Reuben Jones would lead the South team.[43] A week or so later the rosters were announced:

North All-Stars
Cool Papa Bell, Pittsburgh Crawfords, rf
Turkey Stearnes, Chicago American Giants, lf

Mule Suttles, Chicago American Giants, lf
Oscar Charleston, Pittsburgh Crawfords, 1b
Sammy Hughes, Columbus Elites, 2b
Chester Williams, Pittsburgh Crawfords, ss
Willie Wells, Chicago American Giants, ss
Felton Snow, Columbus Elite Giants, 3b
Bill Perkins, Pittsburgh Crawfords, c
Larry Brown, Chicago American Giants, c
Josh Gibson, Pittsburgh Crawfords, c
Kincade, Pittsburgh Crawfords, p
Slim Jones, Philadelphia Stars, p
Willie Foster, Chicago American Giants, p
Willie Cornelius, Chicago American Giants, p
Robert Griffith, Columbus Elite Giants, p
Oscar Charleston, manager
Sam Bankhead, Pittsburgh Crawfords, utility
Jimmy Crutchfield, Pittsburgh Crawfords, utility

South All-Stars
Carlisle, Birmingham Black Barons, 2b
Curry, Monroe Tigers, cf
Jim Ford, Memphis Red Sox, lf
Nat Rodgers, Memphis Red Sox, rf
Red Longley, Memphis Red Sox, ss
West, Nashville, 1b
Leonard Henderson, Claybrook Tigers, 3b
Smith, Memphis Red Sox, c
Lyle, Claybrook Tigers, c
Hampton, Memphis Red Sox, c
Teddy Smith, Claybrook Tigers, p
Bill Howard, Memphis Red Sox, p
Harvey, Memphis Red Sox, p
Adams, Memphis Red Sox, p
Reuben Jones, Memphis Red Sox, manager
Spoon Carter, Birmingham Black Barons, utility
Roosevelt Tate, Claybrook Tigers, utility
Laurant, New Orleans, utility
Pete McQueen, Memphis Red Sox, utility[44]

Kincade was likely Harry Kincannon. There were no first names for several players. They are probably Lick Carlisle, Homer Curry, Jim West, Robert Smith, John Lyles, Bill Harvey, Emery Adams, and Milt Laurent. Jim Taylor and Dizzy Dismukes were named North coaches. South coaches were Rupert Liggons and Eggie Hensley.

On September 16, *Daily World* sports editor Ric Roberts announced yet another South all-star team comprised only of players from the Atlanta Black Crackers and

Jacksonville Red Caps. Roberts said the team would play a North all-star team in a three-game series in Jacksonville on October 1–3, then a two-game series in Atlanta on October 4–5. Roberts selected his team with input from Alonzo "Fluke" Mitchell, manager of the Red Caps. Mitchell would manage the South all-star team.[45]

These games were apparently arranged by Mitchell; Thomas Wilson, owner of the Columbus Elite Giants (formerly from Nashville), and W. B. Baker, owner of the Black Crackers. The story made no mention of the earlier North-South teams selected for the September 29 game in Memphis.[46] "The classiest ball players living in Dixie, ushered into this town from as far north as Chattanooga, Tennessee, as far south as St. Petersburg in this sunny state, as far west as Birmingham, Alabama" began workouts around September 20, according to an unbylined article in the *Daily World*.[47]

Meanwhile, the *Pittsburgh Courier* reported that Memphis was all agog, awaiting the game to be played there on Sunday, September 29.[48] If the game was played, it was not reported in the local newspaper. Several games were played in Jacksonville, Florida, apparently in early October. The *Courier* reported the scores but little detail.[49]

The only game in the series organized by Mitchell, Wilson and Baker which was reported in the *Daily World* was the one of October 2, which the South won, 4–1, behind the pitching of Norman Cross, the star Black Crackers pitcher. Donald Reeves and Bo Williams scored the South team's runs and Red Moore was the top hitter. Fielding honors went to Holliday for the South and North third baseman Snow.[50]

But the *Pittsburgh Courier* reported on October 12 that the NSL stars had taken three out of five contests from the NNL with a sixth game ending in a tie. According to that report, with a Jacksonville dateline, the tie was in the opening game, followed by a 4–3 South win in the second game. The third was won by the North, 5–1, the fourth and fifth were a double-header sweep by the South.[51]

The popularity of these postseason all-stars games was such that the Pittsburgh Crawfords, Negro National League champions, scheduled an October 13 doubleheader in New Orleans against a combined NNL and NSL team. There is no evidence that this game was played.[52]

The probable all-star lineup was given as: Davenport, Philadelphia Stars, or Curry, Memphis, cf; Wright, Nashville, or Rodgers, Chicago, rf; Parnell, lf; Morney, Nashville, or Longley, Memphis, ss; Creasy, Philadelphia, or Smith, Claybrook, 3b; West, Nashville, first base; Carlyle, Homestead, or Jackson, Birmingham 2b; Peppers, Philadelphia, Palm, Brooklyn, or Ippy, Memphis, c, with Parker, Homestead; Howard, Memphis; E. Williams, Brooklyn; and Adams, Memphis, pitchers and Laurent, New Orleans, and McQueen, Memphis, utility. The manager was Red Parnell and his assistant coach was Reuben Jones.[53]

Statistically, the 1935 season was the worst ever for a researcher searching for superlatives. Only 15 box scores and eight additional line scores were located for the entire season. The dispersal was Atlanta 10, Birmingham 9, Memphis 7, Claybrook 2, New Orleans 2, and Chattanooga 1. In fact, results of any kind were found for only 33 league games. The individual leaders are drawn from among Atlanta, Birmingham, and Memphis. Donald Reeves of Atlanta hit .571 in six games while George McAllister of Birmingham hit .368 and Claude Johnson of Memphis it .360 in the same number. For the record, W. H. Mays, the father of Willie Mays, hit .263 in 10 games with Birmingham. Although eventually losing to Claybrook in the playoff, Memphis pitchers dominated the regular season. Howard won all seven Red Sox games for which results were found. Although their won-lost records were not as good, two Atlanta pitchers were impressive in strikeouts. Norman Cross struck out 31 batters in 24 innings while "Rider" Brown struck out 29 in 28.1 innings.

13

1936
The End of an Era

For the first time in three years, the Negro Southern League would attempt to launch its 1936 season with eight teams. The auspicious beginning would be offset by the fact that 1936 was also the last year the league would operate for nine years.

At a league meeting in Nashville in late March the groundwork was laid for the new season. Representatives of a dozen cities attended the organizational meeting. Thomas Wilson, owner of the Negro National League's Elite Giants, was named president and given "full power to act on all matters pertaining to the league." Those in attendance included: William Brown, Montgomery; Bud Hailey, Chattanooga; A. M. Walker, Birmingham; Ed Meneese and Bennie Scales, Nashville; R. H. Penner, Hopkinsville, Kentucky; W. B. Baker, Atlanta; John C. Claybrook, Claybrook, Arkansas; and Dr. J. B. Martin, Memphis.[1]

Strong financial proposals came out of the meeting. Each prospective franchise put up a $100 forfeit fee and pledged to submit at the next meeting a $25 fee for league expenses. Two percent of the gross gate receipts were also committed to the operation of the league, to be turned in by the home team after each game. Guaranteed minimum payments for visiting teams were also established at a rate of $25 for weekday games, $50 for Sundays and holidays, and $12.50 for rainouts. The *Nashville Banner* reported the forfeit fee at $150, and added that the monthly salary limit for each club was $450.[2]

Four teams returned from 1935, the Atlanta Black Crackers, Birmingham Black Barons, Chattanooga Black Lookouts, and Memphis Red Sox. Two other teams were the Cincinnati Tigers, members in 1934, and the Hopkinsville Athletics, members in 1927. The final two teams were the Montgomery Grey Sox and Nashville Black Vols. The latter team was also owned by Wilson of the Elite Giants, now based in Washington, D.C.[3] The Chicago American Giants and the Columbus, Ohio, Buckeyes were listed as associate members.[4]

Meeting a week later at Wilson Park in Nashville, officials released the first-half schedule. The document was peculiar in its nature and proved very quickly to be erroneous. Opening day games on Saturday, May 2, were to be Cincinnati at Nashville and Birmingham at Montgomery with Hopkinsville and Memphis having open dates.[5] In reality, the games reported in newspapers had Cincinnati playing at Nashville, but Chattanooga was at Montgomery. Memphis played a barnstorming team at home. The whereabouts of Atlanta, Birmingham, and Hopkinsville were unclear.

League officials set Sunday, May 10, as opening day in four cities.[6] Results were found for only two games, though. Birmingham won at home against Nashville, 4–1, and Roy Wellmaker hit a home run and pitched a no-hitter in Atlanta as the Black Crackers won, 6–0, over Chattanooga.[7] Chicago beat Cincinnati, 7–6. No results were located for Hopkinsville or Memphis. In addition, Montgomery was reported to be hosting a barnstorming team by the unlikely name of the House of Moses-New York Zulu Cannonball Giants. (It is likely that the word "Cannonball" was a corruption of "Cannibal," the "Zulu Cannibal Giants" was a name used by travelling black teams dressed up as wild Africans for comic effect.)

Despite the confusion over the opening day schedule and, perhaps, even some question about the accuracy of the eight-team lineup, there were interesting stories surrounding the different teams. No story was more dramatic than Atlanta's, where a cheerful outlook was dampered by tragedy even before the first practice could be held.

The Black Crackers, resurrected in 1935 "after thirteen years of absence on a grand scale and five on any sort of scale,"[8] were again to take the field. A meeting at the Auburn Avenue Luncheonette on March 21 resulted in a revised organization with the following officers: Percy Williams, president and treasurer; James "Prince" Andrews, vice president; W. B. Baker, secretary; S. M. Humphrey, business manager; and Lewis L. Means, field manager and assistant business manager.[9]

The team would have "first class transportation and two sets of the best uniforms." All games would be played at Ponce de Leon Park, home of the white Crackers.[10]

Then, on April 26 disaster struck. Williams, popular owner of the Auburn Avenue Luncheonette and who, along with Baker, was credited with bringing the Black Crackers back to the forefront, died suddenly after a short illness. *Atlanta Daily World* sports editor Ric Roberts wrote that his passing made the future look suddenly dark for black baseball in Atlanta.

"In 1935 he spent and lost $800 on the game in Atlanta," wrote Roberts. "In 1936 he was still ready and willing to again venture forward with funds to back and sustain a team. He could take it! Not many men, socked for eight hundred bucks in three months time, would be willing to try such a dubious pastime again. Percy was like that ... he had the courage to hold on to something in which he had faith." In modern dollars, Williams' three-month loss in 1935 would have been $12,375.[11]

"But when Atlanta lost Williams, it lost more than a money man for the team. It was Percy Williams who saved the Black Crackers last July. He was the man who dug down into his pockets and paid off Cracker debts amounting 400.00 and put cash in the coffers. It was Percy who [housed] and fed a half dozen players for two months without one dime coming his way."

For Roberts, Williams' death was obviously a personal loss as well: "It is close to the incredible to think of him gone, vanished, departed for ever. Just two weeks ago Saturday night he served me dinner in his Luncheonette. He showed me the new contract forms for Southern League ball players this season and asked me to tell you that Atlanta would have a baseball team after all.... Percy Williams loved baseball. He thrilled to its eternal matching of wits and its lasting charm. He was willing to spend his money to see it flourish."[12]

Williams' death put the Atlanta club's future up in the air at a time when a team should be in the middle of spring training. Roberts, trying to put a positive spin on a dismal situation, wrote that there was a great opportunity for an enterprising backer to step in. There would be no shortage of good players available, but the immediate needs were "a good bus or two good passenger cars plus two sets of uniforms."[13]

Finally, there was hope. After "rousing baseball meeting at the Butler YMCA," a new Atlanta team emerged. H. H. M. Smith was named club president, "Prince" Albert vice president [sic], W. B. Baker booking agent and business manager, and S. M. Humphrey assistant business manager. James "Prince" Andrews was mentioned as a club official earlier. It could not be ascertained which surname is correct. Lewis Means would be the field manager and Tiny Smith, who had been an All-American end for the Morris Brown College football squad, the team captain. Practice would begin immediately, just a week before opening day.[14]

Birmingham had a new manager and it was not a name with any known connection to black baseball. Andrew M. Walker had not played with Birmingham or any other team as far as can be ascertained. He was possibly a native of Perry County, Alabama. When the Black Barons played a barnstorming game in Marion, the local fans honored Walker as a local boy come home.[15] Because of his surname, it is easy to speculate on whether he was a relative of a Birmingham numbers racketeer named Alfreda "Freddo" Walker. Alfreda Walker was credited with bringing the Black Barons team name back to life after the 1933–34 seasons when the Birmingham team was the Giants, among the names used those years.

"In those days he [Alfreda Walker] was netting himself $750 a day. He put himself up an office in the 'Little Masonic Temple' building and in 1935–36 revived the Black Barons. It is said that the Black Barons operated under a three-man partnership, although Mr. Walker's name was associated as sole owner," wrote Emory O. Jackson in his "Hits and Bits" column in the *Birmingham World*.[16]

Since manager Walker seems to have had no baseball history before or after his two-year stint with the Birmingham club, is it possible he was a brother, a son, or some other relative given a nice job by owner Walker?

Regardless, A. M. Walker was the man reported in the press as representing the team at the Negro Southern League meeting in March, and he was the man in charge when the team began spring training. He would also manage the team again in 1937 when Birmingham joined the new Negro American League.

"From the looks of thing, we are going to be ready to start with a jambup [sic] ball club from opening day," Walker told the *Birmingham News*. "The team has ample financial backing this season, something that it has lacked woefully in other years and every indication points to the fact that the colored fans are hungry [sic] for baseball."

Opening day ceremonies included an unusual first pitch honoree. Instead of a minister or politician, Birmingham selected the female student with the highest grade point average at the Negro Industrial School.[17] Thelma Smith also was "outfitted from head to foot in new Spring ensemble" as part of the honor.[18]

The Montgomery Grey Sox made their exhibition debut in a new venue, the North Decatur Street Park, against the Columbus Giants, possibly an independent team out of Columbus, Georgia, or a misidentified Columbus Buckeyes club. However, no names in the Columbus lineup appeared on the 1935 Buckeyes roster. The game was played as "Name" day when fans could submit names for the ball park. The person whose name was selected would get five dollars.[19] The game was canceled by rain and rescheduled for April 12, but there was no report on the outcome of either the game or the park naming.[20] However, future reports in local newspapers referenced Brown's Park on North Decatur Street. Today there is a Newton Park and Community Center at 1765 North Decatur Street. The facility has a playground, shelters, and picnic tables, but not a baseball park.[21]

The Chattanooga Black Lookouts opened their NSL season on the road at Atlanta, then returned home for three games with the Hopkinsville Athletics. Chattanooga swept the series, winning the Sunday double-header, 6–5 and 3–2, and the Monday game, 16–1. Simpson, who pitched the third game, struck out 18 Athletics while teammates pounded five pitchers for 24 hits. One of them, a home run by catcher Rivers, "hit the Lookout sign in deep center field" At the white minor league Lookouts' Engel Stadium.[22]

As for Hopkinsville, returning to the league after a nine-year absence, very little is known. Only one reference to the team was found in the *Kentucky New Era*, the local newspaper: "The Hopkinsville Athletics, members of the colored southern league, took both ends of a double-header yesterday from the Chattanooga Black Lookouts at Flemings Cave Park. The scores were 7–5 and 8–2, the last game going only five innings before being halted because of darkness. "A five-run rally in the sixth inning enabled Hopkinsville to win the first game Sunday."[23]

Only five scores in all were found for the Athletics. In addition to the doubleheader reported above the team lost three games at Chattanooga in May. Not a single Hopkinsville player was identified in any of the game accounts.

The team was scheduled to play on Saturday and Sunday in Montgomery during the last weekend of May. A local newspaper reported that the Grey Sox would be playing a team called the California Stars instead. The California team was taking the place "of the Hopkinsville club, which disbanded Friday."[24]

There had been great optimism at the beginning of the season for black baseball in the South. Ric Roberts, writing in the *Daily World*, reported that some 6,000 people had turned out in Memphis to witness an exhibition game between the Chicago American Giants and the Claybrook Tigers. He said the amount of revenue generated from tickets was $2,396.50. "Baseball is swinging back to pre-war levels in this southland," wrote Roberts.[25]

On opening day Roy "Snook" Wellmaker of Atlanta had one of the most remarkable performances ever in the Negro Southern League. He not only had a single and home run at bat, but also pitched a no-hitter against the Chattanooga Black Lookouts. Wellmaker struck out 11 and walked only two in shutting down the visitors before a crowd of 2,900 at Ponce de Leon Park.[26] But Wellmaker's stay with the Black Crackers was brief. He joined the Homestead Grays in the Negro National League a few weeks later.[27]

Although no official first-half schedule, except the obviously incorrect one from the *Chicago Defender*, was located it appears that most league games were played on weekends only, thus limiting the total number of games which counted in the standings. Standings published in the *Daily World* on May 30 showed Birmingham (5–1) a game ahead of Memphis (4–2), followed by Atlanta (5–3) and Montgomery (4–4). The other four teams were all under .500. The standings were mathematically balanced even though the number of games played ranged from nine for Chattanooga to only three for Nashville.

13. 1936: The End of an Era

On June 23, Atlanta may have set a Negro Southern League record in a night game with the Memphis Red Sox. The two teams had split a doubleheader on Sunday. Memphis went up two games to one with a 5–4 win on Monday. Atlanta evened the series in possibly the most one-sided game ever played in the NSL, smothering Memphis 29–2. Sam McKibben, writing in the *Daily World*, said "the larruping Atlanta Black Crackers turned the Ponce De Leon Park diamond into a track and the game into a track meet."[28] Atlanta blasted four Memphis pitchers for 39 hits before the game was called after eight innings. James Kemp had two doubles and a triple in five at at-bats. Red Hadley and one of the Howards [there were three Howards on the Atlanta roster] hit home runs. Jim Reese, Cooper, and Maceo Wright hit triples in succession at one point.

With Memphis' only two runs coming on errors, the game finally became a joke: "The Atlanta boys had a merry evening, running the bases backward and down through the pitcher's box. The fans who remained to see the last strike made roared with delight over the antics of the local team.... Are the Crackers hot or has Memphis no team?"[29]

Games of July 5 ended the first-half schedule with Birmingham apparently the winner of the crown. A second-half schedule was distributed by the Scott Newspaper Syndicate out of Birmingham. The July 12–August 10 schedule contained games for Atlanta, Birmingham, Chattanooga, Hopkinsville, Memphis, Montgomery, Nashville, and St. Louis. There was no explanation for the absence of Cincinnati and the appearance of St. Louis, except possibly the writer's mental lapse. The Tigers continued to play league opponents into August. The schedule included many seemingly random open dates for the different teams. There is little evidence that many scheduled games were actually played. On July 12 the *Daily World* referred to the local team as "the orphaned Atlanta Black Crackers."[30] It is unclear if this was a euphemism for the long road trip or a reflection on the demise of the NSL. In either case, when the team was on a North Carolina road trip in late August the newspaper noted, "It seems that the Black Crackers have found it possible to earn more dough while operating in foreign territory than at home." Ric Roberts said local interest had declined considerably after Roy Wellmaker was lost to the Homestead Grays.[31]

Numbers compiled from available box scores show how much Atlanta lost with Wellmaker's departure. His record was 3–1 with four complete games and 49 strikeouts in 38 innings. He threw the team's only shutout. He was also missed at the plate. He had five hits in 14 at-bats for .357 batting average in those five games.

When the team returned to Atlanta in mid–July it was only for a brief respite with another road trip planned for "the Mississippi-Missouri territory." Meanwhile, a former league member, independent Claybrook, had hooked up with the Cuban Stars, and the two teams were travelling together for a time, playing dates throughout the South.[32]

In early August the Black Crackers returned to Atlanta, where local fans were pushing for a series with the Jacksonville Red Caps, supposed winners of 26 out of 28 games on the road. In a rare second-half reference to the pennant race, the *Daily World* noted on August 5 that the Black Crackers were the "second place league team."[33] However, the team did not play a home game after June 30.

Below are first half standings, compiled from various newspaper reports, using the same eight teams published in the *Daily World* in May:

	League Games			*All Games*		
Team	Won	Lost	Pct.	Won	Lost	Pct.
Cincinnati	3	0	1.000	6	3	.667
Birmingham	15	4	.789	17	4	.810
Nashville	5	2	.714	8	2	.800
Atlanta	10	5	.667	12	7	.632
Hopkinsville	2	3	.400	2	3	.400
Memphis	5	9	.357	7	10	.412
Chattanooga	6	12	.333	6	12	.333
Montgomery	4	15	.211	9	15	.375
	50	50				

Although Cincinnati won all of its league games, only three games were reported, making its position in the standings somewhat dubious. Birmingham, on the other hand, played 19 league games and won most of them. Hopkinsville's five games were all with Chattanooga. No results were published for games scheduled with Montgomery and Nashville. The Black Barons can be reasonably declared first half champions of the 1936 Negro Southern League.

With the second-half schedule existing largely on paper rather than on the field, determining a second-half champion is more difficult. Only seven league games were located and some of them are questionable. In fact, only 20 non-league games were located, suggesting that some clubs like Hopkinsville had likely folded and others were doing their ballplaying on extensive barnstorming tours in the East and Midwest. For example, only two games were located for Montgomery for the entire second half of the season, a doubleheader loss at Cincinnati on August 2. Nashville was undefeated in its only game, while Cincinnati was 3–1 and Birmingham 2–1. That would leave Birmingham, the first-half winner, as the author's arbitrary champion in the last pre–World War II season of the Negro Southern League.

The *Nashville Tennessean* reported on August 9 that the Black Vols were going to play a doubleheader with the Southern Grays, "city champs in 1935–36," at Sulphur Dell, the Nashville minor league ballpark. It was said that pitcher "Slow Time" Young might be given an opportunity to pull the iron man stunt if he won the first game. The same article said the local team held a "slim lead in Negro Southern League play."[34]

The sparseness of games played ironically produced some measure of representative individual statistics. Of the 53 league games located, box scores were found for 33 of them. None were found for Hopkinsville and only four for Nashville. The numbers were better for the other teams: Birmingham 18, Memphis 12, Atlanta 9, Montgomery 7, Cincinnati 7, and Chattanooga 6.

Although "Red" Hadley of Atlanta had a higher batting average (16 hits in 32 at bats, .500), hitting honors have to go to David Whatley of Birmingham, for whom 19 box scores were available. Whatley had 31 hits in 77 at bats for a percentage of .403. Six of his hits were for extra bases, giving him a slugging average of .545. Johnny Cowan of Birmingham hit .391 in 12 games, catcher Cooper of Atlanta hit .400 in eight games, and catcher Rivers of Montgomery hit .409 in six games.

Among the pitchers, no one came to close to Wellmaker, the Atlanta hurler who left the team after a few weeks. Porter Moss of Cincinnati was undefeated in three reported games, but had only 10 strikeouts.

13. 1936: The End of an Era

Some of those players would remain in the spotlight in the coming years, although there would be no further attempts to organize a Negro Southern League until 1945. With the advent of World War II, most able-bodied men were in some kind of military service. Consequently, all of baseball was curtailed, even the white major leagues. Some of those players would remain in the spotlight in the coming years although there would be no further attempts to organize a Negro Southern League until 1945. It is possible that the founding of the Negro American League in 1937 made the prospect of a new NSL untenable. At any rate, when World War II came in December 1940 baseball faced radical changes as resources and manpower went toward the war effort. White baseball was affected as much as black baseball. There were 45 white minor league teams operating in 1940. By 1942 the number had dropped to 31.[35]

14

1937–44
The War and Waiting for the Future

Although the collapse of the Negro Southern League during the second half of the 1936 season meant there would be no more NSL for nearly a decade, black baseball in the South was still very much alive—at least in Birmingham and Memphis.

While geographic-specific league ball disappeared in the South, the region was represented in a new league that would not only usher in a measure of stability to black baseball, but would also provide eventually a format for a real, properly organized Negro World Series.

Meeting at the Senate Avenue Branch YMCA in Indianapolis in October 1936, "baseball moguls of the Middlewest and South" met to organize the Negro American League. Cities represented included Birmingham, Chicago, Cincinnati, Detroit, Indianapolis, Kansas City, Memphis, and St. Louis. Major R. R. Jackson of Chicago was elected president of the group. Others officers were Al Monroe, Chicago, secretary; J. L. Wilkinson, Kansas City, treasurer; and Abe Saperstein, Chicago, booking agent and assistant secretary.[1] Saperstein, founder of the Harlem Globetrotters basketball team, was also a major force in Midwestern baseball game booking.

The new Negro American League was comprised of three teams from the 1936 Negro Southern League and five traditional teams that had been playing independent ball or were else being reorganized. The former NSL teams were the Birmingham Black Barons, Cincinnati Tigers, and Memphis Red Sox. The teams returning to league play for the first time in from one to five years were the Chicago American Giants, Detroit Stars, Indianapolis Athletics, Kansas City Monarchs, and St. Louis Stars.[2]

When Birmingham's slot in the new league was announced the *Birmingham News* said black baseball in the city had "reached its biggest moment at last." Returning as manager was the enigmatic A. M. Walker, who announced spring training would begin April 1 and invited walk-ons to come and try out for the team.[3]

The Negro National League members were the Homestead Grays, Newark Eagles, New York Black Yankees, Philadelphia Stars, Pittsburgh Crawfords, and Washington Elite Giants, who had been a Negro Southern League member at one time when located in Nashville. It was the same lineup as 1936 except a seventh team, the New York Cubans, was no longer in the league.[4]

With the founding of the Negro American League the Birmingham and Memphis clubs would have a permanent home for the remainder of their existence over the next twenty-six years. It should be noted, though, that the Black Barons did shut down in 1939, but returned the following year.

14. 1937–44: The War and Waiting for the Future

Still organized and playing independent ball were several familiar names.

As spring training was under way around the country the *Pittsburgh Courier* reported that the Chattanooga Black Lookouts, under the management of Bud Hailey and booking agent E. Claude Camp, were looking for engagements. Players on hand were said to include Ed "Betson" Rivers, Huline "Mule" Smith, "Pitcheye" Smith, Wilbert "Bill" Camp, and Claudine "Schoolboy" Rhodes.[5]

The Atlanta Black Crackers, who had survived the untimely death of benefactor Percy Williams the previous year, had a new owner. Mike Schaine, "theatrical magnate," had purchased the club. In late May the team was reported to have won 22 out of 23 games and was currently touring North Carolina and Virginia before returning home for a five-game series with the Jacksonville Red Caps. Familiar names on the Atlanta roster included Jack Thornton at first base, James Kemp at second base, and Henry "Red" Hadley in the outfield.[6]

In the NAL Kansas City defeated Chicago in a postseason playoff for the league title. Then, a combined team of Monarchs and Giants played a combined Negro National League team in a nine-game series. The combined team of Homestead Grays and Newark Eagles players won eight of the nine games.[7]

The three former NSL teams, Birmingham, Cincinnati, and Memphis, were all bunched in the middle of the NAL standings.

The following year saw Cincinnati drop out and two more former Negro Southern League teams join the Negro American League. The newcomers were the Atlanta Black Crackers and the Jacksonville Red Caps. In the Negro National League Tom Wilson's Elite Giants relocated once again, this time to Baltimore, where they would remain. A new Washington, D.C., team, the Black Senators, joined the league.[8]

The demise of the Cincinnati, Detroit, and St. Louis franchises was due to their failure "to send representatives to the league meeting."[9]

Although Birmingham languished at the bottom of the standings, Memphis and Atlanta each had seminal seasons. The Red Sox won the first-half pennant and Atlanta the second. Memphis won an abbreviated playoff for the overall championship.[10] The two ball teams almost went into the season with the same nickname. The Atlanta club had announced in April that it was going to be called the Red Sox after fans had voted to change the team's name.[11] Shortly afterward, it was announced that the change would not occur. League President R. R. Jackson asked Atlanta to vacate the name change due to conflict with longstanding Memphis Red Sox.[12]

Oblivious to the history of the past few years, the *Birmingham News* reported in August that "one of the most elaborate and probably the most important event ever undertaken in Negro baseball" would take place at Rickwood Field on the coming Sunday. The event? A North-South All-Star game.

The game would match teams drawn from the "North and South sections" of the Negro American League. The southern teams were comprised of players from Atlanta, Birmingham, Kansas City, Memphis, and St. Louis. The north team's players were from Chicago, Indianapolis, and Washington.[13] If this game was played, it was unreported by local newspapers.

In 1939 there was a fruit basket turnover in the NAL. Atlanta, Birmingham, and Jacksonville dropped out and the league was reduced to six teams as a new team, the

Cleveland Bears, and the St. Louis Stars, who had not been in the league in 1938, joined up. The Toledo Crawfords, a reorganization of the former Pittsburgh Crawfords owned by former Negro National League president William "Gus" Greenlee, replaced the Indianapolis ABCs partway through the season.[14]

In 1940 the Birmingham Black Barons were revived and rejoined the Negro American League. Other members were Kansas City, Memphis, Chicago, Cleveland and Indianapolis.[15]

The 1941 NAL lineup saw the return of the Jacksonville Red Caps. The other clubs were Birmingham, Chicago, Kansas City, Memphis, and New Orleans–St. Louis.[16] Later that year war would come and the dynamics of all baseball, white and black, changed for the duration of World War II.

The National Association, the umbrella group for Organized Baseball's minor leagues, had held its annual meeting in Jacksonville on December 5, celebrating the success of 41 leagues that operated in 1941. Two days later the Japanese attacked Pearl Harbor. The number of white minor leagues dropped from 41 in 1941 to 30 in 1942. Only 10 leagues operated in 1943 and 1944.[17] As thousands volunteered or were drafted into the military, the number of available ball players became largely limited to those over 30 years of age or with physical conditions that deemed them unsuitable for service.

Gary Bedingfield's Baseball in Wartime web site lists two major leaguer players and about 150 minor leaguers who were killed during the war. In addition there were hundreds of other baseball players who died, described as semipro, college, high school, or other amateur players.[18] It was during the manpower shortage of World War II that one-armed Pete Gray was able to make his debut as a major league ball player.

Servicemen among the prominent names in black baseball included Monte Irvin, Larry Doby, Leon Day, Hank Thompson, Buck O'Neil, and Lyman Bostock.[19] Negro Southern League players who served included Dan Bankhead, Matthew "Lick" Carlisle, Elmer Carter, Marlin Carter, Howard Easterling, James "Pea" Greene, Paul Hardy, James "Red" Moore, Bill Perkins, Olan "Jelly" Taylor, Roy Wellmaker, and David "Speed" Whatley.[20]

Birmingham and Memphis remained constant members of the Negro American League throughout the war years. In fact, Birmingham became a dominant member of the league. With the arrival of such players as Piper Davis, Artie Wilson, Alonzo Boone, Jimmy Newberry, and Tommy Sampson, the Black Barons won pennants or strongly contended almost every year of the 1940s.

During the war years, all of the clubs had players called into service, often in midseason. There were also opportunities to pump up rosters with soldiers, too. For example, Lyman Bostock was stationed at Fort McClellan in Anniston, Alabama. If he had a weekend pass, he would join the Black Barons for those games.[21]

Gradually the Allied forces began to turn the tide of war. By the summer of 1943 they had cleared North Africa of German and Italian forces. A few weeks later Italian Dictator Benito Mussolini had been deposed and Allied troops were invading Italy.[22] On June 6, 1944, American, British, and Canadian forces landed on the beaches of Normandy, France and began pushing inland.

On the baseball front, by the spring of 1945 the number of white minor leagues had crept back up to 12.[23] That reflected a similar optimism in the black baseball community, where the final revival of the Negro Southern League was now imminent.

15

1945
The League Returns

In January 1945 Sam Brown wrote in the *Birmingham World* that "many baseball leaders are going ahead, making plans to keep the old pastime red hot." And this was despite the uncertainty of the war. Those preparations were being considered in the South as well. A meeting was scheduled on Sunday, February 4, at the Colored YMCA, 4th and Cedar Streets in Nashville to consider "the formation of a Negro Southern League."

Sam Parks of Little Rock and John Harden of Atlanta were reported to be interested in the league proposal. Representatives were also expected from Nashville, Knoxville, New Orleans, and at least one city in North Carolina.[1]

A month later another meeting was scheduled in Nashville to draw up a schedule, adopt a constitution, and discuss a possible working agreement with the Negro American League and Negro National League. The report from the Southern Newspaper Syndicate news service included a list of officers and likely representatives at the meeting: Dr. R. B. Jackson, president, Nashville Black Vols; Allen Page, vice-president, New Orleans; John H. Harden, treasurer, Atlanta Black Crackers; C. J. Kincaide, secretary, Knoxville; J. C. Chunn, director of public relations, Atlanta; Henry N. Lewis, Knoxville Black Smokies; James Cotton, Chattanooga Choo Choos; Sam Parks, Little Rock Greys; Clifford Matthews, New Orleans Black Pelicans; C. L. Moore, Asheville, North Carolina; and Willie Davis, Mobile Black Shippers.[2]

Opening Day was scheduled for Thursday, May 3, for an eight-team lineup.[3] The clubs and their managers were: the Asheville Blues, Moore; Atlanta Black Crackers, Felix Manning; Chattanooga Choo Choos, Cotton; Knoxville Grays, Lewis; Little Rock Greys, Charlie Burgs; Mobile Black Bears, Davis; Nashville Black Vols, Bill Perkins; and New Orleans Black Pelicans, Wesley Barrow.[4] The schedule called for each team to play 40 games in each half of the split season with a post-season playoff between the two winners.[5]

The Asheville Blues, under owner-manager C. L. Moore, had been an independent team for a number of years prior to World War II. When the team prepared for its home opener with Chattanooga, it was announced as a night game "in what is expected to be the largest crowd ever to attend a game" in Asheville. Dr. J. W. Holt, a prominent black physician, was selected to throw out the first pitch and music was provided by the Stevens Lee High School band.[6] The new NSL team would prove to be formidable during the season.

Atlanta had hired Manning as manager after he failed an Army physical exam and

A view, from the 1950s, of McCormick Field in Asheville, North Carolina. Then as in the 1940s, when the Blues played in the NSL, blacks sat in the segregated stands along the third base line (courtesy Bill Ballew).

was exempted from the draft. He announced that spring training would begin on March 23 in Florida.[7] J. C. Chunn, writing for the Southern Newspaper Syndicate, said the Black Crackers would be "the most brilliant ensemble of players ever assembled with an Atlanta professional team." Among the players impressive in camp were outfielders Spencer Alexander, Nathaniel Brannon, and Butch Davis, plus second baseman William "Bull" Howard and a shortstop named Williams.[8]

The Atlanta club was also bolstered by veterans of the Birmingham industrial league, a continuous source of good baseball players for decades. When the Black Crackers played the Baltimore Elite Giants in an exhibition game in Birmingham in April, it was reported that six former industrial league players would be in Atlanta uniforms: second baseman Howard, right fielder Freddie Shepard, catcher Harry Barnes, shortstop "Bozo" Jackson, third baseman "Neckbones" Davis, and pitcher-manager Manning.[9]

Chattanooga owner-manager Cotton's background was in the city's industrial league, where he had been manager of the Churchville Cubs for a number of years.[10] Among the players noted in early signings were shortstop Buster Lovinggood, first baseman "Lefty" Lawson, third baseman Ed Byron, and pitcher Sylvester "Pie" Silvers.[11]

Henry Lewis in Knoxville was also an owner-manager. He was building "a youthful team around the veteran Prim Hall, his field captain and first baseman."[12] The pitching staff was anchored by Gready McKinnis, a left-hander whose career stops would include several Negro League teams as well as a stint in the white minor leagues.[13] One writer said the Grays would "present the local fans with a club blazing with power in all departments."[14] The club was also reported to be a farm team for the Homestead Grays of the Negro National League.[15]

Although the first game was scheduled for a Sunday afternoon, the Knoxville club postponed its Opening Day ceremonies until the following Monday night, May 7. Participants included Professor C. W. Cansler, a longtime black teacher and community leader; NSL Secretary C. J. Kincaide; and the Knoxville city manager.[16]

Little Rock businessman Sam Parks, the team owner, hired veteran player Charlie Burgs as field manager.[17] The team announced a 38-game first-half schedule with 19 of the games to be played at Travelers Field, home of the white Southern Association team in Little Rock.[18] When the season opened with a doubleheader loss to New Orleans in early May, a local newspaper curiously said it was the team's first appearance on the field, whereas New Orleans had been playing for several weeks.[19]

Little Rock, would be replaced by Indianapolis during the season's second half. Other than the identities of owner Parks and manager Burgs, very little other information surfaced about the team, not even a definite team name. The Little Rock newspapers in sparse reports referred to it only as "Little Rock's entry" in the NSL. Both Greys [sic] and Black Travelers showed up in other league city's newspapers, with the latter getting the most mentions. Yet, it is not possible to discern if Black Travelers was really the team's name or if sportswriters simply appropriated a racial variation of the white Little Rock Travelers. Besides Burgs, only a pitcher named Joe Lewis was identified by both given and surname in any game report.

Mobile, under owner-manager Willie Davis, was initially referred to as the Black Shippers, then the Black Bears. Both the Shippers and Bears were names that had been used by white teams in that city and both the Black Bears and Black Shippers popped up from time to time during the season. The Mobile third baseman was William "Bobby" Robinson, reported to be the oldest player in league.[20] Born in the Whistler community near Mobile in 1903, Robinson's career as a premier Negro League third baseman started in 1922 and continued through 1942 with teams that included the Indianapolis ABCs, Birmingham Black Barons, and St. Louis Stars.[21] It would appear that he came out of retirement from his post-baseball career as a brick mason to play for the Black Bears.

Dr. R. B. Jackson, returning as league president, a position he had occupied before the war, was also owner of the Nashville club. Apparently unable to locate one of the players he wanted, he got a sports writer to include the following sentence in a column: "President Jackson of the Negro Southern League and owner of the Nashville Black Vols, is interested in having Catcher Bill Perkins call him collect."[22] It apparently worked, as Perkins was on the Nashville roster when the season began.

But the most notable player on the Nashville team was an infielder named James Gilliam. A native of Nashville, the 17-year-old quit school to sign with the Black Vols for $150 a month. He would move up from there to Baltimore Elite Giants and then follow in Jackie Robinson's footsteps, playing first with Montreal and then with the parent Brooklyn Dodgers. In 1953 He was the National League Rookie of the Year.[23]

New Orleans signed veteran Wesley Barron as manager. His primary pitcher was a left-hander named Frank "Groundhog" Thompson, who had reportedly won 28 of 30 games in local semipro baseball the previous year. "He is small of stature; but he has a fast ball that has plenty of hop on it and a curve that breaks as sharp as a needle point," proclaimed the *Louisiana Weekly*.[24] Strangely, New Orleans newspaper persisted in calling him Thomas throughout the season. In future seasons when he played with other teams, including the NNL's Homestead Grays, his surname was always given as Thompson. Most resources point to that as being the correct name.

Thompson's squat stature led to the nickname "Groundhog." Historian Jim Riley said the Grays Hall of Fame catcher Josh Gibson, cruelly referencing Thompson's hair lip, walleye and chipped tooth, put the pitcher on his "all-ugly" team. During a card game on the Grays team bus, Thompson and firstbaseman Luke Easter swapped accusations of cheating. When Easter threatened to hit Thompson, "Groundhog" pulled out a knife, promising to "cut you down to my size."[25] Thompson was the team's best pitcher and went on to play with the Birmingham Black Barons and Memphis Red Sox, in addition to Homestead.

A poll of 25 "widely known southern sports writers" predicted that Atlanta would be the likely winner of the new league's first pennant with New Orleans a close second. The others, in descending order, were predicted to be Chattanooga, Knoxville, Asheville, Nashville, and Little Rock. Somehow Mobile's finish was left out.[26] The season opened with Atlanta at Knoxville, Chattanooga at Asheville, Mobile at Nashville, and New Orleans at Little Rock. The Nashville game, scheduled for Thursday, May 3, was rained out. On Friday night Asheville swamped Chattanooga, 19–6. Both Atlanta and New Orleans won Sunday double-headers on the road. The second tier of home openers the following weekend saw Little Rock at Mobile, Asheville at Chattanooga, Nashville at Atlanta, and New Orleans at Knoxville.

Preparing for its home opener, the Atlanta club announced its intention of pulling 12,000 fans into Ponce de Leon Park. Club officials said such a crowd would show that Atlanta was the premier baseball city in the South, challenging such claims by Birmingham and New Orleans over the years.

"Years ago the 'front office' of the Black Crackers promised the fans of this city a first-class team second to none in America today. They kept that promise by bringing to you each year a better club and today is said to have the best club in history, barring none of the Black Cracker teams of the past," an SNS story out of the Georgia city proclaimed.[27]

In addition, the Atlanta management had gone to the top for its first pitch ceremony, asking Governor Ellis Arnall to do the honors. Arnall was described as "the youngest state chief executive in America, who has made a remarkable record in office with his liberal views and sympathetic attitude toward the Negro." The response from the governor's office is not known, but Arnall was not at the game. The first pitch was thrown out by NSL President R. B. Jackson to Negro National League President Tom Wilson. "Several widely known society matrons and debutants" were ushers.[28]

Opening Day in Atlanta happened to be Mother's Day, May 13, and the Booker T. Washington High School Band dedicated several selections to the mothers attending the game.[29]

Atlanta, Knoxville, Asheville, and Mobile won the second weekend of the season.

15. 1945: The League Returns

Opening Day in Mobile was a major event with the Negro Elks Club in charge of planning the ceremonies. Alex Herman, exalted ruler of the Elks, was to throw out the first pitch to B. F. Baker, principal of Mobile County Training School. The game was preceded by a parade featuring the St. Peter Claver and Mobile County Training School bands. The route was down Ann Street and Davis Avenue. Negro Boy Scouts were in charge of the flag raising.[30]

After two weeks of play the standings showed Asheville (6–1) on top, New Orleans (5–2) a game back, and Atlanta (5–3) a game and a half behind. Knoxville pitcher McKinnis was said to have pitched a no-hitter against New Orleans.

New Orleans (8–3), Atlanta (8–4), and Asheville (7–4) continued to be the strongest clubs as the third week of the season played out. Knoxville had a surge to tie Asheville for third place. Chattanooga, which had spent the first two weeks of the season in last place, showed signs of improvement. The *Mobile Press* reported that "James Cotton, owner of the Choo Choos and its fiery manager, is rebuilding his club and the weeks [sic] activity issued a warning to the pack that Chattanooga will be a potential threat all the way. Eight new players were added to the staff and several unconditional releases were given." The work of pitchers "Fireball" Franklin and "Pie" Silvers was said to have been a factor in the Chattanooga team's improvement.[31]

By the end of May there was a new league leader, with Knoxville (9–5). Standings published in the *Birmingham World* showed Atlanta (10–6) in second place and New Orleans (9–6) in third. However, there was an obvious typographical error in the standings because Asheville was omitted from the figures.[32] Knoxville had added a big bat to its lineup in early June, obtaining outfielder David T. Harper from the Kansas City Monarchs. Harper made a sensational debut on June 3 against Little Rock. He had four hits in four at-bats, three stolen bases, three runs batted in, and "some fancy ball shagging." Knoxville won the game, 18–3.[33]

Although baseball games were being played again, there was still a war going on. A June doubleheader between Chattanooga and Mobile raised $4,000 for the war bonds campaign.[34] When the Kansas City Monarchs played the Birmingham Black Barons in a Negro American League game in Nashville, it was reported that the Monarchs' shortstop would be Jackie Robinson, "recently discharged from the service after attaining the rank of lieutenant in the tank corps."[35] In Atlanta all wounded war veterans and Boy Scouts in uniform would be admitted free. To carry it a step further, the Black Crackers also said "all hopeless cripples" would also be admitted free.[36] The Knoxville Grays saw their roster weakened when star shortstop Johnny Richardson and first baseman Carl Williams were called into the Army.[37]

On Wednesday, June 6, Mobile beat Chattanooga, 6–5, in a 13-inning game. Harry Simpson, who pitched the entire game, squeezed in Walter Blackman, who had tripled, with the winning run.[38]

A three-team doubleheader, a common occurrence in black major league ball, was played in Knoxville on June 22. The Grays hosted the Mobile Black Bears in the first game, with the winner playing the Atlanta Black Crackers in the nightcap.[39] Fred Miller won a pitching duel with Claude Cruse as Knoxville won the first game, 4–2. The game was punctuated by an argument which required police "to make some of the Bear players leave the field." Atlanta took the second game, which was called an exhibition match, 10–3.[40]

A second three-team doubleheader was scheduled in August, with Asheville playing the Richmond Giants in the first game and the winner facing Knoxville in the nightcap.[41] There was no report on the outcome in the Knoxville papers.

Standings published in late June showed Atlanta in first place. The Black Crackers (21–7) were followed by Knoxville (17–8) and Asheville (12–10). The other five teams were all under .500. The standings were not balanced, however, as they total 95 wins and 98 losses.[42] J. C. Chunn, writing in the *Birmingham World*, reported that the first-half pennant race would likely not be determined until the final games. There were eight games left to play in the first half, but Knoxville had four rained-out games that could possibly be made up before the end of the split season.[43]

On June 30 Atlanta beat the Indianapolis Cardinals, an independent team, 1–0, in an exhibition game played in Columbus, Georgia. The same two teams, plus the Little Rock Black Travelers, played a three-team doubleheader at Ponce de Leon Park the following day.[44] Atlanta won both games, defeating Little Rock, 7–0, in the opener and edging Indianapolis, 6–5, in a 10-inning nightcap.[45] The two Indianapolis games were significant if only because they were precursors to the second half season, when the Cardinals would join the NSL.

There were number of managerial changes during the 1945 season. The earliest one came in late June at Chattanooga where the Choo Choos had struggled throughout the first half of the split season. Jim Cotton obtained former Kansas City Monarchs catcher "Doc" Wingo and turned the reins over to him. The local newspaper reported that Cotton "was forced to give up the manager's job because of heavy office work."[46]

Atlanta won the first half with wins over Little Rock during the final week, and announced that the club had scheduled a road trip to Pittsburgh in late July for a four-game series with the Homestead Grays. The team was also strengthened with the addition of several new players. Among them were first baseman Santiago Salazar, centerfielder Sidney Saucier, third baseman Joe Wiley, and shortstop Pedro Miro. All had been obtained from the New Orleans club. Salazar and Miro later played with the New York Cubans in the Negro National League.[47]

The final first-half standings, as released by the Associated Press, were:

Team	Won	Lost	Pct.
Atlanta	29	9	.763
Knoxville	25	10	.714
Asheville	15	13	.536
New Orleans	17	15	.531
Nashville	14	16	.467
Mobile	9	17	.346
Little Rock	9	22	.290
Chattanooga	7	23	.233[48]

The standings had been provided to the AP by league publicist Chunn, also a regional journalist. The 1945 season was a landmark for the NSL in that regard. Chunn wrote a weekly article on what had happened in the league the previous week, including standings. The final first-half standings, with balanced won-lost columns, indicate that 125 of the schedule 140 games were played. It is known that some games were rained out and on at least two occasions visiting teams missed games because of travel difficulties.

Chunn even monitored individual player statistics. In early July he released team and individual batting leaders as well as pitchers' records. New Orleans, in 19 games, had 149 hits in 628 at-bats for a .334 average. At the bottom was Little Rock with only 80 hits in 616 at-bats (.231) in the same number of games. New Orleans also held the top two spots among individuals, with Miro and Saucier hitting .556 and .500, respectively. Melvin "Slick" Coleman of Atlanta, with a perfect 7–0 record, was the leading pitcher.[49]

Chunn continued to provide standings throughout the second half of the season. They reflect the usual second-half malaise regarding league games, with many teams using the second half for lengthy barnstorming trips, as had been the case in the prewar NSL. The final first-half standings published on August 12 in the *Atlanta Daily World* and the *Mobile Press* show only 56 games having been played.

The second-half season was to start that day with Knoxville at Atlanta, Chattanooga at Little Rock, New Orleans at Asheville, and Mobile at Nashville. Asheville beat New Orleans, Nashville won two from Mobile and the Knoxville-Atlanta double-header was split. At Atlanta fans paid tribute to owner John Harden for bringing baseball back to the city and giving the fans a winning team.[50] There was no report on Chattanooga at Little Rock. However, the previous Thursday Chattanooga had lost at Knoxville, possibly in an exhibition game, by a score of 20–3. The team was reported to be on an exhibition tour the following week.

As the second half got under way there was one franchise shift. The New Orleans club, although a contender throughout the first half of play, had dropped out of the league. Replacing the Black Pelicans were the Indianapolis Cardinals, managed by Rainey Bibbs.

In July the new league team played an exhibition game in Birmingham. The contest drew a caustic review from Emory O. Jackson in the *Birmingham World*: "The game last Sunday between Indianapolis Cardinals and the Jacksonville Eagles was not a topprice promotion although the ticket cost that. Tom Hayes, Black Baron president, who promoted it, claims that he lost money. If he did, that was good for him. Fans who paid to see it lost money and time.

"The usual services that go with the baseball game at Rickwood were absent. The crowd was small and Jay Sims was not hired to announce the batting lineup from the public address system. No official scoring was made. These services were curtailed to cushion the cost. They would have cost no more than $10. Those charges should have been included in the promotion budget, no matter what the size of the turnout.

"If only one fan had attended the game, he was entitled to all of the services that 10,000 would have received. He should not be shackled with the loss of a bad promotion. Had $100,000 been made he would have received no more than what Rickwood promotions calls for. Fans are the only ones who can do anything about this because they foot the bill.

"Incidentally, the Cardinals won both games, 19 to 1 and 4 to 0."[51]

By late July there had been a second franchise change. It was reported that Richmond, Virginia, was replacing Little Rock. "...difficulties with the Little Rock baseball park forced Sam Parks to move his franchise to the Virginia metropolis where fans have assured their whole hearted support," reported the *Daily World*.[52]

The NSL had a presence in Richmond during the first half of the season, with Atlanta and Nashville playing a league game at Mooers Field, home park of the city's white minor league team, on June 19.[53] The Richmond Cardinals, apparently an independent team, played occasional games at Mooers Field, including one against the Baltimore Elite Giants in June.[54] However, the *Richmond Times-Dispatch* never mentioned the local team replacing Little Rock in the NSL. In fact, Little Rock played a three-game series with the Mobile club in Richmond on July 22–23. Little Rock won the Sunday doubleheader by scores of 18–9 and 2–1.[55] There was no report on the Monday game.

On July 26, another NSL games was played in Richmond, this one between Chattanooga and Nashville.[56] On August 5, the *Times-Dispatch* carried a set of standings that showed Richmond in the league and in last place with a record of 1–11.

Still making no reference to Richmond being in the Negro Southern League, the Richmond newspaper reported on August 10 that the Cardinals would play the Vero Beach, Florida, Pelicans in a Saturday game. But, the next day Vero Beach was schedule to play the Norfolk, Virginia, Eagles.[57] The final mention of the Cardinals was on August 17 when it was reported the team would played a three-game weekend series with the Atlanta Black Crackers.[58] There was no report on the outcome of those games.

In none of the stories pertaining to the Cardinals was there any mention of the Negro Southern League. Also, no Richmond manager or player was identified in any of the articles.

Whatever the situation in Richmond, black baseball was not totally gone from Little Rock. In August the Black Travelers, apparently surviving as an independent team, played a series of games in Mobile.[59] That same month they were also scheduled to play a local semipro team at the House of David ball park in St. Joseph, Michigan.[60]

The first published standings for the second half showed Chattanooga, which had struggled during the first half, in the lead. The Choo Choos were undefeated after seven games. Asheville (6–1) was second with Nashville (5–2) and Atlanta (5–2) tied for second. The two new teams, Indianapolis and Richmond, were near the bottom of the standings.[61]

The Choo Choos, perhaps borrowing a page from the showmanship handbook of the white Lookouts owner Joe Engel, put a girl on the mound in their July 17 game against Little Rock. Georgia Mae Williams—a five-foot, six-inch, 105 pounds player—started the game and struck out the first Little Rock batter. She was then replaced by "Junior" Isabella, who pitched Chattanooga to an 18–10 win.[62]

By early August, Nashville (12–3) had moved into first place, followed by Atlanta (9–3). The Black Crackers returned from their Pennsylvania trip with a split in two games with the Homestead Grays. C. L. Moore's Ashville Blues (11–5) were still in contention, also, followed by Knoxville (5–4) and Chattanooga (7–7). Indianapolis (2–7) and Richmond (1–11) had managed only three combined wins in 21 league games, putting them in a struggle with Mobile (1–8) for last place.[63]

Atlanta obviously had been helped by the Cuban players obtained from New Orleans. When Atlanta played the Cincinnati-Indianapolis Clowns of the Negro American League in an exhibition game at Ponce de Leon Park, there were a number of Cubans on both sides. Commenting on their excellent play, sports writer Joel W. Smith speculated that the tropical climate gave Cubans more opportunity to hone their skills. "The most interesting thing about the Cubans, however, is the fact that many of them don't seem to go in for learning the English language, except for a few baseball terms. So, with the large number of Cubans being imported from the islands each year, it may be wise for baseball managers to take a course in Spanish."[64]

The first weekend in August, Atlanta and Nashville squared off in a series at Sulphur Dell. Atlanta shut out the Black Vols in every game, thus regaining first place.[65] J. C. Chunn speculated that "the Atlanta baseball juggernaut" seemed likely to win the season's second half as well. The series sweep dropped Nashville to third place while Asheville moved into second going into a series in Atlanta.[66] Only one game of that series appears to have been played. Behind the four-hit pitching of right-hander Robert Bowman, the Blues won, 3–0. Bowman struck out six, outdueling Melvin "Slick" Coleman. Despite the loss, Atlanta clung to a slim lead in the pennant race.[67] Despite the excellent baseball the Atlanta team had been playing, management made a field leadership change in mid–August. Owner John Harden announced that pitcher Brennan King would replace Felix Manning as manager. King, one of the team's best pitchers, had been athletic director and head football coach at North Carolina A & T College in Greensboro.[68] There was no reason given for Manning's termination except that the club "wanted more aggressive leadership." However, Emory O. Jackson reported in his "Hits and Bits" column in the *Birmingham World* that Manning was fired "when the boss lost a big bet when his team lost to Knoxville 7-to-6 on August 5 in Knoxville."[69] Whether or not that claim is true, it is fraught with errors. On August 5, Atlanta was at Nashville and Chattanooga was at Knoxville.

At any rate, Manning apparently landed on his feet. He was reported to be managing the Chattanooga team by the end of the season.[70]

The announcement of Manning's firing came as the Black Crackers were winding up a three-week barnstorming trip through Virginia and North Carolina.[71] Atlanta, still clinging to a small lead, returned home to face the Knoxville Grays. The Grays and the Asheville Blues were both still in a position to win the second half flag.[72]

The two-game series saw not only the debut of King as Atlanta manager but also the return of Knoxville manager Henry N. Lewis to the Gate City. Lewis had previously managed the Black Crackers. He brought with him for the series James "Red" Moore, a popular Atlanta player who had just been discharged from the Army. Lewis reportedly signed the Atlanta favorite to a two-year contract.[73]

King made his managerial debut on Sunday, August 26, in a 7–4 win over Knoxville at Ponce de Leon Park. Will Thompson scattered eight hits as the Black Crackers moved closer to the second-half pennant.[74]

On Tuesday night at Montgomery King pitched Atlanta to a 5–1 win over Knoxville, setting up the final game of the series in Atlanta on Wednesday, August 29.

Knoxville finally got a victory, scoring twice in the second inning. The big blow was a triple by Leonard Kendricks. Atlanta got a run in the fifth but was unable to do more against James Mitchell's pitching. He gave up only four hits and struck out seven. Will Thompson pitched well in a losing effort, giving five hits and striking out eight.[75]

While Atlanta had taken two out of three from one of the other contenders, the *Daily World* on Thursday, August 30, reported that the Black Crackers needed both games of a Sunday-Monday series with Indianapolis to clinch the second-half pennant. Atlanta was said to have a record of 13–3 in the second half.[76]

But on Sunday the Atlanta paper made no mention of Indianapolis, but rather a two-game series with the Philadelphia Hilldale Giants club on the same dates. It did reference Atlanta winning two of three from Knoxville "to practically seal-off the second half crown."[77] Hilldale was a member of the United States League, which had been organized by Brooklyn Dodgers President Branch Rickey and Gus Greenlee, owner of the Pittsburgh Crawfords. The league functioned for two years, 1945 and 1946. The Black Crackers were listed as a member of the league before the 1945 season began, but in actuality never left the Negro Southern League. Hilldale, which does not appear to have any connection to the Hilldale team of the 1920s and 1930s, won the Sunday game, 1–0, behind the pitching of Richard "Lefty" Mimms. On Monday Alonzo Perry carried a no-hitter into the seventh inning as Atlanta won, 4–2. Hilldale, continuing its Southern tour, split a doubleheader with Asheville the following Sunday.[78]

With still no further reportage on the NSL, the Atlanta club next faced the barnstorming Harlem Globetrotters. After losing, 2–1, at Ponce de Leon Park, the Black Crackers joined the Globetrotters on a barnstorming tour in Texas.[79]

While Atlanta was in Texas, Hilldale returned to Ponce de Leon to play the Pittsburgh Crawfords in a game that was said to have a bearing on the USL pennant race. The winner would then face the Black Crackers when they returned from Texas.[80] The Crawfords won, but Atlanta's foes after the trip were the Tuskegee Army Air Field Warhawks, Birmingham Black Barons, and a nondescript all-star team.[81]

Since Atlanta won both halves of the split season, there was no post-season playoff for the southern title or with the champion of another league.

It is regrettable that not a single box score was found for a 1945 Negro Southern League game. Babe Lawson of Chattanooga appeared to be a formidable power hitter with a number of home runs credited in game accounts. The use of line scores, supplemented by information from some game stories, has enabled the author to compile workable pitching records.

Statistically, there is probably less information available on the 1945 season than any other in the Negro Southern League. No box scores were published, and even line scores were scarce and often incomplete. Indeed, coverage was so sparse that not a single pitcher's name is available for either or the Little Rock or Richmond clubs. The pittance of information available from the line scores and game accounts shows two Atlanta pitchers as the top winners. John Sadler was 6–0 with two shutouts. Melvin Coleman was 6–3. George Franklin of Knoxville was 5–0 with one shutout; Fred Miller of Knoxville was 4–1 with one shutout while Pie Silvers of Chattanooga won four games and lost as many.

A series of all-star games followed the regular season. One, organized by Gus Greenlee and Atlanta owner John Harden, was scheduled for September 16 at Ebbets Field, home of the Brooklyn Dodgers. A North team, managed by Webster McDonald, would be comprised of players from the United States Baseball League. The South team, managed by Henry Lewis, would feature players from the Negro Southern League.[82] However, the *Chicago Defender* reported that the proposed game was canceled when Dr. R. B. Jackson, NSL president, said his league would not participate.

"The Negro Southern League does not endorse any North vs South All-Star baseball game with the United States league," Jackson told the newspaper's sports editor. "The

15. 1945: The League Returns

Southern league will not be affiliated in any way in any all-star attraction with the United States league. Any club holding a franchise as member of the Negro Southern League participating in any way with such an attraction will be fined $2,500 and suspended from the league."

Jackson, in making his vehement statement to the *Defender*, added that the NSL had working agreements with the Negro American League and the Negro National League, the USL's competitors. He said there was a possibility of an all-star game within the structure of those agreements.[83] Another all-star game was organized by Birmingham Black Barons owner Tom Hayes. Also scheduled for September 16, but at Rickwood Field in Birmingham, the game matched a team of NSL all-stars against a Birmingham city industrial league team. Hayes said if the local all-stars won, he would give them another game against the Black Barons the following Sunday. The NSL team, which included a few players from independent southern teams, was managed by C. L. Moore of Asheville. He presented a starting lineup of

Art Haeffer, Asheville, cf
Jim Gilliam, Nashville 3b
J. Price, Louisville Black Caps, 2b
George Lawrence, Chattanooga, 1b
Rainey Bibbs, Indianapolis, c
T. Williams, Little Rock, rf
Frank Russell, Nashville, lf
Rufus Heden, Asheville, c

His pitchers included Edward Derricks, Nashville; Waldo Dunlap, Asheville; P. Johnson, Little Rock; and Nathan Owens, Nashville.

Ed Bynum of Chattanooga was the utility man and Judge Owens of Nashville was assistant coach.[84]

Despite the prominent promotion, it is unclear if the games were played. There was no report in the Birmingham newspapers the following day. When the Black Barons returned to Birmingham, they played games with the Chicago American Giants, New York Black Yankees, and New York Cubans. There was no mention of a game with the industrial league team.

Another all-star game was held in Mobile on Sunday, September 30. This one featured a South team composed of Mobile players, supplemented by others from New Orleans; Gulfport, Mississippi; Pensacola, Florida; and Birmingham. The North team was composed of players from the Cincinnati-Indianapolis Clowns, Kansas City Monarchs, and other Negro American League teams.[85] Apparently rained out, the game was rescheduled for Tuesday, October 2. There was no report in the Mobile newspaper on the outcome, if the game was finally played.

16

1946
Boom Times

Rejuvenated by a reasonably successful season (six of eight teams made it all the way through to the end), a booming post-war economy, and burgeoning manpower from returning military veterans, the Negro Southern League looked to the 1946 season.

Returning 1945 teams were Asheville, Chattanooga, Knoxville, Mobile, and Nashville. A New Orleans club, this time the Creoles, not the Black Pelicans, was mentioned as a possible member. Prospective members from pre-war years were Evansville, Jacksonville, and Montgomery. A likely newcomer was Charlotte, an independent that had played NSL teams often in exhibition games the previous year. Other cities mentioned during the organizational phase were Atlanta; Durham, North Carolina; Helena, Arkansas; Louisville; Pine Bluff, Arkansas; and Winston-Salem, North Carolina.[1]

Evansville, in fact, appeared to be a locked-in member, having been granted a franchise in a December 1945 meeting. However, league President R. B. Jackson called a special meeting in early February to reconsider the Evansville offer because the club had "declared itself unable to meet league obligations." It was also announced that Jackson would attend the joint meeting of the Negro National League and Negro American League in New York on February 20–21 to seek a working agreement for the coming season.[2]

One league official from the 1945 season was lost during the off-season. J.C. Chunn, the Atlanta sports writer whose byline had often appeared on standings and weekly summaries of NSL activity, died after a lengthy illness. Lamenting his loss, the *Chicago Defender* reported: "He could pick more All American players on Morris Brown and Clark from the start of the season than any publicity man in college football. And sometimes Chunn was right.... He was instrumental in getting the *Atlanta Constitution*, a daily newspaper, to donate a huge trophy for the one-mile college relay at the annual Tuskegee relays. Each year we looked for a reunion with our friend "from Georgia." The Peach Blossom Classic was his idea. He had many. "From one end of the South to the other, from Georgia to Texas, Chunn was known to coaches and players alike. He will be missed. He surely will."[3]

Finally, a lineup of eight teams and four associate members was announced. The league members were the Asheville Blues, Charlotte Black Hornets, Chattanooga Choo Choos, Jacksonville Eagles, Knoxville Giants, Mobile Black Bears, Montgomery Dodgers, and Nashville Cubs. The four associate members were the Atlanta Black Crackers, the 1945 champions; Louisville Black Colonels; Pine Bluff Black Cats; and Winston-Salem Grays.[4]

League officers were Jackson, Nashville, president; C. L. Hyatte, Knoxville, vice president; C.L. Moore, Asheville, N.C., treasurer; and C. J. Kincaide, Knoxville, secretary/public relations.[5]

In early May a special meeting was called in Nashville to reconsider the petitions of Atlanta and Louisville for NSL membership. A brief item in the *Defender* said both had been voted into the league.[6] However, while Atlanta played a number of games against the other NSL teams, none were found for Louisville. That item, plus subsequent mentions of Atlanta as a pennant-contender, which it could not have been if an associate members, suggests the league may have operated with nine teams. An odd number of teams in a league is unusual, but then there were many oddities about scheduling and lineups in the NSL. No standings were located to specify Atlanta's position.

When Atlanta hosted Knoxville for a May 26 opener, Joel W. Smith wrote in the *Birmingham World* that the Black Crackers had "their eyes focused on their second straight championship." Owner John Harden started with Brennan L. King pitching and managing the team, then made a change. He hired Bill "Skipper" Yancey, a veteran shortstop who had played with the New York Black Yankees, Philadelphia Stars and other teams and had also coached for several years in the Republic of Panama.[7]

In Asheville, owner-manager Moore mailed out 40 contracts to prospective players. By early March he had nine signed documents back. Among the signees were catcher Rufus Hatten, pitcher Robert Bowman, and outfield Arthur Hefner.[8]

Charlotte, under manager Sam Douglas, prepared for its first league season by signing former NSL players John Sadler and "Early Bird" Ellison.[9] Melvin "Slick" Coleman was the manager. While the team played respectable baseball during the season, coverage was sparse in the local press, usually a paragraph or two before and after the games. Reporting pretty much ceased after a mid–June series with Atlanta. No other leagues games were reported, just an exhibition game with the Washington Black Yankees in early July and one with a semipro team near the end of the month.

Will McClure, vice president of the Chattanooga club, announced in early February that Felix Manning, who had joined the team late in the 1945 season after earlier leading Atlanta to the first-half pennant, would be manager. The team would begin spring training in Florida on March 15. Early signees included catcher Harry Barnes, pitcher Alonzo Perry, and infielder James "Neck Bones" Davis. Perry and Davis had been regulars on the previous year's championship Atlanta club.[10] As it turned out, Davis was a holdout and eventually signed with Atlanta.[11]

Carl "Bubber" Ford, owner of the Jacksonville Eagles, announced that his manager would be veteran third baseman Harry Jeffries, whose career had started in 1920. The field captain would be shortstop Leroy "Phillie" Holmes.[12]

Knoxville, represented by the Grays in 1945, had resumed the Giants name. The new team had purchased the Atlanta Black Crackers franchise, although an Atlanta team with that name continued to play independently. C. L. Hyatte, vice president and business manager, announced that the field manager would be Nat Rogers, the former Memphis outfielder, now in his third decade of Negro League baseball.[13]

Montgomery, operating under the nickname of Dodgers, had signed as its manager veteran pitcher Ernest "Spoon" Carter. Owner John Whatley had to make a change in that nickname before the season was too far along, however.[14]

A staggered Opening Day was scheduled beginning with Knoxville at Asheville on

The 1946 Chattanooga Choo Choos managed by Felix "Chaser" Manning. Willie Mays may have played a few games for them on weekends (courtesy Faye Davis and Birmingham Public Library Archives).

May 1. The Blues would then move to Charlotte for the Hornets' opener. Three other openers were scheduled on May 5 with Montgomery at Chattanooga, Mobile in Jacksonville, and Knoxville in Nashville.[15]

Asheville, Jacksonville, and Chattanooga all opened with great success. The Blues pounded Knoxville, 11–4 and 13–4, then took a doubleheader from Charlotte. Jacksonville won one game and tied one with Mobile. Chattanooga won three straight from Montgomery.

Montgomery spent an inordinate amount of time on the road before having a home game. Their first home series was to be against Asheville, but the first two games were played in Anniston, Alabama, with the third in Gadsden, Alabama. The fourth game, finally scheduled in Montgomery, was rained out. Montgomery was then to host Nashville, but the first two games of the series were played in Selma, Alabama.[16]

The Atlanta management announced that the club would begin spring training on March 15 under manager/pitcher King. Other returning players included John Sadler, Lomas "Butch" Davis, Alonzo Perry, and Nathaniel Brannon. A major newcomer would be Sammy Haynes, veteran catcher with the Kansas City Monarchs. There was no mention of league affiliation.[17]

Atlanta subsequently "opened" its season on May 26 with a doubleheader win over Knoxville before a crowd estimated at 5,000. Robert Branson pitched a five-hit, 3–1, win in the first game and King threw a one-hitter in the second, 2–1, game.[18]

Asheville opened at home against Knoxville, winning 11–4, then adding a 13–4 win the following night. Attorney George Pennell made "a brief speech" and Dr. L. O. Miller, "one of Asheville's outstanding colored physicians," threw out the first pitch in pregame ceremonies. Knoxville manager Nat Rogers hit a homerun and a double among four hits for the visitors in the first game while Spencer Alexander and Nathaniel Brannon each had three hits for the Blues. In the second game, Asheville's Arthur Hefner and Fred Worthy each had three hits.[19] The *Knoxville News-Sentinel* indicated that the Giants might have been handicapped by the fact that two players had been "called home due to illness in their families."[20] Local businesses contributed a number of gifts for outstanding performances. For example, a restaurant offered five dollars for the first home run, another offered five dollars to the first pitcher striking out eight batters. Prizes were also offered for no-hit games, triple plays, and other accomplishments.[21] There was no report on who the prize winners were in the game report the next day.

Advance stories in the newspaper before almost every game noted "a special section of the stands will be reserved for white fans."[22]

Before Knoxville returned home to open its home season against those same Blues, it was reported that the team's management, "noticing that their infield is shot to pieces, sent an urgent S.O.S. to the Memphis Red Sox, appealing for some first class ball players."[23] Apparently Memphis answered the call. New first baseman Robert Boyd (called Bowen in the article) and second baseman George Handy "performed well both afield and at bat" as the Giants split a doubleheader at Nashville, dropping the first game, 4–2, but winning the second on George "Fireball" Franklin's 2–0 shutout.[24]

Boyd would prove to be a major addition to the club. He played for four years, then became the first black player to sign with the Chicago White Sox. He made his major league debut in 1951 and had a nine-year career in the big leagues.[25]

Manager Rogers was reported to be batting .800 prior to the home opener.[26] How he did in the game is not known, but Asheville spoiled the opener, 7–6. Knoxville city officials participated in the pregame ceremonies with City Manager Bill Lockwood batting and another official, C.W. Cansler, pitching.[27]

Although Knoxville was struggling in May, the team received some very uncommon coverage from one of the local newspapers. The *Knoxville News-Sentinel* carried box scores on two games with the Atlanta Black Crackers and ran a feature story on the team, along with photos of catcher Babe Fine, outfielder John Armstrong, and Rogers. A club official was quoted as saying Rogers, at 52 years old, was the oldest active player in the country.

According to the article, Rogers had never hit under .300 in his 19-year career. His high mark was reported to have been .419 with Memphis in 1938. He was also credited with a 31-game hitting streak while playing with the Chicago American Giants. "Although he is still very active in the outfield Rogers' 51 years is beginning to creep up on him and he doesn't play in every game. However, fans can expect to see him either in the outfield or on the coaching lines," the article stated.[28] A few days later, Rogers was the winning pitcher in the second game of a doubleheader against Mobile. The article did not specify if he started the game or pitched in relief.[29]

In August Knoxville celebrated Rogers' fifty-third birthday in conjunction with Emancipation Day ceremonies before a doubleheader with Asheville. Emancipation Day was a holiday celebrated the first week in August in the British West Indies, the Caribbean, and certain sections of the United States. It drew its origin from the Slavery Abolition Act of 1833 that ended slavery in the British Empire. The program was sponsored by the West Tennessee Valley Lodge No. 1152 of the Benevolent and Protective Order of Elks. Ticket prices were announced as grandstand, ninety cents; box seats, thirty cents; bleachers, sixty cents; and children, thirty cents.[30]

Nashville officials trotted out a new wrinkle on the now not uncommon three-team doubleheader in May. The card for Sunday, May 26, featured an opening doubleheader between Charlotte and Mobile. The winner was then to play the local Nashville team in a pair of Monday night games. In the event of a split between Charlotte and Mobile, Nashville would play each team on Monday night.[31] Although Charlotte won both games, Nashville still wound up playing a game against each team on Monday. Nashville's Edward Derrick pitched a shutout in a 4–0 win over Charlotte in the first game and teammate "Bullet" Johnson won the second game against Mobile, 4–1.[32]

Chattanooga started fast, challenging Asheville for first place. The two teams seesawed for several weeks with the Choo Choos finally surging ahead in a doubleheader sweep in late May. Pie Silvers threw a five-hit shut in a 2–0 win. Then, Ernest Long won the nightcap, 2–1, limiting Asheville to a single hit.[33]

But C. L. Moore's Blues quickly got back out front and remained that way. In June the Blues scored 78 runs in four days. The beat the independent Greenville, South Carolina, Black Spinners, 20–4, on June 6. On June 8 they defeated the Spartanburg, South Carolina, Sluggers, 12–2. Returning to league competition on Sunday, Asheville staggered the Montgomery Dodgers with back-to-back 24–0 and 22–0 wins. The Blues had 41 hits and both Frank Flemming and Vernon Phillips pitched no-hit games. Flemming truck out eleven in the first game and Phillips seven in the second. Infielder Herman Taylor hit two home runs and Phillips also hit one. Of the games in which accounts are available, there never was a more decisively won pair in NSL history.[34]

The Blues gave a similar hitting performance in July and August. In July they won league games from Atlanta, 15–7, and Jacksonville, 16–6. That was followed by wins over two more semipro teams, the Martinsville, Virginia, Black Cardinals (14–0) and the Maple Stars (20–5).[35]

A July 31–August 3 series with Montgomery saw the Blues outscore that team 77–39. The scores were 13–6, 15–11, 15–6, 25–11, and 9–5. The line scores are incomplete, but in the third game Montgomery was outhit 28–16.[36]

Asheville's pitching staff was outstanding. In addition to Phillips and Flemming, the Blues had Robert Bowman and Waldo Dunlap. Bowman, a right-hander, had 16 strikeouts in a 13–0 win over Charlotte. Outfielders Fred Worthy and A. C. Neeley had numerous multiple-hit games. Neeley, who also had good power, hit a home run in an exhibition game that "cleared the rightfield bank and finally stopped near the foot of the light pole on top of the hill."[37]

Montgomery, playing just so-so, had a major off-the-field change in early June. The strong Birmingham Black Barons of the Negro American League came to town on June 12 for a game at Hornet Stadium on the Alabama State Teachers College campus. With no explanation for the change, the *Montgomery Advertiser* reported that Birmingham would be playing the Montgomery Red Sox. The change was apparently sudden, because in the pregame story about the contest, the writer referred to Montgomery as the Dodgers.[38]

One can surmise that Montgomery owner John Whatley sought to capitalize on the national attention being accorded Jackie Robinson after he was signed by the Brooklyn Dodgers. That being assumed, one could further assume that Brooklyn officials were not interested in sharing their unique nickname and told the Montgomery owner as much.

Sometimes other events affected Negro Southern League games. Montgomery and Knoxville pledged the proceeds of a Saturday night game at Caswell Park in Knoxville to the United Negro College Fund. "Players of both teams are giving their services," it was reported. Knoxville College was one of 33 historically black colleges and universities benefitting from the campaign.[39] Unfortunately the benefit game was rained out.[40]

A June Knoxville home game was tailored to fit a happening in another sport, boxing.

It was announced that the Giants game with Chattanooga would begin at 7 p.m. an hour earlier than usual. The early start was "to allow fans ample time to witness the games and get back to their radios to listen to the Joe Louis–Billy Conn fight."[41] The fight was a seminal event in boxing history, not only a rematch of two great fighters, but also the first heavyweight championship fight ever televised. An estimated 146,000 people saw the telecast.[42] The ABC broadcast was to begin at 9 p.m. for the bout at Yankee Stadium in New York.[43] In six Knoxville home games for which box scores are available, the time of single games was a little over two hours. Thus fans likely would have been home by 9:30 p.m. Given the usual pre-fight preliminaries, they would have been able to catch the main event. It did not matter, however, as the game was rained out.[44]

A frequent added attraction at a number of NSL and other games during the 1946 season was a running exhibition by Olympic track sensation Jesse Owens. Sometimes Owens raced the fastest ball players, but more often was matched against a horse in an event staged before the game. Most of Owens' appearances were paired with the travels of the Cincinnati Crescents independent team.[45]

On June 23, two NSL teams participated in a four-team doubleheader at Yankee Stadium in New York. The Nashville Cubs scored seven runs in the bottom of the ninth inning to defeat the Jacksonville Eagles, 12–11, in the first game. In the second, the Baltimore Elite Giants defeated the New York Black Yankees, 11–3, in a Negro National League game. The attendance at the June 23 games was reported as 12,000.[46]

The following Sunday a similar NSL/NNL doubleheader was held at the Polo Grounds, home of the New York Giants. In the first game Atlanta defeated Montgomery, 14–4. In the second game the New York Cubans beat Baltimore, 4–1. Another crowd of 12,000 saw the games.[47]

A Fourth of July doubleheader at Yankee Stadium saw Asheville pound out a 15–8 win over the Boston Giants, an independent team, and the Newark Eagles defeated the New York Black Yankees, 3–1. Three Asheville batters—Taylor, Nathaniel Brannon, and Edward Byron—each had three hits in three at-bats in the game.[48]

While on that eastern swing the Blues played at least two white teams. They lost a 6–5 game to the Madison, New Jersey, Kernels, "before 2,575 paying customers." A. C. Neeley hit a 400-foot triple to drive in one Asheville run. There was no report on a game against a white team in Pittman, New Jersey.[49]

Jacksonville's participation in the New York doubleheader was part of an extensive road trip that started June 18 and continued for about a month. All of the games on the trip would be exhibitions except for a selected few with Nashville.[50] The team returned home with a new manager, Harry Jeffries, for a series with Knoxville on July 21.[51]

In late June and early July the Black Crackers went on an exhibition tour with the independent Cincinnati Crescents, managed by Winfield Welch, who had lead Birmingham to NAL championships in 1943 and 1946. Games were played in large venues such as Montgomery, Birmingham, Nashville, Atlanta, and Knoxville, but also in small towns like Lanett, Alabama.[52]

Asheville was apparently the first-half winner of the 1946 season, although sports writer Joel W. Smith lamented the fact that the NSL "has not released to the press the official standings of the various teams comprising the loop." Smith said Asheville finished the first half "well out front" although challenged by a hustling Chattanooga team.[53] The *Asheville Citizen* reported that the local team had clinched the first half with a doubleheader win over Mobile on June 30. Asheville pitching was surprisingly weak, giving up 10 runs and 20 hits in the two games. However, Asheville batters more than made up for the pitching lapse, scoring 25 runs on 25 hits in the 8–2 and 17–8 wins.[54]

In July it was announced that the Blues had been selected for the "seventh annual All-Star game" to be played on August 4 at Memorial Stadium in Greensboro. The Blues would face a Southern All-Star team selected "by popular vote. It was not clear if the all-star team was from the NSL or from a semipro league in which a number of North Carolina cities were members."[55] An advertisement in the *Norfolk Journal and*

Guide listed the Asheville opponent as "South's Selected All-Stars." In conjunction with the game was a "Pin-Up Girl Contest" with the winner receiving a free trip to New York.[56]

As it turned out, the all-star team was selected from among semipro clubs. Bowman pitched a two-hitter as Asheville won the game, 1–0. Both all-star hits were by Dave Campbell, shortstop for the Winston-Salem Pond Giants.[57]

The Nashville Cubs and Mobile Black Bears paired up for an Eastern and Midwestern tour in July.[58] In the season's first half Montgomery had similarly teamed with the Birmingham Black Barons for a tour, playing in Gadsden and Jackson, Mississippi, as well as Birmingham and Montgomery. In the game at Rickwood Field, Birmingham won, 8–2, with future major leaguer Artie Wilson collecting four hits. For Montgomery, outfielder Fred Sims had two doubles against Bill Powell.[59]

In another unusual second-half doubleheader, Asheville and Jacksonville played an afternoon game at Morganton, North Carolina, and a night game in Asheville. The afternoon game was tied, 8–8, after nine innings. It was halted at that point to allow the teams to make about a 50-mile journey to Asheville for the night game, which the Blues won, 4–3.[60]

Asheville continued to play well in the second half but found a more challenging race as Chattanooga, Atlanta, and Jacksonville all played well, also.[61] Joel W. Smith wrote that the season was memorable for the number of outstanding players in the league:

> The pitchers have been particularly impressive, and are far too numerous to mention, yet special honors go to "Big" Bob Bowman, of Asheville; Bob Branson, of Atlanta; and Sylvester Silvers, of Chattanooga. The league is also well stocked with fine catchers, which includes Harry Barnes, of Chattanooga; Rufus Hatten, of Asheville; "Early Bird" Ellison and William Cooper, of Atlanta. For all-around play and consistency, Thomas "Monk" Favors is the outstanding first baseman of the year, with honorable mention going to George Lawson, of Chattanooga, and Boyd, of Knoxville. At second, Dusty Owens, of Atlanta, Ennis Williams, of Chattanooga, and Harris of Jacksonville take the spotlight. Sterling Talley, of Chattanooga, is without a doubt the best shortstop in loop, with Johnnie Richardson, of Knoxville, in second place. At third base, Herman Taylor, of Asheville, gets my vote, followed by Ulyssess Wilkes of Chattanooga, and Denard of Jacksonville. Goins, of Asheville, is tops in leftfield; with honorable mention going to Lomax "Butch" Davis, Atlanta's sensational slugger. In centerfield, David T. Harper, of Atlanta, shares the spotlight with Armstrong, of Nashville. A. C. Neeley, of Asheville, wins the rightfield post by a landslide, with Washington, of Jacksonville taking second place.[62]

The Asheville team was so good, especially at bat, that appreciative fans held an Asheville Blues Night for the final home game against Jacksonville. "Under the sponsorship of Dr. J. W. Holt, one of the city's leading colored physicians, fans have made contributions to a fund for the Blues and the entire proceeds of the drive, including receipts from tonight's game, will be divided evenly between the Blues' players," reported the *Asheville Citizen*.[63] The Blues won both ends of a day-night doubleheader. There was no report on the fund drive, but it seems likely the players received a substantial pay day.

Atlanta played well in the second half, also, holding the lead until early September when a series with Asheville changed the standings. Atlanta blew a two-game lead, dropping all four games to the Blues. Asheville won the first game, 10–8, at Atlanta. The following night the Blues held a 2–1 lead when Atlanta pitcher Roosevelt Davis was ejected "for using an illegal pitch." The Atlanta players left the field in protest and the umpire subsequently awarded Asheville a forfeit win.[64]

The next day Asheville took over first place by winning a 3–2 afternoon game at Morganton and a 5–1 night game at McCormick Field, the Blues home field shared with the white minor league Asheville Tourists. In the night game Bowman struck out 12 Atlanta batters.[65]

There were not nearly as many reports of rowdy behavior in NSL games in 1946 as there had been in some previous seasons. Still, there were occasional problems such as the Atlanta incident above. League President Jackson announced in July that he had levied fines of $25 each on Jacksonville players Taylor and Lamar "for an attack on Base Umpire Patton."[66]

Although the pennant race was not decided until mid–September, Nashville apparently ended its season early. The *Nashville Banner* reported that the Cubs would "conclude their 1946 play at Sulphur Dell" on September 1 against a local independent team.[67] The Cubs played a final series at Asheville afterward, but none of the usual post-season exhibition games against visiting teams from the North and Midwest.

The NSL season came to a close in mid–September when the Asheville Blues took both ends of a doubleheader with Knoxville, thus locking up the second half. It was the second year in a row that the same team had won both halves of the split season. In the opener Will Thompson held Knoxville to five hits in a 5–2 win. In the nightcap, Knoxville jumped out to a seven-run lead in the first two innings. Asheville chipped away at the lead, finally winning, 8–7. The follow day Waldo Dunlap pitched the Blues to a 9–5 win and the regular season came to a close.[68]

Moore's Asheville team, which had challenged Atlanta in 1945, dominated play in 1946. The Blues finished the first half with a record of 23–5 and the second with 25–7, winning 16 consecutive league games at the end. They concluded their season with a doubleheader against NAL runner-up Birmingham at Rickwood Field in October. Asheville's combined first and second-half record of 48–12 gave a remarkable winning percentage of .800 in league games.[69] The team's record in non-league games, drawn from game accounts, was at least 14–4.

The Blues' post-season games include three against the famed Pittsburgh Crawfords, who were playing in the Branch Rickey–generated United States League. The Crawfords were reported to have won the USL pennant two years in a row. In the first game on September 16, the Blues rallied to score seven runs in the bottom of the ninth inning and take a 10–9 victory. Charlie Humber's bases-loaded, two-out double provided the winning margin.[70] The Crawfords won the second game, 5–4, at Valdese, North Carolina. Returning to Asheville to continue the series, the Blues won the third game, 7–2, and the fourth game, 9–7. It was an impressive showing for Moore's team. Although the Blues continued to play games into October, the Crawfords series was a fitting climax to the season for one of the NSL's all-time greatest teams.

The 1946 season was a year with no franchise shifts, although no games were reported for Mobile after July 4 and Montgomery after August 3. Most teams had long gaps during the second half of the season, when far-flung barnstorming trips were traditionally common. Also, there was the peculiar likelihood of a nine-team league including Atlanta, supposedly only an associate member at the season's start, although no standings were published to confirm that.

Remarkably, despite the absence of any standings, more than two dozen box scores were found. The *Chattanooga Times* published box scores of 19 Choo Choos games and the *Knoxville News-Sentinel* published box scores for seven Giants games. That is enough documentation to give some hint of batting superlatives for those two teams.

Catcher Harry Barnes had a batting average of .381 in 18 games for Chattanooga. He also stole 11 bases. First baseman George Lawson hit .318 in 19 games. Third baseman Ulysses Wilkes hit only .270, but he had four home runs and 20 runs batted in in 19 games. When Chattanooga beat Nashville, 5–0, on August 24 the big hit in the game was a two-run home run by Wilkes. It was said to be his 15th of the season.[71]

Knoxville's top hitter was first baseman Robert Boyd with .419 in 11 games. It is unfortunate that more games were not available for Atlanta to give a clearer presentation of left fielder Lomax Davis's season. In four games located he had 10 hits in 18 at-bats for a .556 average. In June it was reported that Knoxville third baseman Herbert Millon had stolen 14 bases in his first nine games after joining the club.

With only two box scores available it is impossible to judge Asheville's batters, but numerous line scores show a superb pitching staff. In games for which a clear outcome could be determined the Blues pitchers were a combined 31–3 with two ties. Robert Bowman's record was 9–1 with three shutouts. Frank Fleming was 7–0 and Vernon "Butch" Phillips was 5–0. Pie Silvers of Chattanooga was second in wins with a record of 8–4, including three shutouts. Ernest Long, also of Chattanooga, had 38 strikeouts in 47.2 innings pitched.

Although Asheville batting is unavailable, game accounts suggest that the team was also very strong at the plate. There were at least 16 games in which the Blues scored runs in double digits. They scored 20 or more four times in league games and once in an exhibition game. A. C. Neeley, who was credited with numerous multiple-hit games and home runs in game reports, hit a three-run homer over the right field fence at Ponce de Leon Park in Atlanta on July 14. The blow was "rated by Atlanta sports scribes as the longest ever hit in the Atlanta park."[72]

Following what the *Chicago Defender* called a "boring season," the NSL sought post-season matchups with the NNL and NAL teams but "due to conflicting dates none could be arranged." Given that situation, the league resorted to the old postseason standby, an all-star game.[73]

NSL President Jackson announced that an East-South all-star game was scheduled for September 22 at the Sulphur Dell park in Nashville. The game would match East and South squads from the league, with each team contributing two players. The East team, managed by C. L. Moore, was comprised of players from Asheville, Charlotte, Knoxville, and Chattanooga. The South team, managed by Carl "Bubber" Ford, the Jacksonville owner, was made up of Atlanta, Jacksonville, Mobile, and Nashville players.[74]

Plans for the game included having "a number of sport, stage and screen celebrities, including some from Hollywood, present." Negro National League President Tom Wilson had been asked to throw out the first pitch.[75] The promise of a celebrity lineup had, perhaps, exceeded reasonable expectations. The two big names were Hattie McDaniel and Clarence Muse. McDaniel was made famous by her role as Mammy in the 1939 Oscar-winning film *Gone with the Wind*. Muse, credited by some with being the first black actor to star in a film, was accomplished in movie circles as an actor, screenwriter, director and composer.[76]

By game weekend Harry Jeffries, the Jacksonville manager, had replaced Ford as manager of the South team. The announced lineups:

East
Kendal Felder, Knoxville, 2b; Herman Taylor, Asheville, 1b; George Lawson, Chattanooga, 1b; Wilbur Adkisson, Nashville, rf; Spencer Alexander, Asheville, lf; Arthur Hefner, Nashville, cf; Sterling Tally, Chattanooga, ss; Harry Barnes, Chattanooga, c; Frazier Robinson, Nashville, c; Lefty Derrick, Nashville, p; Robert Bowman, Asheville, p; Perry, Chattanooga, p; William "Sack" Morgan, Asheville, p; C. L. Moore, Asheville, manager; Wesley Barrow, Nashville, coach.

South
Ray, Jacksonville, ss; Johnson, Atlanta, 3b; Fields, Montgomery, lf; Dickerson, Atlanta, rf; Williams, Montgomery, cf; Kennedy, Montgomery, 1b; "School Boy" Rowe, Atlanta, 2b; Billy Robinson, Mobile, 3b; John Henry, Mobile, cf; Kelly Brooks, Mobile, lf, Thomas Williams, Mobile, p; Adderly Turner, Jacksonville, p; Roggan, Jacksonville, p; Harry Jefferies, Jacksonville, manage; coach unnamed, but likely to be Haynes.[77]

A number of the players, particular some from Atlanta and Montgomery, do not appear to have played on those teams during the regular season. Some of the league's best players, such as Ulysses Wilkes, were not involved at all. It is also possible that the Chattanooga pitcher, Perry, might be Alonzo Perry, picking up another gig after spending the regular season with the Homestead Grays and Birmingham Black Barons.

After a rainout of the Sunday festivities, the game was rescheduled for Monday night. The two entertainers were still on the agenda and the usual "special section … for white people" was available.[78] The East squad won, 6–2, behind the pitching of "Sack" Morgan, who actually started with Atlanta and was sold to Knoxville. The losing pitcher was Bud Wyatt of Atlanta. No player with precisely that name was on the pregame roster, but Atlanta did have a pitcher named Leon Wyatt. There was no question about the batting star, however. Wilbur Adkisson, Nashville's star outfielder, drove in three runs for the winners.[79]

17

1947
Cracks Appearing

With 1946 season's strong finish to build on, the Negro Southern League came back in 1947 with an eight-team lineup again. Five of the teams were familiar: Asheville Blues, Atlanta Black Crackers, Chattanooga Choo Choos, Jacksonville Eagles, and Nashville Cubs. Gone were the Knoxville, Mobile, and Montgomery franchises, to be replaced by the Memphis Blues, New Orleans Creoles, and Shreveport Tigers.

Owners, meeting at the Fourth Street YMCA in Nashville in February, elected Thomas T. Wilson as new president, succeeding Dr. R. B. Jackson. Wilson was owner of the Baltimore Elite Giants and former president of the Negro National League. Other offices were Allen Page, vice president; C. J. Kincaide, secretary; and Dr. R. B. Martin, treasurer. Jackson was owner of the Nashville Cubs, Page was owner of the New Orleans Creoles, and Martin was owner of a new franchise awarded to Memphis. Other baseball club owners at the organizational meeting, including some whose teams did not wind up in the league, were C. L. Hyatte, Knoxville; C. L. Moore, Asheville; John Harden, Atlanta; Carl Ford, Jacksonville; Will McClure, Chattanooga; E. G. Jackson, Montgomery; and Jim Williams, Florida Stars.[1]

An announcement out of Nashville in March said the league had cut back to six teams for the 1947 season. Meeting at the Fourth Street and Charlotte Avenue YMCA, league officials drew up a first-half schedule that included Asheville, Atlanta, Chattanooga, Jacksonville, Memphis, and Nashville. The first half season was to open on May 4 and close on July 4.[2] In early April Asheville Blues owner C. L. Moore told the *Asheville Citizen* that Mobile and New Orleans had been added to the league, raising the membership back to eight clubs.[3] The ownership was Asheville, C. L. Moore; Atlanta, John Harden; Chattanooga, Will McClure; Jacksonville, Carl Ford; Memphis, Dr. M. S. Martin; Nashville, Dr. R. B. Jackson; New Orleans, Allen Page; and Shreveport, Silas Wyrick.[4] Interestingly, two of the owners also owned teams in other leagues. Martin's Memphis Red Sox were in the Negro American League and Wilson's Baltimore Elite Giants were in the Negro National League.

Shreveport never got its team together. In early June the Raleigh Tigers were brought in to fill that vacancy. Raleigh had two very strong black baseball teams at the time, both playing at Chavis Park. The Raleigh Tigers, under Manager Lamb Barbee, appeared to have been fairly well-heeled financially. Owner Arthur Dove's team was playing almost daily in Raleigh and other nearby cities. The team put together a 20-game winning streak that was finally broken by the New Orleans Creoles, apparently in Raleigh's first game as league member.[5]

The 1946 Asheville Blues, champions of the Negro Southern League. Front row, from left: C. L. Moore—manager, Waldo "Cane Creek" Dunlap—p, A. C. Neeley—of, Rufus Hatten—c, Bob Moore (mascot), Fred Worthy—inf, and Spencer Alexander—of. Back row: Dr. White, Herman Taylor—inf, Vernon "Butch" Phillips—p, Frank Flemming—p, Bob Bowman—p, Nat Brannon—1b, Art Hefner—inf, and unidentified (National Baseball Hall of Fame in Cooperstown, New York).

The other team was the Raleigh Grays, a member of the Negro Carolina League. Others in the league included Greensboro, Winston-Salem, Reidsville, and Charlotte in North Carolina; Richmond and Danville, Virginia; and Orangeburg, South Carolina. When the Grays opened their season on May 7, the game was preceded by a parade, first pitch and other traditional ceremonies. Also, seats were reserved for white patrons.[6] As usual, there was a wide array of festive opening day activities planned around the league.

Asheville, the 1946 pennant winner, opened at home against Chattanooga, with a strong nucleus of the championship team returning. Dr. J. W. Holt, "one of Asheville's leading colored physicians," was master of ceremonies for the opening day ceremonies. There was no mention of the first pitch ceremony, but attorney Burgin Pennell was the speaker for the occasion. Music was provided by the Stephens-Lee High School band. A long list of prizes was awaiting players for various accomplishments during the game. Among them:

> ... a pair of Jarman shoes from the Asheville Army Store for the first run; $5 and a free taxi ride from the 970 Taxi for the first pitcher striking out two men in a row; $5 from Slow's Recreation and Billiard Parlor for the player driving in the first run; $5 from H. B. Kilgo of Wilson's Barber Shop for the first homer; a chicken dinner from the Place Grill for the first player reaching first base; $1 from policeman Gilbert Sleight for the

first safe bunt; $5 from the James Keyes Hotel for the first stolen base; $5 from W. H. Avery Shooting Gallery for the first triple; $5 from Ritz Restaurant for the first pitcher striking out seven men ... a marcel wave from Madam Butler's Beauty Salon for the first run of the game.[7]

Asheville won the opener behind the eight-hit pitching of Jess Sanders. Second baseman Charlie Humber and first baseman Nathaniel Brannon each had three singles and a double in five at-bats.[8]

Atlanta opened its home season with a doubleheader against the Nashville Cubs at Ponce de Leon Park, the white Atlanta Crackers field, with the Booker T. Washington High School band under Bandmaster Earl A. Starling providing the National Anthem. Mrs. Walter Mae Bell, of the Atlanta University management staff, threw out the first pitched. Owner John Harden's wife brought as guests a group of "smartly attired young ladies" who posed for photographs with Atlanta players between innings.[9]

The baseball was not nearly as enjoyable as the ceremonies for Atlanta fans. Nashville swept the home team, 6–5 and 4–0, before a crowd of 2,000. Both the performance and the attendance drew the ire of local sports editor Joel W. Smith:

> This would not have been a bad a crowd for a mid-week contest, but it was much too small for a weekend twin-bill to open the season in a metropolitan city....
>
> "Following the doubleheader, it did not take long for the writer to discover that the only people satisfied were the members of the Nashville Cubs' roster. Atlanta fans were disgusted because the Black Crackers booted away the opener, with the game practically in the bag."[10]

The 1946 Nashville Cubs. The team was owned by Tom Wilson, who also owned the Baltimore Elite Giants, formerly of Nashville (courtesy Skip Nipper).

Jacksonville received almost no coverage in the local *Florida Times-Union* newspaper. There was no promotion of opening day or any coverage throughout the season except for one series with Asheville. The paper reported that the Blues would be in town for a single game on Saturday, June 14 and a doubleheader the following day.[11] The two clubs were reported to be "keen rivals and have battled each other all season on even terms." The series might determine the first half championship, the paper said.[12] No results were reported for either date.

Owned by Carl Ford and managed by veteran pitcher Ernest "Spoon" Carter, the few results found for the team were from games played on the road. Jacksonville lost each of these series.

Nashville's home opener was clouded by a tragic blow to the team, the Negro Southern League, and all of black baseball, two days earlier. On May 14 President Tom Wilson died of a heart attack at his farm about 12 miles outside of Nashville. He was 57 years old. Wilson had resigned as president of the Negro National League the year before due to health concerns. Although his physician advised against it, Wilson agreed to take the helm of the NSL as a favor to his friends.

Wilson had been one of the founding members of the Negro Southern League in 1920. His Nashville Elite Giants team was a league regular until he started a series of relocations, which resulted in the club ultimately locating to Baltimore. Among his Nashville business interests was the ownership of the Paradise Ballroom, where he promoted dances, roller skating, and basketball events.[13]

His death came two days before the Nashville Cubs, the minor league team for his Baltimore Elite Giants, were to make their NSL home debut against Jacksonville. His death was noted in a single paragraph on the front of the *Nashville Banner* sports section.[14]

Nashville won the opener, 5–4. It was announced that the Cubs had added to their staff a comedian named Eff Lloyd for additional entertainment.[15]

New Orleans and Memphis opened the season on May 11 in neutral territory, kicking off their pennant runs in Little Rock, Arkansas. The Blues won the first game of a doubleheader, 7–2. New Orleans won the second game, 4–1, behind the two-hit pitching of Winslow Gonzalez. A native of Havana, Cuba, he was a mainstay in the Creoles' challenge to Asheville for 1947 honors, even if no one seemed able to settle on the spelling of his name. The surnames of Gonzalez and Gonzales appeared interchangeably in newspaper reports. The first name frequently used was the anglicized Winslow with a smattering of such Spanish corruptions as Wencesloa, Wensesloa, and Wenessessa.

The Creoles spent the entire first month of the season on the road, not playing a league game in New Orleans until the middle of June. When the home fans finally saw the team, they got their money's worth. Gonzalez beat the Atlanta Black Crackers, 1–0, before a crowd of 5,100. He and Atlanta right-hander Frederick Sheppard pitched four-hitters. New Orleans scored the only run on a throwing error in the sixth inning.[16]

The Atlanta Black Crackers had opened their spring training camp in mid–March at Washington Park in the city. Sammy Haynes, who had taken over as manager in 1946, said he intended to have the team ready for its first exhibition game against the Homestead Grays on March 30.

"After getting the candidates for the team in condition, Manager Haynes will devote much of his time to correcting the crucial weaknesses of 1946. He has made it clear that this year the Black Crackers will have to hit consistently if they intent [sic] to remain on the active roster. Then, too, Skipper Haynes will stress all-around hustle and aggressiveness," sports writer Joel W. Smith reported.[17]

Six pitchers were reportedly on hand; Robert Branson, Brennan L. King, Leon Wyatt, Johnny Roy Brewer, Sack Morgan, and Eugene Jones.[18]

Chattanooga, under veteran Manager Felix Manning, was expected to present the same strong infield it had in 1946. The players were first baseman George Lawson, second baseman Ennis Williams, third baseman Ulysses Wilkes, and shortstop Sterling Talley. The pitching staff would be anchored by a 19-year-old knuckleballer named Ernest Young, "who gets excited at nothing and laughs at everything." Long was starting his third season with the Choo Choos.[19]

The Choo Choos, rated as the league dark horse in a pregame story, lived up to the early billing, taking an opening-day doubleheader from Jacksonville. The attendance for the games was reported at 16,000, probably a typographical error with 6,000 being more likely. Long won the first game, 11–1, pitching a four-hitter. Chattanooga overcame a five-run deficit to win the second game, 9–8, in extra innings. Third baseman Wilkes had four hits, two of them triples, in the first game. Right fielder Freddie Sheppard, who had been acquired from the Birmingham Black Barons, hit "a mighty inside-the-park homer" to win the second game.[20]

Although Chattanooga continued to play decent baseball, showcasing several good players, the team had difficulty attracting a solid fan base. In early August sports writer Sam Seals reported the team had folded due to "poor attendance, bad weather and the failure of various teams to show up" for home dates. As revenues dwindled the team was forced to release stars such as pitchers Long and James "Lefty" Armour, first baseman Lawson and outfielder Shepherd.[21]

Seals said right-hander Long had been scouted by the major league Brooklyn Dodgers. After the Choo Choos played a doubleheader in Atlanta on July 4, Long and Shepherd left the team, joining the Black Crackers on a long barnstorming trip through the Midwest. Both subsequently found positions with a white team in Michigan.[22]

The Memphis Blues are an enigma. All that is really known about the team is its name and the name of the owner, Dr. M. S. Martin. Research did not uncover the names of the manager or a single player. The Blues won a season-opening doubleheader from New Orleans on Sunday, May 11. The games were played in Little Rock, Arkansas. The following Sunday they reportedly lost a doubleheader at home to the Asheville Blues. No other results were reported, suggesting that the team folded early. In fact, its record in early June was reported to be four wins and four losses.[23] The *Memphis World*, the local black newspaper and a sister publication to The *Atlanta Daily World*, did not cover the team. Except for three isolated scores of games with Asheville, published on May 27, The *Memphis World* did not publish a single reference to the Blues the entire season. For that matter, the newspaper did not cover the Memphis Red Sox of the Negro American League either, except for articles pertaining to pitcher Dan Bankhead being sold to the Brooklyn Dodgers.

The New Orleans Creoles added a new element to the season with the introduction of a female coach. Assisting manager Harry Williams was Lucille Bland. "When she takes her place in the coaching box, she gives an active and fiery demonstration of her enthusiasm," reported a Chattanooga newspaper before New Orleans appeared at Engel Stadium.[24] There was no mention of her performance the following day in the game report. New Orleans won the first game, 11–3, behind the pitching of Charlie Daniels. Ernie Long pitched Chattanooga to a 3–2 win in the nightcap.[25]

Meeting in Nashville a few days after Tom Wilson's death, the league named Vice President Page of New Orleans as the new president. At the same meeting it was announced that the Raleigh Tigers were now members of the league. "With Shreveport, La., failing to enter," businessman Arthur Dove was awarded that spot. Shreveport had been listed as the eighth team at the final organizational meeting in May.[26]

Standings released at the meeting showed Asheville and Jacksonville tied for first at 6–1, followed by Atlanta, 6–4. The other teams in the standings were New Orleans, Memphis, Nashville, and Chattanooga.

Although playing respectably, Raleigh found Negro Southern League opponents more formidable than the semipro teams they had been scoring against in double digits. On June 8 the Tigers lost, 5–3, at Nashville, dropping into third place behind the second place Cubs and leader Asheville.[27] Nashville won the second game of the series, 1–0, in a memorable pitching duel between Nashville's Bill Greason and Raleigh's Jimmy Cooper, both of whom went the game's entire 15 innings.[28] Playing almost every day, the Tigers interspersed their NSL schedule with games against nearby semipro teams and barnstormers like the Louisville Congo Zulu Giants. The Louisville team was one

This pennant promotes what is billed as an NSL playoff game between Asheville and Nashville. Curiously, no records from the mid–1940s—when both teams were in the league—indicate that the Cubs won a second-half championship, or that Asheville and Nashville met in a playoff game (courtesy Skip Nipper).

of many barnstormers using the jungle theme. The players generally had single names like Impo and Nyassas, played barefoot and in grass skirts, and occasionally painted their faces to complete the image. Raleigh walloped this particular team, 17–0.[29]

Figuring out the official NSL schedule is a daunting task at times. In July the Atlanta Black Crackers went to Raleigh for a game. "Although both teams are members of the Negro Southern League, the game will not count in the loop standings," the *Raleigh News & Observer* reported.[30]

In June, Asheville opened a home stand with a 16–3 pounding of Jacksonville. Outfielder Spencer Alexander hit a 400-foot, three-run homer and Waldo Dunlap struck out seven. The win put Asheville's NSL record at 14–1 and left the Blues "perched atop the loop standings by a comfortable margin."[31] Assuming the record was correct, Asheville extended it to 17–1 by the time the series was over, winning the second game, 4–3, and then sweeping a doubleheader. Both Will Thompson and Robert Bowman pitched shutouts in the doubleheader. Thompson gave up only one hit in nine innings while Bowman held the Eagles to three in seven innings. In his 13–0 win Thompson retired 16 in a row at one point and finished with six strikeouts. Bowman had 12 strikeouts in seven innings.[32] The Blues outscored Jacksonville 45–6 in the four-game series.

By early July Asheville was reported to have clinched the first half title with a 22–5 record. In fact, in June, the *Chattanooga Times* had reported that Asheville had "gotten away to the longest lead in the league's history."[33] Winding up the first half with a 2–0 shutout against Nashville, the Blues then went on a two-week road trip through the East. The trek included a 5–2 win over Nashville at the Polo Grounds in New York. The team's overall record on the trip was 13 wins in 15 games.[34] Nashville was reported to have finished second in the first half with "a .500 mark."[35]

One of the losses came at the hands of the Carolina All-Stars in Durham. The Carolina team was picked from teams in a semipro league in Virginia, North Carolina, and Southern Carolina. The All-Stars won, 7–6, before a crowd of 5,000.[36]

In August the Blues played another game with the all-stars, this time winning a 4–1 encounter at Winston-Salem, North Carolina. Another NSL team, Jacksonville, played the all-stars in August, losing, 7–6.[37]

Back home the Blues won a pair of games from the Fort Benning Bullets, the 25th Infantry Regiment Army team from Columbus, Georgia. The first game was an exciting 9–8 win and second was a 13–4 trouncing. The 25th Regiment was a segregated Army unit, as was its sister outfit the 24th Regiment, which had produced a number of players in the 1920s and 1930s. Immediately after the second game, Asheville embarked on another typical NSL, lengthy, second half of the season road trip. This one would include a game at Yankee Stadium on August 10. The team was not expected back in Asheville until September 3.[38]

The Jacksonville Eagles, while on a road trip, played a doubleheader in Moultrie, Georgia, with a semipro team called the Atlanta Cardinals. The Cardinals swept the NSL club behind the outstanding play of several men who had been on the Black Crackers' roster earlier. They included David T. Harper, Willie Marvin Terrell, Leon Wyatt, and Eugene "Lefty" Jones."[39] Two days later the Cardinals took a doubleheader from the Charleston Red Birds. Two of the Charleston players were Tom Brown and St. Julian Ladson, both of whom had played with Jacksonville in Moultrie.[40]

In July the Cardinals embarked on a tour of the Northwest and upper Midwest, playing with great success in games in Idaho, Washington, Montana, Minnesota, and other states. Manager Sammy Haynes and other former Black Crackers were still with the team, as were former starters John "Early Bird" Ellison and Johnnie Richardson.[41] Before they returned to Atlanta, the Cardinals also bested another Negro Southern League club, taking two one-run games from the Nashville Cubs. The second game was of particular interest. Playing at Sulphur Dell in Nashville, the Cardinals won, 4–3, in 11 innings. Their starting pitcher was the venerable Satchel Paige. Paige's All-Stars, a barnstorming team, had been scheduled to play the Cubs but for some reason the game was cancelled. The Cardinals filled in and Paige, still in town, hurled the first four innings for the visitors. He struck out nine batters. Victor Johnson came on in relief and finished the game for the Atlanta club.[42] Interestingly, the *Nashville Banner* reported the same account of the game, but still referred to the winning team as the Satchel Paige All-Stars.[43]

The Cardinals returned to Atlanta in early August, breaking a baseball drought as the Black Crackers had been on the road for more than a month. A large crowd turned out to welcome the semipro team home, celebrating its success on the road and honoring the dozen or more former Black Crackers who were on the team by now.[44] The homecoming was spoiled, though, by the visiting Birmingham All-Stars, who swept a doubleheader. The winning pitcher in the first game was Willie Young, a one-armed player from the Birmingham industrial league.[45] Young had played briefly with the Black Barons during World War II.

Although an "overflow" crowd was predicted for the Atlanta Cardinals games with the Birmingham All-Stars, there was no mention of such an outpouring of support in the game reports. That was, perhaps, an indication of a systemic problem with black baseball in Atlanta. Marion E. Jackson, writing in the *Daily World*, noted strong attendance by blacks at the white Atlanta Crackers games:

"Atlanta's Negro fans flock to the Atlanta Crackers games because they can look to no baseball outlet of their own. They want regularly scheduled contests and topnotch performers who can carry on the traditions of the great American game. In addition, the Gate City fans want to see the Big Leaguers of the Negro American and National Leagues. They want to see players qualified and publicized by the local and national sportswriters....

"One of the failures of Atlanta Negro baseball owners is that they have failed to acquaint the public with their stars, their achievements and their successes. News of both the Braves and Black Crackers is spotty and sketchy which suggest that neither the players or owners have any regards for the fans, who might have some interests in them.

"When the teams win local fans are kept in ignorance. When they lose the same is true. Not a dozen horsehide fans in the Gate City know the managers of the two teams, nor could they identify their photographs. Not a single player of the team has kept a record of his batting averages and individual accomplishments. We have no record that the club has a scorer or traveling secretary to keep the newspapers and fans acquainted with the activities of the team."[46]

The Braves team was, of course, not today's Atlanta Braves but rather another semipro team like the Atlanta Cardinals. Jackson's lament over poor publicity and record keeping harks back to similar comments made throughout the history of black league ball, particular the Negro Southern League.

While the Atlanta Braves were traveling successfully with a number of former Black Cracker players, the Black Crackers had filled some of those vacated positions with a group of new players from Texas. All performed well in their debut against Chattanooga at Ponce de Leon Park. Raymond Lacey and Eddie Brigham each had three hits. Charles and James Neal, 16- and 17-year-old brothers, respectively, from Tyler, Texas, excelled at base running and fielding as well as batting.[47] Charlie Neal would go on to the major leagues, signing with the Brooklyn Dodgers in 1950 and batting .370 in the 1959 World Series. He later was among the first black players on the newly-formed New York Mets in 1962.[48]

During none of these transactions on and off the field did the *Daily World* address the Negro Southern League pennant race. Perhaps that was statement enough of the Atlanta team's progress toward a championship. Obviously, the team played no league contests while on its extended July and August road trips. Except for a game with Jacksonville in a four-team doubleheader at the Polo Grounds in New York and a doubleheader with Nashville at Ponce de Leon Park on Sunday, August 17, there were apparently no other league games played by the Black Crackers. Although there was nothing in the Atlanta newspapers to indicate otherwise that the Black Crackers were anything but a league member, the *Nashville Banner* suggested otherwise. On May 18 the paper reported: "The Crackers are associate members of the Negro Southern League. They do not compete for the title, but they still play a full schedule with the other teams in the league."[49]

Asheville again was the first-half winner. Nashville and New Orleans finished second and third, respectively. When the first half ended in early July most of the clubs embarked on a long barnstorming swings. Asheville and Nashville paired up for games in Philadelphia and Baltimore, as well as playing other East Coast teams. New Orleans went east, also, playing the Philadelphia Stars, New York Cubans, and the Bushwicks, a top semipro team from New York.

Although the Nashville newspapers provided only minimal coverage of Cubs games and rarely referenced the pennant race, the local team apparently played good baseball throughout the second half. In August Nashville won a 12–4 decision from Chattanooga behind the seven-hit pitching of Edward Derrick. Center fielder James Armstead by now had replaced Felton Snow as manager, and was said to have hit his 15th home run of the season against the Choo Choos.[50]

On Sunday, June 8, the Atlanta club participated in a three-team doubleheader at Crosley Field in Cincinnati, home of the National League Reds. The other teams were the independent Detroit Senators and the Havana La Palomas. The event was billed as benefit for the Detroit team, which had been involved in a bus accident in Covington, Kentucky, while en route to Cincinnati for a May game with the Cincinnati Crescents. Because of the accident "that temporarily sidelined some of the Senator's [sic] leading players," the game was postponed until June 8. However, the Crescents were unavailable for that date, having booked a game in another city. Atlanta, heading north on an extended road trip, was booked in the Crescents' stead.[51]

Asheville continued to be the dominant team during the second half. The Blues beat New Orleans, 6–4, in the first game of a doubleheader at Pelican Stadium on July 27. They overcame a 3–0 New Orleans lead and played to a 4–4 tie in the second game, which was called because of darkness.[52]

Raleigh, the late-starting member of the league, was never mentioned as a challenger for the pennant, but the Tigers apparently had a very good team. When they went to New Orleans for a series in August a local newspaper wrote: "The Tigers are playing their second season in organized baseball. Last season they compiled the amazing record of 88 victories against 13 defeats. During the month of June the Tigers ran up a winning streak of 21 games before the Creoles snapped that streak. Other winnings streaks have been eight and 10 games, respectively."[53]

The 21-game streak was in May rather than June. On May 23 the Tigers beat Asheville, 2–1, at the Blues' McCormick Field, a win that the *Asheville Citizen* reported as Raleigh's 20th in a row.[54] On June 8–9, the Tigers lost three in a row to Nashville, ruling out June as the month for the streak. Also, a proper perspective on Raleigh's winning streak must include the fact that many of the victories were barnstorming triumphs against semipro teams like the Spartanburg Sluggers. That misnamed team lost to Raleigh, 15–0, getting only five hits while the Tigers were getting 20.[55]

Rain held the series at New Orleans to a single game, which Raleigh won, 1–0, on the three-hit pitching of Cliff Statham.[56] The two teams then played a series of games at neutral sites, with New Orleans winning at least three in a row.[57]

In late August the Creoles were reported to be three games out of first place, going into a home series with the Jacksonville Eagles.[58]

Raleigh, which played well against most NSL teams, had trouble with Nashville. On August 25 the Cubs won a doubleheader at Raleigh, crushing the Tigers, 16–3, in the opener. Ed Derrick then outdueled Cliff Statham 2–0 in the nightcap.[59] Although Nashville continued to play league games into September, that doubleheader seems to have ended the Raleigh league schedule. Curiously, a few days later Raleigh defeated a team billed as the Negro Southern League All-Stars, 9–8. Frank Russell of Nashville and Harry Barnes of Chattanooga were mentioned as All-Star players.[60]

Asheville returned home on September 3 after a month-long road trip through the East. The Blues were reported to have won 15 out of 18 games on the trip, although it seems likely that they would have played more games than that for the length of time they were away from home.[61]

After an exhibition game with the Spartanburg Sluggers, they prepared for an NSL home series against the Nashville Cubs. The pregame story asserted that the Blues were undefeated in second half play.[62] They continued that domination against the Cubs, winning 4–3, 9–8, and 8–0. Waldo Dunlap pitched the shutout, limiting the Cubs to five hits while striking out 10. The Nashville series was followed by yet another road trip, this one for about two weeks "through the south."[63]

When the team returned home, there was a peculiar report that the Blues had won three games out of five from New Orleans for the NSL championship. The story said that New Orleans was the second half winner, a puzzling report if Asheville had been undefeated in the second half less than two weeks earlier.[64] Yet, in early September, when the Creoles took three straight games from Nashville at Sulphur Dell, it was reported that the three losses "tumbled the Cubs out of first place."[65] Playoff or not, Asheville appeared to have won its second consecutive championship.

The Blues' five-game Negro Southern League playoff with New Orleans, called the second-half champion by the *New Orleans Times-Picayune*, was another NSL curiosity.[66] The entire series for Asheville was played on the road.

Asheville won the Friday night opener, 4–3, at Pelican Stadium.[67] After a day off, the second game was played on Sunday afternoon with New Orleans winning, 10–5.[68] The final three games were all scheduled at neutral sites, with New Orleans taking the series lead with a 2–1 victory on Monday night in Baton Rouge.[69] The series was to resume with Game Four at Shreveport on Tuesday night.

Whether or not the series was completed is difficult to determine. An Atlantic Ocean hurricane roared across the Florida Keys and into the eastern Gulf of Mexico late Tuesday and early Wednesday. The Shreveport newspapers carried nothing about the game, raising the question of a washout from the rains preceding the hurricane across the Gulf.[70] By Friday, schools in New Orleans were closed.[71] Even though Shreveport was more than 300 miles northwest of New Orleans and the brunt of the storm, it is still possible that weather caused the cancellation of the series.

On the other hand, as stated above, the *Asheville Citizen* reported that the Blues had take three out of five in the playoff series to win the championship.

The Blues ended their season with an assortment of fall exhibition games. Most notable among them was an 11–6 loss to a Negro National League All-Star team managed by NSL veteran Homer "Goose" Curry. Bob Harvey and Jimmy Wilkes of the Newark Eagles each hit two-run home runs for the winners.[72]

18

1948
Changing Lineup

Although the Negro Southern League had lost a major backer when Tom Wilson died in the spring of 1947, Nashville continued to be the center for league activity. The 1948 organizational meetings were held there in the offices of Dr. R. B. Jackson, who was again named league president.

The two-day session in April resulted in the announcement of a six-team league with two associate members. The core membership teams and their owners were; Atlanta Black Crackers, John Harden; Birmingham Clowns, Tommy Sampson; Chattanooga Choo Choos, Beck Shepherd; Memphis Cardinals, Jim Ford and Amos Mosely; Nashville Cubs, Dr. Jackson; and New Orleans Creoles, Allen Page. The associate members were not named, but W. A. "Pete" Wilder represented the Raleigh Grays at the meeting.[1] Later it appeared that Raleigh and Mobile were the associate members. Missing from the lineup was two-time champion Asheville. C. L. Moore's team had been represented at a meeting in Durham where plans were being made for a Negro American Association. Moore subsequently was named president of the new league.[2] With the exception of Jacksonville and Baltimore, all of the representatives at the meeting were from cities in Virginia or the Carolinas.[3] In May Asheville officials created a bit of a stir when they accused the Chicago American Giants of the Negro American League of "outlaw methods" in signing away shortstop James Pendleton.[4]

Moore had signed Pendleton to a contract in February, paying him $400 a month. Chicago catcher Quincy Trouppe allegedly made at least two overtures to Pendleton while he was in spring training with the Asheville Blues. The shortstop was finally persuaded to jump the club when Trouppe offered the same salary plus a "promise to take him to Puerto Rico this winter." Moore informed NAL President Dr. J. B. Martin that legal steps might be forthcoming.[5]

The 1948 NSL season would be another filled with confusion over just who was officially in the league and who was not. In fact, Birmingham and Memphis carried that confusion to a whole new level. Despite that problem and the usual uncertainty over who won the championship, there was a major highlight. Chattanooga featured a sensational teenage player from Birmingham who caught the fans fancy like no one since Satchel Paige. Indeed, Willie Mays would join Satchel as the two most famous NSL alumni. There is evidence that Mays's father actually started farming the kid out to Chattanooga in 1947, driving him up there to play on weekends. However, the youngster did not appear in any box scores or game accounts during the 1947 season.[6] But it was in 1948 that he blossomed.

Jim Pendleton, Asheville shortstop in 1947, went on to an eight-year major league career with Milwaukee, Pittsburgh, Cincinnati and Houston (courtesy NoirTech Research).

Other league officers besides President Jackson were Allen Page, New Orleans, vice president; Luther Carmichael, Nashville, secretary, statistician, and public relations director; and John Harden, Atlanta, treasurer. A first half schedule was drawn with the season to open on May 2 and close on July 5.

Perhaps more important than the organizational house work was a discussion on the status of the league in relation to the rest of professional baseball. It was urged that league officials work with Baseball Commissioner A. B. Chandler for some kind of recognition by now-integrated Organized Baseball.

Harden, the veteran Atlanta owner, also renewed the call for reliable record keeping. Harden warned fellow owners that recognition from Organized Baseball would not happen if the league did not provide timely, accurate statistics, not only regarding ball playing, but also on attendance.[7]

There were other concerns, also. With Jackie Robinson, who broke the major league color line in 1947, capturing the imagination of baseball fans, the media responded in kind. Coverage of traditional black baseball began to dwindle. There was talk that Robinson's success would hurt Negro League baseball. The issue was of such great concern that Dr. J. B. Martin, Memphis Red Sox owner and president of the Negro American League, was compelled to respond.

"Some seem to think that Robinson's going up into the Major League has and will continue to hurt Negro baseball, while others believe his advancement will be a great help to the Sepia game, I heartily concur with those who think it will benefit Negro baseball," said Martin.[8]

Martin believed that Robinson's success had generated a growth in the number of people becoming baseball fans. He said the breaking of the color barrier was inspiring youngsters to take up the game.

Yet, it is hard to believe that an astute businessman like Martin did not see the dark side. For thousands of black fans the focus was on Jackie and Organized Ball, not on the Kansas City Monarchs, the Birmingham Black Barons and the Homestead Grays. Diminishing press coverage and smaller crowds at Negro League games foretold of disaster.

Joe Black, a Baltimore Elite Giants pitcher who himself advanced to the major leagues and played for six years, saw the handwriting on the wall. "Why is it when I pick up a Negro newspaper there are columns or stories on Jackie Robinson, Roy Campanella and Larry Doby and only a few sentences on the Negro leagues and players?" he asked in an interview with black sportswriter Marion E. Jackson. "You know," he continued, "one of the national papers is running a contest on 'Why I think Colored Baseball Should Be Supported' and yet that same paper has only a few lines on Negro baseball."[9]

Black, a college man who had attended Morgan State College and had already logged five years with the Elite Giants, drew a response from Jackson:

> Our sportswriters cannot give the Dodgers and the Indians headline play week after week without lending a helping hand to the leagues who furnished Campanella, Doby and Robinson to the majors. We cannot forget that these players who cracked Organized Ball's ironclad Jim Crow came up the hard way through the Negro leagues.[10]

Although the Negro American League would hang on until the early 1960s, the Negro Southern League would barely last another four years.

Meanwhile, plans continued for the 1948 season. John Harden's appeal for better record keeping is particularly interesting given the nature of the first-half schedule. For reasons left unexplained, the scheduled called for a five-team rotation each week. For example, the week of May 2–7 listed Chattanooga at New Orleans, Memphis at New Orleans, and Nashville at Atlanta. The week of May 9–16 listed Atlanta at New Orleans, Birmingham at Memphis, and Nashville at Memphis. The peculiar pattern, repeated each week, was arranged around three-team doubleheaders. There was no explanation for one team being left off the schedule each week.[11] However, the struggling NSL was possibly having trouble securing regular venues. In July the *New Orleans Times-Picayune* reported that the Creoles, leading the league with a 24–6 record, were going on an extensive Midwestern trip. They would be on the road until later in the month when promoter Page "is hoping he will be able to secure Pelican Stadium for a series against either Atlanta or Chattanooga."[12] Obviously, the traditional NSL-team-plays-while-white-team-is-on-the-road arrangement was no longer a certainty.

Atlanta opened at home against Nashville on May 2. Ceremonies included the traditional first pitch thrown out by Prof. Charles L. Harper, one of Atlanta's leading educators and president of the local chapter of the National Association for the Advancement of Colored People. King Moore, a retired Atlanta businessman, received the pitch while NSL President Jackson swung the bat. Another unusual first day event was the broadcasting of the game on Radio Station WEAS in Decatur, Georgia.[13] "This will make it possible for shut-ins to keep up with the Black Crackers and find out just what they have to offer in the way of baseball talent," wrote *Atlanta Daily World* sports editor Joel W. Smith.[14]

The Black Crackers made the day a total success by defeating the Cubs, 9–7 and 11–4. In the sixth inning of the first game, Nashville first baseman Butch McCord put the Cubs ahead with a home run over the right field wall. As the first player to hit a home run at Ponce de Leon Park in 1948, McCord was awarded a carton of Old Gold cigarettes, not a premium likely to be seen today.[15]

Two weeks later the Black Crackers hosted a three-team doubleheader that set the stage for more confusion over the makeup of the 1948 Negro Southern League.

In the first game the New Orleans Creoles defeated the Memphis Cardinals, 9–4; Atlanta subsequently defeated New Orleans, 4–0 in the second game.[16]

On the same day, in Memphis, the Memphis Blues "of the newly reorganized negro Southern League" split a doubleheader at Martin Stadium with the Jackson, Tennessee, Giants.[17] So, which team represented Memphis in the NSL? It is not a question easily answered. At no time did the black *Memphis World* or the white *Memphis Commercial Appeal* refer to the team as anything but the Blues. However, by early June, the Memphis press was reporting the Blues to be in the Tri-State League and games were subsequently played with other Mississippi, Tennessee, and Arkansas teams that were said to be members of the league, also. To further confuse the issue, the Blues game with the Chattanooga Choo Choos on June 13 was reported as "a negro Tri-State League doubleheader." And the Blues, with a five-game winning streak, were reported to be leading that league by a half game over the Greenville, Mississippi, Tigers.[18] Other members of the Tri-State League were the Blytheville, Arkansas, Tigers, and Tiptonville, Tennessee, Tigers. All of these teams were called semipro clubs.

Meanwhile, newspapers in every other NSL team referred to the Memphis team in that league as the Cardinals.

The same duality was present in Birmingham. Again, there appear to be two separate teams. Most league newspaper stories about league organization referred to the Birmingham Clowns under Manager Tommy Sampson. However, the name Birmingham All-Stars also surfaced occasionally. Sportswriter Ellis Jones, writing in the *Birmingham World*, suggested the latter name was closer to correct. "The official name of the team Tommy Sampson is managing in [sic] Birmingham Stars."[19] Jones makes no mention of any league affiliation. He reported that the team was currently in the middle of a road trip that would include Jackson and Meridian, Mississippi, Shreveport and Monroe, Louisiana, and an unnamed city in Arkansas.

Players were said to include former Black Barons Lyman Bostock, Freddie Shepherd and Sterling Talley; former industrial leaguers Bennie Griggs and Fred Clarke; and Willie Mays. Whether Mays was playing for both the Choo Choos and Sampson is a matter of conjecture. Historian John Klima quotes Mays as saying he did not recall playing for Sampson. On the other hand, Sampson always claimed that he was the one who really discovered Willie Mays.[20]

Yet, the Birmingham Clowns did play league games. They were in Nashville on May 16 and in Chattanooga on May 30–31 for three-game series. The Clowns, like the All-Stars, were reported to be managed by Sampson. There was a similar overlapping of players. When the Birmingham team played both Nashville and Chattanooga later in the season, it was identified as the Stars. The logical explanation is that the team originated as the Clowns and its name was later changed to the Stars or All-Stars. Because of the uncertainty, both Birmingham and Memphis teams are listed separately in the appendices.

In mid–June the *Birmingham World* reported that the Stars were leaving on a Midwest trip that would carry them into the Dakotas and Manitoba, Canada.[21] Those articles lend credence to the belief that Birmingham's second-tier black baseball team morphed into a barnstorming club rather than a league member. It is also possible that the Clowns folded and Sampson picked up the remnant to form a barnstorming team, which continued to play NSL clubs as well. None of the Birmingham newspapers ever posted news of a scheduled home game or a result. While the *Chattanooga Daily Times* reported on July 5 that Chattanooga had won, 9–5, at Birmingham the previous day, it did not identify the venue. It is the author's belief that the game was played on a neutral site and that all Birmingham games against NSL opponents were barnstorming games.

Chattanooga went into the new season with a lot of promise. After an exhibition game against Nashville, the local newspaper reported that fans were "still talking about the wonderful team they have." The strength of the team was attributed, in part, to owner Beck Shephard hiring veteran catcher Harry Barnes as manager. "...he has a very likeable disposition, is a clean sportsman and a natural leader," reported the *Chattanooga Times*; "Barnes is like perpetual motion while playing the game. He is continually hustling, which certainly is an incentive for the other players."[22]

Other top Chattanooga players included first baseman Jim Canada, shortstop Sterling Talley, and third baseman James Davis. But none of them drew the fans' attention like the young outfielder: "Willie Herman Mayes, [sic], who holds down the center-field position ... is only 16 years old, but packs a lot of power in his 168 pounds. He is a sure fielder and very fast. He is the pride and joy of Manager Harry Barnes and of the fans."[23] Mays, still a student at Fairfield Industrial High School near Birmingham, was being transported by his father, W. H. "Cat" Mays, himself a former NSL player, to Chattanooga on weekends to play for the Choo Choos.[24]

In Memphis, the Blues, playing in Martin Stadium, the only black-owned ballpark in the league, opened on Sunday, May 16. The opponent was the Jackson, Tennessee, Royal Giants. The *Memphis World* reported that in 1947 the two teams had "played their way into the hearts of baseball fans of Memphis and Jackson."[25] There was no reference to the Negro Southern League, and no report on the outcome of the games.

However, the white newspaper, the *Commercial Appeal*, reported both that the Blues were in the "reorganized Southern League" and gave the results of the games. Jackson won the first game, 7–5, and Memphis the second, 4–2. Memphis third baseman Jesse Warren had four hits in the two games.[26]

The *World* did not report on the hometown Red Sox much better throughout the Negro American League season. Only twice were standings published and only twice were scores even given for Red Sox games. Further coverage of the Blues consisted of an announcement that the club would play a game with Chattanooga Choo Choos on June 13 and one that a single game was scheduled with the Blytheville, Arkansas, Tigers the following Sunday. The story on the latter game reported that both teams were "members of the Tri-State League."[27]

The first weekend in June, with the Red Sox on the road, the Blues returned to Martin Stadium for a doubleheader with the Greenville, Mississippi, Tigers. The pregame stories in the *Commercial Appeal* extended the Memphis confusion. The newspaper reported that the Memphis-Greenville game was between semipro teams who were members of the TriState [sic] League. Greenville, managed by Joey Mixon, who was said to be a former Kansas City Monarch. The Tigers were reportedly leading the Blues by a game.[28]

Memphis won both games by identical 9–5 scores with Isaiah Newsome hitting a home run and Ladd White striking out 14 Tigers in the opener.[29]

When the Chattanooga Choo Choos came to Memphis the following weekend, it was again billed as TriState [sic] League doubleheader. The pregame reported focused on the return of former Red Sox Canada to the city. With a five-game winning streak the Blues were leading Greenville by a game with Chattanooga in third place. Chattanooga won both games, sparked in the first one by center fielder Mays' two-run homer.[30]

Later Memphis Blues contests were played with the Blytheville Tigers and with the Tiptonville Tigers, both also said to be members of the Tri-State League.[31]

In late August Chattanooga, still reported as a member of the Negro Southern League, hosted a doubleheader with the Memphis Cardinals. One of the Memphis pitchers was one-armed Willie Young. Young, an industrial leaguer, had played briefly with the Birmingham Black Barons during World War II.

Nashville, under new manager Parnell Woods, had opened its home season on May 16 against the Birmingham Clowns at Sulphur Dell. Pregame ceremonies included the first pitch by Commissioner Seth Mays, a local government official. He tossed the ball to Dr. C. F. Perkins, while Sheriff Garner Robinson served as batter. An added attraction was a "girls' baseball game" to be played prior to NSL contest.[32] Birmingham spoiled the festivities by scoring four runs in the first inning and holding on for a 4–1 win.[33]

Still, Nashville had a strong pitching staff back with 1947 starters "Farmer" Brown and Edward "Lefty" Derrick leading the corps. Derrick was said to have recorded 300 strikeouts during the 1947 season.[34]

The first three-team doubleheader in Atlanta was played on Sunday, May 16. The New Orleans Creoles beat Memphis, 9–4, in the first game. The home fans were treated to a 4–0 shutout in the nightcap as Early King held New Orleans to seven scattered hits.[35]

The following weekend Atlanta was host to the Birmingham All-Stars. Players on this team included familiar Birmingham names such as Johnny Cowan, Sampson, and Canada. Also listed in center field was Mays, who was still a few weeks away from joining manager Lorenzo "Piper" Davis and the Birmingham Black Barons. Pitchers were expected to be "Red" Howard and Nathaniel Brooks.[36]

Presumably, the All-Stars were the team representing Birmingham in the league, rather than the previously named Birmingham Clowns. The All-Stars second baseman, Sampson, had been reported as manager of the Clowns in the preseason period. The games, an NSL doubleheader, would bring to five the official league games for the Black Crackers in the young season. They had previously won two out of three from Nashville.

On the local paper forecast a Birmingham week for the Black Crackers. It was reported that they would host the Birmingham Black Barons on Thursday night, then the Birmingham Clowns of Friday night.[37]

But in the game reports, there was no mention of either Birmingham team. Instead, Atlanta won a doubleheader from the Chattanooga Choo Choos, 7–6 and 3–1. The

A poster promoting a Negro Southern League doubleheader in 1948, held at Louisville's Parkway Field, between the Nashville Cubs and New Orleans Creoles. It was during this series that female players Fabiola Wilson and Lovie Dymond made their debut for the Creoles (courtesy Skip Nipper).

Chattanooga lineup included Canada at first base, Howard on the mound, and Mayes [sic] in center field. Venerable Homer "Goose" Curry, playing centerfield, hit a grand slam home run to spark a six-run ninth inning for Atlanta in the first game. He also had a solo homer in the second game. Mays had three hits and scored three runs in four at-bats in the first game.[38]

On Monday night, Chattanooga blanked the Black Crackers, 3–0, on Bill Barnes' four-hit pitching. The hitting star for winners was "Junior Mayes, the 16-year-old centerfielder." One of his hits was a home run.[39]

Chattanooga returned to Ponce de Leon on Friday night, substituting for the enigmatic Birmingham Clowns. The Alabama team was reportedly stranded in Tennessee after a "wreck" and unable to get to Atlanta in time for the game.[40] There was no coverage of either the Chattanooga game or the one scheduled with the Birmingham Black Barons on Thursday night.

In June, Atlanta went into New Orleans for a single games at Pelican Stadium. The Creoles were reportedly in first place with a 9–1 record. Atlanta's record wasn't given, but the Black Crackers were said to be in second place.[41] Led by shortstop and now manager Tommy Brown, the Creoles won their ninth straight game to strengthen their hold on first place.[42]

The New Orleans team apparently had some difficulty securing Pelican Stadium from the Organized Baseball minor league Pelicans for games at times. In July, it was announced that owner Page was hoping to book the stadium for a series against Atlanta or Chattanooga. Meanwhile, the Creoles, reportedly with a record of 24–6, were on a barnstorming trip to Detroit; Fort Wayne and South Bend, Indiana; Battle Creek, Michigan; and Toledo.[43] When the team returned home, with wins in eight of 10 games, they were reported to have won the first half championship. Because of their outstanding play the Creoles had been invited to participate in the annual all-star game in Durham, North Carolina.[44]

Nashville, which had reportedly tied New Orleans for the lead in late June, faded away in July. The *Nashville Banner* carried no further reports on the team after that New Orleans series. In fact, there were no further reports at all after the Cubs split a doubleheader in Chattanooga on July 13.[45]

New Orleans, which had a female coach in 1947, continued its groundbreaking gender integration of baseball in July. On the Fourth of July, the Creoles played the Nashville Cubs in a doubleheader in Louisville, Kentucky. Two women, Fabiola Wilson and Lovie Dymond, "played three innings and were a hit with the crowd."[46]

In mid–July the Negro Southern League suffered a major setback. After a barnstorming trip through the Midwest and the Atlantic Coast, the Atlanta Black Crackers returned home for a series with the Jacksonville Eagles of the Negro American Association. Atlanta owner John Harden announced that he had removed his team from the NSL and joined the Negro American Association for the second half of the season.[47] In August, Atlanta manager Goose Curry was named manager of an NAA All-Star team that would face the visiting San Juan Stars, champions of the Puerto Rican Winter League.[48]

On August 24, after another month-long barnstorming trip, the New Orleans team returned home for a game against the Black Crackers. After winning the first-half title,

the Creoles were reportedly leading the league in the second half, also. Amos Watson was the leading pitcher with a record of 10–2, followed by Taylor Smith at 7–3 and General Jackson, 5–2. Atlanta was reported to be in second place.[49]

Atlanta came from behind to win the game, 7–4. Although the writing was not specific, it implied that the contest was between two NSL teams. Atlanta's removal to the NAA was not mentioned.[50]

In early September, the Creoles prepared for fall exhibition games against the Cleveland Buckeyes of the Negro American League and the Newark Eagles and New York Black Yankees of the Negro National League. The New Orleans newspaper did not reference the outcome of the NSL second half or any playoff that might have resulted.[51] Chattanooga had spent an inordinate amount of time on the road during the first month of the season. When the club prepared for a May 30 Sunday doubleheader with the Birmingham Clowns, it was only the third and fourth home games for the Choo Choos. But the team reportedly had returned home "red hot." One particular reason manager Harry Barnes had to smile was his center fielder, young Mays. "Mayes [sic] is only 16 years old, but packs a lot of power in his 168 pounds. He is a sure fielder, and very fast. He is the pride and joy of ... Barnes and of the fans."[52]

Mays lived up to expectations. Playing shortstop rather than center field in the first game, he had two hits, a double and a triple, in four at-bats. He drove in five runs and scored four times. He committed one error in four chances in the likely unfamiliar position. Chattanooga won both games, by scores of 17–0 and 6–5. A pitcher identified only as Ramsey limited Birmingham to just three hits in the first game. The games were played before a crowd of 1,198 fans.[53]

The following day, in the second game of a three-team doubleheader, Chattanooga beat Birmingham, 7–4. The losing pitcher was "Pie" Silvers, the mainstay pitcher for the Choo Choos in previous years. Mays, again playing shortstop, had one hit in three at-bats and committed two errors in six fielding chances.[54]

Continuing to awe everyone who saw him play, he produced five hits in seven at-bats in a doubleheader in Memphis in mid–June. One of the hits was a home run.[55]

Although the Chattanooga team continued to play well, local newspaper coverage had declined considerably from a year earlier, when there were box scores for most home games. There was also little or no mention of the NSL pennant race in the 1948 coverage. When the Memphis Cardinals appeared at Engel Stadium in late August it was reported that Chattanooga was attempting "to retain their hold on a first division spot."

The primary attraction was not the pennant race or Willie Mays, who was now with the Black Barons, but the anticipated appearance of Willie Young with Memphis. Young, the one-armed pitcher, was expected to work for the visitors.[56]

With the help of several new positions players, Chattanooga battered Memphis by identical 11–4 scores in the doubleheader. However, there was no mention of Young in the game report or the line scores of the games.[57]

Opposite: **The 1948 Birmingham Black Barons, champions of the Negro American League. The player on the far right is future Hall of Famer Willie Mays, who had started the season earlier with the Chattanooga Choo Choos (National Baseball Hall of Fame in Cooperstown, New York).**

A couple of weeks later Young did play in Chattanooga when Birmingham came to town for a doubleheader. The Birmingham team was now clearly called the All-Stars rather than the Clowns. Young came on in relief and pitched the final four innings of Birmingham's 16–9 opening game win. He "amazed spectators by allowing no hits and only one unearned run in the final four innings," reported the *Chattanooga Daily Times*. The Choo Choos won the second game, 6–4. They were the last reported games in the Chattanooga paper.[58]

Although coverage in the final weeks of the season did not confirm the fact, the pennant was apparently won by the New Orleans Creoles. When the team opened its 1949 season as members of the Negro Texas League, they were referred to as 1948 champions of the Negro Southern League.[59]

In what might be considered a footnote on the season, sportswriter Marion E. Jackson wrote a column in mid–September about a sparsely attended game at Ponce de Leon Park in Atlanta. Citing dwindling attendance and black population shifts to other sections of the city, Jackson predicted that future games would likely be played at neighborhood facilities, Harper Field and Herndon Stadium. "So write it down, for 1950 or 1951, unless there is a drastic reshaping of thinking in Southern mores, we will be more and more inclined to withdraw into self-imposed shells of seclusion, which will be in a sense helpful, but in a social sense harmful."[60]

Jackson's prophecy was unfulfilled in that the black professional baseball teams in Atlanta continued to use Ponce de Leon through the 1950 season. In 1951, it was not a matter of relocation, but simply that the Black Crackers had ceased to exist.

19

1949
The Hyphens Arrive

The confusing membership and the diminishing coverage of the Negro Southern League in 1948 was just a prelude to what was to come or, more accurately, not to come, in 1949.

With more and more cherry picking of top black players by white-owned Organized Baseball, NSL officials sought to stem the tide. League president Dr. R. B. Jackson, Commissioner B. T. Harvey, and others formed a committee to seek an audience with Baseball Commissioner A. B. "Happy" Chandler to discuss the situation.[1]

The amount of coverage given even the so-called black major leagues, i.e., the Negro National League and the Negro American League, was decreasing also in major black newspapers like the *Chicago Defender*, *Pittsburgh Courier*, and *Atlanta Daily World*. In each instance, the success of Jackie Robinson and the subsequent signing of players like Larry Doby and Satchel Paige captured the attention of the fans and the press.

Nevertheless, Jackson pushed forward with NSL organizational efforts, proposing a 10- or even 12-team league for 1949. The larger structure would depend on the Atlanta Black Crackers. Normally a stalwart in the NSL, owner John Harden announced that he was leaning toward fielding an independent rather than a league team.[2]

Meeting in Nashville, Jackson was once again elected president. Other officers were: George E. McCray, Evansville, vice president; H. L. Johnson, Little Rock, secretary; Allen Page, New Orleans, treasurer; and B. T. Harvey, Atlanta, commissioner and director of publicity. Others present at the meeting included Julian Bell and Dr. Hildreth, Jackson, Tennessee, Royal Giants; Dave Slaughter, Montgomery Tigers; Shephard Beck, Chattanooga Choo Choos; Virgil McGraw, Indianapolis ABCs; Ovan Haskins, Lexington, Kentucky, Hustlers; C. Davis, Mobile, Alabama Shippers; Dr. Edgecombe, West Palm Beach, Florida, Rockets; and Kenneth Stuart, Detroit Red Wings.[3]

Jackson still projected a 10-team league with an NSL team in every white Southern Association city. He continued to hold out hope for 12 teams predicated on Atlanta owner John Harden being persuaded to forego his plans to make the Black Crackers an independent team in 1949.[4]

NSL officials met again in Mobile over the weekend of March 13 and 14 to draw up the schedule and finish other organizational details. Clubs present were the Detroit-Mobile Shippers, New Orleans, Nashville, Montgomery, Pensacola, Chattanooga, Evansville, and (Pittsburgh) Homestead Grays. Represented by proxy were Indianapolis; Lexington; Jackson, Mississippi; and Little Rock. Not represented were such mainstay cities as Atlanta, Birmingham, and Memphis.[5]

When the season finally opened, the league was nowhere near the size Jackson had projected. Not only were there only six clubs, but two of them had hyphenated names. These mergers were not the sign of a healthy economy, but rather of a struggle to survive. Opening Day was set for May 15. When the 1949 NSL schedule was published in the *Daily World*, openers were to be the Atlanta-Detroit Brown Crackers and Nashville Cubs, the Gadsden-Florida Tigers at the Pensacola Sea Gulls, and Mobile Shippers vs. Montgomery Tigers at Chattanooga. The newspaper reported that the

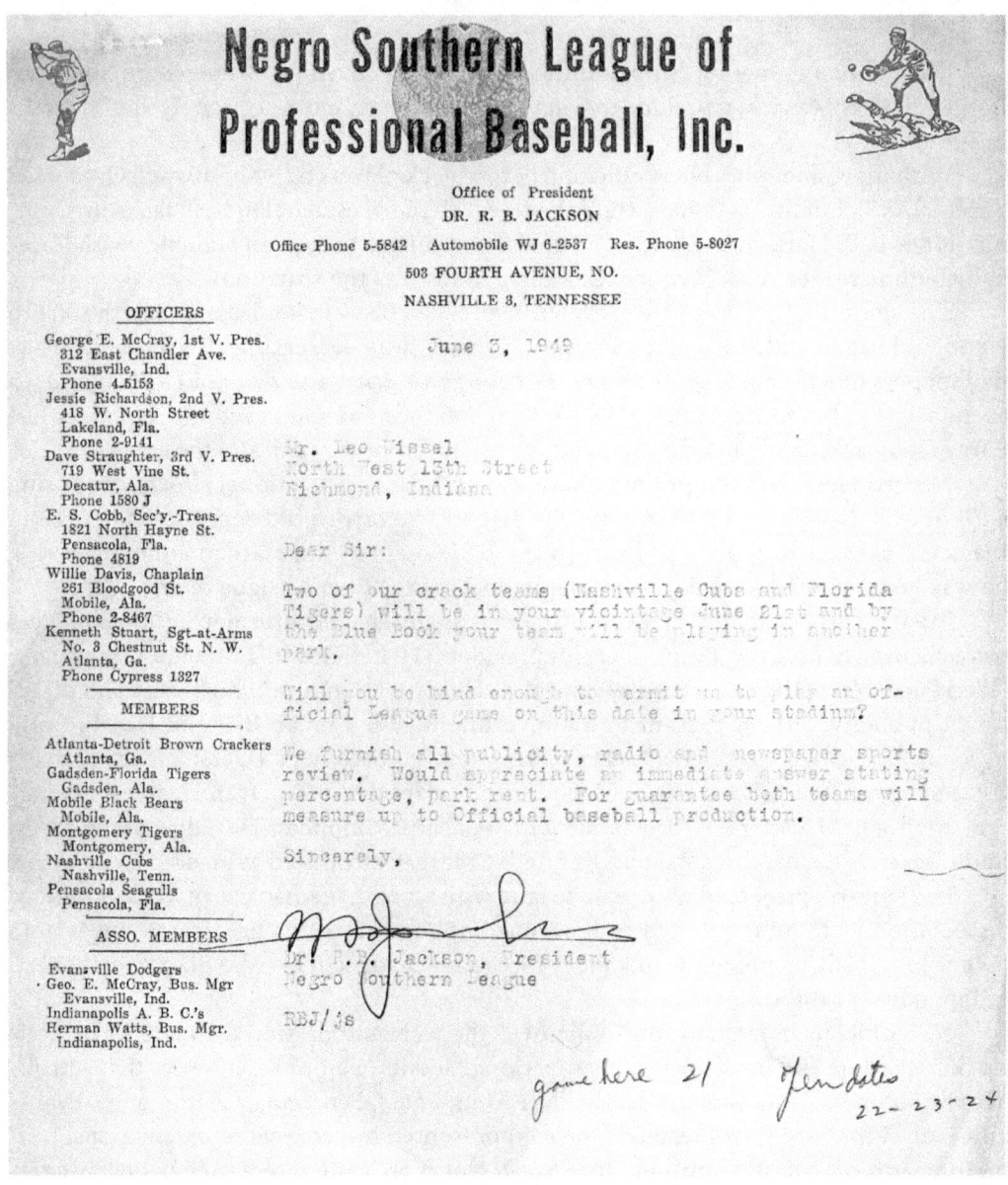

Letter from NSL president Dr. R.B. Jackson to Leo Wissell, owner of the Ohio-Indiana League's Richmond Tigers, seeking a venue for traveling NSL teams (courtesy Center for Negro Leagues Baseball Research).

Atlanta club was an amalgam of the traditional local club and the Detroit Red Wings. The team would "play out of Atlanta and Chattanooga." The Lakeland, Florida, Tigers were being merged with a Gadsden, Alabama, team. Associate members were the Evansville, Indiana, Dodgers and Indianapolis ABCs.[6]

If the Montgomery club even existed, it was tenuously. Neither the *Montgomery Advertiser* nor the *Alabama Journal* ever reported on this team. However, both did frequently report on the Montgomery Giants and the Montgomery Homestead Grays, amateur teams. The Giants were members of the South Alabama Negro League and the Grays were apparently an independent team.

Negro professional teams did play in Montgomery that summer, though. The Birmingham Black Barons played both exhibition and regular league games there occasionally. In June a game was scheduled between the New Orleans Creoles and Shreveport of the Negro Texas League. The New Orleans lineup featured Toni Stone, probably the most notable of several female players the team had in post–World War II years. Another drawing card was Little Sam, "The Wonder Boy," alleged to be a catcher with no hands and feet.[7]

The Creoles were once again in the Negro Texas League along with teams from Oklahoma and Arkansas, as well as Texas. The Creoles were said to be the only team still active when the league folded in early August.[8]

The Mobile was called the Mobile-Detroit Shippers when the team played an exhibition game in April.[9] However, Detroit found the Atlanta pairing more suitable. By May it was the Mobile Black Bears preparing to open the Negro Southern League season with a home game against the Pensacola Sea Gulls.[10] And, like Montgomery, it was a tenuous existence. No results or player names were found for Mobile during the season.

Likewise, no results were found for the Pensacola team, which was owned and managed by Dr. E. S. Cobb. Noted as medical pioneer in the Pensacola area, Dr. Cobb was a black physician trained at Meharry Medical School and the University of Leon in France during World War I.[11]

The Gadsden-Florida Tigers played at City Park in Gadsden, home of the white Gadsden Chiefs of the Southeastern League. The manager was Jesse Richardson and although more results were found for this team than any other, only one played was identified by both first and last name, an infielder named Billy Robe. Reports on the team ceased in mid–June.

The Atlanta-Detroit Brown Crackers club was formed from remnants of former Atlanta teams and the independent Detroit club under Manager Kenneth Stewart. The team trained in Mobile and reportedly won 13 out of 16 exhibition games in preparation for the season. They secured Ponce de Leon Park for their home games.[12] The former Red Wings were said to be champions of the Ohio-Michigan Negro League.[13]

The Nashville Cubs, the only familiar name in the 1949 lineup, had trained in Meridian, Mississippi, under manager Russell Ewing. His top pitcher was Edward "Lefty" Derrick, a mainstay hurler with the Cubs. Otha Bailey, a future Black Baron, was his catcher. As they prepared to open their exhibition season in April they were said to be seeking their fourth consecutive NSL championship. That claim, of course, was nothing more than promotional ballyhoo. Other players included outfielders James Zapp, James

Bransford, and Joe Brooks, left-hander Derrick Brooks, and right-handers Bomber Brown, Cowboy Murray, and Eugene Craig.[14]

The first exhibition game, scheduled with Atlanta-Detroit in late April, was rained out, as was an exhibition game between the New Orleans Creoles and the San Francisco Sea Lions of the Negro Pacific Coast League.[15]

There was no mention of the Gadsden-Florida Tigers in the Gadsden newspaper until May 21. The local sports editor appeared to be surprised to learn that there was a local black professional team: "The first appearance of a Negro baseball team called the Gadsden-Florida Tigers will be held tonight at 8 o'clock at City Park.... The Tigers boast a fast combination of star players formerly connected with the Florida League. They will have one of the fastest infields, headed by hard-hitting Billy Robe...." If the sports editor, Al Fox, was curious about the Gadsden-Florida amalgam, he did not show it.

Still he did report results of a number of games over the coming weeks. The opening game was won by the Tigers, 10–4, over Nashville. A shortstop named Jeff hit a home run and catcher Fisher was three-for-three in the game. Kizer, the Nashville shortstop, had three hits in four at-bats. The winning pitcher was named Turgison.[16] There was no report on the second game of the series.

On opening day in Nashville the Cubs split a doubleheader with the Atlanta-Detroit team. Edward Derrick held the visitors to four hits in the first game. The Brown Crackers out hit the Cubs, 13 to 9, to win the second game, 12–8.[17]

The following weekend in a rematch with the Cubs, Atlanta-Detroit opened its home schedule at Ponce de Leon Park. The Brown Crackers won the game, 5–1, then made it two in a row with a 3–1 win on Monday night in Macon. The two teams played an unreported game in Griffin, Georgia, on Tuesday night. Afterward, Atlanta went to Florida while Nashville returned to Atlanta to play a game with the Gadsden-Florida Tigers.[18] The result was not reported.

Indeed, there was no further coverage of the Atlanta-Detroit team in the *Daily World*, the black community's newspaper. The next reference to a Negro Southern League team was on July 24 when the Nashville Cubs returned to town to play the Original Zulu Giants, a barnstorming team. The game was played at Herndon Stadium on the Morris Brown College campus rather than at Ponce de Leon. The Cubs were reported to have a record of 41 wins in 46 games thus far in the 1949 season.[19]

There was no report in the *Daily World* on the outcome of the game or on the local team the following weekend, when it was to open its home season.

On Sunday, May 29, the Gadsden-Florida team swept a doubleheader from Nashville in Chattanooga, winning, 10–2 and 6–0. The *Gadsden Times* reported that the two wins gave the Tigers "a commanding lead in the loop."

The following weekend Gadsden-Florida won another doubleheader, defeating the Indianapolis ABCs, 9–6 and 3–0, in Louisville.[20] The Tigers then returned home for a Tuesday game with Montgomery Greys at City Park. Admission was 90 cents for adults and 50 cents for children. Montgomery was defeated, 22–4, with Turgison again being the winning pitcher. A local boy named Coates hit a home run for the Tigers.[21]

It is not clear if the Montgomery team was the same as the pre-season Montgomery Tigers or was an independent team. The *Montgomery Advertiser* had no reports on

Negro Southern League games involving a capital city team during the months of May and June. There was also no coverage of a team called the Greys, the longtime nickname for a Montgomery black team.

On Saturday, June 11, Nashville defeated Gadsden-Florida, 8–6, in Anniston, Alabama. Going into a Sunday, June 12, doubleheader at home against Montgomery, the Tigers were reported to have a 10–2 record. They won both games and were next scheduled for a Monday night home game against the Birmingham Giants.[22]

There was no report on the Birmingham game and, indeed, there was no further mention of the Gadsden-Florida Tigers in the *Gadsden Times* the remainder of the summer.

Although the Gadsden-Florida team appeared to be a good one, beating Nashville in most instances that were reported, it apparently did not survive the month of June. Nashville, on the other hand, was still around and playing well as the season wound down. They hosted the Atlanta Black Crackers and the Zulu Giants in a three-team doubleheader on August 7.[23] Was this John Harden's independent team or the misidentified Atlanta-Detroit Brown Crackers? Impossible to say.

By August 15, the Cubs were reported to be in first place with a second-half record of 17–3. Tied for second were the Atlanta Black Crackers and Birmingham Clowns. Again, which Atlanta club is this? And what about the sudden appearance of this Birmingham team? It was reportedly going to play in Nashville on Sunday, August 21, against another mystery club, the Memphis Cardinals. Memphis was said to be bringing with them Willie Young, the one-armed pitcher. The Birmingham club was now called the Black Barons rather than the Clowns. Old bad habits of team identification appeared to die slowly. The games were to be official NSL contests. Then, on Monday night, the Cubs were again to host the Black Crackers.[24]

The rest of the week, the Birmingham club was alternately referred to as the Black Barons and the Clowns. Finally, the game report stuck with Clowns, saying the teams had split a doubleheader. Birmingham won the opener, 7–6, and Willie Young pitched Memphis to a 9–4 win in the second game.[25]

Then, trying for his second win in as many days and with as many clubs, Young was said to be pitching for the Nashville Cubs on Monday night against the Detroit Wolverines. Young was not mentioned in the game report, which said Nashville had beaten not Detroit, but Birmingham, 13–10 the night before. Manager Felton Snow's five-for-five hitting performance powered Nashville.[26]

Perhaps more important is the suggestion that Birmingham and Memphis were members of the Negro Southern League. That would indicate they were replacing other clubs that had folded or that the league had expanded during the second half, a most unlikely occurrence. Or yet again, they were members from the beginning in an incredibly poorly-reported operation.

Only the Nashville Cubs were a constant for the 1949 Negro Southern League season. On September 12 the Cubs hosted the Cleveland Buckeyes at Sulphur Dell in a game that was said to match the Negro American League champion against the Negro Southern League winner. The "inter-league championship" was scheduled to start at 8:15 p.m. "with plenty of seats" reserved for white fans. Admission was one dollar for adults and 40 cents for children.[27] There was no report on the outcome of the game.

While there would be little doubt that Nashville was the 1949 champion, there are a lot of questions about just who the Cubs defeated. Only 19 scores were found for the season, nine of them in games embracing the teams identified early on as members of the league. The other 10 games involved the mysterious Memphis, Birmingham, and Montgomery teams that surfaced mid-season.

The NSL's slide to obscurity, remarkably, would take two more years to complete.

20

1950–51
The End

The declining fan interest and instability of Negro baseball, especially at the minor league level, was plainly evident as efforts were made to form the Negro Southern League in 1950. No fewer than 22 teams in 16 cities were mentioned as possible members of the league during the spring. Among them were two of the increasingly common hyphenated clubs representing two cities.

And it wasn't much better at higher levels. The Negro National League had folded after the 1948 season and the Negro World Series was no more.[1] The Negro American League survived with 10 teams, two from the defunct NNL. In 1951 the number dropped to eight and then six in 1952. Only four teams remained for the 1953 and 1954 seasons.[2]

Every newspaper article about the Negro Southern League's organization efforts seemed to present an entirely different lineup of prospective teams. On February 11, the *Chicago Defender* reported that Evansville, Indiana; Decatur, Alabama; and Pensacola and Lakeland, Florida, had all been dropped from consideration. There was a possibility that the famous Homestead Grays might be accepted as an associate member.[3]

The league's annual winter meeting was held at the Elks Club in Nashville on Sunday, February 26. Teams in the league were reported to be the Atlanta-Detroit Brown Crackers, Gadsden-Florida Tigers, Mobile Black Bears, Montgomery Tigers, Nashville Cubs, and Pensacola Sea Gulls. Commissioner B. T. Harvey had reportedly already set up franchise and player contract mechanics and an umpire rotation schedule. President R. B. Jackson asked clubs to present exhibition schedules and proposed an opening date.[4] Jackson may have been presiding only during the organizational period because later articles report W. S. Martin as NSL president.

On March 11 the *Defender* listed the memberships as the Atlanta Black Crackers; Evansville Braves; Gadsden Red Sox; Jackson, Tennessee, Royal Giants; Nashville Cubs; and an otherwise unidentified Memphis club. By April 25 the *Defender* reported the lineup as the Atlanta Black Crackers; Chattanooga Choo Choos; Gadsden Tigers; Greenville Delta Giants, Louisville/Nashville Cubs; Memphis Red Caps; New Orleans Black Pelicans; and Owensboro, Kentucky, Dodgers. The disparity shows the disarray and the struggle to find some means of survival for black baseball.

Finally, after yet another frantic meeting, officials came up with a plan, in which they agreed "to play regular games, laid the foundation for an all-star game and completed schedules for the coming season." Opening day was set for April 30 with Atlanta at Memphis, Gadsden at Greenville, Nashville at Evansville, and Jackson at New Orleans.[5]

A week before the season was to start a new Opening Day schedule was released: New Orleans at Atlanta, Louisville-Nashville at Memphis, Gadsden at Greenville, Owensboro at Chattanooga. The obvious changes were the replacement of Evansville and Jackson with Owensboro and Chattanooga. Also, the Nashville team was now a consolidated entry.[6] Owensboro is one of the puzzles. Constantly referred to as the Owensboro Dodgers, the team was identified in the *Owensboro Inquirer* as the Braves. Managed by Negro Southern League regular Rufus Hatten, the team was scheduled to open its first NSL season on Sunday, May 7, with the "the Nashville and Louisville All-Stars." The Braves' exhibition schedule had included the following results: a win over the Evansville Dodgers and losses to Waverly, Tennessee, the Booneville American Legion club and the Birmingham Black Braves.[7]

With a roster that contained only one familiar name besides Hatten (infielder Granville Lyons), the Braves were likely comprised of local players. The season opener, first reported to be against the Louisville All-Stars, then the Nashville All Stars, was obviously the Louisville-Nashville amalgam. A doubleheader was scheduled for Sunday, May 7.[8] The games were likely rained out.

The Braves had earlier lost a game to the Atlanta Brown Crackers at Rockport, Indiana, and were scheduled to play a home game against the Louisville Black Colonels on May 13 with the Owensboro Boys Scouts as special guests.[9] Those were the last reports on what might be considered NSL games. All other Owensboro games were against semipro teams and the barnstorming House of David.

On June 1, the *Daily World* reported that Owensboro was one of three teams being dropped from the league for "failure to live up to contractual obligations." The Braves had played only three league games at that point. The other two teams were Chattanooga and Birmingham. Little is known about the Birmingham team. On June 8 a team called the Birmingham Red Sox was scheduled to play the semipro Huntsville Stars at Optimist Park in Huntsville, Alabama. "The Red Sox, newly-formed Negro Southern league aggregation, will be making their first showing here tonight," reported a local newspaper. Birmingham was managed by Jim Canada and supposedly had picked up several former Chattanooga players.[10]

Ever ebullient, league President Dr. W. S. Martin said all of the teams had been strengthened for the new season. He also said the NSL held the future of black baseball: "Negro baseball's future is faced with a challenge, and we feel that the Negro Southern League will eventually prove to be the salvation for our Negro baseball stars trying to make their way in our great National pastime."[11]

The ever-changing schedule saw the opening New Orleans-Atlanta series actually played in Louisville, not Atlanta. The Creoles won the opener, 6–3, and Atlanta the nightcap, 8–2. Al Pinkston, the losing pitcher for New Orleans in the second game, hit a 485-foot home run. Both teams had Cuban shortstops, Chico Farrell for Atlanta and Al Costello for New Orleans.[12]

Two weeks later, the same teams played in Atlanta. There was a great deal of anticipation from local fans to see Miss Toni Stone playing second base for the Creoles after a successful career with all-female teams in California.[13] New Orleans won both games. There was no mention of Stone in the game report.[14]

The Atlanta Brown Crackers opened spring training in Lakeland, Florida, under field manager Vinicius "Nish" Williams, a veteran catcher whose career dated to the mid–1920s. His camp was filled with 18- and 19-year-olds looking to make the team, but also included some who had played in both the Negro American League and the Negro National League.[15]

The earliest gauge on a pennant race was the standings published in the *Daily World* on June 1. They showed the Louisville-Nashville team in first place with a 5–1 record, followed by Atlanta at 7–3, New Orleans 7–5, Greenville 4–3, Memphis 3–5, Chattanooga 0–2, Owensboro 0–3, and Birmingham 0–4.[16]

When Atlanta returned home for a series with Louisville at Ponce de Leon Park in early June, the team faced an odd situation: the inability of fans to get to the ball park because of a transit strike. Owner Jesse Richardson said a public appeal would be made for car pools to get the fans to the stadium if the strike was not settled by game day.[17] And as if the transit strike was not a sufficient disruption, the game added still more to the question of just who was in the league. Atlanta's upcoming opponent was identified as the Louisville Giants, not the Louisville-Nashville Cubs.[18]

When the *Daily World* published the only set of standings on June 1, 1950, it showed a foundering organization with five active clubs among the eight that had started the season. Teams that had been dropped from the league "for failure to live up to contractual obligations" were Birmingham, Chattanooga, and Owensboro.[19]

A league meeting was scheduled for June 11 in Memphis. Agenda items included the consideration of possible additional members, completing a second half schedule, and exploring plans for an all-star game. The meeting announcement listed six teams: Atlanta Brown Bombers, Chattanooga Choo Choos, Greenville Delta Giants, Louisville Stars, Memphis Red Caps, and New Orleans Creoles. Several cities were said to be sending representatives to the meeting to apply for membership. They were: Evansville Dodgers, Indianapolis ABCS, Jackson Tigers, Jacksonville Eagles, Knoxville Tigers, Montgomery Giants, and Savannah Tigers.[20]

It was that morass of confusion that likely lead Atlanta sportswriter Marion E. Jackson to pen this sentence: "The embattled Negro Southern League holds a do-or-die meeting in Memphis, Sunday, June 11."[21]

Although Jackson did not report further on the league's future, it did survive for a while longer. Just a few days after the "do-or-die" meeting, a special meeting was held to draw up more concrete plans for the all-star game.

But when Chattanooga went to Atlanta for a Sunday doubleheader on June 18, it was reported to be the farewell visit for the Choo Choos. The Chattanooga team was said to be dropping out of the league after those games. (Of course, Chattanooga had also been reported to have been previously dropped from the league along with Birmingham and Owensboro.) According to the newspaper report, that move would the league with six (unspecified) teams, but it would be "stronger."[22]

Yet, on June 29, the *Daily World* carried a photograph of legendary Satchel Paige with a caption proclaiming that he would be pitching a few innings for the Chattanooga Choo Choos in a Fourth of July game with the Homestead Grays at Engel Field.[23]

The all-star game was set for Sunday, July 9, at Martin Stadium in Memphis. An NSL team comprised of three members from each league team would play the Memphis Red Sox of the Negro American League. Players would be selected by sportswriters and managers.

In addition to obligatory speeches by league Commissioner Harvey and President Martin, music was to be provided by George Lawson and his "well known radio recording orchestra." Another radio personality was master of ceremonies Dewey Phillips of radio station WHBQ, a disk jockey described as the current "rave among radio personalities," known for his familiar saying, "Tell 'em Phillips sent you."[24]

The game was a success. A crowd of 5,396 filled Martin Stadium to watch the Red Sox win 6–5, scoring the winning run in the bottom of the eighth. Highlights of the game include a home run by Memphis catcher Casey Jones and six innings of play by Toni Stone, the female player from the New Orleans club. Stone walked twice and hit a double to left field. She also handled two fielding chances without an error.[25]

After the game, the Red Sox and the All-Stars were scheduled for a four-game tour that would take them to Eufaula, Alabama, and Atlanta, Macon and Columbus, Georgia.[26] Co-managers of the All-Star team were T. J. Brown of Memphis and Nish Williams of Atlanta. The roster of players was drawn from four clubs: Atlanta, Greenville, Memphis, and New Orleans.[27]

The Memphis Red Sox–NSL All-Stars game in Atlanta had been scheduled for July 12. An advance story with the All-Star roster was the last publication of any Brown Bombers news in Atlanta's black newspaper.[28] The All-Star roster suggests that there were only four active clubs in the league at that time. Certainly no information on a pennant race was published. In August sportswriter Marion E. Jackson wrote that a reader had taken him to task for reporting that the Brown Crackers had ceased to operate. "All we know," wrote Jackson, "is that not one sentence of publicity on the Brown Crackers has come our way and the team hasn't played here in weeks." Jackson said he had checked newspapers from around the Southeast and seen no articles on the team.

Jackson's research not-

By the time Toni Stone signed with the Indianapolis Clowns in 1953, she had played professional baseball for four years, having spent most of the 1949–1952 seasons with the NSL New Orleans Creoles. She is pictured here with heavyweight champion Joe Louis in 1949 (courtesy NoirTech Research).

withstanding, the irate reader reported that he had seen the team play games against Birmingham, Memphis, Miami, and Louisville teams, winning seven out of nine games. Furthermore, he said the Atlanta team was leading the league by five and a half games.[29] It is unclear if the fan was gilding the lily out of civic pride or was sharing real information. In fact not a single score for the Brown Bombers was located after June 29.

The popularity of the All-Star game notwithstanding, the chaotic finish to the 1950 season should have been the Negro Southern League's ignoble end. But, with dogged determination, a handful of baseball men were determined to fly in the face of all odds in 1951.

What they produced was an almost invisible, woefully underfinanced collection of semipro teams playing in obscure venues. Games in traditional Southern Association and similar ball parks were far beyond their means.

In late March, it was reported out of Memphis that the league would operate with a slightly different name in 1951. It would be called the Negro Southern Association instead of the traditional Negro Southern League. The lineup for the NSA at this point was to be Raleigh Tigers, Greensboro Red Wings, Atlanta Braves, Nashville Cubs, Memphis Red Caps, Greenville Delta Giants, New Orleans Creoles, and Columbus Bears. The season was to open on May 14 and close on Labor Day.

The newspaper noted, also, that a similar naming venture in black baseball had failed the year before. A Negro American Association, drawing its name from the white minor league, had started the season with eight teams but only two of them had completed the season.[30]

An April meeting in Atlanta was called by President Allen Page to finalize a first half schedule and, presumably, the lineup of teams. Representatives were expected at the meeting from the Birmingham Eagles, Evansville Dodgers, Greensboro Red Birds, Indianapolis-Atlanta ABCs, Memphis Red Caps, Mobile Black Shippers, Nashville Cubs, and Raleigh Tigers. Associate member representatives were expected from Lakeland and Pensacola, Florida, Jackson and McComb, Mississippi, New Orleans, and Savannah.[31]

A subsequent meeting was scheduled on May 12 at the home of Hill Harris, league treasurer and owner of the Birmingham Black Eagles. Completion of the first half schedule, with a starting date of May 20, topped the agenda. Also, Commissioner Harvey said umpires, roster limits, and other basic business items would be completed at the meeting.[32]

Going into the meeting four franchises were said to be locked in. They were Birmingham; the Evansville Dodgers; Jackson, Mississippi, Cubs; and Nashville Cubs. Expected to attend were representatives from other teams in Indianapolis; McComb, Mississippi;, Mobile; Nashville; New Orleans; and Pensacola, plus the geographically unspecific Florida Cuban Stars.[33]

Mobile was not among the cities projected to participate in the league. Yet, the Mobile Black Bears, called "one of the best independent Colored teams in the south," played an apparent exhibition game with the Nashville Cubs at Hartwell Field in May. Nashville was identified as an NSL member.[34]

Whether or not the meeting at Harris' house was even held is speculative. No newspaper reported on it. In fact, that article, published in the *Birmingham World*, was the only mention of Harris, the Birmingham team, or the league throughout the summer. Neither of the city's white dailies, the *News* or the *Post-Herald*, ever reported anything on those three entities. The only confirmation of the team's existence came from the *Chattanooga Daily Times* and the *Tuscaloosa News*. The former reported that Birmingham lost two games to Chattanooga in early June; the latter reported that the same two teams were scheduled to play a game in Alberta City, a Tuscaloosa suburb in July. No result was reported.

Although listed in all of the preseason organizational stories, the Nashville Cubs were apparently gone. There was no mention of the club in the *Nashville Banner* in May, June, or July. Still, the newspaper was covering a number of Negro American League games scheduled in the city at Sulphur Dell. Most of them involved the New Orleans Eagles. Results were reported for some of those games as well.

Chattanooga, which had apparently had been only an independent team in 1949 and had lasted only a few weeks in the NSL in 1950, was not mentioned as a potential league member. Yet, on June 1 the Chattanooga All-Stars defeated the Birmingham All-Stars, 19–8, at Engel Stadium. Chattanooga won again on Sunday, 7–4. Both games were reported as Negro Southern League contests. Line scores of the two games may say something about the caliber of play in this remnant of the old NSL. Birmingham committed a total of 12 errors while Chattanooga committed 10.[35] In a June 24 game with the Knoxville Packers, each team committed six errors.[36] Albeit a limited sample, the numbers may reflective of the quality of play in the struggling league.

After the Birmingham series Chattanooga was reported to be in first place with a record of six wins and only one loss, that to Knoxville on opening day. The All-Stars were reported to have outscored opponents 63–24 in the seven games played.[37]

In July two series of games were played at Alberta Park in Tuscaloosa. The games did not involve teams listed as likely league members during the preseason meetings. On July 2 the Birmingham Bears and Chattanooga Stars were scheduled.[38] On July 20 a game between the Chattanooga Stars and the Knoxville Packers was scheduled. Entering the game, Chattanooga's record was reported to be 24–3 and Knoxville's 25–2.[39] There was no report on the either game's outcome in the Tuscaloosa newspaper.

The Packers attracted no attention in Knoxville newspapers. There was only one mention of the club throughout the months of the 1951 season: "The Knoxville Packers will meet the Elizabethton Grays in a baseball game at Leslie Street Park at 3 p.m. today. Richardson will pitch for the Packers and Fine will do the catching."[40] There was no report on the outcome of the game.

The pregame article on the Knoxville-Chattanooga contest in the Tuscaloosa suburban park was the final published reference to the Negro Southern League. The end to the storied league had come sadly with very much of a whimper.

Appendix A

Champions, Playoffs, No Hit Games

Champions

1920	Montgomery, disputed by Nashville
1921	Nashville
1922	Nashville
1923	Birmingham
1924–25	no league
1926	Birmingham
1927	Chattanooga
1928	no league
1929	Nashville
1930	no league
1931	Nashville
1932	Chicago, first half, disputed by Monroe
	Nashville, second half
1933	Memphis, first half
	New Orleans, second half
1934	undetermined
1935	Memphis, first half
	undetermined, second half
1936	Birmingham, first half
	undetermined, second half
1937–44	no league
1945	Atlanta
1946	Asheville
1947	Asheville
1948	New Orleans, first half
	New Orleans?, second half
1949	Gadsden-Florida, first half
	Nashville, second half
1950	undetermined
1951	undetermined

NSL Playoffs (number of games)

1921	Nashville 4, Montgomery 1
1926	Birmingham 5, Memphis 2, 3 tie games
1931	Memphis 3, Montgomery 3 (tie)
1935	Claybrook 4, Memphis 2
1946	Asheville 3, New Orleans 2

Negro Dixie Series

1927	Nashville 4, Dallas 1
1932	Monroe 4, Austin 2
1933	Nashville 4, New Orleans 4 (tie)

Negro World Series

1933	Chicago 5, New Orleans 1

No-Hit Games

1920
- May 18 John Dickey, Knoxville 6, Atlanta 0, first game, 9 innings
- July 10 Bud Force, Knoxville 3, Columbus (Ohio) 0, exhibition, 9 innings
- July 17 John Dickey, Knoxville 5 Winston-Salem 2, exhibition, 9 innings
- July 27 Sam Streeter, Montgomery 3, Atlanta 0, first game, 9 innings

1926
- June 27 Bill Gatewood, Albany 7 vs. Birmingham 0
- August 28 Harry Salmon, Birmingham 8, Albany 0

1931
- May 30 Tuggle Dawson, Knoxville 0, Montgomery 1, 7 innings
- July 18 Walter Calhoun, Birmingham 11, Fort Benning 0, 9 innings
- July 27 Homer Curry, Memphis 12, Little Rock 0, 9 innings
- Sept. 5 Homer Curry, Memphis 6, Birmingham 0, 7 innings

1932
- May 7 Barney Morris, Monroe 4, Cleveland 0, 7 innings

1933
- July 9 Son Harvey, Memphis 1, Nashville 0, exhibition, 5 innings

1936
- May 10 Roy Welmaker, Atlanta 6, Chattanooga 0, 9 innings

1945
- May 15 Gread McKinnis, Knoxville W, New Orleans L (unconfirmed)
- June 30 John Sadler, Atlanta 1, Indianapolis 0, exhibition, 9 innings

1946
- June 9 Frank Fleming, Asheville 24, Montgomery 0, first game, 9 innings
- June 9 Vernon Phillips, Asheville 22, Montgomery 0, second game, 9 innings

Appendix B

Yearly Rosters

These rosters were painstakingly compiled from hundreds of newspaper articles and game reports, supplemented by many other resources, including the Internet. A question mark after a name or position indicates that there is a likelihood of correctness, although the information was unconfirmed. If another name follows in parentheses it indicates that both names appeared in contemporary accounts with no clear determination of which was correct.

Information regarding where the team played is presented first, followed by administrators (who may also have been players at some point in their career) and then players and position. The following abbreviations are used throughout: c, catcher; p, pitcher; rhp, right-handed pitcher; lhp, left-handed pitcher; 1b, first base, 2b, second base; 3b, third base, ss, shortstop; inf, infield; of, outfield; rf, right field; lf, left field; cf, center field; util, utility; capt, captain; and x, position unknown. In the case of league officials, the abbreviation NA is "not available."

Team nicknames separated by a slash indicate that contemporary reports often referenced both names with no clear determination of which was correct.

1920

President—Frank M. Perdue, Birmingham
Vice president—J. H. Taylor, Nashville
Secretary—W. M. Brooks, Knoxville
Treasurer—W. J. Shaw, Atlanta

Atlanta Black Crackers

Played at Ponce de Leon Park, Morris Brown field
Rev. T.H. Addison, c-2b-manager by June 8

Anderson, p
Barber, c
Barnes, rf
Cottingham, cf
[Claude?] Cox, ss-capt
Napoleon Cummings, rhp-1b
Big Preacher Davis, 3b
Fred Downer, p, also with Knoxville
McKinney Downs, x
George "Tipper" Fisher, x
Will Flournoy, p
Charley Franklin, x
Frederick, p
Ted Gilliam, 1b
Willie "Lefty" Gisentaner, lhp-rf
Lewis Hampton, rhp-lf-c
[Ben?] Harris, p
Holmes, c
Charles Hudson, p
Will Johnson, p
Johnson, c
Landry, c
Ted Lee, 3b
Americus Lee, 3b
A. J. Lockhart, p
Forest "Wing" Maddox, p
Louis Means, ss
"Suggarty" Murden, c-2b
Omer Newsome, rf
Charles O'Neill, c
Johnny Owens, lhp
Patterson, lf
Ambrose Reid, 3b-cf
[B.?] Rodriguez, p
Sanders, p
Mack Smith, c
Scott Smith, p
Sotolongo, c
Tremble, c
Fred Wiley, p
Williams, p
Gerard Williams, inf
David "Mingo" Wingfield, cf-lf

Birmingham Black Barons

Played at Rickwood Field
Frank M. Perdue, manager-president

Brown, 3b
Canella, ph
P. Cardenas, c
John Cason [Casey], c-2b
John "Red" Charleston, c-rf, also with Nashville
Clemmons, ph
Willie Dozier, 2b-rf
[Jesse "John"?] Edwards, 2b-3b
Will Holt, rf
[Stanford?] Jackson, 2b
Eusebio Jeminez, 2b
John Kemp, lf-rf
Forest "Wing" Maddox, p
Martini, c
Bob McCormick, 3b, also with Montgomery
Buford "Geechie" Meredith, ss-3b
Juanelo Mirabal, rhp-cf-3b
Estaban Montalvo, lf-cf
Myals [Miles], 2b
Perez, 1b-ss
Pickens, lhp

Rochelle, cf
Rodriguez, p
Rogers, p
B. Rosella, cf
Russell, 3b
Harry Salmon, rhp-rf
Samson, p
Sotalongo, c
Tantaros [Tanano], c
Taylor, p
G. Taylor, x
Matthew Taylor, 1b
Tubbs, rf
Warner, p
Eugene Wesley [Westley], c-rf
Young, p, also with Montgomery
Gordon Zeigler, lhp

Jacksonville Stars
Played at Barrs Field
———

Cardle, 2b
Dawkins, c
Dawson, 1b
Willie Gisentaner, lhp-rf, also with Atlanta
Harris, p
Howard, p
Johnson, p-lf-cf
Johnston, p
Jones, ss
Alonzo "Fluke" "Hooks" Mitchell, p-cf-rf, also with Knoxville
Charles O'Neill, c-3b, also with Atlanta
Patterson, lf
Preacher, c-3b
Preston, rf
Roynord, ss
Smith, 2b-ss
Tipp, 1b
Wise, ss-2b-rf-cf
Zipp, cf

Knoxville Giants
Played at Booker T. Washington Park
Monroe D. Young, secretary
William M. Brooks, manager
———

Ralph "Pete" Cleage, 1b
Dana [Diana?], rf
John "Steel Arm" Dickey, p
Fred Downer, lf, also with Atlanta

William "Buddie" Force, rhp
Grimes, c
Peewee Hamilton, ss
Harris, p, from Winston-Salem
Howe, rf
Lloyd [Loyd?], cf
Long, inf, added for playoffs
Forest "One Wing" Maddox, p-cf, also with Atlanta
May, c
Alonzo "Fluke," "Hooks" Mitchell, rhp, also with Jacksonville
H. Moore, 2b
J. Moore, p
Pete "Bun" Moore, lhp
"String Bean" Moore, p
Moseley, rf
Johnny Ray, x
Russell, 3b
Sanders, c
Sims, c
"Black Babe Ruth" Smith, lhp
Smith, lf
Pete Widener, 1b
Tom Williams, p

Montgomery Grey Sox
Played at South Holt Street Park
John Staples, president Henry Hannon, manager-1b-lf
Marion "Daddy," "Red" Cunningham, 1b-3b-manager by Aug. 11
———

Anderson, p
Brown, p
Clay Carpenter, cf, also with Nashville
Cotton, p
Herman "Rounder" Cunningham, ss
[Walter "Newt"?] Joseph, p
Mason, p, also with Nashville
Bob McCormick, 3b, also with Birmingham
Hub McGavock, lf, also with Nashville
George "Deacon" Meyers, p, also with Nashville
Miles, p
Jimmy Moss, p-rf
O'Neil, p
Patton, cf
Preston, c-rf-1b

George "Tubby" Scales, 3b-rf
Seals, 1b, traded to Nashville for Carpenter
Stern, p
Sam Streeter, lhp
Charles "Two-Sides" Wesley, 2b
Poindexter Williams, c-rf
Young, p

Nashville White Sox
Played at Sulphur Dell
Marshall Garrett, manager
———

Amos Allison, ss-2b-rf
Clay Carpenter, cf, also with Montgomery
John "Red" Charleston, c, also with Birmingham
Crowder, p
W. Dixon, 3b
Russell "Columbus" Ewing, lf-3b
Hall, p
Harper, c
Johnny Holt, rf, also with Pensacola
Hunt, 1b-2b
Hurt, 1b
Johnson, c
E. Johnson, 1b
S. Johnson, 1b
V. Johnson, rf
Mason, p, also with Montgomery
McCall, rf
Fred McCarver, p-ss
Hub McGavock, cf-lf-2b, also with Montgomery
Meyer, p, also with Montgomery
Meyers, of
Miles, p
Nesbitt, p
Newell, cf
Eddie Noel, p
Norris, p
Amos Otis, of
Sam Peters, cf
Phillips, ss
Seals, cf, also with Montgomery
Simpkins, p
Norman "Turkey" Stearnes, lf-cf-p
Leroy Stratton, 3b
Albert Street, 2b
Thompson, c

Appendix B: Yearly Rosters 1921

Joe Ware, c
Wayers, p
Williams, p

NEW ORLEANS CAULFIELD ADS

Played at Heinemann Park
Fred Caulfield, p-manager

Badeau, p
Chase, ss
George "Bowlegs" Collins, ss-3b-rf
Cowens, ss
Davis, cf-rf
Dondell, p
Durand [Durant], 2b-ss
[Glover "Gus"?] Gardner, rf-ss
John George, 3b-cf-ss-2b
Lawrence "Cannonball" Graves, p
Hoomer Hall, c
Jackson, ss
Legnea, cf
"Chief" Lewis, rf-c
Margues, lf
Marquis, c
Lewis "Mo-feet" Moffett, p
Pardo, lhp
Robertson, lhp-rf
Robinson, p
Herman "Bobby" Roth, c
Percy Segula, cf
Watson, cf
Winfield S. Welch, lf-c
Williams, 1b-rf
Percy Wilson, 1b-p-2b-cf
John Woods, p

PENSACOLA GIANTS

Played at Moro Castle Park
Dr. A. J. Kerr, owner
C. J. Lawson, official scorer
Dan Brown, manager

Arnold, 2b-p-rf
Rudolph Ash, p
Cowin [Cowen], ss-3b
Cummings, p
Dawson, cf-3b-rf
Finley, 1b
Frederick[son], p
Glover "Gus" Gardner, rf-c
R. Harris, lf
Herman[s], ss
Johnny Holt, cf-3b, also with Nashville

Johnson, c-rf
Lumpkin[s], 3b 2b
Mays, 3b
Milton, rf
Johnny Owens, p-1b
Pardo, p
Patterson, ss
Pope[Poke], 3b
Price, 2b-ss-c-3b
Raggor, c
Ross, c
Sanford, rf-lf
"Vodie" Smith, 3b-c-2b-ss
Tally, p-cf-rf-lf
Tommy, ss-2b-1b-c
Tompkins, 3b-2b
Watts, ss-rf-lf-3b
Wright, 1b-2b
A. Wynder, rf-p
P. Wynder, p-ss

1921

President—F. M. Perdue, Birmingham
Vice president—R. H. Tabor, Nashville
Secretary—Prof. W. M. Brooks, Knoxville
Treasurer—W. J. Shaw, Atlanta

ATLANTA BLACK CRACKERS

Played at Ponce De Leon Park and Morris Brown campus
Negro Southeastern League, moved to NSL, replacing Gadsden c. May 7
Black, club official
Harper, club official
Mobley, club official
Sol Rivers, manager in August
W. J. Shaw, club official

Austin, 3b
Barnes, 2b-p
Bradley, cf
Clay, 3b-p-rf
Cox, ph
A__ Cox, lf
Claude Cox, 1b-ph-3b
"Big Preacher" Davis, 3b-25
Dixon, rf
Edwards, ss
George "Tipper" Fisher, rf
Ted Gilliam, 1b

Willie Gisentaner, lhp-rf-ph
Grimes, c, also with Birmingham
[Lewis?] Hampton, p-lf-rf
Ben Harris, p
G. Jackson, lf
M. Jackson, 2b
James, rf
A. J. Lockhart, p-1b-cf
Maxwell, c-p
Lewis Means, c-ss-pr-2b
Jim Hugh Moss, p, also with Bessemer
"Suggarty" Murden, p-2b
Myers, ss
[Charles?] "Little Preacher" O'Neil [O'Neal], c
Reese, cf
Ambrose Reid, lf-ph
Joe Robinson, p
Smith, rf-cf
Sam Streeter, lhp
Watson, cf
Charles "Twosides" Wesley, cf-2b-ss

BESSEMER [ALA.] STARS

Played at Garfield Park
B. Mason, club official

Arnold, lhp
Barker, c-cf, also with Montgomery
Binder, 3b
Blanchard, c
Chisholm, rf
Gordon, 3b
Jackson, 2b
Jordan, ss
[George?] McAllister, 1b
Miles, ss-3b
Moorer, lf
Jim Hugh Moss, p-3b, also with Atlanta
T. Nicks, lf
J. Nix [Nicks], c
Parker, p-lf
Smith, rf-p
A. Watson, c
Tom Watson, p
Wilson, c

BIRMINGHAM BLACK BARONS

Played at Rickwood Field
Frank Perdue, manager

Brown, c
Cardenas, c-lf
John "Steel Arm" Dickey, lhp-rf, also with Mobile and Montgomery
Gray, 1b
Gray, p
Grimes, c, also with Atlanta
Will Holt, lf-cf-rf
Eli "Lefty" Juran, lhp-rf, also with Gadsden and Knoxville
John "Buck" Juran, rhp, also with Gadsden and Knoxville
John Kemp, cf
Forest "Wing" Maddox, lf
Bob McCormick, ss-lf-3b
Buford "Geechie" Meredith, 2b-3b
Juanelo Mirabal, rhp-rf, also with Memphis
Morris, rf
Pickens, lhp, with Atlanta last year
Rassler, p
Rhodes, c
Rosella [Rouselle], 2b-cf
Rudolph, rhp-rf-lf
John Henry Russell, 3b-ss, also with Montgomery]
Harry Salmon, rhp-rf-lf
Smith, 2b-lf-cf
Matthew Taylor, 1b, also with Mobile
"Babe Ruth" Tubbs, rf
"Honeyboy" Williams, lf-3b-ss
Winston, c

Chattanooga Tigers

Played at Andrews Field
A. W. Bishop, president, manager by July 17
Carl Bradley [Bodley?], manager
Curtis, secretary

———

W. Anderson, 2b-ss
Bains, 2b
Samuel Billings, c
Boman [Bonam], lf-3b
Bridges, c
Buggs, lf
Davis, cf
Gentry, 1b
Glass, p-1b
Grimes, p

James Earl "Coming Cyclone" Gurley, p-rf
T. Hall, ss
G. Henderson, p
Jack "Shadow" Henderson, p
H. Johnson, 2b-rf-cf
W. E. Jones, p-3b
Joseph, 1b
Lamb, ph
R. Martin, util
Andrew Morris, c
Neal, cf
Nelson, c
Garrett Norman, lf-p-3b
O'Neill, rf
Reed [Reid], 3b-ss
J. F. Scott, c
Stewart, ss-2b-lf
Tatum, 3b
White, c-1b
"Black Babe Ruth" Williams, cf
Wright, p-cf
Young, lhp

Gadsden Tigers

Played at League Park
Replaced by Atlanta c. May 7
John Tyler, manager?- business manager

———

Edward[s], 2b
James, p
Eli Juran, lhp, also with Also with Birmingham and Knoxville
Johnny Juran, rhp, also with Birmingham and Knoxville
Kemp, c-lf
McEntyre, 1b
Miller, 3b, also with Knoxville
Mitchell, cf
Norman, ss, also with Knoxville
Pickens, p
Taylor, rf
Toplin, c

Knoxville Giants

Played at Booker T. Washington Park
Chris Contax, president
Howard Armstrong, coach
Monroe D. Young, club official?
William M. Brooks, manager

Ralph "Pete" Cleage, 1b-mgr by June 11

———

Adams, p
Anderson, c
Appleby, ph
Armstrong, rf
Bains, 3b
Beatty [Bady, Baty], c
Bedford, x
Brown, p
Cannon, c
Carell, inf
Clay, p
Downey, c
DuBois, c
Gallaher, 3b
Gibson, p
Graves, p
Green, c
Grimes, c
Gross, 2b-3b-rf
Hale, p
"PeeWee" Hamilton, 1b-ss-2b
Hilton, 2b
Hobson, c
Johnson, x
Jones, rf
Eli Juran, lhp, also with Birmingham and Gadsden
John Juran, rhp, also with Birmingham and Gadsden
Lloyd, cf-p
Forest "Wing" Maddox, cf
Martin, ss
McIntyre, 2b
Miller, 3b, also with Gadsden
Molle, rf
June Moon, rf
Moore, p
Moseley [Mosley], lf-rf
Nesbit, p
Eddie Noel, p
Norman, ss-lf, also with Gadsden
Oden, c
Riddle, 1b
"Babe Ruth" Rivers, lf
Sampson, lhp, 6–0
Samson, lf
Shaw, c
"Big Smitty" Smith, x
Spencer, p-lf-rf
Toplin, c
Warren, lhp
Pete Widener, 1b
Williams, p
Pete Wimmes [Wimmer], p

Win[g]field, 3b
Young, p, ex–Montgomery
Zanier, p

Memphis Red Sox

Played at Fay Avenue Park and Russwood Park
W. P. Martin, club official
Miller, manager by August

Andrews, ss-3b
George "Jew Baby" Bennette, lf
Billings, p
Blackman, p
Blackwell, p
Bowman, lf-3b
Breakly [Breakby], p
Brown, 2b
Cox, 3b
Crawford, rf
Dykes, c
Glass, 1b-lf
Grimes, c
Huey, 2b-ss
Jones, p
Leader, c
Martin, rf-lf
McCrary, rf
Juanello Mirabel, rhp, also with Birmingham
Ralph Moore, p
Morris, c
Moss, 3b
Pippen, p
Reid, 3b-ss
Riley, p
Robinson [Roberson], lhp
Calvin Rodgers, p
Rodgers, ss
Rogers, c
Rollie, cf
Sharp, 3b
Sutton, c
Trim, 1b
Williams, c-1b-2b

Mobile Braves

Played at Dixie Park
Joe McCoy, club official

Arnold, p-lf
Bass, p
Billings, p
Blanchard, ss
Chester, p
John "Steel Arm" Dickey, lhp, also with Birmingham and Montgomery
Golden, p
Joe Hall, lf-cf
Herman, ss-3b
Hill, cf-lf
Jones, p
Kemp, lf-cf
Leslie, c
McCoy, ss-2b
Newton, p
Price, c
Retton, p
Roach, p
Rogers, p
Roscoe, cf
Sheffield, rf
Smith, 3b
Streeter, p
Tally, p
Mathew Taylor, 1b, also with Birmingham
Thomas, c
Tommy, 2b-c
Wesley, ss-3b-c
Wiley, c
Windham [Wynder], p
Young, p

Montgomery Grey Sox

Played at Southside Park
John Staples, president, and apparently manager by end of year
David Cotton, p-cf-manager
Jim Patton, cf-manager

Larry Brown, c
Burden, x
P. Cardena[s], c
Clay Carpenter, 2b-3b-cf, also with Nashville
John "Red" Charleston, c-rf
Cotton, lf
Herman "Rounder" Cunningham, ss
Johnnie Cunningham, 2b
Marion "Red" Cunningham, 1b-capt
John "Steel Arm" Dickey, p, also with Birmingham and Mobile
Dixon, p
Ellis, c
Lee Gordon, inf
Lucas, lhp
Mays, 1b
Fred McCarver, rf-2b
"Hub" McGavock, lf
George "Deacon" Meyers, p
Eddie Noel, p, also with Nashville
Parker, 1b-p-3b
Preston, rf-ss-c
John Henry Russell, 3b, also with Birmingham
"Slim" Sallee, p-rf-cf
George Sanford, p
George "Tubby" Scales, 3b
Norman "Turkey" Stearnes, cf-rf-lf
Tally, p

Nashville Elite Giants

Played at Sulphur Dell, Athletic Park and Greenwood Park
Marshall Garrett, owner?
J. A. Newton, manager by July 24
William Webster, manager?
Amos Allison, 1b-2b-3b-capt, manager?

Bas[s]ham, cf
"Kid" Billings, p
Carney, rf
Clay Carpenter, cf-assist mgr, also with Montgomery
Daltie "Bullet" Cooper, p-cf-lf
[Will?] Crowder, p
J__ Davis, p
W___ Dixon, of-ss-2b
Ellis, 1b
Foster, p
"Frenchy" Gibson, p
Grady, lf
Gratton, 3b
Lawrence "Cannonball" Graves [Groves], rf-2b
Vernon "Baby" Green, c
Greer, c
G. Griffin, 2b-3b-1b
Jordan, lf
Lloyd, c
Malloy, cf-lf
Marable, p
Means, ss
Moorer, lf
[Wild Bill?] Nesbitt, p-rf-lf
Eddie Noel, p, also with Montgomery
Amos Otis, of

"Hooty" Phillips, ss-c-3b
Roberts, rf
Smith, ss
Norman "Turkey" Stearnes, of
Leroy Stratton, 2b-3b
Wade, p
Wallace, 3b
Joe Ware, 1b-c-rf
Wilson, p

New Orleans Caulfield Ads

Played at Heinemann Park
Fred Caulfield, manager

———

"Babe" "Black Babe Ruth," Bryant, 2b
George "Bow-Legs" Collins, ss-3b-2b
Ducet, rf
Durand, 3b-2b
Glover "Gus" Gardner, c
John George, ss
Harris, lf
[George?] Harney [Horney], p
"Chief" Lewis, lf-rf-c
S. Lewis, 3b-c
Marquez, c
Lewis Moffett, p
Aubrey Owens, p-rf
B___ Platt, p
Richard, ss
Rober[t]son, lhp
Robinson, p
Bobby Roth, c-rf
Rouesselle, lf
Samson, ss
Percy Segula
Whippett, p
Williams, 1b
Percy Wilson, 1b

1922

President—F.M. Perdue, Birmingham?; J.W. Miller, Memphis?
Vice president—NA
Secretary—NA
Treasurer—NA

Birmingham Black Barons

Played at Rickwood Field
Frank Perdue, manager

———

Edwards, x
Ellington, p
Will Holt, of, also with Nashville
Eli Juran, lhp
Johnny "Buck" Juran, rhp
Lewis, c, in Negro Texas League last year
Mason, x, also with Memphis
George McAllister, 1b-c
Bob McCormick, 3b
Buford "Geechie" Meredith, 2b
Miller [Miles], 2b-ss
Mitchell, cf
Jim Hugh Moss, p
Pickens, p
Sellers, lf
"Black Babe Ruth" Tubbs, rf
A. Watson, c
Tom Watson, p
Wilkes, rf
Woodal, p
Young, rhp, also with Memphis and Nashville

Chattanooga Tigers

Played at Andrews Field
Robert "Soo" Bridgeforth, president
Thomas Wilson, owner?
J. A. Newton, manager

———

"Lefty" Bohannon, lhp
Brown, c
Carrothers, c
Jim Hall, p, also with Montgomery
Hall, c
McCreary, p
Hub McGavock, x
"Parson" Miller, p
Momand, p
Montgomery, p
Mooreman [Morman], c
Andrew Morris, c
Nelson, x
Wild Bill Nesbitt, p-cf
Ray, p
Thomas, p
Young, c

Knoxville Giants

Played at Booker Washington [formerly Brewer's Park] Park

Ralph "Pete" Cleage, 2b-manager

———

Amos, lf-cf
Atken, p
Brown, c-rf
Brown, p
Clay, 1b
John "Steel Army" Dickey, lhp
Fine, c
Fleer, 1b
L. Hamilton, rf-ss
R. Hamilton, ss-rf
Harris, p
Lee, 2b
Forest "Wing" Maddox, lf-rhp
McCrary, x
Miles [Mite?], cf-ss-3b
Miller, 3b-ss
B. Miller, p
Mills, p
H. ["Dee"?] Moore, 2b, from Morristown
Johnny Ray, p
"Home Run" Rodgers, of, also with Memphis
Rogers, p
Harry Salmon, rhp
Sampson, p-1b
Toplin, rf-c
Warren, p-rf-1b
Williams, 3b

Louisville Stars/ White Sox

Played at Eclipse Park
E. Arnold, club official
J. A. Arnold, president
Thomas Wilson, owner
Piedmont Bell, manager

———

Bradley [Brady], cf
Brocky, cf
D. Brown, p
H. Brown, 1b
Cooper, c
Cooper, p
Hamilton, lf
Hayson, p
Hessen, p
Hogan, p
Hoys, rf
Hughes, c
Lannom, ss
Lennie, 2b
Lewis, 2b
Lowe, 3b

Marable, p
Moore, p
Riley, p
Roulette, p
Taylor, cf-ss
Toler, cf
Turley, lf
Winston, rf
J. Young, rf
R. Young, c-ss

MEMPHIS RED SOX

Played at Russwood Park and Fields Park
R. A. Lewis, club official
J. Miller, manager?
Chick Cummings, manager

Bateman, p
C. Beard, 3b-ss-2b
William "Kid" Billings, p-lf
Buford, f-cf
Burney, ss
Clay Carpenter, cf-lf
John "Red" Charleston, c, also with Montgomery
Clay, cf
Cooper, p
Cooper, c
Cooper, rf-lf
Johnny Cunningham, 2b, also with Montgomery
Marion "Red" Cunningham, 1b, also with Montgomery
Carl Glass, lhp-lf
Green, c
Green, 1b-2b-ss
William Griffin, 1b
Hamilton, c
Eppie Hampton, c
H. Hampton, c
J. Hampton, c
L. Hampton, 1b-2b-ss-3b
Jones, p
Lee, 2b
Lewis, c
William "Kid" Lowe, ss, also with Nashville
Mason, p, ex-B'ham
Ralph "Squire" Moore, rhp-rf, also with Nashville and New Orleans
Garrett Norman, rf
Rea, lf
Robertson, p
C. Robinson, p
"Home Run" Ro[d]gers, lf-rf-c-ss, also with Knoxville

John Henry Russell, 3b-ss
Sharp, rf
C. Spearman, rf
William Spearman, rf
Norman "Turkey" Stearnes, lf
W. Tee, 1b
R. E. Williams, lf
Young, p, also with Birmingham and Nashville

MONTGOMERY GREY SOX

Played at Southside Park
Will Newsome, vice president
John Staples [Samuels], president
A.E. Wells, secretary-treasurer
Marion "Daddy" Cunningham, 1b-manager by Aug. 19?, also with Memphis

---

Amos, ss
Bender [Binder], 3b
Charleston, c, traded to Memphis
Herman "Rounder" Cunningham, ss
Johnnie Cunningham, 2b, also with Memphis
Walter "Steel Arm" Davis, lhp
Ewing, cf
Golden [Goshen], p-rf
Green, c
Jim Hall, p, also with Chattanooga
Henry Hannon, mgr
Hughes, p
Kemp, cf
Forest "Wing" Maddox, rhp
"Big" Mason, p
Moffet, p-2b, ex–New Orleans
"String Bean" Parker, 1b
Starke, p
Norman "Turkey" Stearnes, rf-lf
Stone, x, traded to Memphis
Thomas, 2b-cf
Ware, 3b-1b
Gordon? Zeigler, lhp
Zimmerman [Zinnerman], lf-cf-3b

NASHVILLE ELITE GIANTS

Played at Sulphur Dell
Tom Wilson, owner
Leroy Stratton, ss-3b-mgr

George "Jew Baby" Bennette, x
Daltie Cooper, p
[James?] Ellis, 1b-p
Evans, c
Geer, c
Noel Graves [Grover, Groves], p-2b
Green, p
Green, c
Grimes, 2b
[Jim?] Gurley, p-rf-lf
Hall, rf-lf
Harris, c
Hogan, c?
Will Holt, lf, also with Birmingham
William "Kid" Lowe, 3b-capt, also with Memphis
Malloy [Moloy], cf
Marable, p
S. "Parson" Miller, p-rf
Money, c
Roy "Square" Moore, rhp, also with Memphis and Orleans
Andrew Morris, c-1b-rf
Eddie Noel, p-rf
"Bughouse" Norman, lf
"Hooty" Phillips, ss, also with New Orleans
Pool[e], 2b
Percy Segula, [see Percy Wilson]
Spratt, c-lf-2b
Trimble, p
Percy Wilson, x, also with New Orleans Ads and New Orleans Crescent Stars
Wynne, p
Young, rhp, also with Birmingham and Memphis

NEW ORLEANS CAULFIELD ADS

Played at Heinemann Park
Replaced by Crescent Stars in Late May/early June
Fred Caulfield, owner-manager

Beasley, p
Bryant, c-1b

Carver, 2b
Durand, 3b
Harris, lf
Lewis, c
Fred McCarver, ss, from Nashville
Roy "Squire" Moore, p, also with Memphis and Nashville
Leroy "Hooty" Phillips, ss, also with Nashville
Platt, p
Richardson, ss
Robertson [Robinson], lhp
Rousell [Russell], rf-1b
Percy Segula, of
Wesley, c-1b
Johnny Wight, of
Percy Wilson, c-cf, also with Nashville and New Orleans Crescent Stars

New Orleans Crescent Stars

Played at "local negro ball park, Hope and Allen streets" [Crescent Star Park?]
Replaced Caulfield Ads in late May/early June
Fred Fauria, club official
W.C. [R.C.] Marine, president and owner
Charlie Stevens, manager

———

Calvin Alexander, p
Anderson, p
George Collins, 2b-3b-rf-cf
Durand, 3b
Galloway [Callaway], cf-lf
Richard Gee, c-cf
Johnny George, ss, ex–Chicago
Harris, lf
Bruce Hill, cf
M. Hill, p
Stanaford "Jambo" Jackson, 3b-ss
Milt Laurent, p-lf-rf
Miles Lucas, p
Lupan, p
Miller, p-cf
Aubrey Owens, p
Anderson Pryor, cf-ss-3b-2b
[Bobby?] Roth, c
J. Tee, c
Wallace, rf-3b
George Wilson, lf-rf

J. Wilson, rf
Percy Wilson, 1b, also with Nashville and New Orleans Ads

———

1923

President—J. T. Suttles [Settles], Memphis
Vice president—
Secretary—W.C. Marine, New Orleans
Treasurer—Joe Rush, Birmingham

Atlanta Black Crackers

Played at xxxx

———

Clark, lf
Cotten, cf
Cox, 3b-2b
Daniel[s], lf
Ealey, cf
Fields, ss-p
"Tipper" Fisher, ss
Ted Gilliam, 1b
Godley, 2b-3b
Golden, 3b
Green, c
Irene, 1b
Jackson, p-rf-2b
Jones, ph
Lloyd, c
A. J. Lockhart, p
Forest "One Wing" Maddox, cf-rhp, also with Birmingham
Shugarty Murden, c
F. Robertson [Robinson], cf-p
H. Robinson, 2b-rf
Smith, ph-3b
Stevens, ph-rf
Watts, ss
Young, 1b-p

Birmingham Black Barons

Played at Rickwood Field
Joined Negro National League second half
Baby Lee King, business manager
Joe Rush, owner
Poindexter Williams, c-2b-1b-ss-manager by July 5

———

Fred Bell, rf-lf
A. Brown, c
John Cason, c
John "Red" Charleston, c
Fred Daniels, p
Dougherty, p
Carl "Butch" Glass, lhp, also with Memphis
Curtis Green[e], 1b-lhp
Walter Harper, c
Stanford Jackson, ss
Reuben Jones, rf
Eli Juran, lhp-rf
Johnny "Buck" "Bubber" Juran, rhp
John Kemp, cf-lf
Forest "Wing" Maddox, p-cf-rf, also with Atlanta
George McAllister, 1b-ss
C. B. "Bob" McCormick, 3b, also with Memphis
Lewis Means, c
Buford "Geechie" Meredith, ss-c
Joe Mitchell, lf-cf-rf
Juan Padrone, p
Charles "Rags" Robertson, p
Harry Salmon, rhp
Leroy Stratton, 3b
George "Mule" Suttles, lf
David Watson, p
L. Williams, p
Gordon Zeigler, lhp

Chattanooga Tigers

No results found

Memphis Red Sox

Played at Lewis Athletic Park
Joined Negro National League second half
R. S. Lewis, president
Greeney Wall [Walls], lf-mgr

———

Larry Brown, c
Carpenter, cf-lf-c
John "Red" Charleston, c-rf
John Edwards, lf-p-rf
James Ellis, 1b-2b
William Foster, p
Carl "Butch" Glass, lhp-lf-cf, also with Birmingham
James Earl Gurley, rhp
George Hamilton, c
L. Hamilton, 3b-cf-2b-ss
C.B. "Bob" McCormick, ss, also with Birmingham
Ralph "Square" Moore, p
Garrett Norman, rf-c-cf-lf

Parker, 1b
John Henry Russell, 2b
T. Russell, 3b-rf-lf-2b
William Spearman, p
Ware, rf
John Young, p

MOBILE

No results found

NASHVILLE ELITE GIANTS

Played at Sulphur Dell and Greenwood Park

Allison, c
Barker, cf-lf
Dandy, p-ss
Dudley, rf
Edwards, ss-2b-3b
Erskine, p-rf
Green, c
Haney, p
Harris, rf-3b-lf-cf
Hicks, 1b
Jones, p-rf
Malloy, lf
McIntyre, ss
H. McMillan, 1b-2b-ss-3b
Miller, ss-rf-3b
Mitchell, rf-lf
Murphy, p
Parker, lf
Ridley, 1b
Shelton, lf-rf
Stanton, 1b
[Leroy?] Stratton, 2b-ss-3b
Thomas, lf-rf-cf-3b
Toplin [Topman], c-rf
Weston, 3b

NEW ORLEANS CAULFIELD ADS

Played at Heinemann Park and Crescent Stars Park
Fred Caulfield, manager

Anthony, p-rf
Bissant, lf-p
Bryant, c
H. Davis, cf
Ducey, c
Durand [Durant], 2b-3b
Farris, 2b-lf
Gallagher, 1b
Handy, rf-cf-lf

Harris, rf-lb-lf
Hensley, 3b-ss-rf-cf
Hyde, ss
Jackson, ss-2b
C. Johnson, c
M. Johnson, p
Jones, 1b-2b
Milt Laurant, cf-p-ss-lf-c
McNeal, 1b-rf
Moffett, rhp
Nelson, c
Platt, rhp
Richard[s] [Ritchett], ss-2b-1b
Robertson, lhp-rf
Roussell, lf-cf-p-rf
Rudolph, 3b-ss
Smith, p
Weber, 3b-2b
Wilson, c
Winebury, ss-3b-2b-lf
Young, p-rf

1926

President—Bert M. Roddy, Memphis, founder of Solvent Savings Bank of Memphis and president of National Negro Business League
Secretary-treasurer—R. T. Jackson, Birmingham
Directors—Oscar W. Adams, Birmingham

ALBANY GIANTS

Played at Southside Ball Park
John S. Montgomery, club official
Bill Gatewood, ph-p-manager

John "Red" Charleston, c-1b
Chesnutt, p
Davis, p
John? Fenner [Finner], p-rf
Fisher, cf
Franklin, 1b
Gaither, ss
Ross Hay[e]s [Haze], rf-c-1b-2b
"Booty" Jackson, p
James C. Jeffries, lhp-cf, also with Birmingham
Johnson, 3b-c
McDonald, rf-p, from Texas
Miles, 2b

Pascal, ph
Pondeck, cf
Red, p
Redding, 1b-rf
Ross, cf-rf
Rouslin, 1b
Tomlin [Tumblin], ss-cf-2b-rf
Umblch, cf
Peter Washington, lf
Williams, c
Williams, p

ATLANTA BLACK CRACKERS

Played at Spiller Park
H.J. Peek, club official
J. H. Reese, co-owner
Sol Rivers, club official
Sharp[e], business manager
George Stewart, club official
W. J. Johnson, c-rf-cf-mgr
Lewis Means, manager by June 10

Broughton, rf-lf
Canty, p
Cattan, cf
Charlie Clark, p-2b-rf
Clay, lf-1b
Cotton, cf
"Jumping Joe" Daniels, lhp
[John?] Finner [Fenner], rhp-rf
Forbes [Fobbs], p
Ted Gilliam, 1b
Gillings, p
Graham [Grimm], ss
Harrold, 1b
"Little" Charlie Hawkins, 2b-ss
J. Henderson, lf-rf
Louie Henderson, lf-rf-lhp
Leroy Idlett, 3b
M. "Booty" Jackson, p-3b-1b-rf-2b
J. Jennings, p
Will Johnson, 1b
Lenny, p
Hubert Lockhart, p
Forest "One Wing" Maddox, cf-p-lf
Manuel, c
Ma[r]sden, 2b
Maxwell, rf-lf-cf
McFarland, 1b
"Suggarty" Murden, 3b-p-2b
Reese, c
Rivers, p

Robinson, p-3b
Price Sheppard [Sheppard Price?], c-lf
Smith, 2b-3b
Stallworth, 3b-1b
Melvin Sykes, rf
J. Williams, p-rf-1b
"Nish" Williams, c
T. Williams, 2b-c
Young, ss-p-lf

BIRMINGHAM BLACK BARONS
Played at Rickwood Field
Oscar W. Adams, president
A. G. Benning, club official
Oscar Buchanon, club official
J.T. Jackson, club official
R. T. Jackson, secretary
H. Strawbridge, treasurer
Joe Rush, manager?
Clarence Smith, 2b-cf-c-lf-ss-manager

———

Charles "Hooks" Beverly, lhp
Leo "Eight Rock" Birdine, rhp-lf
Calhoun, p
Fred Daniels, ph
Saul Henry "Dixie" Davis, lf-ss, also with Memphis
Curtis Harris, p-1b-2b-lf
James "Lefty" Jeffries, lhp-pr-rf, also with Albany
Reuben Jones, lf
Juran, p
John Kemp, lf-cf-rf
John Lilly, lf
George McAllister, 1b
McIntyre, ss
Lewis Means, c
Buford "Geechie" Meredith, 2b
Joe "Goose" Mitchell, rf
J. Webb Oden [Odum], 3b
DeWitt Owens, ss
Robert Poindexter, p
Carl Roland, c, also with Memphis
Harry "Fish" Salmon, p-rf
Poindexter Williams, c
Williford, ss
Wilson, c

CHATTANOOGA BLACK LOOKOUTS
Played at Andrews field
C. M. [Mal] Carter, owner

William Lowe, 3b-ss-c-manager

———

Austin, p
Bell, p-1b
Burrows [Burrow], p
Clark, rf-lf-p-cf
Ralph "Pete" Cleage, rf-1b-lf
Anthony Cooper, lf-p-rf
Dixon [Hixon?], p
B. Fields, 2b-ss-p-rf
Finis, p
Gray, lf-cf
James Earl Gurley, cf-p
Henderson, 2b
A. Henderson, 2b-rf
C. Henderson, p
H. Henderson, p-rf
L. Henderson, 2b-3b-c
Alex Herman, 2b-rf
Hixon, p
Hudson, p
L. Jackson, p
Jasper, p
Jones, p
Lane, ss
Leonard, p
Levanshawn, 1b2b-rf
Lyons, 1b
Leonard "Otto" Mitchell, ss
Moffat, p
Mort, c
Nelson, c
Newsom, 2b
Lefty Nichols, lhp
Odum, c
Leroy "Satchel" Paige, p-rf-lf
Richards, p
Stine, c
Stone, c-1b-rf
Strickney [Stricklin], rf
Frog Thomas, p
H. Young, c-cf

MEMPHIS RED SOX
Played at Lewis Park
R. S. [R. L.] Lewis, club official
Charles "Two-Sides" Wesley, rf-2b-manager

———

Augustus, p
Bell, c
Billings, rhp
Boswell, c
Brooks, p
Larry Brown, c
Black Bottom Buford, 3b

Calhoun, p
Clark, ph-rf-lf
Saul "Dixie" Davis, ss-3b, also with Birmingham
Bill "Emery" Drake, p, ex–KC
[Johnny?] Edwards, p
Fields, p-ph
Fisher, lf-rf
Carl "Butch" Glass, p-1b-rf-lf
[George?] Hamilton, ph-p-lf-c
Lewis Hampton, c
Harris, p
Hines, 3b
Howe, ph
Hyde, ss-c-3b-rf-cf
Tom Jackson, p
Lucas, p
Maywhether, p
McEntyre, ss-3b-lf
J. C. "Mack" McHaskell, 1b
Bob "Ruby" Miller, 2b-ss-3b-captain
Moore, c
Ralph "Steel Arm" Moore, lf-p
Overalls, lf
Parker, ph-p-c
Patterson, ss
[Carl?] Robinson, 1b
Carl Roland, c, also with Birmingham
Pythias Russ, ss-c
Rutherford, ss
Hulan "Lefty" Stamps, lhp
Toney, ph
Nat Trammell, rf-p
William "Steel Arm" Tyler, p
Walker, c-1b-rf-lf
C. "Pinky" Ward, cf-2b
Findall Williams, lf
Williford, ss
Reb Willis, p

MONTGOMERY GREY SOX
Played at Northside Park
J. H. [M. J.] Bailey, secretary
Will Newsome, vice president
John Samuels, president
A.E. Wells, secretary-treasurer
Henry Hannon, manager

———

Anderson, rf-cf-p
Cooley, 1b-c
Marion "Dad" Cunningham, ss

Appendix B: Yearly Rosters 1927

John [Jeff?] "Steel Arm" Davis, p
Drew, p-cf-rf
Fields, p
Hall, c
Hardy, p
Holt, 2b-lf
Jackson, p
Joseph, 1b
Long, c-3b-2b
Forest "One Wing" Maddox, p-lf-p
Milton, p-ph
Morrow, ph
Newsome, cf-p-rf-lf
Norwood, rf-lf-2b
Perkins, c-cf
Sammy Routt, p
Doug Smiley, rhp
O. Smith, c-2b-3b
Spalding, lf
Thomas, 1b
Tony, 1b
Washington, 2b
Wesley, c-2b
Westmoreland, c-1b, also with Nashville
Williams, lf

NASHVILLE ELITE GIANTS

Played at Sulphur Dell
Green, secretary
T. W. Wilson, club official
Leroy Stratton, 3b-ss-manager
Wilson, p-lf-rf-manager by Aug. 15

———

Anderson, lf-cf
Russell Bailey, c
Bell[e], p-rf
[Clay?] Carpenter, cf-lf-rf
Cummings, c-1b
R. Edwards, 2b-lf
Ellis, 1b-2b-rf
Hillis, ss
"Big" Jasper, p-rf
Jones, lf
William McNeil [McNeal], lf-cf
W. Mitchell, rf
Nichols, lhp
Eddie Noel, p-lf-cf
Phillips, ss-3b
Powers, p
Jack Ridley, 1b-2b
Russell, rf

Sharp, c
E. Thomas, p-ph
Toplin[g], c
Westmoreland, ph-c, also with Montgomery
Clarence White, lhp
Young, lf

NEW ORLEANS CAULFIELD ADS

Played at Heinemann Park
Fred Caulfield, manager and club official

———

Harvey "Chuffy" Alexander, 2b-1b-lf
Benjamin, 1b-lhp-cf
Jean Bissant, p
Black, ph
Breaux, 2b-rf-ss
Brussell, p
[George?] Collins, 3b-2b
Garrett, 1b-cf
Otis Henry, ss-3b-c
Jackson, p
James, 1b
Milt Laurent, cf-lf-1b-2b
Roy "Red" Parnell, cf-rf
Powe, rhp-rf
Roberts, ph
Robinson, ss-c
Bobby? Roth, c-rf
Roussell, cf;-p-lf-rf
Stokes, p
Thomas, rf-rhp
Jim "Smokey" Willis, rhp

———

1927

President—N/A
Vice president—N/A
Secretary—N/A
Treasurer—N/A

ATLANTA BLACK CRACKERS

Played at Spiller Field
T. F. Fortson, owner

———

Albert, rf
Burton [Burden], p
Cornelius, p-ss-cf
[Joe?] Daniels, lhp
Siley Doon, 3b
Fish, c
Fobb, cf
Fobb, p

Forbes, lf
Harrell, 2b
Harris, p
Hayes, c
Jackson, 3b-ss
Johnson, rf
Manuel, c
Matthews, p-cf-lf
Mitchell, ss
Moffett, p
Moore, lf
Moore, p
J. Parker, p-3b
T. Parker, c
W. Parker, lf-p
C. Price, ph-c
Redd, p
Suggs, p
Thomas, 1b
Washington, ss
Wiggins, 3b
Nish Williams, cf
Young, ss

CHATTANOOGA BLACK LOOKOUTS

Played at Andrews Field
W. R. Abrahams, owner-manager [business manager?]
Pete Cleage, manager

———

Anderson, rf
Baker, lf
Clay Carpenter, cf
Clark, rf
Cloustan [Coston], p
Edwards, 2b
Frederick, p
Guney, 3b
Haydon, c
C. Henderson, p
Lenon Henderson, 3b
High, cf
Jennings, p
Johnson, 2b
Levenshaw, 2b
Lynch, c
Lyons, 1b
Forest "One Wing" Maddox, p
Satchel Paige, p
Peters, 1b
Phillips, ss
Price, c
[Doug?] Smiley, p
Sota, rf
Thomas, 1b

Warner, p
Young, lf
Young, p
Aldo Young, x

DECATUR GIANTS

Played at Malone Park
Frank Johnson, promoter-
 business manager
———
Joe Martin, c

EVANSVILLE LOUIS REICHERT GIANTS

Played at Bosse Field
Robert Murray, business
 manager
Charles Baker, manager
———
Raymond Austin, p
*Bell, lf
John "Red" Charleston, c,
 also with Nashville
Clint, cf-lf
George "Hippo" Collins, 2b,
 also with Nashville
Cornelius, cf
Craig, 1b
Dyer, lhp
Dyes, lf
Dykes, ph
Edwards, rf
English, c-rf
*[John?] Finner, rhp
Froggie, p
Griffin [Guffin], cf-rf-2b-
 captain
*[James Earl?] Gurley, rf
Harris, ss
Harris, p
*Hensley, rhp
King, p
Knight, p
McNeal, p-rf-f
Miller, 3b
Otto Mitchell, ss-2b
Pritchett [Pritchell, Puchett],
 lf
J. Scott, 1b
*Settles [Settler], 3b
Adolph Spratt, c
Swift, ph
"Babe" Terry, p-rf
C. Thomas, p
*Trent, rhp
Ward, lhp
*Wells, ss

White, ph
C. [Clarence?] White, p
* all added to roster for
 postseason play

HOPKINSVILLE

Played at Boose Field
Barker, mgr
———
Baker, c
Brewer, c
Briggs, 3b
Cole[s], 2b-ss
Cunningham, ss
Daniels, lhp
Herrel[l], p
Herrod, p
Howell, rf
Hudson, p
Johnson, x
Joplin [Toplin], c
Lefty Kaiser [Kizer], p
Kendrick, p-lf
Landers, 2b-1b
Mack, 1b
Marsh, cf-rf
McCarley, p
Mitchell, cf
Morris, rf
Morrow, lf
Spaulding, c
Suggs, 3b
Toplin, c
Williams, p-cf
Wilson, p

JACKSON, TN, CUBS

Played at Lakeview Park
———
Belle, p
[Black Bottom?] Buford, 3b
Clark, 2b
Clark, lf
[John?] Finner, p
Groves, ss
Mack, 1b-p
Morios, c
Peoples, p
[Ted "Double Duty"?]
 Radcliff, p, c
Richards, p
Russell, cf
Searcy, p
Smith, ss
C. Smith, 2b
G. Smith, c
Steckler, p

Stretson, p
Thomas, lf
Wilson, rf
Wilson, p

MEMPHIS GIANTS

Played at Lewis Park
———
Cliff Bell, p-of
Haley, ss
Harris, p
Martin, c
Bill Pryor, p
William "Nat" Rogers, lf
A. Smith, rf
A.S. [A. J.] Smith, c-2b
J. Smith, 2b
J. Smith, cf
Weston, 3b
Wilson, 1b

NASHVILLE ELITE GIANTS

Played at Sulphur Dell
Owen Wilson, club official
Tom Wilson, owner
Joe Hewitt, ss-2b-lf-mgr
———
William Anderson, rf-lf-cf
Bell, p
Charles Beverly, p
Brown, c
Black Bottom Buford, 3b-ss
Carpenter, cf
John "Red" Charleston
 [Charlton], c, also with
 Evansville
George "Hippo" Collins, 2b-
 3b, also with Evansville
[John?] Finner, p
Hall, 2b-rf
Milfred "Rick" Laurant, cf
Al Morris, ss-c-cf
Pennock, p
Phillips, 2b
Pruett, p
Jack Ridley [Risley], 1b-lf
[Sammy?] Routt, rf-p
William Spearman, p-lf
Leroy Stratton, ss-3b
Ware, 1b
White, p
Williams, p
Nish Williams, c
Williams, lf-rf
Jim "Smokey" Willis, lhp-rf
Wilson, lhp

1929

President—Thomas T. Wilson, Nashville
Vice president—Charles Baker, Evansville
Secretary—C.M. Carter, Chattanooga
Recording secretary—Benny D. Scales, Nashville
Treasurer—T. F. Fortson, Atlanta

ATLANTA GREY SOX

Played at Spiller Field
Independent team?
T. F. Fortson, owner

———

Cannady, 2b
Canty, p
Cantrell, p
Clay, rf
Cotton, lf
Hayes, c
[Tolusha?] Howard, p
[John?] McFarland, 1b
Mitchell, ss
Moore, p
Omiels, cf
Wiggins, 3b
"Lefty" Williams, lhp
Nish Williams, c

CHATTANOOGA BLACK CATS

Played at new Lincoln Park
[James Earl?] Gurley, 1b-cf-manager

———

Brown, 1b
Chestnut, cf
Pete Cleage, rf-3b
Cunningham, lf
Ego [Igo], p
Emillo, ss
Gigo, p
Hayes [Hoyes], c
C. Henderson, lf- p
Henry Henderson, lf-rf
Lenon Henderson, 3b
S. [E.] Henderson, 2b-lf
T. Henderson, x
W. Henderson, cf
Hogan, lf
Howard, ss
Johnson, 2b
Long, 2b
Lungalow, c
Lefty Lynn, lhp
Lyons, lhp-1b
Marshall, rf-cf
["Suggarty"?] Murdon [Murden], ss
O'Neil, rf
Riners, p
Singlong [Sing Long, Singalong], 2b
[Doug?] Smiley, p
Strickland, p
Teasoy, c
Lefty Williams, p

EVANSVILLE REICHERT GIANTS

Played at Bosse Field
Charles Baker, manager

———

Raymond Austin, rhp
Bailey, c, p?
Bell, 3b-1b-2b
"Bullet" Cannon, p
Cates, ss
Clint, cf
Cole, 2b-lf
Cornelius, cf
["Dusty"?] Decker, ss-3b
Dukes, ss-p
Louis English, c, also with Louisville
John Finner p
Golpin, c
Granville, c
Griffin, 2b-3b
[Cecil?] Kaiser, c-p, from Kentucky
Kenan, p
Levell [Leavell], rf
[Granville?] Lyons, 3b-1b
Lyons, p
Massey, rf-p-lf, from Kentucky
McNeal [McNeil], p-rf
Miller, ss-3b
Owens, c
Porter, p-rf-lf
Pritchett, lf-ss
Russell, rf-lf
Rustin, p
Scott, 1b
Skinner, p
Smiley, p
Stone, c-rf
"Baby" Terry, p-rf-2b-lf
Toplin [Troplin], c
Williams, lhp-r

LOUISVILLE BLACK CAPS

Played at Parkway Field
Independent team?
John Dixon, club official
Jim Morris, c-manager
W. Griffin, 2b-cf-manager

———

R. Bobo, lf
Brown, 1b
Cannon, p
English, c-cf-rf, also with Evansville
[Russell?] Ewing, rf-cf
Hudson, p
Sammy T. Hughes, 2b-cf
McKenna, p
[William?] McNeal [McNeil?], rf-cf
Morris, x
Nichols [Nickle], cf-rf
Norris, 3b
Palmer, lf
Ragland, p
Scott, 1b
Felton Snow, ss-rf
Toplin, c

NASHVILLE ELITE GIANTS

Played at Wilson Park and Sulphur Dell
Thomas T. Wilson, owner
Joe Hewitt, ss-mgr

———

Charles Blackwell, cf
William Bobo, ss-1b
Black Bottom Buford, 3b
John "Red" Charleston, c
William "Sug" Cornelius, p-rf-lf
Jessie Edwards, 2b
Evitt, 2b
Gray, 3b-rf
Kid Harvey [Lit Harvell, Harney], ss
Al Morris, rf
Eddie Noel, p
Jack Ridley, lf-ss
Russell, rf
Singlong [Sing Long, Singalong], ph
William Spearman, p
Felton [Leroy] Stratton, ss
Clarence Threallkill, ss-lf
Clarence "Red" White, lhp
Jim "Bullet" Williams, lhp-rf
Nish Williams, c-rf
Jim Willis, p

Henry "Red" Wright [Sid Wright], p

New Orleans Black Pelicans

No results found

1931

President—R. T. Jackson, Birmingham [ex–Negro National League president]
Vice president—Dr. R.B. Jackson, Nashville
Secretary—Joe Vaughn, Chattanooga
Treasurer—Thomas Wilson, Nashville

Atlanta Panthers

Played at Ponce de Leon Park?
Second half member?
No results found

Cotton, cf
Cox, 1b
Daniels, p
Jones, p
Means, 2b
Payne, lf
Scott, rf
Shepherd, c
Smith, ss
Williams, 3b

Birmingham Black Barons

Games played at Rickwood Field
Charlie Johnson, club official
Frank Perdue, owner
Buford "Geechie" Meredith, c-3b-2b-manager

Hank Anderson, cf-rf
C.F. "Jabo" Andrews, rf-cf
Sam Bankhead, 2b-ss
Bealle, p
Jerry Benjamin, 2b-3s, also with Knoxville
Bradshow, x
Black Bottom Buford, 3b
Bumble, 2b
J. [Leo?] "Eight Rock" Burdine, rf-lf-cf-p
Walter Calhoun, p, also with Chattanooga and Montgomery
Matthew "Lick" Carlisle, 3b-ss
Carter, p-2b
A. Carter, p-3b-ss
Elmer "Willie" Carter, p
J. Carter, p
Z. Carter, 2b-3b
Clark, lf, also with Louisville
Walter Cooley [Coolie], 3b-rf-c
Anthony "Peewee" Cooper, ss
B. Cooper, p
Tommy Dukes [Duke], c
Jesse Edwards, ss
William Howard, 1b
C. Huber[t], cf-lf, also with Nashville
Jim Jeffries, cf-lhp-1b-lf
[John?] Kemp, cf
George McAllister, 1b
[Bob] McCormick, 3b]
Terris McDuffie [McDuff], lf-cf
Miller, x
Mott, 3b-lf
[William?] Nash, p
Martin Oliver, rf-2b-c
Bill Perkins, c-rf
Harvey Peterson, p-cf, also with Knoxville and Montgomery
Petway, ss-3b
Harry "Fish" Salmon, p-lf
Robert "Bob" Smith, c-rf
T. Smith, lf-cf-1b
Felton Stratton, cf
Sam Streeter, ph-p
S' van [Sullivan??], cf
Columbus Vance, rp-rf-lf-cf
Robert Veale Sr., rhp-rf, also with Montgomery
Charley Wright, p

Chattanooga Black Lookouts

Played at Engel Stadium
Bo Carter, club official
Joe Vaughn, owner, club official?
Pete Cleage, 1b-manager
Jesse Edwards, 2b-cf-manager
William "Professor" Lowe, ph-3b-manager?, also with Memphis

Bell, c
Walter Calhoun, p-rf, also with Birmingham and Montgomery
Clark[e], lf
Colie [Coley, Cooley], p
Cunningham, lf- rf
J. [Johnny?] Cunningham, rf
L. Cunningham, lf
Andrew Drake, c
Eddings, lf
Flippins, ss-p
Gannet [Gant], p
Gray, x
Henry "Hank" Henderson, 1b-p
Leonard [Lenon] Henderson, 3b-lf-rf-ss
M. "Long" Henderson, 1b
Huber, 2b
Igou [Igon], p
Jim Jeffries, p-rf
Martin, c
McFarlane, 1b
A. Owens, lf
Claude "Dusty" Rhodes [Rowe], p
Rowe, pr
Strand, 3b
Strong, c
Ely [Roy] Underwood, cf-2b-ss-3b
Willis, cf
Wright, rf-p-cf
Zollie Wright, lf-cf, also with Memphis

Knoxville Giants

Played at Vestal Park and Leslie Street Park
W. M. Jenkins, club official
J. T. Holland, owner?
J. A. Nance, manager in May
W.F. Hilliard, manager by June 21

Allen, 1b
C. F. "Jabbo" Andrews, of
Jerry Benjamin, 3b-2b, also with Birmingham
Joe Borden [Bordin, Boders], c-ss-p-lf
[Barney?] "Burley" Brown, p
Cade, x
Cole, c
Crook[s] [Cook], p
Tuggle Dawson, p-rf
Den[i]son, 2b-rf

Eagle, cf
Fate, cf
Luther Green, cf
Cecil Gross, p
Tom W. Jackson, p
Clarence Keith, rf-lf
Luque, rhp
Red Eye" Lynch, c
J. Webb Oden, ss-3b-of-c
Patterson [Peterson], ss
Roosevelt "Speed" Tate, lf-cf
Vick, p
White, p

LITTLE ROCK BLACK TRAVELERS

Played at Kavanaugh Field
Buddy Nolan, co-owner
J. J. Powell, co-owner
F. A. Snodgrass, co-owner
Earl [S.?] Taylor, manager
J. J. Floyd, owner-mgr by mid–July

———

Earl Ackerson, lhp
Lewis Anderson, c, ex–CAG
Bland, p
Buford, x
"Chink" Childs [Chiles, Childes], p
Cobb[s], c
Horace "Sonny Boy" Cole, rhp
Conway, rhp
Bob Cooke, 3b
Eagle, cf
Faison, 3b
Murray Gillespie, p, also with Memphis
Hawkins, cf
Jackson, c
Jackson, rf
Byron Johnson, ss-3b
J. Johnson, 3b-p
C. Jones, 2b
R. Jones, rf-2b
[Ray?] Longley, 1b-3b
McGruger, 3b
Pete McQueen, cf-rf
Moore, rf
Buford Nunley, 1b
Richardson, 2b
[Johnny?] Robinson, rf-2b-c
B[?]. Robinson, p
Stallworth, lf
Thomas, lf
Sammy "Runt" Thompson, 2b-ss, also with Memphis

Wilbourne [Wilburne], p
Young, c

MEMPHIS RED SOX

Played at Lewis Park
Dr. B. B. Martin, owner
E. B. Nesbitt, president
Larry Brown, c-manager
Homer "Goose" Curry, rf-lf-p-manager c. Aug. 9

———

Blow, 3b
Burgos [Burgis], cf
Chevlier, 3b
Willie "Sug" Cornelius, p-rf-lf
Harry "Baby" Cunningham, rhp
C. Cunningham, p-rf
W. Cunningham, lf
Bennie Fields, of
Jimmy Ford, 2b-3b
Murray "Lefty" Gillespie, lhp-1b, also with Little Rock
Bill Harvey, ph-p
Otis Henry, 3b
Oscar "Heavy" Johnson, rf-1b
Jim "Lefty" Johnson, 1b-rf-p
Johnston, p-1b
Reuben Jones, cf
"Rookie" Jones, cf-3b
Clarence "Foots" Lewis, ss-3b
William Lowe, 3b-ss, also with Chattanooga
Moody, ss
Elvin Powell, 3b-2b
Purro, rf
Purvis, lf-cf-rf
Robinson, 1b
Harry Salmon, p, in postseason
Ted Shaw, p
Raymond Taylor, c
Terrell, cf
Sammy "Runt" Thompson, 2b, also with Little Rock
H. Thornton, of
Bill Van Buren, rf
David Wingfield, ss
Zollie Wright, rf-cf, also with Chattanooga

MONTGOMERY GREY SOX

Played at Cottage Hill Park,
Alabama State campus; also Cramton Bowl
Will T. Brown, president and owner
Marion "Red," "Daddy" Cunningham, manager-1b
Henry Hannon, manager? by mid–July

———

Anderson, p
Frank Bradley, ph-lf-p-rf
Brooks, p
Burns, 3b-ss-2b
Walter Calhoun, p, also with Birmingham and Chattanooga
Capres ["Lefty" Capers?], p
[Matthew "Lick"?] Carlisle, ss
Carter, x
Herman "Rounder" Cunningham, ss-3b
Dokes, p
Paul Hardy, c
Wheeler Hardy, p
[Matthew?] Jackson, 3b-ss
Johnson, c
Lockhart, p
Felix "Chaser" Manning, 1b
McNeal, cf
Milton, p
Alonzo "Hooks" Mitchell, c-lf-cf-p
Neal, p-cf
Everett Nelson, p-cf-2b-rf
Peek[s] [Peaks], p-lf
Harvey Peterson, 2b-cf-p-rf-3b, also with Birmingham and Knoxville
Johnny Ray, cf-rf-c
Horace "Zeke" [Claude "Dusty"?] Rhodes, p
Otto Scott, 3b
Singalong [Sing Long, Singlong], 2b
[Nat?] Trammell [Trimble], 2b
Turner [Turney], lhp
Robert Veal [e, Sr.], rhp-rf, also with Birmingham
White, p, in postseason
B. Williams, rf
David Wingfield, 2b

NASHVILLE ELITE GIANTS

Played at Wilson Park and Sulphur Dell
Vernon Green, secretary

Tom Wilson, owner
Leroy Stratton, 3b-ss-cf-lf-manager

Clarence Adkins, of
Clifford "Cliff" Bell, p
Black Bottom Buford, 2b-ss-3b
Richard Cannon, p
John "Red" Charleston, c
Coley, rf
Comer "Hannibal" Cox, 2b-rf-3b
Jesse Edwards, 2b
Gray, 3b
Lenon Henderson, of
"Slim" Henderson, lf, from Chattanooga
C. Huber[t], cf-c, also with Birmingham
Jasper, p
Claude "Hooks" Johnson, 3b-ss
Jones, 3b
Wiliam "Kid" Lowe, 3b-ss, from Memphis
Granville Lyons, 1b
Dempsey "Dimp" "Lefty" Miller, p
Albert "Dumpy" Owens, p
Owensby, p
Petway, ss-2b
Piller, ss
Jack Ridley, cf
Ronsell, of
Russell, lf-cf
Clarence "Harvey" Threakill, cf-rf
Jesse "Hoss" Walker, ss
Joe Wiggins, pr-3b
Nish Williams, c
Jim Willis, rhp-rf
Will [Bill?] Wright, ph-p
Henry "Red" Wright, p

1932

President—Dr. R. B. Jackson, Nashville
Vice president—Robert Cole, Chicago
Secretary—L. S. N. Cobb, Birmingham
Treasurer—Thomas T. Wilson, Nashville

ALCOA ALUMINUM SLUGGERS

Played at Alcoa Park?
Second half member
Flash Miller, club official-manager?

Bailey, c
James Bright, p
James Carr, p
Melford Carr, x
Carter, p
Dean, p
Eddie Dowell, x
Ralph Dowell, 2b
James Green, x
Hall, p
Roy Henry, 1b
Miller, c
Leroy Miller, x
Ralph Miller, cf
Randolph Miller, x
Simpson, p
Simpson, c
George Tolbert [Talbert], x
Watkins [Watson], c
Clarence Watson, c
Wood, x

ATLANTA BLACK CRACKERS

Played at Ponce de Leon Park and Morehouse College
T. J. Fortson, owner, and apparently field manager by late May
A. J. Peeks, club official

Hipolito Torrento Arenas, ss-lf-cf-3b
Tank Austin, p
Red Bradley, p, ex–Morris Brown
Bo Briggery, ss-1b-cf
Campson, ss
Carter, p
J. "Flash" Frazier, ss
James Joe "Pig" Green[e], c-1b
Herman "Red" Howard, p
Leon Toloshus Howard, p
Jones, cf
Emory "Bang" Long, 3b
John McFarland, 1b-2b
Lewis Means, 2b
Merriweather, 3b
James "Red" Moore, cf
Lamar Potter, p-ph-rf-2b-lf
Frank Ray, lf
Ambrose Reid [Reed], lf-rf-p
Robertson, p

"Papa Charlie" Robinson, lhp-lf
Ormond Sampson, ss
Stinson, cf-lf
Jack Thornton, p-lf-1b
Strico Valdez, 2b
Roy Wellmaker, p
James Winston, rf-lf-p
Geech Yarbrough, c-1b

BIRMINGHAM BLACK BARONS

Played at Rickwood Field
Folded by early June. Franchise transferred to Lexington, Ky., for second half
L. S. N. Cobb, owner
Poindexter Williams, c-manager

Sam Bankhead, p-2b, also with Louisville and Nashville
Alonzo Boone, p
J. Borden [Boyden], 3b-lf-rf
Walter Calhoun, p, also with Memphis
Richard Cannon, p, also with Louisville
Ernest "Spoon" Carter, p, also with Louisville and Memphis
[Elmer "Willie"?] Carter, 3b-ss
Harry Cunningham, p
Davis, 2b
Andrew Drake, c, also with Chicago and Louisville
Lenon Henderson, 3b-ss, also with Louisville
John Jasper, p
Milt Laurent, 2b, also with Nashville;
George McAllister, 1b
George Nash, lhp, with BBB in '31
William Nash, p
Martin Oliver, rf-cf-b-2b, also with Louisville
Harvey Peterson, lf-3b-c
Petway, ss-3b-lf-rf, also with Louisville and Nashville
Harry Salmon, p, later with Homestead
[Buster?] Smith, c
Roosevelt "Speed" Tate, cf, also with Louisville

Jim West, of-1b, also with Memphis

CHICAGO AMERICAN GIANTS
Played at Cole's 39th Street Park
Robert Cole, owner
Dave Malarcher, 3b-manager

———

Ameal Brooks, c
Brown, ph
Robert "Buddy" Campbell, c
Norman Cross, p
J. Davis, 1b
Walter "Steel Arm" Davis, 1b
Kermit Dial, p-2b-3b
Andrew Drake, c-p, also with Birmingham and Louisville
Willie Foster, p
John Hines, c-lf
Joe Lillard, p-1b-lf
William "Jack" Marshall, 2b
Clarence "Spoony" Palm, c
A. Powell, p
Malvin "Putt" Powell, p
Alex Radcliff, 3b
William "Nat' Rogers, rf
Ross, p
Norman "Turkey" Stearns, cf-pr-rf
James "Sandy" Thompson, lf
Tines, ph
E.C. "Pop" Turner, ss
Wash, 2b
Williams, 1b

COLUMBUS TURF CLUB STARS
Played at Neil Park
Second half member
A. H. Howle [Howie], business manager-manager?

———

Bill Byrd, p
Fisher, p
Gilchrist, x
Griffin, x
Jackson, x
John Kerner, lf-p
Duke Lattimore, c
Mimms, p
Minn, p
Morse, p
Pagie, p
Smith, c

Williams, p
[James?] Womack, x

INDIANAPOLIS ABCs
Played at Perry Stadium
Candy Jim Taylor, 3b-manager

———

Ralph Anderson, of
Herman "Jabo" Andrews, rf
Henry Baker, rf-lf
Bashum, c
Jimmy Binder, 3b-cf
Binson, ss
Brammell, c
J. Burdine [Burden], 3b
Davis, ph-lf
Saul Davis, rhp
Wilson "Connie" Day, 2b-ss
Charles "Dusty" Decker, ss-3b
Denson, ss
Eddie Dwight, of
Dennis Gilchrist, ss-p
Gladney, ss
Bob Graves, p
Jack [Leo?] Hannibal, p
Logan "Slap" Hensley, p
Jackson, c-cf
Johns[t]on, p-1b
John Lyles, c-ss
Henry Milton, ss
Moss, p;
Mitch Murray, c
Williams Owens, ss-p
Willie Lee "Joe" Scott, 1b
Lefty Smart, p-lf-cf-1b
Spann, 2b
Taylor, p-ph
J. Thomas, 2b-lf
Samuel "Sad Sam" Thompson, p-lf
Columbus Vance, p-lf
Irving "Lefty" Waddy, p
B. Williams, lf
H. Williams, lf
I. Williams, cf-ph
John "Big Boy" Williams, lf-rf-cf
P. Williams, ph
R. Williams, lf

KNOXVILLE GIANTS
Played at Leslie Street Park
Second half member half
Joe Borden, manager in June
J. A. Nance, manager by July

———

Avery, p
Bailey, p
Benson, c
Bowden, ss
Brantley, x
Carter, c
Den[i]son, inf
Early [Ealey], p
Gibbs, p
Cecil Gross, p
Ted Gross, x
Jackson, p
G. Johnson, p
"Red Eye" Lynch, p-c
Miller, x
J. C. Sharpe, c-of
Simpson, p
Spencer, p
Taylor, cf

LEXINGTON HARD HITTERS
Played at Stivers Field
Replaced Birmingham second half

———

"Red" Cade, p-cf, former Knoxville player
Caldwell, rf
Crooks, p, former Knoxville player
Gibson, p
Glass, lf
"Stumpy" Harris, 1b-ss
Houston, p
Tom Jackson, p
"Shorty" McClain, 2b
Mims, lhp
"Paps" Murdine [Nundine], ss
J. Webb Oden, p-3b-c
Ransom, c
Rogers, cf
Webster, c
Whitley, p
Yost, ss

LITTLE ROCK GRAYS
Played at Kavanaugh Park and Crump Park
D. J. Dubisson, club official
J. J. Floyd, club official
Sug Jones, 1b-cf-manager

———

Newt "Red Fox" Blevins, 3b
Buford, 1b
Carr, lf

Appendix B: Yearly Rosters 1932

William Carter, 2b
Cobb, c
Cross [Coss], ss
Faisson, ss
Willie "Bill" Haynes, 1b-p
Herman "Red" Howard, p-rf-lf
Robert Hughes, x
Edgar Jackson, c-rf
Byron Johnson, ss-ph
Reuben Jones, c-cf-rf-lf
James Liggons, lhp-lf
Wayman "Red" Longley, cf-ss
Pete McQueen, rf-lf
Buford Nunley, 1b-p
Albert Overton, p-cf-ph
Andrew Porter, p
Johny Robinson, cf
Tommy Young, c

Louisville Black Caps

Played at Parkway Field
Disbanded around July 24
William Scott, club official
Jim Brown, lf-rf-manager
Jimmie Lyons, cf-manager by May 16

———

Sam Bankhead, p, also with Birmingham and Nashville
Richard Cannon, p, also with Birmingham
Ernest "Spoon" Carter, p, earlier with Birmingham
Cummings, c
Curtis, c
Andrew Drake, c, also with Birmingham and Chicago
Louis English, c
Willie "Lefty" Gisentaner, lhp-rf
George Harris, 2b
Henry Harris, ss
Lenon Henderson, 3b, also with Birmingham
Alto Lane, p
Granville Lyons, 1b
William "Red" McNeil, rf-lf-cf
Charlie Miller, 2b
A. C. Neely, p
J. Webb Oden, lf-2b-rf
Martin Oliver, cf-2b, also with Birmingham
Petway, lf-c, also with Birmingham and Nashville

Andrew Porter, p, also with Nashville
Claude "Dusty" Rhodes, p
Felton Snow, 3b-cf
Roosevelt "Speed" Tate, of, also with Birmingham
Raymond Taylor, c-cf-1b, also with Memphis
Thomas, c
Jim Thurman, rf-p
Torenti, p
C. Pinky Ward, lf
Whitney, p

Memphis Red Sox

Played at Lewis Park
Dr. B. B. Martin, owner
Homer "Goose" Curry, lf-p-manager

———

Emery "Ace" Adams, p-lf-rf
Herman "Jabo" Andrews, rf-p-lf-2b
Jerry Benjamin, 2b-rf-cf
Walter Calhoun, p-rf, also with Birmingham
Ernest "Spoon" Carter, p, also with Birmingham
Cosa [Coss, Cass], rf-1b-2b
Harry Cunningham, rhp-cf
Tommy Dukes, c, also with Nashville
Gardner, 2b
Murray Gillespie, lhp-rf
David "Bill" Harvey, p-rf
Haskins, inf
Otis Henry, 3b
J. "Lefty" Johnson, 1b-p-rf, from Texas
Josh Jones, cf-3b-2b
Reuben Jones, cf-3b
Clarence "Foots" Lewis, ss
Red Murray, rhp
Guy Ousley, 2b-3b
Harvey Paterson, of, ex–Columbus
Harvey Peterson, rf-cf-lf-p
Raymond Taylor, c-ph, also with Louisville
Bill Van Buren, x
Jim West, 1b, also with Birmingham

Monroe Monarchs

Played at Casino Park
H. D. English, business manager
Fred Stovall, owner
Frank Johnson, lf-rf-p-manager

———

Harve "Chuffy" Alexander, 1b
Willie Burnham, p
Homer "Goose" Curry, of
Porter "Big Boy" Dallas, 3b-ss
Harry Else, c
Leland Foster, p
Murray Gillespie, lhp
Samuel Harris, of-p
David "Bill" Harvey, p
Maher, lf
Dick Matthews, p
Leroy Morney, ss
Barney Morris, p
Roy "Red" Parnell, cf-p
Bob Saunders, 2b
Ray Sheppard, 1b-3b-ss-2b-cf
George Sias, 3b
Hilton Smith, p
H. Walker, lf-c, ex–Milwaukee Giants
W. C. Walker, 1b-lf
Elbert Williams, p
Graham H. Williams, p
Zollie Wright, rf-lf

Montgomery Grey Sox

Played at College Hill Park
Will M. Brown, president and owner
Henry Hannon, manager

———

James "Steel Arm" Bell, c-cf-rf-p
Brown, p
Walter "Bearcat" Calhoun, p-cf-lf
Matthew "Lick" Carlisle, ss-lf
Charles "Dusty" Decker, ss
Albert Frazier, 2b
Oren Frazier, 2b
Walter Goins, p-c
James Gurley, 1b-p
Paul Hardy, c-cf-lf
H. Harris, cf
Jackson, 3b
A. Matthew Jackson, 3b
F. Lewis, lf-rf-cf
Chaser Manning, 1b-2b
Mitchell, 1b
Alonzo "Hooks" Mitchell, p
C. Mitchell, p
George Mitchell, p-rf

Johnny Mitchell, c-cf-rf
S. Mitchell, p
Everett Nelson, rhp-ph
James Pope, p
John Ray, 2b-rf-lf-cf
Tremble [Frank Trimble?], 2b
Clarence "Red" White, p
S. White, p

Nashville Elite Giants

Played at Wilson Park and Sulphur Dell
Thomas "Tom" T. Wilson, owner
Joe Hewitt, manager

Sam Bankhead, p-cf-lf-ss, also with Birmingham and Louisville
Black Bottom Buford, 2b-3b
Richard Cannon, p
John "Red" Charleston, c
Tommy Dukes, c-cf, also with Memphis
H. Long Henderson, 1b
Lenon Henderson, 3b
Robert "Frog" Holsey, p
Hosea, p
Sammy T. Hughes, ss-2b
Milton Laurent, rf-1b-cf, also with Birmingham
Lester, p
Louie, ph
Granville Lyons, 1b
Marsh, rf
Charlie Miller, 2b-3b
William Nash, p
Petway, ss, also with Birmingham and Louisville
Andrew Porter, p, also with Louisville
Posey, p
Jack Ridley, cf-lb-lf
Rowe, p
Robert Smith, c
Leroy Stratton, lf-ss-3b
Roosevelt "Speed" Tate, cf-rf-lf-3b
Jesse "Hoss" Walker, ss
Joe Wiggins, 3b
E. Williams, 2b
M. Williams, ph-of
Nish Williams, c-rf
Jim Willis, p-lf
Burnis "Bill" Wright, rf-lf
Henry L. "Red" Wright, p-rf

1933

President—N/A
Vice President—N/A
Secretary—N/A
Treasurer—N/A

Alexandria Lincoln Giants

Played at Lincoln Street Park
Glen Bradford, owner
R. D. Marcus, owner
Winfield Welch, ph-lf-rf-manager
Allen [C. D.?] "Iron Man" Moseley, p-manager by July 8, also with Crescent Stars
J. A. Morrison, manager, by July 24

Adams, 2b
Bennett, 3b-2b
[Sam?] Blake, ss-2b
Gamble, p
Hawkins, ss
Hickman, 3b
Holtz, c
Irving, c
A. "Fats" Johnson, p
Arthur "Pretty Boy" Floyd Kranson, p
John Markham, p
Edward "Head" Mayweather, 1b
B. Miller, 2b-ss
Mitchell, 2b-rf-3b
"Lefty" Mouton, p
Thomas "Big," "Steel Arm" Parker, p-cf, also with Crescent Stars
Patterson, 3b
Shaw, p
Sim[m]s, p-rf-lf-1b
E. Smith, c-rf
"Shorty" Walker, lf-3b-c-2b
Wyatt, lf

Algiers Giants

Played at West Side Park
Pete "Creole Pete" Robertson, general manager by Aug. 5, manager on Aug. 13, also with Crescent Stars
E. E. Muse, ss-manager
Welsh [Winfield Welch?], manager

Charley Beverly, lhp
Green Beverly, cf-p-ss
Brougille, p
Brown, x
Porter Dallas, 3b-1b-2b
Diamond, c
Dunbar, c-1b-3b
English, rf
Harris, 2b-ss
Hill, p-lf-ph
Johnson, p
Kirkwood, p
Lobat[s], [Lobart] c
George Markman, p
Milton, p-ph
Barney Morris, p
Robert "Black Diamond" Pipkin, p-cf
Rabbs, rf
Reed, lf-ph
Wilson, 1b
Woods, 1b

Jackson Senators [Bear Cats?]

Played at League Park and Bailey Avenue park
Replaced by Pine Bluff by July 15
Dr. R. L. Johnson, president
Frank Ralton, secretary
J. W. Wilson, vice president
Clarence Winters, treasurer

Bassett, c
Brown, p
Cox, 2b-35
Dunn, cf
Green, ss
Hannen [Hanney], 1b
Hyde, lf
Johnson, c
Long, 2b
Moore, rhp
John Pepper, c
Powell, rf
Vaughan, p
Wade, p

Little Rock Stars

Played at Crump Park, Bailey Avenue Park, and Hicks Field in England, Ark
Reuben Jones, p-cf-lf-rf-mgr
Ira Jones, p-mgr, mgr by June 17

Bill Young, manager on July 2

Battle, lhp
Big Train, c
Fox Blevins, 3b
Callahan, 3b-rf-2b
[James?] "Stump" Carter, 2b-3b
Childress, p-2b
Cook, ss-2b
Curley, x
J. C. Freeman, p
[James Earl?] Gurley [Gulley], lf-cf
Hawkins, c-lf
Haynes, p
Higgins, lhp
William Howard, p-rf-lf, also with Memphis
Jackson, p
Johnson, p
Byron "Mex" Johnson, ss-3b
J. Jones, p
Sug Jones, cf-lf
Lewis, 2b
James Liggons, p
Lindsey, p
Waymon "Ray" Longley, lf
Madison, 3b
McCarroll, p
McCarter, 2b
Morris, p
Nickerson, 3b
Buford Nunley, 1b-p
Pickett, ss
Porter, p
Robinson, c
F. Sims, p
Smith, p
E. Smith, p
Stringer, of
Tate, rf
H. Underwood, c
Underwood, p-c

Memphis Red Sox

Played at Lewis Park
Dr. W. S. Martin, owner
Homer Curry, lf-p-rf-3b-manager
Frank Johnson, manager by early June, also with Monroe
Reuben Jones, cf-2b-lf-3b-manager by September

Barney "Lefty" Brown, lhp

Matthew [Lick] Carlisle, ss-2b
Ernest Carter, p
Marlin "Spoon" Carter, rhp-3b
Count, x
Louis English, rf-1b
Jim Ford, 2b-3b-ph-lf
Gardner, ph
Griffin, lhp
Harney, ph-p
David [Bill] "Lefty" "Son" Harvey, p-lf-rf-ph
William Howard, p, also with Little Rock
Jasper, p
[Oscar "Heavy"?] H. Johnson, 1b
J. Lefty Johnson, ph-p-rf-1b
John "Hooks" Johnson, lhp
Landers, p
Lewis, ss
William "Kid" Lowe, 3b
Jim Mason, 1b-rf-lf
McAllister, 1b
McKenzie, 1b
Eddie Peoples, p
Harvey Peterson, cf-3b
Peterson, rhp
Bob Sa[u]nders, 2b
Robert Smith, c-rf-3b-pr
[Rooevelt?] Tate, cf-rf
Raymond Taylor, c-ph
Underwood, c

Monroe Monarchs

Played at Casino Park
Replaced by Montgomery second half
Frank Johnson, lf-mgr, also with Memphis

Bennett, lf
Harry Else, c, also with Shreveport
Evans, c
[Luther?] Gilliard, cf-p
Hellar, 2b
Hickman, ss
Hudson, p
J. Johnson, lf
Madison, p-rf
Jiggs Maxwell, 3b, also with Shreveport
McHellar, 1b, also with Shreveport
Barney Morris, p, also with Shreveport

Bob Saunders, 2b
[Hilton?] Smith, p-lf, also with Shreveport
Williams, c
Elbert Williams, p, also with Monroe and Shreveport
Zollie Wright, rf, also with Shreveport

Montgomery Grey Sox

Played at College Hill Park and Cramton Bowl
Replaced Monroe second half
[James Earl?] Gurley [Curley], 1b-mgr

James Bell, cc
"Lefty" Glover, lhp-cf
Gresham, rf
Grey [Gray], 2b-3b
Leonard Henderson, ss
Lamar, 3b
George Mitchell, p-2b
J. Mitchell, cf-lf-rfp
Murray, 3b
Nelson, p
[Johnny?] Ray, c-lf-rf
Claude Rowe [Rhodes?], 2b-p-cf
Snowden, p
Tyson, c
[Johnny?] Washington, 3b-1b

New Orleans Crescent Stars

Played at Crescent Park and Heinemann Park
Roy "Red" Parnell, p-cf-manager

[Harvey "Chuff"?] Alexander, 1b
"Wee Willie" Brimmer [Bremer], p
"Red" Brouguille [Bougille], p
Bryant, x
George Collins, 3b-2b
"Shorty" Cooper, ss
Lloyd "Bearman" Davenport, lf
Harry Else, c
Hamilton, c-ph
Eppie Hampton, c
Chick "Moocher" "Popsickle" Harris, p-lf-rf
Milt Laurent, rf-ph-lf
Dickie Matthews, p

Barney "Rocking Chair" Morris, p
Allen [C.D.] "Iron Man" Moseley, p, also with Alexandria
E. E. Muse, ss-3b
William Nash, p
O'Bryant, ss
Palmer, rf
Thomas "Big Train" Parker, p, also with Alexandria
Robert "Black Diamond" Pipkins, p
Bobby Roth, c
Russell, p
George Sias, 3b, ex–Washington
Smith, p
Hilton Smith, p
Morris Smith, p
Wade, p
Elbert Williams, p, also with Monroe and Shreveport
Percy Wilson, 3b-1b
Zollie Wright, lf

PINE BLUFF BOOSTERS

Replaced Jackson by July 15

———

Duncan, c
Gardner, p
Hinton, p
Neal, p

SHREVEPORT CUBS

Played at Palace Park
[Frank?] Johnson, manager

———

T. Alexander, c
Booker, cf
R.C. Canady, 3b
"Shorty" Cooper, ss
Davis, p
Else, c
"Red Shirt" Gibson, p
B. Gipson, rf-cf-p-lf
L. Gipson, p
Theodore Gipson, cf-rf-rhp-1b
Booker T. Harmon [Herman], 3b
Willie Johnson, 1b-cf-p-ph
Jones, c
Alvin "Bubber" Jonnard, p
Maxwell, 3b, also with Monroe
McHellar, 1b, also with Monroe
Barney Morris, p-ph, also with Monroe
Estor Nabors [Nabels] [Nabus], lf
Peterson, p
Shaw, cf-p-ph
Shaw, lhp-cf
Sims, lf-pr-p
Smith, p-ph-rf, also with Monroe
Elbert Williams, p, also with Monroe and New Orleans
Wright, rf, also with Monroe

———

1934

President—Dr. J. B. Martin
Secretary—L.S.N. Cobbs

ATLANTA ATHLETICS

Played at Ponce de Leon Park and Morris Brown College
C. E. Jackson, manager in early preseason
W. L. Joseph, general manager-manager on April 30

———

Allen, p
Raymond Bonner, lf
Evan Bradon, inf
"Lefty" Bridges, lhp
[Ernest "Spoon"?] Carter, p
Willie Carter, ss
Chinn, cf-p
"Smokey Joe" Donell, rhp
English, ss
Hap Glenn, 3b-ss
Melvin Haley [Hailey], of
Leonard Henderson, inf
Ingram, 2b
J. Jackson, 2b
Clarence Keith, 2b
John McFarland, x
[William "Red"?] McNeil, of, also with Louisville
Muff Moffitt, x
James "Red" Moore, 1b
"Lefty" Pollard, lhp
Robert Porter, p
Johnny Ray, of
"Lefty" Reid, lhp
Ripper, 2b-ss
E. Rivers, c
R. Rivers, lf
Robinson, c
Rowe, p-3b
John Henry Sampson, ss
Ed Seitz, cf
Sims, 3b
Smith, p
Jesse Tyner, p-rf, ex–Montgomery
James Valentine, cf-p-ss

BIRMINGHAM BLACK BARONS

Played at Rickwood Field
Frank Perdue, owner Ludie Keys, owner
Charles Walker, secretary
Freddo Walker, owner
W.G. "Bill" Perkins, c-manager, pre-season
Herman Andrews, rf-manager

———

Jerry Benjamin, cf-1b
Matthew "Lick" Carlisle, 2b
Walter Carlyle, 2b
Earnest Carter, p
Frank Collins, p
Anthony Cooper, cf-ss
Johnny Cowans, 3b
Willie Crawford, rf
Dawson, ph
Felix "Chin" Evans, p-of
Walter Glover, lhp
Paul Hardy, c-rf
A. Matthew Jackson, ss
Johnson, lf-rf
Hamp Johnson, of
Arthur "Mutt" Jones, p
Bill Jones, p
C. Jones, p
W. Jones, rf-cf
Morris, p
Mosley, rf
George Nash, p
Martin Oliver, c-rf-2b
Harvey Peterson, lf
Columbus "Dazzy" Vance, p
Vines, p
John Washington, 1b
Worthington, 1b [Washington?]

CINCINNATI TIGERS

Played at Crosley [Redland] Field
M. Jones, president
DeHart Hubbard, manager or business manager
Bill Evans, ss-manager
Jim Glass, manager

Appendix B: Yearly Rosters 1935

"Dizzy" Dismukes, manager by early June

Bert Blakely, cf-c
Burdell, p
["Dusty"?] Decker, 2b
Dunson, 3b
Euell, c
Carl Green, ss-lf
Harris, 1b
J. "Sonny" Harris, ss
Virgil Harris, p
Joe Henderson, rhp
E. Houston, lf
Jesse Houston, p-lf-3b-ss-cf
F. Jackson, 1b-lf
Alto "Big Train" Lane, p
Ed Lyons, 3b
Helburn Meadows, cf
Miller, 2b
Porter Moss, p
Nicholson, lf
Roy Partlow, p-lf
Postell, 2b
Redden, c
Rice, lf-cf
Ridley, cf
"Sneaky" Ro[d]gers, p-ph-rf
Milton "Mighty Blood" Smith, c
Bob "Turkey" Smith, 1b
Spears, 1b
Taylor, c
George Terry, ss-2b
Dan Tye, 3b-2b
Harry "Wu Fang" Ward, rf
Yost, lf

LOUISVILLE CAPS [BLACK SOX]

Played at Parkway Field
Russell "Columbus" Ewing, business manager
A.F. Scott, club official
Joe Hewitt, manager

Black Bottom Buford, 3b
Richard Cannon, p
Joe Cates, ss
Bill Charter, lf
Diemer, p
Louis English, c
William Gill, rf
Willie Gisentaner, lhp
"Rookie" Jones, of, also with Memphis
Lyons, p-1b
McNeil, x, also with Atlanta

Miller, 1b-2b
Jack Ridley, cf
Saunders, 2b-rf, also with Memphis
Raymond Taylor, c, also with Memphis

MEMPHIS RED SOX

Played at Red Sox Park
Dr. A. B. Carter, club official
Dr. B. B. Martin, owner
Reuben Jones, rf-mgr

Don Bennett, 2b-3b
Homer "Goose" Curry, lf-rf-cf-p-3b
Benny Fields, ss
Jimmy Ford, lf-ph
Luther Gilliard, rf-lf-cf-p
Eppie Hampton, c
William [David?] "Bill" "Son" Harvey, lhp-cf
Herman "Red" Howard, lhp
William Howard, rhp
"Rookie" Jones, cf, also with Louisville
Rufus Liggon, p
Emory "Bang" Long, ss
Wayman "Red" Longley, 2b-lf-ss-3b
Jim Mason, rf-1b-p-lf
Beauford Nunley, 1b
Sa[u]nders, 2b-3b, also with Louisville
Robert Smith, 3b-c-2b
Raymond Taylor, c, also with Louisville

MONROE MONARCHS

Played at Casino Amusement Park
C. W. Nalls, club official
Stovall, owner
Frank Johnson, of-mgr

"Kid" Brown, ss
Carter, 3b-2b
Lloyd "Bear Man" "Stomp" Davenport, cf, also with New Orleans?
Harry Else, c-3b
Leland Foster, p
Ben Gilliard, lhp-of
Griffin, lhp-rf, from Texas
Otis "Red" Henry, 2b-3b
Floyd [Arthur] Kranson, rhp
Jimmy "Slim" Liggons, rhp

James Madison, p
Ed "Head" Mayweather, 1b
Jack Moore, of
Leroy Morney, ss
Barney "Rocking Chair" Morris, p
George "Dirty Shirt" Sias, lf
Sim[m]s, lf
E. Smith, rf-c-lf
Hilton Smith, p
Elbert Williams, p, also with New Orleans

NEW ORLEANS CRESCENT STARS

Played at Crescent Park and Heineman Park
Associate member?
H. D. English, owner
Roy "Red" Parnell, cf-mgr

Lloyd "Pepper" Bassett, c-1b
Charles "Streak" Beverly, p-rf-lf
Willie Bremmer [Brimmer], lf
Lloyd Davenport, cf
Milt Laurent, 1b-lf
Charlie Miller, 3b-ss
Moore, p
C.D. "Iron Man" "Gatewood" Mosley, p-rf
E. E. Muse, 2b
Thomas "Big Train" Parker, lf
Reed, lf
Elmo "Rookie" Remi [Renney or Remy], p
George Sias, 2b-cf
Sims, 2b
Elbert Williams, p, also with Monroe
Graham H. Williams, p
Zollie Wright, ss-2b

1935

President—Dr. J. B. Martin, Memphis
1st vice president—Milton H. Grey, Birmingham
2nd vice president, W.B. Baker, Atlanta
Secretary—L. S. N. Cobb, Memphis
Treasurer—Dr. W. S. Martin, Memphis
Corresponding secretary—B.

T. Harvey, Morehouse
  College
Schedule Committee
  Chairman—Dr. B. B.
  Martin, Memphis

ATLANTA BLACK CRACKERS

Played at Spiller Field, Ponce de Leon
Winfred B. Baker, owner
Percy Williams, co-owner as of June 12
Sammy Thompson, 2b-mgr
George "Jew Baby" Bennett, rf-lf-mgr by mid–June
Norman Cross, p-mgr by July 28
Gabby Stephens, manager by May 17

"Scotty" Barnhead [s], c
J. James[?] Brooks, rhp
Brown, 2b
"Black Rider" Brown, p-rf-ph
Jimmy Brown, p
Clayton, 3b
"Curver" Colton, p
Jimmy "Babe" Davis, ss
Jeff Drake, 3b
Felix "Chin" Evans, p-rf-1b-lf
Oran "Duckey" Frazier, ss
Oscar Glenn, ss
James Green[e], c
Charles "Texas Flash" "Flit" Holliday, cf
George Humphrey, lf-c
"Geech" Jennings, p
James "Gabby" Kemp, ss-2b-lf
James "Red" Moore, 1b, also with Chattanooga
Donald Reeves, lhp-rf
[Neil?] Robinson [Roberson], 3b-ss
"Mule" Smith, ss
Tiny Smith, 1b-2b
Thedore Smith, 1b
Jack Thornton, 2b
Lefty Williams, p
Nish Williams, c

BIRMINGHAM BLACK BARONS

Played at Rickwood Field
Gus Allen, owner
C. Chisholm, assistant manager
Molton H. Gray, business manager
Poindexter Williams, ph-mgr
George McAllister, 1b-2b-cf-rf-mgr by mid–May

Fred Bankhead, ss
Harry Barnes [Bonds], c
Jerry Benjamin, x
Good Black, 2b
Erwin Boyd, p
Matthew Carlisle, 2b
Cliff Carr, 3b
Ernest "Spoon" Carter, x
Atkins "Yak" Collins, p
Davis, lf
Ellis, c
James Fields, cf-rf
Gresham, rf-p
S. Howard, 1b
Mack Jackson, 3b
Johnson, rf-cf-lf
Hamp Johnson, rf, p
Keepy, 2b
Kemp, ss
Maya, p
W. H. Mays, lf-cf-3b
Mitchell, 2b
Jodie Mitchell, p
Wild Bill Mitchell, p
"Hog" Mosley, 3b
George Nash, p
Sylvester Owens, 2b
Jeff Posey, p-ph
Smith, rf-ss
Howard Smith, util
John Smith, util
Threat[t][s], cf
C. Threats, p
Bob Walker, p
Watson, c, p
White, rf
Williams, ph
Wrencher, 1b

CHATTANOOGA BLACK LOOKOUTS

Played at Engels Stadium
C. M. Carter, owner
W. L. Joseph, business manager
James Earl Gurley, manager, preseason
[Bud?] Hailey, ph-2b-manager

Camp, 2b
Fitch, p
Floyd, p
Gantt, x
Grant, lf
"Long Henry" Henderson, 3b
Henry, 1b
Kirby, lf
Lagin, rf
Lawrence, rf
Lungelow, c
Martin, p
Miller, ss
James "Red" Moore, 1b-p, also with Atlanta
Newsome, 3b
Rivers, c
[Claude] "Speedball" Rowe, p
Smith, ss-2b
"Mule" Smith, inf
Webb, cf
Welsh, cf

CLAYBROOK TIGERS

Played at Claybrook Park
John C. Claybrook, owner
L.S.N. Cobb, business manager

Bill Adams, x
Jesse Askew, 1b-ss
Bill "One Arm" Ball [Bell], rf
Walter "Lefty" Calhoun, lhp
"Handful" Davis, x
Geechie Donald, p
Espie, x
Hall, lf
Charlie Henderson, x
Leonard "Duckey" Henderson, ss-3b
Logan "Eggie" Hensley, p
John Hundley [Huntley], c
John "The Brute" Lyles [Liles], 3b-c-2b
Robert "Trip" Merritt, c
Johnnie Ray, lf
Russell, lf
Alfred "Grey Hound" Saylor [Sailor], 1b-c
Theolic "Teddy," "Fire Ball" Smith, p
Roosevelt "Bill" Tate, cf
Taylor, 1b, from Memphis
Dan Wilson, 2b
Emmett Wilson, lf

MEMPHIS RED SOX

Played at Martin Stadium

B. B. Martin, business manager
Dr. W. S. Martin, owner
Reuben Jones, rf-mgr

———

[Emory?] Adams, p-2b
Arthur, p
Jim Canada, 2b
Marlin Carter, ss
Downer, p
Jim Ford, ph-lf-rf-2b
Fox, x
Eppie Hampton, c
Bill Harvey, p
Bill Howard, p
Claude Johnson, 3b
J. W. Jones, cf
Johnny Jones, p
Red Langley [Longley], rf-ss
Rupert Liggons [Ligon], lhp
Pete McQueen, rf-lf
Nash, p
Beauford Nunley [Nunnalley], 1b
M. Owens, x
Nat Rodgers, rf
L. Smith, lf-1b
Robert Smith, c-1b, from B'ham
[Jim?] West, 1b

Montgomery Grey Sox

Played at Cramton Bowl
Independent team? Associate member?
William M. Brown[e], president

———

E. Brown, rf
Burk [Burch, Buck], 2b
Burke, p
Carter, 3b
Crosby, 3b
Ellis, 1b
Glover, p
[Paul?] Hardy, c
Johnson, 1b
Lamar, ss
Lett, ss
Lloyd, p
Lloyd, c
Mitchell, c
Mitchell, p
Edgar Poole, lf
Pryor, cf
Pyrus, p
Reed, cf

Richardson, lf
Rogers, rf
Stokes, lhp
Joe Turner, p
White, p

New Orleans Black Pelicans

Played at Crescent Park
Independent team? Tri-State League?
Allen Page, owner
Sandy Thompson, p-manager

———

Clifford Allen, p
Lloyd "Pepper" Bassett, c
Bradford, lf
J. Brookes, p
[Horatio?] Cotton, x
Cross, p
Downs, x
Fisher, 1b
Gates, 3b
Lefty Glover, p
Green, c
Humphrey, c
Leroy Idlett, x
Jennings, p
Johnson, c
Lorant [Milt Laurent?], x
McIntosh, 2b
Bob Miller, p
Miller, ss
Moore, rf
Smith, cf-p
Taylor, p-rf
Wilbur, c
Booker Williams, p

1936

President—Thomas Wilson, Nashville

Atlanta Black Crackers

Played at Ponce de Leon Park
James "Prince" Andrews, vice president
W. B. Baker, secretary
S. M. Humphrey, business manager
H. H. M. Smith, treasurer, named president on May 2
Percy Williams, president-

treasurer, co-owner, died April 26
Lewis L. Means, manager and assistant business manager
Tiny Smith, lf-2b-manager by June 19

———

Red" Bradley, p
James Brooks, p
"Black Rider" Brown, rhp
Cooper, c
Jimmy "Babe" Davis, ss
Roseborough Downs, p
Felix "Chin" Evans, p
Oran "Duck" Frazier, ss-2b
Glover, p
James "Pig" Green[e], c
Henry "Red" Hadley, cf-rf
Hicks, c
Howard, 3b
C. Howard, lf
J. D. Howard, lf
Leroy Idlett, 3b
"Brer" Jones, 3b, ex–Jax
James "Ripper" ["Gabby"?] Kemp, c
John McFarland, 1b
Jim "Slim" Reese, lhp-ph-rf
Donald Reeves, rf
Smith, ss
Jack Thornton, 1b
Roy "Spook" Welmaker, lhp-lf-cf
Maceo "Squabbler" Wright, rf-lf

Birmingham Black Barons

Played at Rickwood Field
Andrew M. Walker, manager

———

Fred Bankhead, 2b-3b-ss-c
Harry Barnes, c
Barnes, Harry, rhp, New York Zulu Giants last year
Jack "Dizzy" Bruton, rhp-lb
Pit "Daffy" Bruton, p
James Canada[y], 1b
[Melvin "Slick"?] Coleman, ss
Johnny Cowan, 3b-2b
Cox, cf
Willie Truehart "Red" Ferrell, p
Benny Fields, cf-ss
Lefty Glover, lhp, also with Montgomery
Tom "Pop-Eye" Hollins, rhp

Herman "Red" Howard, lf
Johnson, ph
Kimbroe, c
Owens, cf
Dewitt Owens, 2b-3b
Jeff [Ray] Posey, p
Quicksey, 3b-c
Robertson, p
Armand Tyson, 3b-2b
David "Hammer Man" Whatley, rf
Wilson, ss
Parnell Woods, 3b-ss

Chattanooga Black Lookouts

Played at Engel Stadium
Bud Hailey [Haley], owner? manager?

———

Bill Brooks, rhp
Brown, lf-p-1b
Camp, ss
Coles, lf-p
Tom Craig, c
["Dusty"?] Decker, 2b
[Felix?] "Slim" Evans [Evins], p
Fields, rf
Gantt, cf
Glenn, ss
Gorge, 1b
Humphrey, lf-c-rf
"Sticks" Johnson, 3b
"Pitcheye" Lawrence, rf-p
Martin, p
McGee, 3b
"Lefty" Reid [Reed], lhp
Ed "Betson" Rivers, p-c
Claude Rowe, p
Simpson, p-rf, p
E. Smith, 1b-p-3b-ss, from Pensacola, 47-year-old ex–big leaguer
H. "Horse" Smith, 3b-p-ss
Spencer, p
Marion Stafford, 2b-ss
Webb, rf-cf-1b
Williams, p

Cincinnati Tigers

Played at Crosley Field
DeHart Hubbard, manager [probably general manager]
Jim Glass, manager by May 17

———

Rainey Bibbs, 2b-3b
Marlin "PeeWee" Carter, ss-3b
Childes [Childers?], c
Clark, rf-lf
Lionel Decuire, c
Howard Easterling, ss
Frank Edwards, 2b
A. [Jerry] Gibson, rf
J. "Sonny" Harris, ph-ss-2b
Virgil "Schoolboy" Harris, p
Jesse "Alibi Ike" Houston, p-rf
John Johnson, p
Johnson, c
Arthur Maddox, p
Jasper Miller, p
Roy Partlow, p
Harvey Peterson, lf
Neal "Shadow" Robinson, cf
Russell, p
"Reb" Russell, 3b
Willy Sim[m]s, rf
Simons, rf
Bob "Turkey" Smith, c
Olan Jelly Taylor, 1b
Donald "Tippy" Tye, lhp

Hopkinsville Athletics

Played at Flemings Cave Park
Reported to have disbanded on May 22
R. H. Penner, club official

Memphis Red Sox

Played at Russwood Park and Martin Park
Dr. B.B. Martin, business manager
Dr. J. C. Martin, club official
Robert Smith, 1b-c-3b-manager as of May 16
William "Nat" Rogers, lf-manager by early August

———

Allen, p-ss-3b
Roosevelt Cox, c-p
Saul Davis, x
Charles "Dusty" Decker, 3b-2b
Easley, lf
Evans, lf
Bill Evans, of
Felix "Chin" Evans, p
Jimmy Everett, p
Jim Ford, rf-ss

Gibbs, 1b
C___ Hall, p
Hamilton, 1b
Eppie Hampton, c-1b
Howard Hassett, p
Claude Ha[y]slett, p
Hazle [Hazle Thomas?], p
Otis Henry, rf-lf-cf-c
Herman "Red" Howard, lhp
Humphrey [Humphries], rf
Jackson, p-rf
Livingston "Winky," "Wimpy" James, ss-3b-1b
"Rookie" Jones, cf
Kelly, p
Clarence Lewis, 2b
Joe Ware, cf

Montgomery Grey Sox

Played at North Decatur Street Park [Brown's Park?]
William M. Brown, president and owner
[Paul?] Hardy, c-lf-mgr

———

Arrington [Arlington], p
Bever [Beaver] [Beverly?], p
Blackwell, 1b
Brown, rf-c
W. [William?] Carter, 3b
[Joe?] Cates, 3b
Crickett, lf
Crockett, p-lf-3b
Dewitt, lf-p
Duncan, p
Howard Easterling, 2b
Louis English, c
Fair [Fain, Fairly], lf-3b
Frazier, ss
[Herbert?] Gay, rf
Lefty Glover, lhp, also with Birmingham
Harris, p
[Harry?] Jefferson [Jeffers], 2b-rf-lf-1b
Jones, p
[Clarence?] Lamar, ss
Lester?] Lockett, p
[Hubert?] Lockhart, p
[Jim?] Mason, p
McCracken, lf-cf-p
Nichol[a]s, ss-2b
Pendleton, 1b
Poole, lf
DeWitt Prickett, p-of, ex–Jax Red Caps
Ray, cf

Reed [Reid], cf
R. Taylor, lf-rf-cf
Tye, p
White, p
Williams, lhp

NASHVILLE BLACK VOLS

Played at Wilson Park and Sulphur Dell
Ed Menesse, owner?
Joe Myers, owner?
Benny Scales, owner
Jesse "Hoss" Walker, ss-manager

———

Bender, c
Black Bottom Buford, 3b
Gray, rf-2b
J. Jackson, c
Johnson, p-rf
Jones, c
Henry Kimbro, lf
Red Longley, 2b, ex–Memphis
Love [William "Kid" Lowe?], 3b
Granville Lyons, 1b
Frank McAllister, p
Stokes, p
Thriekill, cf
Johnnie Williams, ph-p
Woodrow, ph
"Slow Time" Young, p

———

1945

President—Dr. R. B. Jackson, Nashville
Treasurer—John H. Harden, Atlanta
Secretary—C. J. Kincaide, Knoxville
Director of Public Relations—J. C. Chunn, Atlanta

ASHEVILLE BLUES

Played at McCormick Field
C. L. Moore, 1b-owner-manager
Charles Jones, p-manager?

———

Anderson, c
Robert Bowman, rhp
Howard Cleveland, cf

Waldo "Cane Creek" Dunlop, lhp
Eugene Dunn, 3b
Evans, c
Russ Evans, p
Frank Flemming, lhp-lf
Doug Graeber, lf
Charlie Green, 2b-3b
Charlie Harris, 2b-lf-cf
Rufus Hatten, c
Arthur Heffner, ss
Hefferies [Jeffries?], p
Clarence Lamar, ss-2b
Robert Lee Madison, rhp
A C. Neeley, rf
Booker Neeley, p
Owen, c
Robinson, 2b
Joe Royal, c
Eker Sewell, p
Herman Taylor, 3b

ATLANTA BLACK CRACKERS

Played at Ponce De Leon Park and Harper's Field
John Harden, owner
Felix "Chaser" Manning, p-1b-mgr, also with Chattanooga
Brennan King, manager as of Aug. 15

———

Spencer Alexander, cf, also with Knoxville
Harry Barnes, c
Nathaniel Brannon, rf
Melvin "Slick" Coleman, rhp
James "Neckbones" Davis, 3b
Lomax "Butch" Davis, lf
John "Early Bird" Ellison, c
William Otis "Bull" Howard, 2b
Rozo "Babe" "Bozo" Jackson, ss
Brennon King, rhp
Early King, p, also with Nashville
Willie Marvin, 3b, also with Knoxville
Pedro Miro, ss, also with New Orleans
[William "Slack"?] Morgan, p
Alonza Perry, rhp
Bobby Robertson, x
John Sadler, p
Santiago Salazar, 1b, also with New Orleans

Sidney Saucier, lf, also with New Orleans
George "Jitter" Scales, of, also with Chattanooga
Clarence "Hambone" Sims, rhp
Will Thompson, p
Lazarus Vernez, ss
Joe Wiley, 3b, also with New Orleans
Ennis Williams, ss-2b

CHATTANOOGA CHOO CHOOS

Played at Engel Stadium
Bino Boger, club official?
Will McClure, club official
Mrs. Will McClure, club secretary
James Cotton, manager and owner
"Dock" Wingo, c-manager by June 28
Ed Byrom, manager by July 15
Felix Manning, manager by Aug. 26, also with Atlanta

———

Thomas Acken [Aekin, Ackin, Atken], c
"Baldy" Adkins [Akins, Atkins], c
James "Lefty" Armour, lhp
Ed Bryon [Byroki, Byrron], 3b
L__ Byrron, rf
Harper Clark, inf
Dave, cf-lf
Dennard [Dillard], 2b-ss
George "Fireball" Franklin, p, also with Chattanooga
Frazier, rhp-lf
Pete Harris, p
"Junior" Isabella [Isabel, Isabelle], 1b-p
Jackson, 2b
Jenkins, cf, also with Mobile?
"Babe" "Lefty" Lawson, 1b
Phil Lindsey, p
Emory "Schoolboy" Long, 2b-of-inf-p
Ernest Long, p
Longalow [Longalon], c
"Buster" Lovingood, ss-rf
Mauson, x
Will "Foots" McClure, cf-rf
Patterson, p
Rollins, rf
George "Jitter" Scales, lf, also with Atlanta

Sellers, p
"Speed" Shepherd, ss
"Pie" Silver[s], p, also with Mobile
Simpson, p
West, c
Georgia Mae Williams, p

INDIANAPOLIS CARDINALS

Played at Mooers Field [Victory Field?]
Replaced Little Rock by mid–July. B'ham World of July 24 says replacing New Orleans Black Pelicans
Rainey Bibbs, manager

———

Bus Allen, p
Jim "Bimbo" Bennett, p
Charleston, x
Coachman, c
Cowan, x
Duke Duncan, ss
"Lefty" Finch, lhp
Hall, p
Harrington, c
Haynes, x
Hill, p
Hooker, p
Jordan, p
[Lester?] Lockett, 3b
[Hank?] Mainor, p
Royale, c
Shelby, x
Leroy Sutton, rhp
Bill Thomas, p
Herman Watt[s], lhp
Williams, lhp

KNOXVILLE GRAYS

Played at Caswell Park [and Smithson Stadium?]
Henry N. Lewis, p-c-cf-manager and owner
Harry Jeffers, manager on Aug. 26

———

Spencer Alexander, of, also with Atlanta
Walter "Plug" Bester, p-rf
William Bradford, [Braddock] 2b-3b
Robert Burney, p
Martin Crue, p, also with Mobile
Taylor Erwin, x

Clifford Fields, inf
Roy "Babe" Fine, c
George "Fireball" Franklin, p, also with Chattanooga
Prim[e] Hall, 1b-capt
David T. Harper, of
James Horton, p
Bill Howard, 2b
Taylor Irwin, lf
Thomas Jackson, p
Harry Jeffries, c
Lennard "Double Duty" Kendricks [Kendrix], c
C. J. Kincaide, p
Willie Marvin, 3b, also with Atlanta
Earnest Mason, p
Gread "Lefty" McKinnis, lhp
Fred Miller, p
James "Lefty" Mitchell, p
James "Red" Moore, 1b
Willie Morgan, c
Roselle Murray, p
Newson, c
Henry [James] Panion, 3b
Lonnie Pearson, c
"Peaches" Peele, p
Johnny Richardson, ss
Freddie Shepherd, rf-cf
Clyde "Boone" Smith, ss
Quincy "Whirlwind" Smith, x
Erwin Taylor, lf
James "Shoe-String" Taylor, cf-lf
Carl Williams, 1b
Erwin [Eddie] Williams, lf-rf

LITTLE ROCK BLACK TRAVELERS

Played at Travelers Field
Replaced by Indianapolis Cardinals by mid–July
Sam Parke, owner
Charles Burgs, manager
Elbert Walker, manager, also with Mobile

———

[Joe or Garanett?] Bankhead, rhp
Coachman, c
Curry, c
Duncan, p
Hall, p
Hill, p
Hooker, p
Hyde, ss

Joe Lewis, p
Mainor, p
McCarthy, c
Peaches, p

MOBILE BLACK BEARS

Played at Hartwell Field
Willie Davis, business manager and owner
Julius Payton, of-manager by early July
Elbert Walker, manager by early August, also with Little Rock

———

Wesley "Racehorse" Attenbury, x
Ferdinand R. Berty, c-of
Walter Blackmon, x
Clyde Bonnie, p
M. H. Brown, ss
Byron, 3b
Bertis Carlton, x
Carson, p
Martin Crue, lhp, also with Knoxville
Fred Douglas, x
Franklin, ss
Hackle, rf
Houston, 2b
Jenkins, rf, also with Chattanooga
Carl Jenkins, 1b
Matthew [Martin?] Jenkins, rhp
Lawson, 1b
Otis Martin, p
Roy McCarther, inf
McNair, c
Robinson [Murphy] "Steel-Trap" Morgan, c
Nathan Owens, p, also with New Orleans
Rocking Chair Rabbit, c
Willie Richbourg, p
E. Roberts, p
Robertson, x
William Bobby Robinson, 3b
Sanders, 3b
Sylvester "Pie" Silvers, p, also with Chattanooga
Harry Simpson, rhp
Oliver Smith, rhp
"Wild Bill" Stevens, rhp
Bill Tate, x
Verdis "Midnight" Thomas, cf
Charles West, c, ex–BBB

Eddie Williams, util
Eric Williams, lf

Nashville Black Vols

Played at Sulphur Dell
Dr. R. B. Jackson, owner and president
Bill Perkins, manager
Granville Lyons, manager by July 28
Dusty Owens, manager by Sept. 7

Brown, p
Leon Childress, p-c
Edward "Ace" "Lefty" Derrick, lhp
James Gilliam, 3b
Grimes, 1b
"Smokey Joe" Hall, p
Johnson, p
Early King, p, also with Atlanta
Lyons, p
Patton, p
Bill "Pa" Perkins, c
Richardson, p
Frank Russell, ss
Doc Wingo, c
Harvey Young, ss

New Orleans Black Pelicans

Played at Pelican Stadium
Clifford Matthews, owner
Wesley Barrow, manager
Ernest English, lf-manager by early July?

Bennett, rf
Bob Bissant, x, a Cuban, captain
Moffitt "Lefty" Brooks, lhp
Davis, 2b
Walter Dearhart, p
Robert English, lf-1b
Clarence Ferndudez, 2b
Eugene "Mule" Hardin, c-1b
Stamps "Jelly" Holl[e]y, cf
"Steel-Trap" Johnson, c
Letcher, p
Herbert [Thompson] "Jitterbug" Luther, p
Pedro Miro, ss, also with Atlanta
Mitchell, p
James "Jimmy" Murphy, p

Parke O'Neal, x
Nathan Owens, p, also with Mobile
Tom "Big Train" Parker, rhp
Rogers Pierre, p
Douglas Rome, p
Santiago Salazar, 1b, also with Atlanta
Sidney "Popeye" Saucier, lf, also with Atlanta
Frank "Mighty Ground Hog," Thompson, lhp
Britt Ward [Word, Wood], c
Joe Wiley, 3b, also with Atlanta

Richmond Cardinals

Played at Mooers Field
Replaced New Orleans in second half
Few results reported, no personnel named

1946

President—R. B. Jackson, Nashville
Vice president—C. L. Hyatte, Knoxville
Treasurer—C.L. Moore, Asheville, N.C.
Secretary/public relations— C. J. Kincaide, Knoxville

Asheville Blues

Played at McCormick Field
C. L. Moore, manager

Thomas Acken, c, with Chattanooga last year
Spencer Alexander, rf-lf
Richard Banks, c
Robert Bowman, rhp
Nathaniel Brannon, 1b-lf
Mack Briggs, p
Burns, x
Edward Byron [Byron, Byrum, Byram], 2b-3b
Cooper, c
Covington, rhp
Waldo "Cane Creek" Dunlap, lhp
Frank Fleming, lhp-rf
Walter Goins, lf
Charlie Green, 2b
Charlie Harris, 2b

Rufus Hatten, c
Arthur Hefner, ss?-cf, also with Montgomery
William "Snag" Henderson, c
Charlie Humber [Humbler], 2b
Jeffries, p
Charles[?] Jones, c
A. C. Neeley, rf-p-c
Booker Neeley, p
Jasper Perkins, inf
Vernon "Butch" Phillips, rhp
Jesse [John?] Sanders, p, also with Charlotte
Edward Sim[m]s, p-c, also with Charlotte and Knoxville
Richard "Red" Stewart, cf, also with Charlotte?
Herman Taylor, 3b-2b
Will Thompson, p, also with Charlotte
Williams, inf
Fred Worthy, ss-3b

Charlotte Black Hornets

Played at Griffith Park
Melvin "Slick" Coleman, p-manager
Sam Douglas, manager

Alexander, c
Willie Brannon, x
Johnny Brown, x
Nat Caldwell, x
Ben Camel, x
Dave Campbell, x
Davis, p
Grier, p
Prim Hall, x
Charlie Harris, inf, also with Knoxville
Herrion, p
Johnson, c
Johnson, p
Willie Johnson, x
Graham Johns[t]on, x
Mackey, c
Auburn Nelson, p
John Sadler, p
Jesse T. Sanders, p, also with Asheville
Edward Sim[m]s, p-c, also with Asheville and Knoxville
Richard Stewart, x, also with Asheville?
Will Thompson, p, also with Asheville

Appendix B: Yearly Rosters 1946

Wallace, c
Tommie Woods, x

Chattanooga Choo-Choos
Played at Engel Stadium
Will McClure, president and owner
Felix Manning, p-1b-ph-manager

———

James Armour, lhp
"Toots" Arnold, lhp
Harry Barnes, c
Brown, c
Cole[s], c
Melvin "Slick" Coleman, p
James "Neck Bones" Davis, p
Dennard, x
Clarence Dodd[s], lf
Waldo Dudley, x
Edward Gamble, of
Edward Grisely, inf
Harris, lf-2b
John High, rhp
Howard, p
Jenkins, p
Matthew Jenkins, cf-rf
Jones, p
George "Babe" Lawson, 1b-lf
Lloyd, lf
Ernest "Early" Long, p
B. Lovingood, ss-lf-ph
Nathaniel McClinic, lf
McGee, cf-lf
Werby McGhee, x
McNealie, lf-ph
Motay, p
Owens, lf
Alonzo Perry, p
Rowe, p
Silvester "Pie" Silvers, rhp
Big Red Smith, 1b
Harry Sneed, rf-ph-lf
Sterling Talley, ss
B. Toats, lhp
Ulysses Wilkes, 3b
H. Wilks, lf-rf
Ennis Williams, 2b

Jacksonville Eagles
Played at City Ball Park on Myrtle Avenue
Carl "Bubber" Ford, president and owner
Edgar Campbell and Fluke Mitchell co-managers on July 2
Harry Jeffries, manager by mid–July Phillie Holmes, p-manager

———

"Schoolboy" Allen, rhp
Brooks, c
Brooks, rf-cf
Edward Dennard, 3b
"Spec" Ellis, lhp
Everett, lf
Golden, p
Grimes, x
Harris, 2b
Leroy "Phillie" Holmes, p
Johnson, c
[Clarence?] Lamar, 2b
[Felix?] McLarin, c-ss
Mitchell, p
Poole, x
[Johnny?] Ray, cf-1b-ss
Early Richburg, rhp
Richland, p
J__ Robinson, cf
K__ Robinson, 1b
Roggan, p
Ben Taylor, lhp
[Henry?] Turner, rf
Adderly Turner, rhp
Washington, rf

Knoxville Giants
Played at Caswell Park
C. L. Hyatte, vice president and business manager
Walt E. Kennedy, Jr., president
C. J. Kincaide, secretary
Nat Rogers, rf-lfe-ph-manager, ex–Memphis

———

John Armstrong, rf-1b
Bandy, 2b
Walter "Tojo" Bester, p-util
Robert Boyd, 1b
Brooks, lhp
Cartwright, rf
Daniels, c
P [Fount] Dickerson [Dickson], p
Fair, c
Kendal Felder, 3b
Roy "Babe" Fine, c
George "Fireball" Franklin, p-ph
Grimes, 1b-of
George "Red" Handy, 3b-2b
Charlie Harris, 3b, also with Charlotte
David T. Harper, cf
Hettor, x
Edward Horne[r], lf
James Horton, p
H. A. Jefferson, p
"Red" Jenkins, lhp
Jones, p
Cecil Jordan, lf-cf-ss
James "Tut" Lockman, cf
Long, 3b
Harry Milton, ss-3b
William "Sack" Morgan, lhp
Arthur Ramsay, 2b-lf
Fount Richardson, p
Johnnie Richardson, ss
Willie "Schoolboy" Rowe, rhp
Sewell, p
Edward Sim[m]s, p-lf, also with Asheville and Charlotte
Simpson, util
Smith, p
Vickers, lhp
Ward, 1b
Williams, lhp

Mobile Black Bears
Played at Hartwell Field
Sam [Willie] Davis, owner or promoter
Claude "Baby Face" Green, p-manager

———

Alexander, p
Ataberry [Attlebury], lf
Beck, p
Berty, c
Kelly Brooks, lf
Chestnut, p
Davis, 1b
Edwards, p
John Henry, cf
George Hunt, c
Jones, c
Matthews [Mathis], c
Owens, rf-p
"Fireball" Panther, rhp
Parker, 2b
Porter, ss
Billy Robinson [Roberson], 3b
Sims, x
Smith, c
Smith, p

Snead [Speed], lhp
Thomas, cf
Thomas, p
H__ Thomas, x
Washington, c
Thomas Williams, p

Montgomery Dodgers/ Red Sox

Played at Cramton Bowl, Hornet Stadium
Jake Whatley, owner
Ernest "Spoon" Carter, lf-rhp-manager
Kendall "Buck" Felder, 2b-p-ss-35-manager by late July?
Ernest Robinson, p-manager by mid–August

———

Allen, p
Anderson, p
John Avery, 1b-p-lf-rf
Jim "Butch" Bolden, rhp
Bonnes [Bonner], p
Jim Brown, 2b-ss-3b
Camp, c
Jim Can[n]ady, 1b
James Carter, 3b-2b, ex–BBB
Cody, c
Peter "Fireball" Cole, rhp
Carvin Crowe, 3b-rf-c-lf
Donaldson, 1b-ph-c
Jack Edwards, of
Ellis, p
Fields, lf, in AS game
Melvin Foson [Fosom], ss
Gibson, ss
Harris, p
Arthur Hefner, ss?, also with Asheville
Higgins, p-ph-rf
Holloway, rf
Houser, 3b
Taylor Irving, x
Jalreath, p
Hamp Johnson, cf-rf
Joseph, 3b-2b
Kennedy, 1b
McGee, cf
James "Dudder" "Dude" Mitchell, cf-lf
Mitchell, c
Murphy, p
Henry Newberry, p-lf
Laymon Ramsey, cf-rhp-lf
Jake Robertson, of?-ss
[Sylvester "Pie"?] Silvers, p
Fred Sims, cf

Smith, c
H. Taylor, rf-cf
Thomas, c
Jim Tolbert, c
Vaughan, c
Veall, p
Williams, p
Williams, lf-cf-rf
C. Williams, of
Orrin Williams, of

Nashville Cubs/ Black Vols

Played at Sulphur Dell
Tex Burnett, ph-manager
Frazier Robinson, manager by Aug. 16
Wesley Barrow [Barron], manager by September?

———

Roy Acklin [Aiken], p
Wilbur "Yank" Adkisson [Atkinson], rf-c
James Armistead, cf
Armstrong, cf
Norman Banks, 2b
Alfred "Bomber" Brown, p
Burnett, ph
Claiborn Cartwright, x
Col[y]vin, p
James Daly, 1b
Clarence Davis, 1b
Edward Derrick, lhp
Edmundson, c
Edmundson, p
Nathaniel Edwards, p
Carl Emerson, ss
Ferras, ph
Roscoe Germany, p
Gibson, lf
Gilby, of
Arthur Hefner, cf
Henton, lf-c
Archie Hinton, rhp
Floyd Jackson, p
"Bullet" Johnson, p
Early King, p
James Knight, p
Lanier, x
Richard "Cowboy" Murray, p
Bill [John] Newberry, p-cf
[Nathan?] Owens, lf
Frazier "P-80" Robertson, c
Russell, 2b
Frank Russell, lf
John Russell, p
William Scott, ss
Stratten, lf

Roy Swanson, c, p
Williams, p
James Zapp, 3b

———

1947

President—Tom Wilson, died in office on May 16, replaced by Allen Page
Vice president—Allen Page, New Orleans
Secretary—S. J. Kincaide
Treasurer—Dr. B. B. Martin, Memphis

Asheville Blues

Played at McCormick Field
C. L. Moore, manager, owner-manager

———

Spencer Alexander, rf-cf
Richard Banks, c
Harry "Bunny" Barnes, c, also with Chattanooga and Raleigh
Robert Bowman, rhp
Nathaniel Brannon, lf-of
Byrd, p
Edward Byron [Byrum, Bryon], 2b-p, also with Jacksonville
Cooper, c
M___ "Babe" Daniels, c
Font [Fount] Dickerson, p
Tom Dickson, p
Dillard, p
Waldo "Cane Creek" Dunlap, p
Ellison, c
Babe Fine, c
Frank Fleming, lhp
Walter Goins, lf
Charlie Harris, 1b, also with Jacksonville and Raleigh
Rufus Hatten, c, also with Raleigh
Arthur Hefner, cf
Leroy "Phillie" Holmes, inf, also with Atlanta
Charlie Humber, 2b
Sonny Jeffries, p
A.C. Neeley, rf, also with Raleigh
James Pendleton, ss
Vernon "Butch" Phillips, p
Font Richardson, p
Jesse [John?] Sanders

[Saunders], p, ex–
  Charlotte
Richard "Red" Stewart, cf-lf
Herman Taylor, 3b
Will "Gene" Thompson, p
Willie Williams, util
Fred Worthy, ss-lf-cf-1b

ATLANTA BLACK CRACKERS

Played at Ponce de Leon Park
Associate member, according
  to Chatt Times, 5–18–47
John Harden, owner
Claud Malcolm, becomes co-
  owner in March
Sammy Haynes, manager
Spoon Carter, manager mid–
  May
William Perkins, c-manager,
  debut on May 14
Melvin "Slick" Coleman, rhp-
  manager, by Aug. 10

———

Robert Branson, lhp
Eddie Brigham, 2b
Thaddeus Christopher, c
Eddie Daniels, rhp
Roosevelt "Duro" Davis, rhp
Deakins, ph
Theodore Dillon, p, also with
  New Orleans
Clyde Golden, lhp
David T. Harper, cf
Alonzo Hicks, p-rf
Holden, p
Leroy "Phillie" Holmes, 2b,
  also with Asheville
Jackson, p
Babe "Bozo" Jackson, 3b
Eugene "Lefty" Jones, lhp
Ralph Jones, p
Brennan L. King, p
Raymond Lacey, x
William Makell, x
William "Sack" Morgan, lhp
Charles Neal, rf, 16, brother
  of James Neal
James Neal, ss, brother of
  Charles Neal
Maurice Peatross, 1b
John Ray, ph-util-cf
Johnny Richardson, ss
Russell, x
Frederick Shepherd, rhp
Jimmy Thompson, of
Leon Wyatt, rhp
James Zapp, lf

CHATTANOOGA CHOO CHOOS

Played at Engel Stadium
Will McClure, owner
Felix Manning, p-manager

———

James "Lefty" Armour, lhp
Harry Barnes, c, also with
  Asheville and Raleigh
James Bolden, p
T. Bolden [Bolen], p
Claiborne [Jimmy?]
  Cartwright, rf-lf-ph, also
  with Raleigh
James Dailey, p-ph
Kendel "Buck" Felder, ss-util
Elbert Gamble, rf-ph
Roland Gay, 3b-2b
Acie Griggs, rhp
Bennie Griggs, rhp
Wiley Griggs, lf-3b
Harper, cf
Norton Hudson, c
Hamp Johnson, rf
George "Babe" Lawson, 1b
Ernest Long, rhp-ph
Nathaniel McClinic, cf-lf
Patterson, lf-rf
Richardson, p
Ripple, pr
N. [D.?] Rivers, rf-ph
William "Schoolboy" Rowe, p
Freddie Shephard, rf-lf-ph
Sylvester [Lindsey?] "Pie"
  Silvers, p
Smith, 3b
Sterling Talley, ss
Ulysses Wilkes, 3b
Eddie Williams, lf
Ennis Williams, 2b

JACKSONVILLE EAGLES

Played at Jacksonville Park
Carl Ford, owner
Ernest "Spoon" Carter, rhp-
  manager
Clarence Lamar, manager by
  Aug. 17

———

Bar[r]on, 2b
Edward Brown, x
Tom Brown, x
Edward Byron, 2b, also with
  Asheville
Davis, 3b
Edward Dennard, 2b-3b
Elmer Edwards, p

Elmore, p
Evans, c
Thomas "Monk" Favors, x
George Gerideau, lhp
Tom Greer, of
Charlie Harris, 1b, also with
  Asheville and Raleigh
Hatten, x
Howard, p
St. Julian Ladson, x
Lamar, ss
Lemar, c
H__ [John] McLaurin
  [McLeron], c-3b
Ramsey, p
Ray, lf
Eddie Richb[o]urg, p
Robinson, lf-ph-cf
Walt Rogers, of
Tommy Sampson, rf
Sims, cf-lf-3b
Albert Smith, x
Benny Taylor, p
Allen Turner, p
Ted Turner, rhp
Washington, p
Washington, 1b
White, x

MEMPHIS BLUES

Played at Martin Stadium
Dr. M.S. Martin, owner

———

No player names found

NASHVILLE CUBS

Played at Sulphur Dell
Dr. R. B. Jackson, owner
Eff Lloyd, comedian
Felton Snow, 3b-manager
James Armstead, cf-manager
  by early August

———

Wilbur Adkis[s]on, ph-rf
[Hoses?] "Buster" Allen, p
Black, c
Alfred "Bomber" "Farmer"
  Brown, p
Luther "Sleepy" Colvin, p
Clarence "Spike" Davis, lf-
  3b-rf
Gabriel Davis, x
Edward "Lefty" Derrick, lhp
Foster, x
William "Double Duty"
  Greason, p-c
Herman Howard, lhp

James Jones, cf-rf-lf
Brennan King, p
Early King, p
Wesley [Frank] Logan, c
Clinton "Butch" McCord, 1b
Fred Miller, rhp-rf
Judge "Dusty" Owens, 2b
Nathaniel Owens, p
Bill Patterson, c
Johnnie Richardson, ss
Frank Russell, ss
William Scott, ss
Roy Swanson, c
James Zapp, lf

New Orleans Creoles

Played at Pelican Stadium
Allen Page, owner
Lucille Herbert, coach
Harry Williams, 2b-ph-manager

———

Oliver Andry [Andray, Andrews], c-rf
Charles Byrd, 3b
Francisco Cas[s]anova, c
Chapman, p
Charlie [Eddie] Daniels, rhp
F. Daniels, c
Theodore Dillon, p, also with Atlanta
Bobbie Fields, p
James Ford, 3b
Edouard Gavelin [Gavalan], ss-3b
Wencesloa [Wensesloa, Wenessessa, Winslow] Gonzalez [Gonzales], lhp
Archie Hinton, rhp
Billy Horne, ss
Shirley Jackson, util
Bernie Jefferson, p
Wesley Logan, c
Logan, p
Grady Manning, rf
Fred McDaniels, rhp
B. [Charles] McLaurin, p
Miller, p
Tom Parker, of
Merrill Porter, 1b
Tom Purvis, rhp
Sam Robinson, p
Archie [Rudolph] Ray [Ray Rudolph?], p-pr
Joe Spencer, 2b
Johnny [Herb] Stamps, p
James Watts, lf

Eddie Williams, lf-rf
Dan Wilson, x

Raleigh Tigers

Played at Chavis Park
Arthur Dove, owner
Pete Wilder, business manager
Lamb Barbee, of-manager

———

Wiley Bailey, x
Harry Barnes, c, also with Asheville and Chattanooga
Robert Barnes, p
"Red" Baskerville, 2b
Brewington, x
Bobby Burns, p
Harold "Red" Burton, lhp
Jimmy Cartwright, util, also with Chattanooga
Hazell Clark, 3b-2b
Jimmy Cooper, p
John Cooper, rhp
"Big Train" Cozart, x
Austin Davis, inf
Nat Davis, x
Sam Davis, 1b
Ralph Donley, lhp
Evans, x
Roy Fine, c
Bill Hall, of
Charlie Harris, 1b, also with Asheville
Rufus Hatten, c, also with Asheville
Sonny Jefferies, p
Marvin Johnson, rhp
Jones, x
Henry [Bro] Knuckles, lf
Clarence Lamar, x
Jimmy [Johnny] Mack, rhp
Murphy Morgan, c
Murl Mortan, x
[Booker?] Neeley, p
A. C. Neeley, cf, also with Asheville
Ollie Paige, inf
Ray Robinson, lhp
Wiggins Springfield, ss
Cliff Statham [Staton], rhp
Bobby Stephenson, p
Bill Stevenson, rhp
Benjamin Taylor, lhp
Vines, c
Eugene White, ss
Bill Wilder, p
L__ Williams, c
S__ Williams, p

Womack, p
Robert Womble, lf

Shreveport?

Failed to enter league, franchise awarded to Raleigh, N.C. in early June

———

1948

President—Dr. R.B. Jackson, of Nashville
Vice president—Allen Page, New Orleans
Secretary, statistician and public relations—Luther Carmichael, Nashville
Treasurer—John Harden, Atlanta

Atlanta Black Crackers

Played at Ponce de Leon Park
Negro American Association in second half
John Haden, owner
Lewis Means, manager
Homer Curry, manager, by May 22

———

Charley Bell, x
James Bell, lhp
Homer "Goose" Curry, cf-lf
Lomax "Butch" Davis, lf-cf
Edward Dennard, 3b
Emory "Bo" Dickerson, ss
James "Early Bird" Ellison, c
Thomas "Monk" Favors, 1b
Cliff Hardaway, p
David T. Harper, cf
Harry Hatcher, x
"Butch" Hubert, p
Neal Jackson, x
Ralph Jones, p
Early King, rhp
Leonard, p
Nathan McClinic, cf
Odell McCoy, p
Julius "Junior" McFarlin (McFarland), p
Major Metts, x
Sack Morgan, lhp
James O'Kelley, 1b
Judge "Dusty" Owens, 2b
Ramsey, p

John Ray, rf
Johnnie Richardson, ss
Milton "Chip" Smith, 3b
Roy Swanson, c
Willie Marvin Terrell, 3b
Terry Thomas, x
Welch, 1b;
James B. Williams, lhp
Stew Williams, 2b, also with Nashville
Leon Wyatt, p
Charley (Clarence) Wynder, p-c, also with New Orleans

Birmingham All-Stars

Ballpark undetermined
Tommy Sampson, manager

———

Harry Barnes, c
Nathaniel Brooks, p
Jimmie Canady, 1b
Johnnie Cowan, ss
James Davis, 3b
Bennie Griggs, x
"Red" Howard, p
Clarence King, lf
Willie Mays, cf, also with Chattanooga
Tommy Sampson, 2b
Freddie Shepard, rf

Birmingham Clowns

Ballpark undetermined
Tommy Sampson, owner-manager

———

Collins, 2b
Cooper, rf
Diddley, p
Felder, ss
Foster, c
T__ Gardner, cf
Grattis (Gattis), p-2b
Haines, lf
Heigh, ss
Manning, ph
Oliver, 3b
Payne, p
Scott, lf
"Pie" Silvers, p
Sims, rf
Thomas, 1b
Williams, ph
Willie Young, p, also with Memphis

Chattanooga Choo Choos

Played at Engel Stadium
Harry Bonds, manager
Beck Shepherd, owner

———

William "Popeye" Barnes, p
Harry Bonds, x-manager
Booker, p
Jim Canady, 1b
Charles, lf
Chissom (Chism), 2b
James "Neck Bones" Davis, 3b
Evans (Evins), cf
Felton, 2b
Herman Gorman, of
Red Howard, p
John "Butch" Hubert, c-p
Isbel (Isabella), p
Johnson, c
Dave Lawson, ss
George "Babe" Lawson, 1b
Lillie, p
Lloyd, cf
Willie Herman Mays, cf-ss
McCoy, rf
Means, 3b
Willie Patterson, c-3b-p
Ramsey, p
Roy Rivers, lf
Frank Rosso, p
Tom Smith, 1b
Sterling Talley, ss
Stew Williams, 2b

Memphis Blues

Played at Martin Stadium
Charlie Burg(s), manager

———

Alexander, p
Carter Bell, c
Jimmy Bradberry, ss-2b
Charlie Burg(s), c-manager
Craig, lf
Robert Daniel, 2b
Marion Dovine, rf
Casey Evans, inf-p
Frank Garrett, x
Mose Garrett, lf
Earnest Harris, p-utility
Earl(e) Houston, p
Johnson, c
Jones, 1b
Cecil Jordan, x
Landers, 2b
Freddie Lockhart, 1b
Red Longley, of-c

Isaiah Newsome, x
John Ray, lf
Sammy Sanders, rhp
L__ Sanford, x
John Smith, 3b
Cleo Tate, rf
Jessie Warren, 3b-p
Ladd White, p

Memphis Cardinals

Ball park undetermined
Jim Ford, owner
Amos Mosely, owner

———

Bell, c
Bradbury (Bradberry), ss
Bradsbury, p
Alex Brown, x
Craig, lf
Dovine, rf
Johnson, c
Jones, 1b;
William Landrum (Landers, Landred), 2b
Mosley, c; John Henry Oliver, cf
Ral, lf
Sanders, p
Scott, p
Smith, 3b
Snedecor (Snedeker), p
Ishmael Taylor, x
Clarence Threatts, p
Willie Young, p, also with Birmingham Clowns

Nashville Cubs

P, games played at
Dr. R.B. Jackson, owner
Parnell Woods, manager
Shelton Snow, manager by June 22?

———

Kelley Brooks, rf
Brooks, p
"Bomber" "Farmer" Brown, p
Cervantes?, c
Curtis Clark, cf
Melvin "Slick" Coleman, p
Clarence "Spike" Davis, 3b
Edward "Lefty" Derrick, lhp
Manning, x
"Butch" McCord, 1b
Sack Morgan, p
Nathan Owens, p
Pat(t)erson, c
Frazier Robinson, x

Harold Robinson, ss
Frank Russell, x
__ Scott, lf
Segraves, c
Serves, p; Roy Swanson, c
"Horse" Thompson, p
"Horse" Walker, p
Bob Williams, c
E__ Williams, 2b
Stew Williams, 2b, also with Atlanta
Harvey Young, ss
R__ Young, x
James Zapp, x

New Orleans Creoles
Played at Pelican Stadium
Allen Page, owner
T. J. "Tommy" Brown, manager by June 5
Dennis Gordon, manager by June 17
Jesse Richardson, owner? general manager?

―――

"Buster'" Allen, p
"Shorty" Andry, of
"Buddy" Armour, cf
Andrew Bellamy, p
John Bissant, lf
Lincoln Boyd, lf-cf
Thomas Brown, 3b-ss
Lovie Dymond, x
Johnny Edmond, p
Thomas Favoris, x
Dennis Gordon, c
Curtis Hardaway, rf-1b-p
Harry Hatcher, lf-3b
Jim Hill, p
Billy (Bobby) Horne, ss
Bob "General" Jackson, p
James Jackson, ss
Bill Jefferson, p
Bob Johnson, inf
Agar (Edgar) Leonard (Lennard), p
Vince Lombard, p
Major Metts, 2b
Terry Moore, rf
James Neil, ss
James Pearson (Pierson), cf
Pinkston, c;
Bob Pleasant, p
Tom Purvis, rhp;
Reuben Reddick, ss
Milton Smith, 2b-3b
Taylor Smith, p

Holly "Jelly" Stamps, x
Terry Thomas, rf
Amos (Aron)Watson, p
Isaac Welch, 1b
John B. Williams, p;
Reuben Williams, inf;
Fabiola Wilson, x
Clarence "Double Duty" Wynder, c-p, also with Atlanta

―――

1949

President—Dr. R. B. Jackson, Nashville
Vice president—George E. McCrary, Evansville
Secretary—H. L. Johnson, Little Rock; Dr. E. S. Cobb, Pensacola
Treasurer—Allen Page, New Orleans; B. T. Harvey, Atlanta
Commissioner and Public Relations—B. T. Harvey, Morehouse College, Atlanta

Atlanta-Detroit Brown Crackers
Played at Ponce de Leon Park
Kenneth Stewart, manager

―――

John [Clarence] Barnes, c
Joseph Burns, c
Clarence Crocker, rf
Wilson Dortch, x
Emanuel Driver[s], 3b
Amos English, p
Ralph Flowers, 2b
Louis Ghee, p
Tommy Hester, lf
Gaston Johnson, p
Wilbur Lockett, p
Albert Pugh, cf
John Sadler, p
Robert Shelton, ss
White, p, also with Nashville
Walter Williams, p-1b
Roosevelt Young, p

Gadsden-Florida Tigers
Played at City Park
Jesse Richardson, manager and owner

―――

Cleveland, p
Coates, x
Ferguson, p
Fisher, c
Gordon, p
Jackson, of
Jeff, ss
Jones, p
Billy Robe, inf
Taylor, 2b
Turgison, p

Mobile Shippers
Played at Hartwell Field
Willie Davis, owner-manager
Bill Perkins, manager by May 21

―――

No players identified

Montgomery Tigers
Played at [undetermined]
Dave Shoughter, owner-manager

―――

No players identified

Nashville Cubs
Played at Sulphur Dell
Dr. R. B. Jackson, president and owner
Russell Ewing, manager
Felton Snow, manager by Aug. 15

―――

Otha Bailey, c
James Bransford, 2b-cf
Derrick Brooks, lhp
Joe Brooks, rf-p
Alfred "Farmer" "Bomber" Brown, rhp
Jack Bruton, 3b
Calhoun, p
Chyslom, ss
Eugene Craig, lhp
"Lefty" Derrick, lhp
Scottie Drake [Duke], rf
Hatten, x
Clayton Holt, 3b
Gerry Kizer, ss
McKenzie, 3b
Cowboy Murray, lhp
Naples [Napier], cf
Nelson, p
James Nelson, p
Parker, 1b
Rufus "Junior" Patton, cf

Potter, x
Pugh, lf
Russell, rf
Sapp, x
James Sapp, lf
Hosea Thomas, p
Hoss Thompson, x
Washington, p
White, p, also with Atlanta
Bob Williams, c
Stew Williams, 2b

Pensacola Sea Gulls

Played at [undetermined]
Dr. E. S. Cobb, manager-owner

No players identified

1950

President—Dr. R. B. Jackson, Nashville; Dr. W. S. Martin, Memphis
Vice president—N/A
Secretary-treasurer—Allen Page
Treasurer—N/A
Secretary-commissioner—B. T. Harvey, Atlanta

Atlanta Brown Crackers

Played at Ponce De Leon Park
Jessie Richardson, co-owner
Arthur J. Williams, co-owner
Nish Williams, manager

Jerry Adams, 3b-cf
James Baldwin, p
James Bell, rhp
Lincoln Boyd, rf
Jim Canada, 1b
Cartwright, lf
Joe Chism [Chisholm], util
William Cooper, c
"Inky" Craig, p
James "Neckbone" Davis, of
Jim "Smokeyes" Davis, 3b
Frank Gibbs Davis, c
Dixon, p
Frank Evans, lf
John H. Fisher, c
Jimmy [Lewis] Gillis, c
George Gray, rhp
Beck Gregg, p

Paul Harris, x
Henry Hatcher, 2b
Barnett Hodges, p
Curtis Hollingsworth, p
James "Gabby" Kemp, 2b
Early King, p
Jimmy Marberry, x
William [M. E.] McCray [McQueary, McCrary], p
Orlando "Chico" O'Ferrell, ss
Dusty Owens, x
Nat Pollard, p
Grady Ross, x
Roland Silva, 2b
Jerry Taylor, 3b
Noah Taylor, 2b
Odell Taylor, x
Charlie Webster, cf

Birmingham

Played at [undetermined]
No results found or players identified
Dropped from league for failure to meet contractual obligations

Chattanooga Choo Choos

Played at Lookout Field
Dropped from league for failure to meet contractual obligations
Leroy Valentine, club official
Beck Shephard, owner?

No results found or players identified

Greenville Delta Giants

Played at Frisby Stadium
Boyce Jennings, club official?
Dr. Noble Frisby, owner
Homer "Goose" Curry, manager?

Joe Bond, rhp
Larry Denson, c
Isaah Harris Newsome, rf
George Robinson, x
Alvin Taylor, ss
Frank White, 3b

Louisville/Nashville Giants

Played at Parkway Field

[Louisville] and Sulphur Dell [Nashville]
Wildabert Keeple, club official
Ezel Leach, club official
Jesse "Hoss" Walker, owner-manager

Yank Adkisson, rf
Black, cf-c
Bunch, cf
Wesley Dennis, x
[Edward?] Derrick, lhp
Folk, ss
Freeman, rhp
Harris, c
Holt, 3b
Kell[e]y, lhp
Nelson, p
Rous, 2b
Frank Russell, 3b
Hoss Thompson, rhp
West, 1b
Young, ss
James Zapp, lf

Memphis Red Caps

Played at Martin Field
Matty Bresela, club official
Dr. W. S. Martin, owner
T. J. Brown, 2b-manager

Sam Billinger, p
Bobby Braden [Brados], 2b-3b
Ollie Brantley, rhp
Larry Cunningham, cf
Joe Henry, 3b
Percy Howard, c
Vernall Jackson, p
George Kaufman, rhp
Fred McDaniels, cf
Curtis McGowan, p
Gilbert Varona, 1b

New Orleans Creoles

Played at Pelican Stadium
A. Cant[r]ey, co-owner
Allen Page, club official, co-owner?
Chester Risby, co-owner
Wesley Barrow, p-manager
Felton Snow, manager by Aug. 13

Harry Barnes, c
John Bisanti, ss

James [Ernest] Bradford, lf
Joseph Brooks, rf
Cleveland Cartwright, cf
Irvin Castille, ss
John Diamond, lhp
"Big" Dollar, x
Eddie Gavalan, x
Paul Harris, x
Gene Jackson, x
Ed "Gravel" Jarrin, p
Charles Johnson, c
J. Johnson, ss
Joe Johnson, x
John Johnson, p
"Lefty" Johnson, lhp
Ralph Johnson, x
Gene Jones, p
Al "Buddy" Lombard, p
Don Mitchell, x
Roy Partlow, p
Nat Peoples, ss-of
Al Pinkston, p-1b-of
Everett Riley, p
James [John] Rushton, p
Joe Spencer, 2b
Toni Stone, 2b
Roy Swanson, c
James [Bill] Terrell, cf
Marvin Terrell, 3b
James "Junior" Williams, p

Owensboro Braves

Played at Miller Field
Dropped from league for failure to meet contractual obligations
Rufus Hatten, c-rf-manager

———

Otto Blay, of
Nathan Bussey, 2b
C. W. Christian, p
Scotty Drake, lf
"Showboat" Gilbert, 1b
C. Hackman, 1b

"Hack" Hackworth, ss
Raymond Haggdon, p
L. W. Harlin, ss
Clayton Holt, 3b
Marshall Holt, p
Paul Jackson, p
Tennis Johnson, k of
Granville Lyons, 2b
Art Pugh, cf
John Ray, of
R. T. Sutherland, c-rf

1951

President—Allen Page
President and director of public relations—Dr. R.B. Jackson
Vice president—Arthur Dove
Treasurer—Hill Harris, treasurer
Secretary—N/A
Commissioner—B. T. Harvey

Birmingham Black Eagles/Bears

Played at [undetermined]
Hill Harris, owner

———

No players identified

Birmingham All-Stars

Played at [undetermined]

———

Dobbs, p
Julian, p
Logan, c
Taylor, c
Thompson, p

Chattanooga Stars

Played at [undetermined]
Raymond [Claude] Roberts, ss-manager

———

Clarence "Bill" Dodd[s], c-of
Elliott, c
Roosevelt Fernandis, of
L__ Gooden, of
Leon Jackson, of
John Logan, p
John Macon, x
Woodrow Means, 3b
Louis Robertson, c
Robinson, p
J. D. Sims, 2b
Tom "Lefty" Smith, 1b
Willie Stalling, p
Stalling, c
Harry Taylor, ss
James Thornton, p
Walker, p

Knoxville Packers

Played at Leslie Street Park

———

Fine, c
Richardson, p

Nashville Cubs

Played at [undetermined]
Jesse "Hoss" Walker, possible manager

———

No players identified

Nashville Stars

Played at [undetermined]
"Soo" Bridgeforth, owner

———

No players identified

Chapter Notes

Introduction

1. http://www.entertainment.howstuffworks.com/negro-leagues-hall-of-fame-members.htm.
2. *Chattanooga Times*, 18 July 1945.
3. Ibid., 9 June 1947.
4. Martha Ackman, *Curveball, the Remarkable Story of Toni Stone* (Chicago: Lawrence Hill Books, 2010).
5. http://www.wikipedia.org/wiki/Pete.Gray, last modified on 9 October 2013.
6. William B. Ruggles, *The History of the Texas League of Professional Baseball Clubs, 1888–1951* (No city: The Texas Baseball League, 1951).
7. http://www.baseball-reference.com/bullpen/Bob_Riesener, last modified on 13 January 2011, at 15:05.
8. *Birmingham Reporter*, 29 May 1929.
9. *Birmingham World*, 8 July 1941.
10. Ibid., 29 July 1941.
11. *Atlanta Daily World*, 30 April 1946.
12. Wentworth, Harold and Flexner, Stuart Berg, editors, *Dictionary of American Slang* (New York: Thomas Y. Crowell Company, 1960).
13. *Birmingham World*, 11 April 1941.
14. Ibid., 18 April 1941.
15. *Montgomery Advertiser*, 21 August 1920.
16. *Birmingham News*, 11 July 1920.
17. *Atlanta Constitution*, 4 September 1920.
18. *Birmingham News*, 18 July 1920.
19. *New Orleans Times-Picayune*, 23, 24 July 1920.
20. *Atlanta Daily World*, 23 July 1936.

Chapter 1

1. Bill O'Neal, *The Southern League, Baseball in Dixie 1885–1994* (Austin, TX: Eakin Press, 1994, 2; Marshall D. Wright, *The Southern Association in Baseball 1885–1961* (Jefferson, NC: McFarland, 2002, 5).
2. Bill Plott, "The Southern League of Colored Baseballists," *Baseball Research Journal* (Cleveland: The Society for American Baseball Research, 1974).
3. Dick Clark and Larry Lester, eds., *The Negro Leagues Book* (Cleveland: The Society for American Baseball Research, 1994, 15).
4. James A. Riley, *The Biographical Encyclopedia of the Negro Baseball Leagues* (New York: Carroll & Graf, 1994, 294–5).
5. *The Sporting News*, 11 April 1896; Jeffrey Michael Laing, *Bud Fowler: Baseball's First Black Professional* (Jefferson, NC: McFarland, 2013), 131–134.
6. Clark and Lester, *The Negro Leagues Book*, 17.
7. *Atlanta Independent*, 6 March 1920.
8. *Chicago Defender*, 6 March 1920.
9. Clark and Lester, *The Negro Leagues Book*, 17.
10. Ibid., 17.
11. *Montgomery Advertiser*, 9 May 1920.
12. *Atlanta Constitution*, 20 May 1920.
13. *Knoxville Journal and Tribune*, 18 June 1920.
14. Ibid., 1 July 1920.
15. Ibid., 31 July 1920.
16. *New Orleans Times-Picayune*, 15 August 1920.
17. *Atlanta Independent*, 6 March 1920.
18. *Chicago Defender*, 17 April 1920.
19. *Birmingham Reporter*, 20 March 1920.
20. *Constitution*, 8 April 1920.
21. *Journal and Tribune*, 29 April 1920.
22. Ibid., June 28, 29, 30, 1920.
23. Bill Plott, interview with James Hannon, Montgomery, AL, 27 September 1997.
24. *Journal and Tribune*, 10 May 1920.
25. *The Constitution*, 26 April 1920.
26. Ibid., 27 April 1920.
27. *The Montgomery Advertiser*, 1 May 1920; *The New Orleans Item*, 4 May 1920.
28. *The Pensacola Journal*, 30 April 1920.
29. *The Constitution*, 15 August 1920.
30. Ibid., 3 September 1920.
31. Ibid., 5 September 1920.
32. *The Birmingham News*, 4, 5 May 1920.
33. Ibid., 4 May 1920.
34. *The (Knoxville) Sunday Journal and Tribune*, 9 May 1920.
35. *Atlanta Constitution*, 23 May 1920.
36. *Journal and Tribune*, 2 June 1920.
37. *Alabama Journal*, 25 June 1920.
38. *Pensacola Journal*, 27 May 1920.
39. *Birmingham News*, 3 June 1920.
40. *Journal and Tribune*, 3 June 1920; *Knoxville Sentinel*, 3 June 1920.
41. *Journal and Tribune*, 5 June 1902.
42. Ibid., 6 June 1920.
43. *Birmingham News*, 3 September 1920.
44. Ibid., 3 June 1920; *Birmingham Reporter*, 12 June 1920.
45. Riley, *The Biographical Encyclopedia of the Negro Baseball Leagues*, 748.
46. *Montgomery Advertiser*, 23 July 1920.
47. *Journal and Tribune*, 7 July 1920; *Knoxville Sentinel*, 7 July 1920.
48. *Knoxville Sentinel*, 5 July 1920.
49. *Journal and Tribune*, 25 June 1920.
50. Ibid., 19 June 1920.
51. *Alabama Journal*, 16 April 1920; Bill Plott, interview with Jesse Gosha, Montgomery, AL, 17 September 1997; Bill Plott, telephone interview with Jesse Gosha, 2 September 1998 Bill Plott, interview with James Hannon, Montgomery, AL, 27 September 1997.
52. Riley, *The Biographical Encyclopedia of the Negro Leagues*, 699–700.

239

53. *Chicago Defender*, 31 July 1920.
54. *Montgomery Advertiser*, 31 July 1920.
55. *Journal and Tribune*, 30 July 1920.
56. Ibid., 19 June 1920, 2 July 1920.
57. Ibid., 2 July 1920.
58. *Montgomery Advertiser*, 15 July 1902.
59. *Atlanta Constitution*, 5 August 1920.
60. *New Orleans Times-Picayune*, 1 May 1920.
61. *Montgomery Advertiser*, 18 July 1920.
62. Riley, *The Biographical Encyclopedia of the Negro Leagues*, 321.
63. *Birmingham News*, 6, 22 June 1920.
64. Ibid., 27, 28 July 1920.
65. *Birmingham News*, 22 June 1920.
66. *New Orleans Times-Picayune*, 24 May 1920.
67. Ibid., 20 May 1920.
68. *New Orleans Item*, 23 June 1920.
69. Ibid.
70. Ibid., 24 July 1920.
71. *New Orleans Times-Picayune*, 13 June 1920.
72. *Atlanta Constitution*, 12, 13 June 1920.
73. *New Orleans Times-Picayune*, 9 July 1920; *New Orleans Item*, 9 July 1920.
74. *New Orleans Times-Picayune*, 25 July 1920.
75. Ibid., 22 July 1920.
76. Ibid., 10 August 1920.
77. *Atlanta Constitution*, 30 April 1920.
78. Ibid., 28 May 1920.
79. Ibid., 22 June 1920.
80. "Turkey Stearnes" last modified 7 September 2011, 15:21, http://www.baseball-reference.com/bullpen/Turkey_Stearnes.
81. Riley, *The Biographical Encyclopedia of the Negro Leagues*, 739–40.
82. *Journal and Tribune*, 8 August 1920.
83. *Birmingham News*, 30 June 1920.
84. *Montgomery Advertiser*, 21 August 1920.
85. *Journal and Tribune*, 6 September 1920.
86. *Chicago Defender* 11 September 1920.
87. *Journal and Tribune*, 12 September 1920.
88. Ibid., 30 August 1920.
89. Ibid.
90. Ibid., 6 September 1920.
91. *Alabama Journal*, 4 October 1920.
92. "Turkey Stearnes" last modified 7 September 2011, 15:21, http://www.baseball-reference.com/bullpen/Turkey_Stearnes.

Chapter 2

1. *Chicago Defender*, 2 April 1921.
2. Ibid., 12 April 1921.
3. *Alabama Journal*, 24 April 1921.
4. *Montgomery Advertiser*, 4 May 1921.
5. Riley, *The Biographical Encyclopedia of the Negro Leagues*, 544–5.
6. *New Orleans Times-Picayune*, 22, 23 April 1921.
7. *Nashville Tennessean*, 23 April 1921.
8. *Birmingham News*, 26 April 1921.
9. Ibid., 27 April 1921.
10. *Chicago Defender* 14 May 1921.
11. *Nashville Banner*, 15 May 1921.
12. Riley, *The Biographical Encyclopedia of the Negro Leagues*, 875.
13. *Chicago Defender*, 2 April 1921.
14. *Times-Picayune*, 17 May 1921.
15. Ibid., 20 May 1921.
16. Ibid., 26 May 1921.
17. Ibid., 24 July 1921.
18. Ibid., 30 June 1921.
19. *Chicago Defender*, 14 May 1921.
20. *Gadsden Times*, 30 March 1921.
21. Ibid., 19 April 1921.
22. *Atlanta Constitution*, 15 May 1921.
23. *Chicago Defender*, 11 June 1921.
24. Ibid., 16 July 1921.
25. *New Orleans Times-Picayune*, 29 July 1921.
26. Knoxville *Journal and Tribune*, 26 April 1921.
27. Ibid., 2 May 1921.
28. Ibid., 19 May 1921.
29. Ibid., 24 May 1921.
30. Ibid., 30 May 1921.
31. Ibid., 25 June 1921.
32. Ibid., 23 June 1921.
33. Ibid., 6 June 1921.
34. Ibid., 22 June 1921.
35. *Chicago Defender*, 18 June 1921.
36. *Chattanooga Times*, 8 June 1921.
37. Ibid., 14 August 1921.
38. Ibid., 17 July 1921.
39. *Chicago Defender*, 11 June 1921.
40. *Birmingham News*, 11 September 1921.
41. *Chicago Defender*, 17 September 1921; *Birmingham News*, 11 September 1921.
42. Ibid., 24 September 1921.
43. *Nashville Tennessean*, 14 September 1921.
44. *Montgomery Advertiser*, 28 August 1921.
45. Ibid., 3 September 1921.
46. Ibid., 14 September 1921.
47. *Chicago Defender*, 1 October 1921.
48. Ibid., 15 October 1921.
49. *Montgomery Advertiser*, 17, 19 August 1921.

Chapter 3

1. *Birmingham News*, 28 May 1922.
2. *Chicago Defender*, 6 May 1922.
3. *Chattanooga Times*, 4 May 1922.
4. *Chicago Defender*, 13 May 1922; *Nashville Tennessean*, 4 May 1922.
5. Ibid., 20 May 1922.
6. *Nashville Banner*, 17 May 1922.
7. *Chicago Defender*, 27 May 1922.
8. Ibid., 3 June 1922.
9. *Times-Picayune*, 8 May 1922.
10. *Memphis Commercial-Appeal*, 12 June 1922.
11. Riley, *The Biographical Encyclopedia of the Negro Leagues*, 178.
12. *Knoxville Journal*, 28 June 1978.
13. *Birmingham News*, 30 April 1922.
14. *Commercial-Appeal*, 8 May 1922.
15. *Birmingham News*, 2 May 1922.
16. http://www.baseball-reference.com, last modified on 24 April 2013, 9:56.
17. Ibid; Riley, The *Biographical Encyclopedia of the Negro Leagues*, 33.
18. *Birmingham News*, 5, 6 May 1922; *The Commercial-Appeal*, 5–6 May 1922.
19. *Montgomery Journal*, 21 May 1922.
20. Ibid., 19, 20 Aug, 1922.
21. *Birmingham News*, 23 April 1922.
22. *Birmingham News*, 16 May 1922.
23. *Nashville Banner*, 12 June 1922.
24. Ibid., 19 June 1922.

25. *Nashville Tennessean*, 17 June 1922.
26. Ibid., 19 June 1922.
27. Riley, *The Biographical Encyclopedia of the Negro Leagues*, 107–08.
28. *Chattanooga Times*, 3 May 1922.
29. Ibid., 9 June 1922.
30. Ibid., 1 July 1922.
31. *Nashville Banner*, 6 July 1922.
32. Ibid., 6 July 1922.
33. Ibid., 7 July 1922.
34. Ibid., 29 July 1922.
35. *Birmingham News*, 23 May 1922.
36. *Commercial-Appeal*, 26 June 1922.
37. *Birmingham News*, 21 May 1922.
38. Ibid., 22 June 1922.
39. Ibid., 25 June 1922.
40. Ibid., 27 June 1922.
41. Ibid., 19 June 1922.
42. *Nashville Banner*, 28, 29, 30 July 1922; *Nashville Tennessean*, 28, 29, 30 July 1922.
43. *Nashville Banner*, 30 July 1922.
44. Ibid., 1 August 1922.
45. Ibid., 6, 7 August 1922.
46. *Chattanooga Times*, 3 June 1922.
47. *Memphis Commercial-Appeal*, 17 June 1922.
48. *Chicago Defender*, 19 August 1922.
49. Ibid., 7 September 7, 1922.
50. *Commercial-Appeal*, August 7, 1922.
51. Ibid., August 7, 1922.
52. *Montgomery Journal*, 19 August 1922.
53. *Chicago Defender*, 7 September 1922.
54. *Nashville Banner*, 12 June 1922.
55. http://agatetype.typepad.com, posted by Gary Ashwill, 3 May 2012.
56. baseballhistoryblog.com
57. http://agatetype.typepad.com, posted by Gary Ashwill, 3 May 2012.

Chapter 4

1. *Birmingham News*, 29 April 1923.
2. Ibid.
3. Ibid.; *Pensacola Journal*, 11, 17 June 1923.
4. *Birmingham News*, 24 June 1923.
5. Ibid., 1–3 May 1923.
6. *Memphis Commercial-Appeal*, 13, 19 May 1923.
7. Ibid., 3 June 1923.
8. Riley, *The Biographical Encyclopedia of the Negro Leagues*, 122–3.
9. http://www.baseball-reference.com, "Squire Moore."
10. *Memphis Commercial-Appeal*, 3 July 1923.
11. Riley, *The Biographical Encyclopedia of the Negro Leagues*; http://www.baseballhall.org, "Suttles, Mule."
12. *Birmingham News*, 27 May 1923.
13. Ibid., 27 May 1923.
14. Ibid., 7 June 1923.
15. *Times-Picayune*, 25 May 1923.
16. *Memphis Commercial-Appeal*, 25 July 1963.
17. Clark and Lester, *The Negro Leagues Book*, 1994.
18. John Holway, *The Complete Book of Baseball's Negro Leagues: The Other Half of Baseball History* (Fern Park, FL: Hastings House, 2001).
19. *New Orleans Times-Picayune*, 9 July 1923.
20. *Memphis Commercial-Appeal*, 28 August 1923.
21. Holway, *The Complete Book of Baseball's Negro Leagues: The Other Half of Baseball History*, 197.

Chapter 5

1. *Norfolk Journal and Guide*, 3 April 1926.
2. Ibid.
3. *Pittsburgh Courier*, 16 January 1926.
4. *New York Times*, 18 February 1997.
5. *Birmingham Reporter*, 6 March 1926.
6. *Birmingham Reporter*, 13 March 1926; *Pittsburgh Courier*, 10 April 1926.
7. *Chicago Defender*, 3 April 1926.
8. *Nashville Tennessean*, 30 June 1926.
9. *Memphis Commercial-Appeal*, 3 June 1926.
10. Riley, *The Biographical Encyclopedia of the Negro Leagues*, 309–10.
11. Ibid., 422–23.
12. *Atlanta Independent*, 13 May 1926.
13. *Pittsburgh Courier*, 30 April 1926.
14. Lloyd Johnson and Miles Wolff, eds., *The Encyclopedia of Minor League Baseball* (Durham, NC: Baseball America, 126).
15. *Chicago Defender*, 15 May 1926.
16. *Birmingham News*, 2 May 1926.
17. Ibid., 9 May 1926.
18. Ibid., 11 May 1926.
19. *Birmingham Reporter*, 8 May 1926.
20. *Memphis Commercial-Appeal*, 2 May 1926.
21. *Atlanta Independent*, 20 May 1926.
22. Ibid., 20 May 1926.
23. *Montgomery Advertiser*, 21 May 1926.
24. http://www.waymarking.com, Pickett Springs Resort.
25. *Atlanta Independent*, 20 May 1926.
26. *Memphis Commercial-Appeal*, 14 June 1926.
27. Ibid., 16 June 1926.
28. Ibid., 26 June 1926.
29. *New Orleans Times-Picayune*, 20 August 1926.
30. *Chicago Defender*, 12 June 1926.
31. Ibid., 19 June 1926.
32. Ibid., 26 July 1926.
33. Ibid., 14 August 1926.
34. Ibid., 3 July 1926.
35. *Albany Herald*, 28 June 1926.
36. Ibid., 6 July 1926.
37. *Chicago Defender*, 17 July 1926.
38. Ibid.
39. *Birmingham News*, 27 June 1926.
40. *Pittsburgh Courier*, 24 July 1926.
41. *New Orleans Times-Picayune*, 13 July 1926.
42. Ibid., 14 July 1926.
43. *Birmingham News*, 20 June 1926.
44. Ibid., 18 July 1926.
45. *Atlanta Constitution*, 25 July 1926.
46. Riley, *The Biographical Encyclopedia of the Negro Leagues*, 865.
47. *Birmingham News*, 18 July 1926.
48. Ibid., 20 July 1926.
49. *Chattanooga Times*, 30 July 1926.
50. *Atlanta Independent*, 15 July 1926.
51. Ibid., 22 July 1926.
52. Ibid., 5 August 1926.
53. Ibid., 19 August 1926.
54. *Commercial-Appeal*, 16 August 1926.
55. Ibid., 15 August 1926.
56. *Times-Picayune*, 19 August 1926.
57. *Albany Herald*, 24 July 1926.
58. Ibid., 24 July 1926.
59. Ibid., 27 July 1926.
60. *Memphis Commercial-Appeal*, 31 July 1926.

61. *Chattanooga Times*, 7 August 1926.
62. *Atlanta Independent*, 27 May 1926.
63. Ibid., 3 June 1926.
64. *Atlanta Constitution*, 23 May 1926.
65. Ibid., 20 July 1926.
66. *Nashville Tennessean*, 4 September 1926.
67. Riley, *The Biographical Encyclopedia of the Negro Leagues*, 619.
68. http://www.astrosdaily.com, Gene Elston's Journal, 8 August 2010.
69. *Nashville Tennessean*, 30 June 1926.
70. *Birmingham News*, 27, 28, 29, 31 August 1926, 1 September 1926.
71. *Memphis Commercial-Appeal*, 5 September 1926.
72. Ibid., 5 September 1926.
73. Holway, *The Complete Book of Baseball's Negro Leagues*, 198, 209.
74. Riley, *The Biographical Encyclopedia of the Negro Leagues*, 248.
75. *Chicago Defender*, 28 August 1926.
76. Ibid., 4 September 1926.
77. *Birmingham News*, 9 September 1926.
78. Ibid., 19 September 1926.
79. *Memphis Commercial-Appeal*, 12 September 1926.
80. Ibid., 13 September 1926.
81. Ibid., 14 September 1926.
82. Ibid., 22 September 1926; *Birmingham News*, 22 September 1926.
83. *Birmingham* News, 23 September 1926.
84. Ibid., 23 September 1926.
85. *Memphis Commercial-Appeal*, 26 September 1926.
86. *Birmingham News*, 29 September 1926.
87. Ibid., 30 September 1926.
88. *Atlanta Independent*, 3 June 1926.
89. *Atlanta Journal*, 1 July 1926.
90. *Chattanooga Times*, 3 August 1926.
91. *Nashville Tennessean*, 30 June 1926.
92. *Albany Herald*, 24 May 1926.
93. *Birmingham News*, 11 June 1926.
94. *Albany Herald*, 6 July 1926.
95. *Birmingham News*, 13, 14 July 1926.

Chapter 6

1. *Evansville Argus*, 31 October 1942.
2. *Chattanooga Daily Times*, 6 July 1927.
3. *Atlanta Independent*, 3 March 1927.
4. Ibid., 10 March 1927.
5. Ibid., 5 May 1927.
6. Ibid., 2 June 1927.
7. *Atlanta Constitution*, 14 June 1927.
8. *Evansville Courier*, 3 May 1927.
9. Ibid., 5 May 1927.
10. *Memphis Commercial-A*ppeal, 14 May 1927.
11. Ibid., 16 May 1927.
12. Ibid., 17 May 1927.
13. Ibid., 17 May 1927.
14. Ibid., May 10–11, 1927.
15. baseball-ref.com
16. http://www.wikipedia.org, "Ted Radcliffe, last modified 7 August 2012, 03:57; Bill Plott, interview with Ted Radcliffe, 17 August 1996, Montgomery, AL.
17. Kyle P. McNary, *Ted "Double Duty" Radcliffe* (Minneapolis: McNary Publishing, 1994, 24).

18. *Nashville Banner*, May 15–19, 1927.
19. Ibid., May 22–23, 1927.
20. Ibid., May
21. *Chattanooga Daily Times*, 26 May 1927.
22. *Chicago Defender*, 1 May 1927.
23. *Chicago Defender*, 4 June 1927.
24. *Evansville Courier*, 12 June 1927.
25. *Nashville Banner*, 18 June 1927.
26. *Nashville Tennessean*, 18 June 1927.
27. *Nashville Banner*, 22 June 1927.
28. *Nashville Tennessean*, 21 June 1927.
29. *Chicago Defender*, 25 June 1927.
30. *Evansville Courier*, 26 June 1927.
31. Ibid., 27 June 1927.
32. Ibid., 28 June 1927.
33. *Nashville Banner*, 13 July 1927; *Chattanooga Times*, 6 July 1927.
34. *Evansville Courier*, 27 July 1927.
35. *Nashville Banner*, 12 August 1927.
36. *Nashville Tennessean*, 11 August 1927.
37. *Chattanooga Daily Times*, 14 August 1927.
38. http://www.wikipedia.org, "St. Louis Stars," last modified 1 September 2013, 07:05.
39. *Evansville Courier*, 23 August 1927.
40. http://www.three-eye.com, last modified 20 August 2008.
41. *Evansville Courier*, 19 September 1927.
42. *Evansville Courier and Journal*, 25 September 1927.
43. *Evansville Courier*, 30 September 1927.
44. Ibid., 26 September 1927.
45. Ibid., 3 October 1927.
46. Ibid., 10 October 1927.
47. http://www.politicalgraveyard.com, "Refermat to Reickenback."
48. *Evansville Courier*, 17 October 1927.
49. Ibid., 16 October 1927.
50. *Nashville Tennessean*, 4 September 1927.
51. *Chicago Defender*, 27 August 1927.
52. Charlie Hurth, *Southern Association Baseball Records* (No city: Southern Association, 136).
53. *Nashville Tennessean*, 1 September 1927; *Nashville Banner*, 30 August 1927.
54. *Nashville Tennessean*, 11 September 1927.
55. Ibid., 13 September 1927.
56. Riley, *The Biographical Encyclopedia of the Negro Leagues*, 747.
57. http://www.nlbpa.com, "Short-lived Milwaukee Bears didn't get much play," from www.onmilwaukee.com, 6 May 2003.

Chapter 7

1. *Nashville Tennessean*, 20 June 1928.
2. *Memphis Commercial Appeal*, 22 April 1928.
3. *Chicago Defender*, 7 July 1928.
4. Ibid., 7 July 1928.
5. Ibid., 8 September 1928.
6. *Birmingham Reporter*, 17 March 1928.
7. *Louisville Courier-Journal*, 5 May 1929; Clark and Lester, *The Negro Leagues Book*, 160.
8. *Louisville Courier-Journal*, 5 May 1929; Clark and Lester, *The Negro Leagues Book*, 161.
9. *Chicago Defender*, 8 June 1992.
10. Ibid., 27 April 1929.
11. *Nashville Tennessean*, 2 June 1929.
12. *Nashville Banner*, 16 June 1929.

13. Ibid., 22 June 1929.
14. Ibid., 28 July 1929.
15. *Chicago Defender*, 10 August 1929.
16. *Evansville Courier*, 20 May 1929.
17. Ibid., 21 May 1929.
18. *Atlanta Constitution*, 6 May 1929.
19. Ibid., 24 May 1929.
20. *Atlanta Constitution*, 26 May 1929; *Chicago Defender*, 1 June 1929.
21. *Nashville Tennessean*, 20–21 May 1929.
22. *Nashville Banner*, 3–4 June 1929.
23. *Evansville Courier*, 10–11 June 1929.
24. Ibid., 11 June 1929.
25. Richard Bak, *Turkey Stearnes and the Detroit Stars, the Negro Leagues in Detroit, 1919–1933* (Detroit: Great Lakes Books, 1994; http://wikipedia.org, "Black Bottom, Detroit," last modified 17 November 2013, 07:06.
26. http://www.theblackbottom.wordpress.com/communities,/blackbottom/history, last modified on 20 July 2013, 20:47.
27. *Atlanta Constitution*, 29 June 1929.
28. *Chattanooga Daily Times*, 12 May 1929.
29. Ibid., 2 July 1929.
30. *Evansville Courier*, 30 July 1929.
31. Ibid., 8–19, 1929, 3 September 1929.
32. *Chicago Defender*, 31 May 1930.
33. Ibid., 31 May 1930.
34. Ibid., 31 May 1930.
35. http://www.wikipedia.org, "Houston Riot (1917), last modified 15 November 2013, 21:43.
36. Riley, *The Biographical Encyclopedia of the Negro Leagues*, 534–36; L. Albert Scipio, *The 24th Infantry at Fort Benning* (Silver Spring, MD: Roman Publications, 1986, 169–70). Photocopy provided by Donovan Research Library, Fort Benning, GA.

Chapter 8

1. *Pittsburgh Courier*, 31 January 1931.
2. Riley, *The Biographical Encyclopedia of the Negro Baseball Leagues*, 290–92.
3. Clark and Lester, *The Negro Leagues Book*, 160–61.
4. *Pittsburgh Courier*, 21 March 1931.
5. *Pittsburgh Courier*, 4 April 1931; *Chicago Defender*, 14 March 1931.
6. *Chicago Defender*, 16 May 1931.
7. *Chicago Defender*, 11 April 1931; *The Alabama Journal*, 8 April 1931.
8. *Chicago Defender*, 11 April 1931.
9. *Memphis Commercial Appeal*, 5 April 1931.
10. *Montgomery Advertiser*, 1–2 May 1931.
11. *Alabama Journal*, 3 May 1931.
12. *Nashville Tennessee*, 3 May 1931; *Chattanooga Daily Times*, 3 May 1931.
13. *Chattanooga Daily Times*, 2 May 1931.
14. *Alabama Journal*, 11 May 1931; *Memphis Commercial Appeal*, 17 May 1931.
15. *Memphis Commercial Appeal*, 1 June 1931.
16. *Chicago Defender*, R13 June 1931.
17. *Birmingham Reporter*, 12 June 1931.
18. *Birmingham News*, 31 July 1931.
19. Ibid., 2 June 1931.
20. *Alabama Journal*, 17 June 1931.
21. Ibid., 18 July 1931.
22. *Chicago Defender*, 8 August 1931.
23. *Nashville Banner*, 8 July 1931; *Pittsburgh Courier*, 18 July 1931.
24. *Memphis Commercial Appeal*, 3 July 1931.
25. *Chattanooga Daily Times*, 5 July 1931.
26. *Knoxville News-Sentinel*, 31 July 1931.
27. *Chicago Defender*, 4 July 1931.
28. Ibid., 4 July 1931.
29. *Arkansas Gazette*, 3 June 1931.
30. *Commercial Appeal*, 10 June 1931.
31. *Arkansas Gazette*, 17 July 1931.
32. Ibid., August 26, 31, 19131.
33. *Memphis Commercial Appeal*, 28 July 1931.
34. Ibid., 6 September 1931.
35. *Chicago Defender*, 1 August 1931.
36. Ibid., 22 August 1931.
37. *Arkansas Gazette*, 19 July 1931.
38. *Chattanooga Daily Times*, July 25–26, 1931.
39. *Nashville Banner*, 27 July 1931.
40. Ibid., 8 August 1931.
41. Ibid., 13 August 1931.
42. Ibid., 14 August 1931.
43. *Nashville Banner*, 14 August 1931; Riley, *The Biographical Encyclopedia of the Negro Baseball Leagues*, 91.
44. *Chattanooga Daily Times*, 1 July 1931.
45. Ibid., 1 July 1931.
46. *Commercial Appeal*, 2 August 1931.
47. Ibid., 24 August 1931.
48. *Memphis World*, 20 September 1931.
49. *Alabama Journal*, 13 September 1931.
50. *Memphis Commercial Appeal*, 21 September 1931.
51. Ibid., 21 September 1931.
52. *Nashville Banner*, 31 August 1931.
53. *Pittsburgh Courier*, 5 September 1931.
54. Clark and Lester, *The Negro Leagues Book*, 104–06.
55. *Nashville Tennessean*, 24 July 1931.
56. *Nashville Banner*, 27 July 1931.
57. *Monroe World*, 2 September 1931; *Nashville Banner*, 2 September 1931.
58. *Monroe World*, 4 September 1931; Clark and Lester, *The Negro Leagues Book*, 105; Holway, 275.
59. *Monroe World*, 7 September 1931.
60. *Monroe World*, 8 September 1931; *Monroe News-Star*, 8 September 1931.
61. *Monroe World*, 9 September 1931.
62. Ibid., 10 September 1931.
63. Holway, *The Complete Book of Baseball's Negro Leagues*, 272.

Chapter 9

1. Clark and Lester, *The Negro Leagues Book*, 161–164.
2. Ibid., 164.
3. Holway, *The Complete Book of Baseball's Negro Leagues*, 292.
4. *Atlanta Daily World*, 7 December 1932.
5. *Knoxville News-Sentinel*, 27 June 1932.
6. *Pittsburgh Courier*, 4 February 1932.
7. Clark and Lester, *The Negro Leagues Book*, 164; *Monroe Morning World*, 28 February 1932.
8. *Atlanta Daily World*, 11 March 1932.
9. *Monroe Morning World*, 20 March 1932.
10. *Atlanta Daily World*, 20 March 1932.
11. Ibid.

12. Clark and Lester, *The Negro Leagues Book*, 164.
13. Riley, *The Biographical Encyclopedia of the Negro Leagues*, 186.
14. *Nashville Tennessean*, 5 June 1932.
15. *Atlanta Daily World*, 6 July 1932.
16. *Chicago Defender*, 23 July 1932.
17. *Chicago Defender*, 30 July 1932.
18. *Birmingham News*, 16 January 1932; State of Alabama Certificate of Death, 17 January 1932, official copy issued on 27 August 1998.
19. *Birmingham Reporter*, 9 April 1932.
20. *Louisville Courier-Journal*, 4 June 1932.
21. *Monroe News-Star*, 21 April 1932.
22. Ibid., 6 May 1932.
23. Ibid., 7 May 1932.
24. Ibid., 8 May 1932.
25. Ibid., 9 May 1932.
26. Ibid., 24 May 1932.
27. *Nashville Tennessean*, 23 April 1932.
28. Ibid., 23–24 April 1932.
29. *Memphis Commercial-Appeal*, 22 April 1932.
30. *Indianapolis News*, 30 April 1932.
31. Ibid., 1 May 1932.
32. Ibid., 18 May 1932.
33. *Louisville Courier-Journal*, 8 May 1932.
34. *Atlanta Daily World*, 6 April 1932.
35. Ibid., 6 April 1932.
36. Ibid., 15 April 1932.
37. Ibid., 3 May 1932.
38. Ibid., 4 May 1932.
39. Ibid., 5 May 1932.
40. *Pittsburgh Courier*, 4 June 1932.
41. *Monroe Morning World*, 12–14 June 1932.
42. Ibid., 2 July 1932.
43. Ibid., 3–5 July 1932.
44. *Monroe Morning World*, 6 July 1932; *Atlanta Daily World*, 6 July 1932.
45. *Pittsburgh Courier*, 9 July 1932.
46. Ibid., 9 July 1932.
47. *Chicago Defender*, 16 July 1932.
48. http://www.wikipedia.org," Alcoa, Tennessee," last modified on 11 December 2013, 17:37.
49. Telephone interview with historian Cato Clowney, 26 July 2012.
50. *Aluminum Bulletin*, June 1920, "Base Ball," 10–11.
51. *Lexington Leader*, 17 July 1932.
52. Ibid., 24 July 1932.
53. Ibid., 31 July 1932.
54. Ibid., 1–2 August 1932.
55. *Lexington Leader*, 14 August 1932; *Lexington Herald*, 14–15 August 1932.
56. *Knoxville News-Sentinel*, 28 June 1932.
57. *Knoxville Journal*, 8 July 1932.
58. Ibid., 2 July 1932.
59. Ibid., 12 August 1932.
60. *Knoxville News-Sentinel*, 12 June 1932.
61. Ibid.
62. *Atlanta Daily World*, 22 July 1932.
63. *Columbus Dispatch*, 18 July 1932.
64. *Atlanta Daily World*, 22 July 1932.
65. *Chicago Defender*, 23 July 1932.
66. *Monroe Morning World*, 28 July 1932.
67. *Chicago Defender*, 30 July 1932.
68. *Indianapolis News*, 25 July 1932.
69. *Montgomery Advertiser*, 13 August 1932.
70. *Chicago Defender*, 23 July 1932.
71. Ibid., 30 July 1932.
72. *Louisville Courier-Journal*, 25 July 1932.
73. Ibid., 1–2 August 1932.
74. *Chicago Defender*, 13 August 1932.
75. Ibid., 13 August 1932.
76. *Columbus Dispatch*, 20 August 1932.
77. Ibid., 13 August 1932.
78. *Knoxville Journal*, 6 September 1932; *Knoxville News-Sentinel*, 6 September 1932.
79. *Atlanta Daily World*, 31 August 1932.
80. *Chicago Defender*, 27 August 1932.
81. *Monroe Morning World*, 19 August 1932.
82. Ibid., 21 August 1932.
83. Ibid., 29 August 1932.
84. *Monroe News-Star*, 29 August 1932.
85. Ibid., 30 August 1932.
86. *Monroe Morning World*, 31 August 1932.
87. *Monroe Morning World*, 31 August 1932; *Atlanta Daily World*, 1 September 1932.
88. *Monroe Morning World*, 5 September 1932.
89. Ibid., 10 September 1932.
90. Ibid., 10 September 1932.
91. Riley, *The Biographical Encyclopedia of the Negro Baseball Leagues*, 723–725.
92. *Chicago Defender*, 24 September 1932.
93. *Atlanta Daily Word*, 23 September 1932.
94. *Nashville Tennessean*, 22 September 1932.
95. *Chicago Defender*, 10 October 1932.
96. Ibid., 3 October 1932.

Chapter 10

1. *Atlanta Daily World*, 8 June 1933.
2. Clark and Lester, *The Negro Leagues Book*, 161.
3. Riley, *The Biographical Encyclopedia of the Negro Leagues*, 577.
4. *Chicago Defender*, 22 April 1933.
5. Holway, *The Complete Book of Baseball's Negro Leagues*, 299.
6. *Chicago Defender*, 20 May 1933.
7. Ibid., 26 May 1933.
8. http://www.wikipedia.org, "Memphis Red Sox," last modified on 12 May 2013, 15:10.
9. *Pittsburgh Courier*, 11 March 1933.
10. Ibid.
11. *Chicago Defender*, 8 April 1933.
12. *Montgomery Advertiser*, 1 July 1933.
13. *Birmingham Reporter*, 27 May 1933.
14. Ibid., 3 June 1933.
15. *Shreveport Times*, 14 May 1933.
16. Ibid., 31 May 1933.
17. Ibid., 7 June 1933.
18. *Monroe News-Star*, 11 April 1933.
19. *Monroe World*, 12 April 1933.
20. *Monroe News-Star*, 17 April 1933.
21. Ibid., 19 April 1933.
22. *Arkansas Gazette*, 2 April 1933.
23. Ibid., 21 April 1933.
24. Ibid., 23 April 1933.
25. *Jackson Clarion-Ledger*, 1 April 1933.
26. Ibid., 23 April 1933.
27. Ibid., 28 May 1933.
28. *Memphis Commercial-Appeal*, 2 July 1933.
29. *Monroe News-Star*, 4 May 1933.
30. *Memphis Commercial-Appeal*, 15 May 1933.
31. *Monroe News-Star*, 22 May 1933.
32. *New Orleans Times-Picayune*, 24 May 1933.
33. *Chicago Defender*, 12 August 1933; *Pittsburgh Courier*, 8 July 1933.

34. *Monroe News-Star*, 23 May 1933.
35. *Chicago Defender*, 3 June 1933.
36. *Pittsburgh Courier*, 10 June 1933.
37. Ibid., 8 July 1933.
38. *Memphis Commercial Appeal*, 30 June 1933.
39. Ibid., 15 July 1933.
40. *Chicago Defender*, 24 June 1933.
41. *Pittsburgh Courier*, 15 July 1933.
42. *Montgomery Advertiser*, 15 July 1933.
43. *Arkansas Gazette*, 2 July 1933.
44. Ibid., 23–24 July 1933.
45. *Chicago Defender*, 12 August 1933.
46. *Pittsburgh Courier*, 26 August 1933.
47. *New Orleans Times-Picayune*, 1 September 1933.
48. Ibid., 3, 4, 5, 7 September 1933.
49. *Nashville Banner*, 9 September 1933.
50. *Arkansas Gazette*, 9 September 1933.
51. *New Orleans Times-Picayune*, 6 September 1933.
52. Ibid., 11 September 1933.
53. Holway, *The Complete Book of Baseball's Negro Leagues*, 302.
54. *New Orleans Times-Picayune*, 23–27, 30 September 1933, 2–3 October 1933.
55. *Chicago Defender*, 7 October 1933.
56. *New Orleans Times-Picayune*, 18 September 1933.
57. Ibid., 21 September 1933.
58. Ibid., 24 September 1933.
59. Ibid., 25 September 1933.
60. Ibid., 26 September 1933.
61. Ibid., 27 September 1933.
62. Ibid., 2 October 1933.
63. Ibid., 3 October 1933.
64. *Pittsburgh Courier*, 7 October 1933.

Chapter 11

1. *Pittsburgh Courier*, 3 March 1934.
2. Ibid., 10 March 1934.
3. Ibid., 10 February 1934.
4. Ibid., 3 February 1934.
5. Ibid., 3 March 1934.
6. *Atlanta Daily World*, 1 April 1934; *Pittsburgh Courier*, 31 March 1934.
7. *Atlanta Daily World*, 1 April 1934.
8. *Pittsburgh Courier*, 31 March 1934.
9. *Chicago Defender*, 7 April 1934.
10. *Louisiana Weekly*, 10 March 1934.
11. Ibid., 28 April 1934.
12. *Pittsburgh Courier*, 3 February 1934.
13. *Atlanta Daily World*, 10, 15 April 1934.
14. Ibid., 15 April 1934.
15. Ibid., 2 May 1934.
16. http://www.thehistorymakers.com/biography/howardmoorejr, posted 14 April 2007.
17. *Atlanta Daily World*, 4 May 1934.
18. Ibid., 6 May 1934.
19. Ibid., 29 March 1934.
20. Ibid., 1 May 1934.
21. *Birmingham News*, 20 May 1934.
22. Ibid., 23 May 1934.
23. Ibid., 14 May 1934.
24. Riley, *The Biographical Encyclopedia of the Negro Baseball Leagues*, 323.
25. *Birmingham News*, 21 May 1934.
26. Ibid., 24 May 1934.
27. *Atlanta Daily World*, 8 June 1934.
28. *Birmingham News*, 10 June 1934.
29. *Atlanta Daily World*, 18 May 1934.
30. *Courier-Journal*, 17 May 1934.
31. Ibid., 27 May 1934.
32. Ibid., 28 May 1934.
33. *Louisiana Weekly*, 21 April 1934.
34. Ibid., 28 April 1934.
35. *Chicago Defender*, 30 June 1934.
36. Ibid., 23 June 1934.
37. *Louisiana Weekly*, 14 July 1934.
38. Ibid., 23 June 1934.
39. Ibid., 15 September 1934.
40. Ibid., 30 June 1934.
41. *Louisiana Weekly*, 2 June 1934.
42. Ibid., 30 June 1934.
43. Ibid., 14 July 1934.
44. Ibid., 9 June 1934.
45. Ibid., 28 July 1934.
46. Ibid., 4 August 1934.
47. Ibid., 28 July 1934.
48. *Monroe World*, 1 July 1934.
49. *Louisiana Weekly*, 21 July 1934.
50. *Atlanta Daily World*, 6 July 1934.
51. Ibid., 24 July 1934.
52. *Chicago Defender*, 7 July 1934.
53. Ibid., 14 July 1934.
54. Ibid., 21 July 1934.
55. *Chicago Defender Courier*, 18 August 1934.
56. Ibid., 4 August 1934.
57. *Chicago Defender*, 1 September 1934.
58. Ibid., 1 September 1934.
59. Ibid., 15 September 1934.
60. *Pittsburgh Courier*, 6 October 1934.
61. *Nashville Banner*, 8 October 1934.
62. http://www.siouxcityhistory.org/art-a-leisure/125-sioux-city-ghosts.
63. *Chicago Defender*, 15 September 1934.

Chapter 12

1. *Pittsburgh Courier*, 6 April 1935; *Chicago Defender*, 13 April 1935.
2. *Chicago Defender*, 13 April 1935.
3. *Arkansas Democrat-Gazette*, 4 July 2002.
4. *Chicago Defender*, 2 March 1935.
5. Ibid., 27 July 1935.
6. *Montgomery Advertiser*, 28 August 1935.
7. *Chicago Defender*, 2 March 1935.
8. Ibid., 22 June 1935; *New Orleans Times-Picayune*, 13 June 1935.
9. *Chicago Defender*, 6 April 1935.
10. *Atlanta Daily World*, 10 March 1935.
11. Ibid., 20 March 1932.
12. Ibid., 31 March 1932.
13. *Birmingham News*, 28 April 1935.
14. Ibid., 28 April 1935; *Atlanta Daily World*, 10 April 1935.
15. *Birmingham News*, 28 April 1935.
16. Ibid., 1 May 1935.
17. *Atlanta Daily World*, 20 April 1935.
18. http://www.athletics.morehouse.edu/sports/201112/btharvey.aspx!id+10.
19. *Atlanta Daily World*, 28 June 1936.
20. *Chicago Defender*, 13 April 1935.
21. *Commercial Appeal*, 8 May 1935.
22. *Atlanta Daily World*, 13 May 1935.

23. Ibid., 7 May 1935.
24. Ibid., 7 May 1935.
25. Ibid., 9 May 1935.
26. http://www.baseball-fever.com/showthread.php?57538.Meet-the-Sports-Writers.
27. *Atlanta Daily World,* 18 May 1935.
28. Ibid., 4 June 1935.
29. Ibid., 28 August 1935.
30. *Chicago Defender,* 25 May 1935.
31. Ibid., 22 June 1935.
32. Ibid., 6 September 1935.
33. *Birmingham News,* 19 May 1935.
34. Ibid., 20 May 1935.
35. *Memphis Commercial Appeal,* 1 July 1935.
36. Ibid., 4 July 1935.
37. Ibid., 30 August 1935.
38. Ibid., 3 September 1935.
39. Ibid., 17 September 1935.
40. *Monroe Star-News,* 22 September 1935.
41. *Atlanta Daily World,* 2 September 1935.
42. Ibid., 2 September 1935.
43. Ibid., 7 September 1935.
44. *Atlanta Daily World,* 14 September 1935; *Pittsburgh Courier,* 28 September 1935; Clark and Lester, *The Negro Leagues Book,* 115–17.
45. *Atlanta Daily World,* 16 September 1935.
46. Ibid., 16 September 1935.
47. Ibid., 20 September 1935.
48. *Pittsburgh Courier,* 28 September 1935.
49. Ibid., 12 October 1935.
50. *Atlanta Daily World,* 3 October 1935.
51. *Pittsburgh Courier,* 12 October 1935.
52. Ibid., 12 October 1935.
53. Ibid., 12 October 1935.

Chapter 13

1. *Chicago Defender,* 4 April 1936.
2. *Nashville Banner,* 24 April 1936.
3. Clark and Lester, *The Negro Leagues Book,* 119.
4. *Birmingham News,* 3 May 1935.
5. *Chicago Defender,* 4 April 1936.
6. *Birmingham News,* 3 May 1936.
7. Ibid., 11 May 1936; *Atlanta Daily World,* 11 May 1936.
8. *Atlanta Daily World,* 13 March 1936.
9. Ibid., 22 March 1936, 15 April 1936.
10. Ibid., 15 April 1936.
11. http://www.westegg.com/inflation.
12. *Atlanta Daily World,* 27 April 1936.
13. Ibid., 28 April 1936.
14. Ibid., 3 May 1936.
15. *Birmingham News,* 10, 12 June 1936.
16. *Birmingham World,* 20 May 1948.
17. Ibid., 8 May 1936.
18. Ibid., 10 May 1936.
19. *Montgomery Advertiser,* 11 April 1936.
20. Ibid., 13 April 1936.
21. http://www.motgomeryal.com.
22. *Chattanooga Times,* 19 May 1936.
23. *Kentucky New Era,* 8 June 1936.
24. *Alabama Journal,* 23 May 1936.
25. *Atlanta Daily World,* 6 May 1936.
26. Ibid., 11 May 1936.
27. Ibid., 5 July 1936.
28. Ibid., 24 June 1936.
29. Ibid., 24 June 1936.
30. Ibid., 12 July 1936.
31. Ibid., 30 August 1936.
32. Ibid., 17 July 1936.
33. Ibid., 5 August 1936.
34. *Nashville Tennessean,* 9 August 1936.
35. Lloyd Johnson and Miles Wolfe, eds. *The Encyclopedia of Minor League Baseball.* (Durham, NC: Baseball America, 1993, 200–202, 204–206).

Chapter 14

1. *Pittsburgh Courier,* 31 October 1936.
2. Clark and Lester, *The Negro Leagues Book,* 162; *Birmingham News,* 21 March 1937.
3. *Birmingham News,* 21 March 1937.
4. Clark and Lester, *The Negro Leagues Book,* 161.
5. *Pittsburgh Courier,* 3 April 1937.
6. *Chicago Defender,* 29 May 1937.
7. Holway, *The Complete Book of Baseball's Negro Leagues,* 341–2, 346.
8. Clark and Lester, *The Negro Leagues Book,* 161–62; Holway, *The Complete Book of Baseball's Negro Leagues,* 351, 352.
9. *Chicago Defender,* 27 February 1938.
10. Holway, *The Complete Book of Baseball's Negro Leagues,* 351; Clark and Lester, *The Negro Leagues Book,* 165.
11. *Chicago Defender,* 2 April 1938.
12. Ibid., 16 April 1938.
13. *Birmingham News,* 8 August 1938.
14. Clark and Lester, *The Negro Leagues Book,* 163; Holway, *The Complete Book of the Negro Leagues,* 359.
15. http://www.baseball-reference.com, last modified 21 January 2009 11:52.
16. Holway, *The Complete Book of Baseball's Negro Leagues,* 383.
17. Lloyd Johnson and Miles Wolff, *The Encyclopedia of Minor League Baseball,* 204–216.
18. http://www.baseballinwartime.com/baseball_in_wwii.
19. http://www.wikipedia.org/wiki/negro_league_baseball.
20. http://www.baseballinwartime.com/baseball_in_wwii.
21. *Birmingham News,* 11 May 1942.
22. http://www.wikipedia/wiki/timeline_in_world_war_ii.
23. Johnson and Wolfe, *The Encyclopedia f Minor League Baseball,* page 216.

Chapter 15

1. *Birmingham World,* 30 January 1945.
2. Ibid., 20 March 1945; *Louisiana Weekly,* 14 February 1945.
3. *Louisiana Weekly,* 7 April 1945.
4. *Birmingham World,* 4 May 1945.
5. *Chicago Defender,* 20 January 1945.
6. *Birmingham World,* 4 July 1945; *Asheville Citizen,* 4 May 1945.
7. *Birmingham World,* 19 January 1945.
8. Ibid., 27 March 1945.
9. Ibid., 3 April 1945.
10. *Chattanooga Times,* 9 May 1945.
11. Ibid., 13 September 1945.
12. *Atlanta Daily World,* 2 May 1945.

13. Riley, *The Biographical Encyclopedia of the Negro Leagues*, 538.
14. *Atlanta Daily World*, 5 May 1945.
15. *New Orleans Times-Picayune*, 12 May 1945.
16. *Knoxville News-Sentinel*, 8 May 1945.
17. *Atlanta Daily World*, 2 May 1945.
18. *Arkansas Democrat*, 4 May 1945.
19. Ibid., 7 May 1945.
20. *Mobile Press*, 1 July 1945.
21. Riley, *The Biographical Encyclopedia of the Negro Leagues*, 675; http://www.baseball-reference.com/nlb/player.cgi?id=robins000bob.
22. *Birmingham World*, 16 March 1945.
23. Riley, *The Biographical Encyclopedia of the Negro Leagues*, 319–20.
24. *Louisiana Weekly*, 14 April 1945.
25. Riley, *The Biographical Encyclopedia of the Negro Leagues*, 778–9.
26. *Atlanta Daily World*, 3 May 1945.
27. *Birmingham World*, 11 May 1945.
28. *Atlanta Daily World*, 13 May 1945.
29. Ibid., 10 May 1945.
30. *Mobile Press*, 11 May 1945.
31. Ibid., 29 May 1945.
32. Ibid., 5 June 1945.
33. *Knoxville News-Sentinel*, 5 June 1945.
34. *Mobile Press*, 4 June 1945.
35. *Nashville Banner*, 3 June 1945.
36. *Atlanta Daily World*, 16 April 1945.
37. *Knoxville News-Sentinel*, 16 June 1945.
38. *Mobile Press*, 7 June 1945.
39. *Knoxville News-Sentinel*, 18 June 1945.
40. Ibid., 23–24 June 1945.
41. Ibid., 19 August 1945.
42. *Birmingham World*, 26 June 1945.
43. Ibid., 26 June 1945.
44. *Atlanta Daily World*, 1 July 1945.
45. Ibid., 6 July 1945.
46. *Chattanooga Times*, 28 June 1945.
47. *Atlanta Daily World*, 8 July 1945; *Birmingham World*, 20, 24 July 1945.
48. *Birmingham News*, 8 July 1945.
49. *Louisiana Weekly*, 7 July 1945.
50. *Atlanta Daily World*, 8 July 1945.
51. *Birmingham World*, 27 July 1945.
52. *Atlanta Daily World*, 24 July 1945.
53. *Richmond Times-Dispatch*, 19 June 1945.
54. Ibid., 24–25 June 1945.
55. Ibid., 21, 23 July 1945.
56. Ibid., 26 July 1945.
57. Ibid., 10 August 1945.
58. Ibid., 17 August 1945.
59. *Mobile Press*, 12 August 1945.
60. *Herald-Press*, 16 August 1945.
61. *Birmingham World*, 27 July 1945.
62. *Chattanooga Times*, 18 July 1945.
63. *Birmingham World*, 7 August 1945.
64. Ibid., 14 August 1945.
65. *Atlanta Daily World*, 14 August 1945.
66. *Birmingham World*, 17 August 1945.
67. *Atlanta Daily World*, 14 August 1945.
68. *Birmingham World*, 21 August 1945.
69. Ibid., 7 September 1945.
70. Ibid., 7 September 1945.
71. Ibid., 28 August 1945.
72. *Atlanta Daily World*, 22 August 1945.
73. Ibid., 23 August 1945.
74. *Birmingham World*, 31 August 1945.
75. *Atlanta Daily World*, 30 August 1945.
76. Ibid., 30 August 1945.
77. Ibid., 9 September 1945.
78. *Knoxville News-Sentinel*, 10 September 1945.
79. *Atlanta Daily World*, 11, 13 September 1945.
80. Ibid., 16 September 1945.
81. Ibid., 26, 28, 29 September 1945, 2 October 1945.
82. Ibid., 7 September 1945.
83. *Chicago Defender*, 8 September 1945.
84. *Birmingham News*, 16 September 1945; *Birmingham Age-Herald*, 16 September 1945.
85. *Mobile Register*, 30 September 1945; *Atlanta Daily World*, 18 September 1945.

Chapter 16

1. *Chicago Defender*, 2 February 1946.
2. Ibid., 2 February 1946.
3. Ibid., 2 February 1946.
4. *Pittsburgh Courier*, 4 May 1946.
5. *Norfolk Journal and Guide*, 4 May 1946.
6. *Chicago Defender*, 18 May 1946.
7. *Birmingham World*, 19 May 1946; Riley, *The Biographical Encyclopedia of the Negro Baseball Leagues*, 888–89.
8. *Norfolk Journal and Guide*, 2 March 1946.
9. Ibid., 13 April 1946.
10. *Chicago Defender*, 2 February 1946.
11. *Birmingham World*, 3 March 1946.
12. *Birmingham World*, 5 March 1946.
13. *Chicago Defender*, 23 March 1945; Riley, *The Biographical Encyclopedia of the Negro Leagues*, 679.
14. *Chicago Defender*, 20 April 1945; *Norfolk Journal and Guide*, 20 April 1946.
15. *Chicago Defender*, 4 May 1946.
16. *Montgomery Advertiser*, 11–12 May 1946.
17. *Birmingham World*, 5, 28 February 1946.
18. *Chicago Defender*, 1 June 1946.
19. *Atlanta Daily World*, 14 May 1946; *Asheville Citizen*, 1 May 1946.
20. *Knoxville News-Sentinel*, 4 May 1946.
21. *Asheville Citizen*, 1 May 1946.
22. Ibid., 21 May 1946.
23. Ibid., 5 May 1946.
24. Ibid., 6 May 1946.
25. https://www.coe.ksu.edu/annex/nlbmuseum/history/players/boyd.html.
26. Ibid., 4 May 1946.
27. Ibid., 9 May 1946.
28. Ibid., 26 May 1946.
29. Ibid., 30 May 1946.
30. Ibid., 4 August 1946; http://www.wikipedia.org/wiki, "Emancipation Day," last modified 25 November 2013, 16:20.
31. *Nashville Banner*, 24 May 1946.
32. Ibid., 27–28 May 1946.
33. *Chattanooga Times*, 29 May 1946.
34. *Norfolk Journal and Guide*, 22 June 1946; *Asheville Citizen*, 10 June 1946.
35. *Norfolk Journal and Guide*, 3 August 1946.
36. Ibid., 24 August 1946.
37. *Asheville Citizen*, 14 June 1946.
38. *Montgomery Advertiser*, 9 June 1946.
39. *Knoxville News-Sentinel*, 26, 31 May 1946.
40. Ibid., 2 June 1946.
41. Ibid., 19 June 1946.

42. http://www.wikipedia.org/wiki/Billy_Conn, last modified 9 January 2015, 09:07.
43. *Chattanooga Times*, 19 June 1946.
44. *Knoxville News-Sentinel*, 20 June 1946.
45. Ibid., 5 July 1946.
46. *Chicago Defender*, 29 June 1946.
47. Ibid., 6 July 1946.
48. *Asheville Citizen*, 5 July 1946.
49. Ibid., 13–14 July 1946.
50. *Florida Times-Union*, 14 June 1946.
51. Ibid., 18 June 1946.
52. *Chicago Defender*, 19 June 1946.
53. *Birmingham World*, 20 August 1946.
54. *Asheville Citizen*, 1 July 1946.
55. *Norfolk Journal and Guide*, 20 July 1946.
56. Ibid., 27 July 1946.
57. Ibid., 10 August 1946.
58. *Chicago Defender*, 6 July 1946.
59. *Birmingham News*, 14 June 1946.
60. *Asheville Citizen*, 22 August 1946.
61. *Birmingham World*, 20 August 1946.
62. Ibid., 2 August 1946.
63. *Asheville Citizen*, 23 August 1946.
64. *Norfolk Journal and Guide*, 14 September 1946; *Asheville Citizen*, 1 September 1946.
65. *Asheville Citizen*, 1 September 1946.
66. *Nashville Banner*, 15 July 1946.
67. Ibid., 28 August 1946.
68. *Norfolk Journal and Guide*, 21 September 1946; *Birmingham World*, 17 September 1946; *Asheville Citizen*, 9 September 1946.
69. *Chicago Defender*, 5 October 1946; *Asheville Citizen*, 9 September 1946.
70. *Asheville Citizen*, 17 September 1946.
71. *Chattanooga Times*, 25 August 1946.
72. *Ashville Citizen*, 16 July 1946.
73. *Chicago Defender*, 14 September 1947.
74. Ibid., 5 October 1946; *Asheville Citizen*, 9 September 1946.
75. *Chicago Defender*, 4 September 1946.
76. Ibid., 21 May 1946; http://www.wikipedia.org/wiki/Clarence_Muse, last modified 11 December 2013, 03:22.
77. *Nashville Banner*, 20 September 1946.
78. Ibid., 23 September 1946.
79. Ibid., 24 September 1946.

Chapter 17

1. *Chicago Defender*, 8 February 1947.
2. *Atlanta Daily World*, 9 March 1947.
3. *Asheville Citizen*, 4 April 1947.
4. *Atlanta Daily World*, 15 May 1947.
5. *Raleigh News and Observer*, 27 May 1947.
6. Ibid., 7 May 1947.
7. *Asheville Citizen*, 8 May 1947.
8. Ibid., 9 May 1947.
9. *Atlanta Daily World*, 13 May 1947.
10. Ibid., 11 May 1947.
11. *Florida Times-Union*, 14 June 1947.
12. Ibid., 15 June 1947.
13. *Chicago Defender*, 24 May 1947.
14. *Nashville Banner*, 16 May 1947.
15. Ibid.
16. *Times-Picayune*, 18 June 1947.
17. *Atlanta Daily World*, 12 March 1947.
18. Ibid.
19. Ibid., 2 May 1947.
20. *Chattanooga Times*, 5 May 1947.
21. Ibid., 3 August 1947.
22. Ibid.
23. *Memphis World*, 10 June 1947.
24. *Chattanooga Times*, 8 June 1947.
25. Ibid., 9 June 1947.
26. *Atlanta Daily World*, 3 June 1947; *Chicago Defender*, 31 May 1947.
27. *Raleigh News and Observer*, 9 June 1947.
28. Ibid., 10 June 1947.
29. Ibid., 16 June 1947.
30. Ibid., 7 July 1947.
31. *Asheville Citizen*, 18 June 1947.
32. Ibid., 20 June 1947.
33. *Chattanooga Times*, 20 June 1947.
34. *Asheville Citizen*, 22 July 1947.
35. *Nashville Banner*, 9 July 1947.
36. *Chicago Defender*, 26 July 1947.
37. Norfolk *Journal and Guide*, 16 August 1947.
38. *Asheville Citizen*, 25 July 1947.
39. *Atlanta Daily World*, 3 June 1947.
40. Ibid.
41. Ibid., 20, 24 July 1947.
42. Ibid., 31 July 1947.
43. *Nashville Banner*, 25 July 1947.
44. *Atlanta Daily World*, 1 August 1947.
45. Ibid., 6 August 1947.
46. Ibid., 14 August 1947.
47. Ibid., 1 July 1947.
48. http://www.nlbpa.com/the-athletes/neal-charlie.
49. *Nashville Banner*, 18 May 1947.
50. Ibid., 12 August 1947.
51. *Atlanta Daily World*, 7 June 1947.
52. *New Orleans Times-Picayune*, 28 July 1947.
53. Ibid., 6 August 1947.
54. *Asheville Citizen*, 24 May 1947.
55. Ibid., 23 May 1947.
56. *New Orleans Times-Picayune*, 13 August 1947.
57. Ibid., 17 August 1947.
58. Ibid., 24 August 1947.
59. *Raleigh News and Observer*, 26 August 1947.
60. Ibid., 30 August 1947.
61. *Asheville Citizen*, 3 September 1947.
62. Ibid., 5 September 1947.
63. Ibid., 10 September 1947.
64. Ibid., 22 September 1947.
65. *Nashville Banner*, 2 September 1947.
66. *New Orleans Times-Picayune*, 8 September 1947.
67. Ibid., 13 September 1947.
68. Ibid., 15 September 1947.
69. Ibid., 16 September 1947.
70. Ibid., 18 September 1947.
71. Ibid., 19 September 1947.
72. *Asheville Citizen*, 1 October 1947.

Chapter 18

1. *Birmingham World*, 30 April 1948.
2. *Atlanta Daily World*, 12 May 1948.
3. *Birmingham World*, 27 February 1948.
4. Ibid., 1 June 1948.
5. *Atlanta Daily World*, 12 May 1948.
6. John Klima, *Willie's Boys, the 1948 Birmingham Black Barons, the Last Negro League World Series, and the Making of a Baseball Legend* (Hoboken, NJ: John Wiley & Sons, 2009, 45).

7. *Birmingham World*, 30 April 1948.
8. *Memphis World*, 19 March 1948.
9. Ibid., 20 April 1948.
10. Ibid.
11. *Birmingham World*, 30 April 1948.
12. *New Orleans Times-Picayune*, 11 July 1948.
13. *Birmingham World*, 7 May 1948.
14. *Atlanta Daily World*, 2 May 1948.
15. Ibid., 4 May 1948.
16. Ibid., 17 May 1948.
17. *Memphis Commercial-Appeal*, 17 May 1948.
18. Ibid., 17 June 1948.
19. *Birmingham World*, 25 May 1948.
20. *Birmingham World*, 25 May 1948; Klima, *Willie's Boys*, 45.
21. *Birmingham World*, 18 June 1948.
22. *Chattanooga Times*, 2 May 1948.
23. Ibid., 30 May 1948.
24. Riley, *The Biographical Encyclopedia of the Negro Baseball Leagues*, 523–24.
25. *Memphis World*, 14 May 1948.
26. *Memphis Commercial Appeal*, 15, 17 May 1948.
27. *Memphis World*, 8 June 1948, 18 June 1948.
28. *Commercial Appeal*, 6 June 1948.
29. Ibid., 7 June 1948.
30. Ibid., 13, 14 June 1948.
31. Ibid., 20, 24 June 1948.
32. *Nashville Banner*, 22 April 1948, 12 May 1948.
33. Ibid., 17 May 1948.
34. *New Orleans Times-Picayune*, 17 June 1948.
35. *Atlanta Daily World*, 18 May 1948.
36. Ibid., 20 May 1948.
37. Ibid., 23 May 1948.
38. Ibid., 26 May 1948.
39. Ibid., 26 May 1948.
40. Ibid., 28 May 1948.
41. *New Orleans Times-Picayune*, 10 June 1948.
42. Ibid., 11 June 1948.
43. Ibid., 11 July 1948.
44. Ibid., 25 July 1948.
45. *Chattanooga Times*, 14 July 1948.
46. *New Orleans Times-Picayune*, 11 July 1948.
47. *Atlanta Daily World*, 15 July 1948.
48. Ibid., 11 August 1948.
49. *New Orleans Times-Picayune*, 22 August 1948.
50. Ibid., 25 August 1948.
51. Ibid., 7 September 1948.
52. *Chattanooga Times*, 30 May 1948.
53. Ibid., 31 May 1948.
54. Ibid., 1 June 1948.
55. Ibid., 14 June 1948.
56. Ibid., 22 August 1948.
57. Ibid., 23 August 1948.
58. Ibid., 30 August 1948.
59. *New Orleans Times-Picayune*, 24 April 1949.
60. *Memphis World*, 17 September 1948.

Chapter 19

1. *Chicago Defender*, 26 March 1949.
2. Ibid., 3 March 1949.
3. *Birmingham World*, 11 March 1949.
4. *Chicago Defender*, 26 March 1949.
5. *Birmingham World*, 11 March 1949; *Chicago Defender*, 26 March 1994.
6. *Atlanta Daily World*, 12 May 1949; *Chicago Defender*, 21 May 1949.
7. *Montgomery Advertiser*, 6 June 1949.
8. *Atlanta Daily World*, 4 August 1949.
9. *Mobile Press*, 10 April 1949.
10. Ibid., 22 May 1949.
11. http://www.devilliersmuseum.com/Florida_Black_Tourism_Center.html.
12. *Birmingham World*, 17 May 1949.
13. *Gadsden Times*, 28 April 1949.
14. Ibid., 28 April 1949.
15. Ibid., 28 April 1949.
16. Ibid., 22 May 1949.
17. *Atlanta Daily World*, 19 May 1949.
18. Ibid., 25 May 1949.
19. Ibid., 24 July 1949.
20. *Gadsden Times*, 6 June 1949.
21. Ibid., 30 May 1949, 6 June 1949.
22. Ibid., 13 June 1949.
23. *Nashville Banner*, 3 August 1949.
24. Ibid., 15 August 1949.
25. Ibid., 23 August 1949.
26. Ibid., 24 August 1949.
27. Ibid., 10 September 1949.

Chapter 20

1. Heaphy, I, 1869–1960, 241.
2. Clark and Lester, *The Negro Leagues Book*, 162–63.
3. *Chicago Defender*, 11 February 1950.
4. *Birmingham World*, 24 February 1950; *Chicago Defender*, 25 February 1950.
5. *Birmingham World*, 21 March 1950.
6. Ibid., 25 April 1950.
7. *Owensboro Inquirer*, 3 May 1950.
8. Ibid.
9. Ibid., 7 May 1950.
10. *Huntsville Times*, 8 June 1950.
11. *Chicago Defender*, 29 April 1950.
12. *Atlanta Daily World*, 2 May 1950.
13. Ibid., 14 May 1950.
14. Ibid., 16 May 1950.
15. *Birmingham World*, 11 April 1950.
16. *Atlanta Daily World*, 1 June 1950.
17. Ibid., 31 May 1950.
18. Ibid., 4 June 1950.
19. Ibid., 1 June 1950.
20. *Birmingham World*, 30 May 1950; *Atlanta Daily World*, 30 May 1950.
21. *Birmingham World*, 9 June 1950.
22. *Atlanta Daily World*, 16 June 1950.
23. Ibid., 29 June 1950.
24. *Birmingham World*, 7 July 1950.
25. Ibid., 11 July 1950.
26. *Atlanta Daily World*, 8 July 1950.
27. Ibid., 9 July 1950.
28. Ibid.
29. *Birmingham World*, 11 August 1950.
30. Ibid.
31. Ibid., 28 April 1951.
32. *Birmingham World*, 1 May 1951.
33. Ibid; *Atlanta Daily World*, 1 May 1951.
34. *Mobile Register*, 11 May 1951.
35. *Chattanooga Times*, 2, 4 June 1951.
36. Ibid., 25 June 1951.
37. Ibid., 7 June 1951.
38. *Tuscaloosa News*, 2 July 1951.
39. Ibid., 20 July 1951.
40. *Knoxville News-Sentinel*, 3 June 1951.

Bibliography

Books

Aaron, Hank, with Lonnie Wheeler. *I Had a Hammer.* New York: HarperCollins, 1991.

Ackmann, Martha. *Curveball: The Remarkable Story of Toni Stone.* Chicago: Lawrence Hill Books, 2010.

Aiello, Thomas. *The Kings of Casino Park: Black Baseball in the Lost Season of 1932.* Tuscaloosa: University of Alabama Press, 2011.

Ashe, Arthur. *A Hard Road to Glory: The History of the African American Athlete,* volumes 1 and 2. New York: Amistad Books, 1988.

Bak, Richard. *Turkey Stearnes and the Detroit Stars: The Negro Leagues in Detroit, 1919–1933.* Detroit: Great Lakes Books, 1994.

Bankes, James. *The Pittsburgh Crawfords.* Dubuque, IA: Wm. C. Brown, 1991.

Barra, Allen. *Rickwood Field: A Century in America's Oldest Ballpark.* New York: W. W. Norton, 2010.

Brashler, William. *Josh Gibson: A Life in the Negro Leagues.* New York: Harper & Row, 1978.

Bruce, Janet. *The Kansas City Monarchs: Champions of Black Baseball.* Lawrence: University Press of Kansas, 1985.

Chalk, Ocania. *Black College Sports.* New York: Dodd, Mead, 1976.

Charlton, Jim, and Mike Shatzkin. *The Ballplayers.* New York: Arbor House, 1990.

Clark, Dick, and Larry Lester, eds. *The Negro Leagues Book.* Cleveland: Society for American Baseball Research, 1994.

Cook, Ben. *Good Wood: A Fan's History of Rickwood Field.* Birmingham, AL: A. H. Cather, 2005.

Darnell, Tim. *The Crackers: Early Days of Atlanta Baseball.* Athens, GA: Hill Street Press, 2003.

Debono, Paul. *The Indianapolis ABCs: History of a Premier Team in the Negro Leagues.* Jefferson, NC: McFarland, 1997.

Dixon, Phil, and Patrick Hannigan. *The Negro Baseball Leagues: A Photographic History.* Mattituck, NY: Amereon House, 1992.

Einstein, Charles. *Willie's Time: Baseball's Golden Age.* Carbondale: Southern Illinois University Press, 1979.

Faulkner, David. *Nine Sides of the Diamond: Baseball's Great Glove Men on the Fine Art of Defense.* New York: Times Books, 1990.

Filichia, Peter. *Professional Baseball Franchises: From the Abbeville Athletics to the Zanesville Indians.* New York: Facts on File, 1993.

Fullerton, Christopher. *Every Other Sunday.* Birmingham, AL: R. Boozer Press, 1999.

Grabowski, John. *Willie Mays.* New York: Chelsea House, 1990.

Gregorich, Barbara. *Women at Play: The Story of Women in Baseball.* New York: Harcourt Brace, 1993.

Guzman, Jessie Parkhurst, ed. *1952 Negro Year Book.* New York: Wm. & Wise, 1952.

Hano, Arnold. *Willie Mays: The Say-Hey Kid.* New York: Bartholomew House, 1961.

Heaphy, Leslie A. *The Negro Leagues, 1869–1960.* Jefferson, NC: McFarland, 2003.

Henderson, Edwin Bancroft. *The Negro in Sports.* Washington, D.C.: Associated Publishers, 1939.

Heward, Bill, with Dimitri V. Gat. *Some Are Called Clowns: A Season with the Last of the Great Barnstorming Baseball Teams.* New York: Thomas Y. Crowell, 1974.

Hogan, Lawrence. *Shades of Glory: The Negro Leagues and the Story of African American Baseball.* Washington, D.C.: National Geographic, 2006.

Holway, John B. *Black Diamonds: Life in the Negro Leagues from the Men Who Lived It.* Westport, CT: Meckler, 1989

_____. *Blackball Stars: Negro League Pioneers.* Westport, CT: Meckler, 1988.

_____. *Bullet Joe and the Monarchs.* Washington, D.C.: Capital Press, 1984.

_____. *The Complete Book of Baseball's Negro Leagues: The Other Half of Baseball History.* Fern Park, FL: Hastings House, 2001.

_____. *Josh and Satch: The Life and Times of Josh Gibson and Satchel Paige.* Westport, CT: Meckler, 1991.

_____. *Smokey Joe and the Cannonball.* Washington, D.C.: Capital Press, 1983.

_____. *Voices from the Great Black Baseball Leagues.* New York: Dodd, Mead, 1975.

Irvin, Monte, and James A. Riley. *Nice Guys Finish First.* New York: Carroll & Graf, 1995.

Johnson, Lloyd, and Miles Wolff, eds. *The Ency-*

clopedia of Minor League Baseball. Durham, NC: Baseball America, 1993.

Kelley, Brent. *I Will Never Forget.* Jefferson, NC: McFarland, 2003.

_____. *The Negro Leagues Revisited: Conversations with 66 More Baseball Heroes.* Jefferson, NC: McFarland, 1998.

_____. *Voices from the Negro Leagues: Conversations with 52 Baseball Standouts.* Jefferson, NC: McFarland, 1998.

Klima, John. *Willie's Boys: The 1948 Birmingham Black Barons, the Last Negro League World Series, and the Making of a Baseball Legend.* Hoboken, NJ: John Wiley & Sons, 2009.

Laing, Jeffrey Michael. *Bud Fowler: Baseball's First Black Professional.* Jefferson, NC: McFarland, 2013.

Lebovitz, Hal, with Satchel Paige. *Pitchin' Man: Satchel Paige's Own Story.* Cleveland: Cleveland News, 1948.

Lester, Larry. *Black Baseball's National Showcase: The East-West All-Star Game, 1933–53.* Lincoln: University of Nebraska Press, 2002.

Lowry, Philip J. *Green Cathedrals: The Ultimate Celebration of All 271 Major League and Negro League Ballparks Past and Present.* Cleveland: Society for American Baseball Research, 1992.

Luke, Bob. *The Baltimore Elite Giants: Sport and Society in the Age of Negro League Baseball.* Baltimore: Johns Hopkins University Press, 2009.

Mays, Willie, with Charles Einstein. *Born to Play Ball.* New York: G. P. Putnam's Sons, 1955.

Mays, Willie, with Lou Sahadi. *Say Hey: The Autobiography of Willie Mays.* New York: Simon & Schuster, 1988.

McCann, Kevin D. *Jackson Diamonds: Professional Baseball in Jackson, Tennessee.* Dickson, TN: Three Star Press, 1999.

McNary, Kyle P. *Ted "Double Duty" Radcliffe: Thirty-Six Years of Pitching and Catching in Baseball's Negro Leagues.* St. Louis: McNary, 2005.

Newman, Zipp, and Frank McGowan. *House of Barons.* Birmingham, AL: Cather Brothers, 1948.

O'Neal, Bill. *The Southern League.* Austin, TX: Eakin Press, 1994.

Overmyer, James. *Queen of the Negro Leagues: Effa Manley and the Newark Eagles.* Lanham, MD: Scarecrow, 1998.

Paige, Leroy "Satchel," as told to David Lipman. *Maybe I'll Pitch Forever.* Garden City, NY: Doubleday, 1961.

Peterson, Robert. *Only the Ball Was White: A History of Legendary Black Players and All-Black Professional Teams.* Englewood Cliffs, NJ: Prentice-Hall, 1970.

Porter, David D. *Biographical Dictionary of American Sports: Baseball.* Westport, CT: Greenwood, 1987.

Powell, Larry. *Black Barons of Birmingham: The South's Greatest Negro League Team and Its Players.* Jefferson, NC: McFarland, 2009.

Pride, Charley, with Jim Henderson. *Pride: The Charley Pride Story.* New York: William Morrow, 1994.

Retort, Robert D. *Pictorial Negro League Legends Album.* New Castle, PA: self-published, 1992.

Ribowsky, Mark. *A Complete History of the Negro Leagues.* Secaucus, NJ: Carol, 1995.

_____. *Don't Look Back: Satchel Paige in the Shadows of Baseball.* New York: Simon & Schuster, 1994.

Riley, James A. *All-Time All-Stars of Black Baseball.* Cocoa, FL: TK Publishing, 1983.

_____. *The Biographical Encyclopedia of the Negro Baseball Leagues.* New York: Carroll & Graf, 2002.

_____. *Dandy, Day and the Devil: A Trilogy of Negro League Baseball.* Cocoa, FL: TK Publishing, 1987.

Robinson, Frazier "Slow," with Paul Bauer. *Catching Dreams: My Life in the Negro Baseball Leagues.* Syracuse, NY: Syracuse University Press, 1999.

Rogosin, Donn. *Invisible Men: Life in the Negro Leagues.* New York: Atheneum, 1993.

Ruggles, William B. *The History of the Texas League of Professional Baseball Clubs, 1888–1951.* Dallas: Texas League of Baseball Clubs, 1952.

Scipio, L. Albert. *The 24th Infantry at Fort Benning.* Silver Spring, MD: Roman Publications, 1986.

Shatzkin, Mike, ed. *The Ballplayers.* New York: Arbor House/William Morrow, 1990.

Shirley, David. *Satchel Paige: Baseball Great.* New York: Chelsea House, 1993.

Spatz, Lyle, ed. *The SABR Baseball List and Record Book.* New York: Scribner, 2007.

Swanton, Barry. *The Mandak League: Haven for Former Negro League Ballplayers, 1950–1957.* Jefferson: McFarland, 2006.

Tygiel, Jules. *Baseball's Great Experiment: Jackie Robinson and His Legacy.* New York: Oxford University Press, 1983.

Walker, James R., and Robert V. Bellamy, Jr. *Center Field Shot: A History of Baseball on Television.* Lincoln: University of Nebraska Press, 2008.

Watkins, Clarence. *Baseball in Birmingham.* Charleston, SC: Arcadia, 2010.

Wentworth, Harold, and Stuart Berg Flexner, comps. *Dictionary of American Slang.* New York: Thomas Y. Crowell, 1960.

White, Sol. *Sol White's History of Colored Base Ball, with Other Documents on the Earliest Black Games, 1886–1936.* Introduction by Jerry Malloy. Lincoln: University of Nebraska Press, 1995.

_____. *Sol White Baseball Guide.* Philadelphia: H. Walter Schlichter, 1907; reprint, Columbia, SC: Camden House, 1984.

Wolff, Rick, ed. *The Baseball Encyclopedia*, Ninth Edition. New York: Macmillan, 1993.

Wright, Marshall D. *The Southern Association in Baseball: 1885–1961*. Jefferson, NC: McFarland, 2002.

Young, A. S. *Negro Firsts in Sports*. Chicago: Johnson Publishing Group, 1963.

____. *Mets from Mobile: Cleon Jones and Tommie Agee*. New York: Harcourt Children's Books, 1970.

Newspapers

ALABAMA
Alabama Citizen
Anniston Star
Birmingham Age-Herald
Birmingham Journal
Birmingham Ledger
Birmingham News
Birmingham Post
Birmingham Post-Herald
Birmingham Reporter
Birmingham Times
Birmingham World
Centreville Press
Decatur Daily
Gadsden Times
Gadsden Times & Daily News
Huntsville Mirror
Huntsville Times
Jasper Daily Mountain Eagle
Mobile News-Item
Mobile Press
Mobile Press-Register
Mobile Register
Montgomery Advertiser
Montgomery Alabama Journal
Selma Times-Journal
Talladega Daily Home
Tuscaloosa News

ARKANSAS
Arkansas Democrat
Arkansas Gazette

DISTRICT OF COLUMBIA
Washington Post

FLORIDA
Florida Times-Union
Pensacola Journal

GEORGIA
Albany Herald
Atlanta Constitution
Atlanta Daily World
Atlanta Independent
Atlanta Journal
Augusta Chronicle
Macon News
Macon Telegraph
Moultrie Observer
Savannah Morning News
Savannah Press
Thomasville Daily Enterprise
Waycross Journal-Herald

ILLINOIS
Chicago Defender

INDIANA
Evansville Courier
Indianapolis News
Indianapolis Star

KENTUCKY
Kentucky New-Era (Hopkinsville)
Lexington Herald
Lexington Leader
Louisville Courier-Journal
Owensboro Inquirer

LOUISIANA
Alexandria Daily Town Talk
Louisiana Weekly (New Orleans)
Monroe Morning World
Monroe News-Star
New Orleans Item
New Orleans Times-Picayune
Shreveport Journal
Shreveport Times

MICHIGAN
Detroit Free Press
St. Joseph Press-Herald

MISSISSIPPI
Jackson Clarion-Ledger

MISSOURI
Kansas City Call
The Sporting News (St. Louis)

NEW YORK
New York Times

NORTH CAROLINA
Asheville Citizen
Asheville Citizen-Times
Asheville Times
Charlotte Observer
Raleigh News & Observer

OHIO
Akron Beacon-Journal
Alliance Review
Cincinnati Enquirer
Cleveland Plain Dealer

Columbus Citizen Journal
Columbus Dispatch

PENNSYLVANIA
Harrisburg Patriot-News
Philadelphia Daily News
Pittsburgh Courier
Pittsburgh Post-Gazette
Pittsburgh Press
Sporting Life (Philadelphia)

SOUTH CAROLINA
Charleston News & Courier

TENNESSEE
Chattanooga Daily Times
Jackson Sun
Knoxville Herald
Knoxville Journal & Tribune
Knoxville News-Sentinel
Knoxville Sentinel
Memphis Avalanche-Appeal
Memphis Commercial Appeal
Memphis World
Nashville Banner
Nashville Globe & Independent
Nashville Tennessean
Public Guide (Knoxville)

TEXAS
Austin American-Statesman

VIRGINIA
Journal and Guide (Norfolk)
Richmond Times-Dispatch

WEST VIRGINIA
Wheeling Register

Periodicals

Aiello, Thomas. "The Fading of the Greys: Black Baseball and Historical Memory in Little Rock." *The Arkansas Historical Quarterly*, Winter 2006, 360–84,
"America's Only Negro Daily," *Negro Digest*, December 1945, 67–8.
"Base Ball." *Aluminum Bulletin*, June 1920, 10–11.
Baseball Future." *Negro Digest*, March 1944, 41.
Bates, Bryan L. "The New Migration to the South." *Ebony*, September 1998, 58–63.
Brashler, William. "The Honky Writer." *Newsweek*, 20 February 1978, 21.
Chadwick, Bruce. "Color Blind Collectibles." *Topps Magazine*, Fall 1992, 42–43
Cohen, Haskell. "Ace of Diamonds," *Negro Digest*, July 1944, 31–33.
Craft, David. "Memphis Red Sox Spotlighted in New Video." *Sports Collectors Digest*, 12 June 1998, 130–31.

Cummiskey, Joe. "Baseball's Biggest Drawing Card," *Negro Digest*, August 1944, 69–70.
"Diamond Dazzler." *Negro Digest*, October 1946, 56.
Frank, Stanley. "No Diamond Dimout." *Negro Digest*, July 1943, 17–18.
Fullerton, Chris. "Striking Out Jim Crow." *The Reader*, February-March 1995, 1–2.
Harwell, Ernie. "Found: A Popular Umpire." *Negro Digest*, April 1944, 10.
"Homerun Josh." *Negro Digest*, October 1945, 79.
Horick, Tandy. "They Might Have Been Heroes: Memories of Nashville and the Glory Days of Baseball's Negro Leagues." *Nashville Scene*, May 2, 1996, 23–30.
"Josh the Basher." *Negro Digest*, September 1943, 45–6.
"Judy Johnson (1899–1989)." *Negro Digest*, 26 June 1989.
"Judy Johnson (1899–1989)." *Sports Illustrated*, 26 June 1989.
Kessler, Gene. "Boogie on the Diamond." *Negro Digest*, February 1946, 9–10.
"The Legend of Bismarck, N.D." *Negro Digest*, November 1944, 83–85.
Lewis, Lloyd. "Hesitation Ball." *Negro Digest*, January 1945, 37–38.
Mann, Arthur. "24 Letter-Man." *Negro Digest*, May 1946, 31–35.
Monroe, Al. "Panic Is Seen Within the Ranks of Organized Baseball." *Abbott's Monthly*, August 1932.
_____. "What Is the Matter with Baseball?" *Abbott's Monthly*, April 1932.
Morse, George C. "Iron Men of Baseball." *Negro Digest*, September 1946, 23–66.
"No Average Ball Players." *Negro Digest*, August 1943, 91–2.
Paige, Satchel, as told to Ernest Mehl. "My Biggest Baseball Day." *Negro Digest*, May 1943, 7–10.
Plott, Bill. "The Southern League of Colored Base Ballists." *Baseball Research Journal*, 1974.
Reynolds, James E. "The Batboy Who Swung for Equality." *Sports Illustrated*, 2 July 1990.
Rosengarten, Theodore. "Reading the Hops: Recollections of Lorenzo Piper Davis and the Negro Baseball League." *Southern Exposure*, Summer/Fall 1977.
Rozin, Skip. "Two Worlds." *Topps Magazine*, Fall 1992, 36–39
Rushin, Steve. "A Life Well-Lived." *Sports Illustrated*, 20 January 2003, 15.
Smith, Shelley. "Remembering Their Game." *Sports Illustrated*, 6 July 1992.
Smith, Wendell. "Baseball on Diplomatic Rocks." *Negro Digest*, April 1943, 71–2.
Turkin, Hy. "Foul Bawl," *Negro Digest*, April 1945, 35–6.
_____. "No Black Ball for Black Jackie," *Negro Digest*, March 1946, 41–43.
Woodward, Stanley. "Satchel's Ambition," *Negro Digest*, August 1943, 41–43.

VHS/DVD

Dawson, David W. *Swingin' Timber*. Fayetteville: University of Arkansas, 2001. VHS recording.

Haddock, John R., and Steven J. Ross, prods. *Black Diamonds, Blues City: Stories of the Memphis Red Sox*. Memphis, TN: University of Memphis, 1998. VHS recording.

Ward, Connie Cameron, producer. *Safe at Home*. Atlanta Public Television, 1974. VHS recording.

Interviews

All interviews were conducted by the author.

Otha Bailey. Birmingham, AL, 16 May 1999.
Ralph Banks. Telephone interview, 10 September 1998.
Lyman Bostock, Sr. Birmingham, AL, 16 June 1993; telephone interview, June 14, 1997.
"Birmingham Sam" Brison. Birmingham, AL, 3 June 2010.
John Brown. Telephone interview, 18 June 1997.
Joe Caffee. Telephone interview, 6 June 2003.
Bill "Ready" Cash. Harrisburg, PA, 8 August 1998.
Cato Clowney. Telephone interview, 26 July 2012.
Bubba Cunningham. Montgomery, AL, 5 October 1997
Lorenzo "Piper" Davis. Montevallo, AL, 24 February 1983.
Charlie Dees. Telephone interview, 30 October 2010.
Henry Elmore. Birmingham, AL, 17 February 2011.
Frank Evans. Birmingham, AL, 13 August 2009 and 3 June 2010.
Severn Frazier. Telephone interview, 11 January 1992.
Severn Frazier, Jr. Telephone interview, 13 October 1998.
Jesse Gosha. Montgomery, AL, 26 September 1997; telephone interview, 2 September 1998.
Willie Grace. Telephone interview, 16 June 1997
Bill Greason. Birmingham, AL, 1 February 1995.
Bennie L. Griggs. Birmingham, AL, 6 June 2002
Wiley Griggs. Birmingham, AL, 14 April 1995.
Raymond Haggins. Montevallo, AL, 15 April 1994.
James Hannon. Montgomery, AL, 26 September 1997.
Sam Jethroe. Telephone interview, 18 June 1997.
Mamie "Peanut" Johnson. Harrisburg, PA, 8 August 1998.
Ethel Klep. Telephone interview, 17 June 1997.
Joseph Klep. Telephone interview, 17 June 1997.
Elnora Frazier Lee. Telephone interview, 5 November 1998.
Tony Lloyd. Birmingham, AL, 3 June 2010.
Buck O'Neil. Asheville, NC, 7 July 1996.
David Pope. Telephone interview, 18 July 1996.
Charley Pride. Telephone interview, 6 May 1999; interview, Birmingham, AL, 16 May 1999.
Ted "Double Duty" Radcliffe. Montgomery, AL, 17 August 1996.
Tommy Sampson. Telephone interview, 18 June 1997.
Jake Sanders. Birmingham, AL, 17 February 2011.
Al Smith. Telephone interview, 18 June 1997.
Willie Smith. Anniston, AL, 20 January 1970 and 10 December 1993.
Thomas "High Pockets" Turner. Harrisburg, PA, 8 August 1998
Bob Veale. Montevallo, AL, 24 February 1983; Birmingham, AL, 20 May 1998.
Claude Walker. Telephone interview, 20 September 1998.
Ernest Waters. Telephone interview, 20 September 1998.
Bessie Williams (widow of Poindexter Williams, Jr.). Telephone interview, 4 February 2004.
Charles L. "Coot" Willis. Telephone interview, 23 August 2010.
Artie Wilson. Telephone interview, 20 July 1996.
Bill Wilson (Knoxville Giants researcher). Telephone interview and correspondence, various dates, September 1998.
Willie Young. Birmingham, AL, 16 May 1999.

Web Sources

"Alcoa, Tennessee." *Wikipedia*. Last modified 8 May 2014. http://en.wikipedia.org/wiki/Alcoa, Tennessee.

Ashwill, Gary. "Jim Hugh Moss." *Agatetype* (blog), 3 May 2012. http://www.agatetype.typepad.com, 3 May 2012.

Bedingfield, Gary. "Baseball in World War II." *Baseball in War Time* (blog). http://www.baseballinwartime.com/baseball_in_wwii.

"Billy Conn." *Wikipedia*. Last modified 27 February 2014. http://en.wikipedia.org/wiki/Billy Conn.

"The Black Bottom." *Black Bottom* (blog). Accessed, 20 July 2013. http://theblackbottom.wordpress.com/communities/blackbottom/history.

"Black Bottom, Detroit." *Wikipedia*. Last modified 26 April 2014. http://en.wikipedia.org/wiki/Black Bottom, Detroit.

"Bob Riesener." Baseball Reference. Last modified 13 January 2011. http://www.baseball-reference.com/bullpen/Bob_Riesener.

"Bobby Robinson." Baseball Reference. Accessed 13 January 2011. http://www.baseball-reference.com/nlb/player.cgi?id=robins001bob.

"B. T. Harvey Stadium." Official Website of Morehouse College Athletics. Accessed 19 May 2014. http://www.athletics.morehouse.edu/sports/2010/11/22/btharavey.aspx?id=10.

Burgess, Bill. "Meet the Sports Writers." Baseball Fever. Accessed 19 May 2014. http://www.baseball-fever.com/showthread.php?57538.Meet-the-Sports-Writers.

"Carl Glass." Baseball Reference. Last modified 24

April 2013. www.baseball-reference.com/bullpen/Carl Glass.
"Charlie Neal." Website of the Negro Leagues Baseball Players Association. Accessed 19 May 2014. http://www.nlbpa.com/the-athletes/neal-charlie.
"Clarence Muse." *Wikipedia*. Last modified 18 May 2014. http://en.wikipedia.org/wiki/Clarence Muse.
Curren, Dan. "Short-Lived Milwaukee Bears Didn't Get Much Play." Online Milwaukee. Accessed 6 May 2003. http://www.onlinemilwaukee.com.
"Devilliers Museum." Website of the Devilliers Cultural Heritage e-Museum. http://devilliersmuseum.com/Florida_Black_Tourism_Visitor_s_Center.html.
Elston, Gene. Gene Elston's Journal (online collection of papers and interviews). Astros Daily. Accessed 8 August 2010. http://www.astrosdaily.com/history/elston.
"Emancipation Day." *Wikipedia*. Last modified 26 April 2014. http://en.wikipedia.org/wiki//Emancipation_Day.
"Houston Riot (1917)." *Wikipedia*. Last modified 5 May 2014. http://en.wikipedia.org/wiki/Houston_Riot_(1917).
"Howard Moore, Jr." The History Makers (online video oral-history collection). Accessed 14 April 2007. http://www.thehistorymakers.com/biography/howard-moore-41.

"Illinois-Indiana-Iowa League." Illinois-Indiana-Iowa League (baseball-history website). Accessed 20 August 2008. http://www.three-eye.com.
"Memphis Red Sox." *Wikipedia*. Accessed 12 May 2013. http://en.wikipedia.org/wiki/Memphis Red Sox.
"Montgomery, AL." City of Montgomery, Alabama, Website. Accessed 19 May 2014. http://www.montgomeryal.gov.
"Negro League Baseball." *Wikipedia*. Last Modified 8 May 2014. http://en.wikipedia.org/wiki/negro_league_baseball.
"Picket Springs Resort." Waymarking Website. Accessed 19 May 2014. http://www.waymarking.com/waymarks/WMEPKW_Pickett_Springs_Resort_Montgomery_Alabama.
"Refermat to Reickenback," *Political Graveyard*. http://politicalgraveyard.com/bio/refermat-reickenback.html.
"St. Louis Stars." *Wikipedia*. Last modified 15 February 2014. http://en.wikipedia.org/wiki/St. Louis Stars.
"Ted Radcliffe." *Wikipedia*. Last modified 4 April 2014. http://en.wikipedia.org/wiki/Ted_Radcliffe.
"Timeline of World War II." *Wikipedia*. Last Modified 29 April 2014. http://en.wikipedia.org/wiki/Timeline_of_World_War_II.

Index

Author's note: Due to the fact that first names could not be ascertained for a number of Negro Southern League players, those individuals are identified in the index by the team and year of their association. Similarly, some team names reappear many years apart with no tangible connection. They are likewise identified by year. Finally, because teams are mentioned numerous times over the course of a season, the author has chosen not to identify them for each game reference reported during the baseball season, just the more important references. Page numbers in bold italics indicate pages with illustrations.

A. G. Spalding baseball 9
Abrahams, W. R. 68
Acipco team 127
Adams (Memphis player, 1935) 132, 133
Adams, Bill *126*
Adams, Oscar W., Jr. 49
Adams, Oscar W., Sr. 43, 49–50
Adkisson, Wilbur 166
Alabama State Teachers College 54, 83, 161
Albany Giants 24, 51, 67
Albany Pecans 60
Alberta City Park 200
Alcoa Aluminum Company 97
Alcoa Aluminum Sluggers 91, 96, 97
Alcorn State College 83
Alexander, Chuffy 58, 93
Alexander, "Smut" 89
Alexander, Spencer 146, 159, 166, *168*, 173
Alexandria Lincoln Giants 101, 106
Algiers Giants 101, 106, 127
Allen (Knoxville Smokies secretary, 1932) 98
Allen, Gus 127
Allison, Amos 26
American Association 2, 7, 94, 98
American Broadcasting Company 161
American Negro League 91
Anderson (Nashville outfielder, 1926) 65
Anderson, Hank 84
Anderson, Sam *53*
Anderson, William 75
Andrews, Bill 117
Andrews, Herman 116, 117, 124
Andrews, James "Prince" 136, 137
Andrews Field 37, 40
Appalachian League 37
Arkansas Travelers 43
Armour, James "Lefty" 171
Armstead, James 175
Armstrong, John 160

Arnall, Governor Ellis 148
Arnold, E. 33
Arnold, Luke 116
Ash, Rudolph 13, 25
Asheville Army Store 168
Asheville Blues 145, 156, 157, 159, 160–61, 162, 163, 164, 167, *168*, *172*, 173, 175, 176–77, 178
Asheville Giants 40
Asheville Tourists 164
Askew, Jessie *126*
Associated Negro Press 3, 49
Associated Press 150
Atlanta Athletics 114, 115, 119, 127
Atlanta Black Crackers 8, 9, 10, 24, 43, 48, 51, 60, 67, 76, 91, 92, 96, 114, 125, 127, 128, 129, 132, 135, 136–37, 139, 143, 145–46, 148, 149, 150, 153, 154, 156, 157, 159, 162, 167, 169, 170–71, 173, 174, 175, 178, 180–81, 183–84, 185, 187, 188, 189, 191, 192, 195
Atlanta Braves 174–75, 199
Atlanta Brown Bombers 197, 198, 199
Atlanta Brown Crackers 196, 198
Atlanta Cardinals 173–74, 175
Atlanta Crackers 5, 8, 116, 127, 129, 136, 174
Atlanta Cubs 24, 59
Atlanta-Detroit Brown Crackers 190, 191, 192, 193, 195
Atlanta Grey Sox 76, 77, 79, 80
Atlanta Panthers 82, 83
Atlanta University 9, 51, 116, 169
Attendance 10, 12, 34, 44, 47, 54, 59, 61, 80, 83, 95, 98, 105, 106–107, 116, 117, 118–19, 121, 125, 129, 138, 148, 159, 162, 169, 170, 171, 173, 174, 187, 188, 192, 198
Auburn Avenue Luncheonette 136
Augusta, Georgia, team 36

Augustus (Memphis pitcher, 1926) 59
Austin Black Senators 101, 102, *119*
Austin, Raymond 69
Avery Shooting Gallery 169

Bacharach Giants 76
Bailey, H. J. 50
Bailey, Otha 191
Bailey Avenue Park 108
Baker, B. F. 149
Baker, Charles 70, 74, 80
Baker, W. B. 125, 133, 135, 136, 137
Ball, Bill "One-Arm" *126*, 129
Baltimore Black Sox 76, 105
Baltimore Elite Giants 10, 16, 143, 146, 147, 152, 162, 167, 170, 180
Bankhead, Dan 144, 171
Bankhead, Sam *122*, 123, 132
Barbee, Lamb 167
Barber, L. L. 8
Barker (Montgomery outfielder, 1921) 30
Barnes, Bill 85
Barnes, Harry 106, 146, 157, 163, 165, 166, 176, 182, 187
Barnett & Lewis 41
Barrow, Wesley 145, 147–48, 166
Bassett, Lloyd "Pepper" *115*
Bell, Clifford 89
Bell, James "Cool Papa" 51, 123, 131
Bell, Julian 189
Bell, Mrs. Walter Mae 169
Benevolent and Protective Order of Elks 160
Benjamin (New Orleans pitcher, 1926) 65
Benjamin, Jerry 90, 117, 121, 122, 123
Bennett, George "Jew Baby" 35
Bessemer Gray Sox 71, 76
Bessemer Stars 24
Beverly, Charles "Nunny" 116, 122

257

Bibbs, Rainey 155
Billings "Kid" 31
Birdine, Leo 4, 58, 62, 63, 64, 65, 87
Birmingham All-Stars (1932) 99
Birmingham All-Stars (1947) 174
Birmingham All-Stars (1948) 181–82, 183, 188
Birmingham All-Stars (1951) 200
Birmingham Barons 58
Birmingham Bears 200
Birmingham Black Barons 2, 5, 8, 9, 24, 43, 48, 51, 76, 82, 91, 92, 96, 106, 109, 114, 120, 126–27, 126, 127, 132, 135, 142, 144, 147, 148, 155, 161, 163, 164, 166, 171, 180, 181, 183–84, 185, *186*, 191, 193
Birmingham Black Braves 196
Birmingham Clowns (1948) 178, 181–82, 183–84, 185, 187, 188
Birmingham Clowns (1949) 193
Birmingham Eagles 199
Birmingham Foxes 109
Birmingham Giants (1908) 9, 10
Birmingham Giants (1934) 114, 115, 116, 117, 123, 137
Birmingham Giants (1949) 193
Birmingham Grey Sox 37
Birmingham Industrial League 127, 146, 155, 174, 181
Birmingham Monarchs 109
Birmingham Red Sox 196
Birmingham Stars 181–82
Bishop, A. W. 30
Bissant, Jean 65
Black, Joe 180
Blackman, Walter 149
Blackwell, Charles 48, 73, 78
Bland, Lucille 1, 171–72
Blue Front Baseball Headquarters 116
Blytheville Tigers 181, 182–183
Bobo, William 78, 87
Bogalusa, Louisiana team 28
Booker T. Washington Community Center Band, Louisville 118
Booker T. Washington High School (Memphis) 128
Booker T. Washington High School Band (Atlanta) 148, 169
Booker T. Washington High School field (Atlanta) 127
Booker T. Washington Park 9
Boone, Alonzo 93, 94, 144
Boone, Ike 3
Booneville American Legion club 196
Bosse Field 77
Bostock, Lyman 144, 181
Boston Giants 162
Boudreau, Lou 73
Bowman, Robert 153, 157, 161, 163, 164, 166, *168*, 173
Boyd, Blain 25
Boyd, Robert 159, 163, 165
Brachey, Judge John B. 118

Bradley (Royal Ponciana Hotel club player, c. 1920) *53*
Brannon, Nathaniel 146, 159, 162, *168*
Bransford, James 192
Branson, Robert 159, 163, 171
Brewer, Johnny Roy 171
Brewer's Park 9
Bridgeforth, Robert 33, 37
Bridgeforth, William "Soo" 37
Brigham, Eddie 175
Brinson, Henry 8
Britton, Johnny 4
Brooklyn Dodgers 154, 161, 171, 175
Brooks, Derrick 192
Brooks, Joe 192
Brooks, Kelly 166
Brooks, Nathaniel 183
Brooks, W. M. 8, 9, 25, 28
Brown, B. 122
Brown, "Bomber" 192
Brown, Dan 8, 10
Brown, Dave 30
Brown, "Farmer" 183
Brown, H. *53*
Brown, Jim 95, 100
Brown, "Kid" 121, 122
Brown, Larry 44, 51, 62, 83, 84, 90, 132
Brown, Mordecai "Three Finger" 19, 73
Brown, "Rider" 134
Brown, Sam 145
Brown, T. J. 198
Brown, Tom 173
Brown, Tommy 185
Brown, William M. 110, 114, 125, 135
Brown's Park 138
Bryant, "Baby" 25
Buffalo Soldiers 35, 80
Buford, Black Bottom 78–9
Burgs, Charlie 145, 147
Burnett, M. B. 76
Burnham, Willie B. 89
Butler YMCA 137
Byron (Byrom, Bynum), Ed 146, 162

Calhoun, Walter 84, *126*
California Stars 138
California winter league 87
Camp, E. Claude 143
Camp, Wilbert "Bill" 143
Campanella, Roy 180
Campbell, Dave 163
Canada, Jim 129, 182, 183, 185, 196
Cannon, Richard 88, 89, 118
Cansler, C. W. 147, 160
Canty (Atlanta pitcher, 1926) 65
Carbon Hill, Alabama 28
Cardenas (Montgomery catcher, 1921) 30
Cardenas, Francisco "Panchito" 19
Carlisle, Matthew "Lick" 110, 113, 116, 121, 122, 123, 132, 133, 144

Carmichael, Luther 179
Carolina All-Stars 173
Carpenter (Memphis outfielder, 1922) 41
Carpenter (Nashville outfielder, 1926) 55
Carpenter, Clay *14*, 26
Carter (Memphis third baseman, 1934) 122
Carter, C. M. 50, 114
Carter, Elmer 144
Carter, Ernest "Spoon" 93, 157, 170
Carter, Mal 8, 54
Carter, Marlin "Spoon" 110, 127, 144
Carter, "Spoon" 132
Cash, Bill "Ready" 61
Casino Park 89, 93, 94, 99, 101, 120
Caswell Park 161
Caulfield, Fred 8, 10, *11*, 19, 22, 28, 33, 34, 46, 47, 50, 52, 80, 115, 116, 119, 120
Chandler, A. B. 179, 189
Chapman, Ray 5, 21
Charleston, John "Red" 30, 36, 46, 48, 66, 79, 87
Charleston, Oscar 102, 103, 131, 132
Charleston Red Birds 173
Charlotte Black Hornets 156, 157, 160
Chattanooga All-Stars (1927) 72
Chattanooga All-Stars (1951) 200
Chattanooga Black Caps 77
Chattanooga Black Lookouts 48, 67, 76, 80, 82, 114, 135, 142
Chattanooga Choo Choos 1, 145, 146, 149, 150, 152, 156, 157, *158*, 167, 175, 178, 181, 182–83, 184–85, 187, 188, 189, 195, 197
Chattanooga Lookouts 37, 138
Chattanooga Stars 200
Chattanooga Tigers 24, 30, 43
Chattanooga White Sox 1, 51, 64
Chavis Park 167
Chicago American Giants 8, 22, 27, 30, 40, 45, 46, 47, 67, 76, 82, 91, 92, 95, 115, 122, 129, 131, 132, 133, 135, 142, 143, 155, 178
Chicago Black Sox 16
Chicago Giants 8
Chisholm community 55
Chunn, J. C. 145, 146, 150–51, 153, 156
Church, Robert R., Jr. 94
Churchville Cubs 146
Cincinnati Crescents 161, 175
Cincinnati-Indianapolis Clowns 152
Cincinnati Tigers 67, 114, 115, 119, 135, 139, 142
Citizen Congress Association 107
City of David 124
City Park 191
Civic Association, Birmingham 54

Index

Civil War 7
Clark, John 113
Clark College 9, 128
Clarke (Chattanooga outfielder, 1931) 83
Clarke, Fred 181
Clay (Atlanta player, 1926) 64
Claybrook, John C. 122, 125, 135
Claybrook Tigers 125, *126*, 129, 132, 139
Claybrook Park 125
Cleage, Ralph "Pete" 9, 15, 23, 28, 33, 35, 67, 72, 86, *86*
Cleveland Bears 144
Cleveland Buckeyes 187, 193
Cleveland Cubs 82, 88, 89, 92, 93
Cleveland Giants 105
Cleveland Indians 5, 21
Cleveland Red Sox 117
Cleveland Stars 93, 115
Coates (Gadsden player, 1949) 192
Cobb, Dr. E. S. 191
Cobb, L.S.N. 114, 115, 121, 122, 125
Cohen, Octavus Roy 20
Cohen, Walter 40
Cohen Stars 47
Cole, Horace 76–77
Cole, Robert A. 93, 103
Cole, W. C. 76
Coleman, Melvin "Slick" 151, 153, 154, 157
Cole's American Giants 93, 98, 101, 103, 105, 112
College Hill Park 83, 111
Collins, George *11*, 19–20, 58, 66, 122
Collins Chapel Hospital 122
Colored Citizens League, Birmingham 49
Colored YMCA, Nashville 145
Columbia Broadcasting System 101
Columbus Bears 199
Columbus Blue Birds 105
Columbus Buckeyes 51, 135, 137
Columbus Elite Giants 132
Columbus Giants 137
Columbus Turf Club 98
Columbus Turf Stars 67, 91, 96, 98
Comiskey Park 121–22
Conley, Jimmy 73
Conn, Billy 161
Contax, Chris 28
Cooley, Walter 106
Cooper (Atlanta catcher, 1936) 139, 140
Cooper, Anthony 122
Cooper, Daltie 30, 31, 32
Cooper, Jimmy 172
Cooper, William 163
Corbin Hill, Alabama 28
Cornelius, Willie "Sug" 78, 83, 90, 132
Costello, Al 196
Cotton (Atlanta outfielder, 1926) 54, 56
Cotton, James 145, 146, 149, 150
Council Bluffs, Iowa, tournament 124
Cowan, Johnny 122, 140, 183
Cox, Comer 88
Craig, Eugene 192
Cramton Bowl 54, 84, 111
Crawford, Sam 49–50
Creacy, Dewy 133
Crescent Park 112, *119*, 125
Crescent Stars Athletic Club 34
Crisby, W. N. *see* Kritzky, W.N.
Crosley Field 175
Cross, Norman 128, 132
Crossett Athletics 131
Crump, A. 114
Crump Park 111
Cruse, Claude 149
Crutchfield, Jimmy 132
Cuban All-Stars 19
Cuban House of David 87, 109
Cuban Stars 8, 23, 46, 130, 139
Cuban Stars (East) 19, 76
Cuban Stars (West) 19, 76
Cummings, Chick 35
Cunningham, Harry "Baby" 90
Cunningham, Herman "Rounder" *14*, 16, 30, 35
Cunningham, Johnnie 16, 30, 35
Cunningham, Marion "Daddy" *14*, 16, 25, 26, 30, 35, 36, 38, 51, 83
Cunningham family 16
Curry (Monroe outfielder, 1935) 132
Curry, Homer "Goose" 86, 88, 90, 110, 115, 122, 123, 132, 133, 177, 185

Dallas, Porter 101, 122
Dallas Black Sox 74
Daniels, Charlie 172
Daniels, Fred 58
Daniels, Joe 59, 65
Davenport, Lloyd 133
Davis (Albany player, 1926) 66
Davis, Benjamin J. 54
Davis, C. 189
Davis, "Handful" *126*
Davis, James "Neck Bones" 146, 157, 182
Davis, Lomax "Butch" 146, 159, 163, 165
Davis, Lorenzo "Piper" 144, 183
Davis, P. D. 54
Davis, Roosevelt 164
Davis, Rev. S. 54
Davis, Saul 66
Davis, Walter "Steel Arm" 103, 104
Davis, Willie 145, 147
Dawson, Tuggle 83, 85
Day, Leon 144
Dayton Marcos 8
Decatur Royal Giants 67
Dejoie, C. C. 40
DeMoss, Bingo 105
Dennard (Jacksonville third baseman, 1946) 163
Derrick, Edward 155, 160, 166, 175, 176, 183, 191, 192
Deselles, Elsie 107
Detroit Red Wings 189, 191
Detroit Senators 175
Detroit Stars 8, 46, 51, 62, 76, 82, 105, 142, 175
Detroit Wolverines 193
Dickerson (Atlanta outfielder, 1946) 166
Dickey, John "Steel Arm" 9, *12*, 12–13, 15, 16, 17, 18, 22, 23, 25, 26, 29, 30, 31, 32, 34, 35
Dirskell, William 80
Dismukes, Dizzy 132
Dixie League 106
Dixie Series 74, 84, 129
Dixon, John 80, 92
Doby, Larry 144, 180, 189
Dortch (New Orleans player, 1934) 121
Douglas, Sam 157
Douglass, Ernest 24
Dove, Arthur 167, 172
Downs, Richard 92
Drake, Andrew 87
Drake, Bill "Emery" 62, 63, 64, 73
Drake, Raymond 3
Dubisson, Dan 107
Dukes, Tommy 85, 86, 122, 123
Dunlap, Waldo 155, 161, 164, *168*, 173, 176
Durand (New Orleans infielder, 1920, 1923) 20, 46, 48
Durand *see* Juran
Durand, Mack *11*, 46, 48
Durant *see* Juran
Durham, Joe 61
Dymond, Gloria "Lovie" 1, *184*, 185

Earle, Charles *53*
East St. Louis Giants 73
East-South All-Star game 165
East-West All-Star Game 121, 122
East-West League 8, 91, 105
Easter, Luke 148
Easterling, Howard 144
Eastern Colored League 8, 76, 91
Ebbets Fields 154
Economics 9, 30, 37, 38, 41, 49, 50, 59, 60, 61, 67–68, 76, 92, 98, 105, 108, 113, 121, 135, 136–37, 138, 139, 151, 160, 163, 193, 197
Edgecombe, Dr. 189
Edwards, James 83
Edwards, Jesse 23, 88
Elizabethon Grays 200
Elks Club, Nashville 195
Ellis (Memphis infielder, 1923) 46, 48
Ellis (Nashville infielder, 1926) 55
Ellis (Nashville pitcher, 1926) 65
Ellison, John "Early Bird" 157, 163, 174
Else, Harry 121, 122, 123

Elston, Gene 61
Engel, Joe 98, 107, 152, 200
Engel Stadium 137, 172, 187, 197
English (Evansville catcher, 1927, 1929) 69, 78
Evangeline League 3
Evans, E. H. 107
Evansville Braves 195
Evansville Dodgers 191, 196, 197, 199
Evansville Eagles 73
Evansville Reichert Giants 67, 76, 77
Ewing, Russell 191

Fair Park 106
Fairfield Industrial High School 182
Farrell, Chico 196
Favors, Thomas "Monk" 163
Felder, Kendall 166
Fields (Montgomery outfielder, 1946) 166
Fields, Loubie *11*
Fine (Knoxville catcher, 1951) 200
Fine, Babe 160
Fisher (Gadsden player, 1949) 192
Flemings Cave Park 138
Flemming, Frank 160, 161, 165, **168**
Florida Cuban Stars 199
Florida Stars 167
Floyd, J. Ernest 41
Forbes (Atlanta pitcher, 1926) 54–55
Force, William "Bud" 12–13, 16, 23
Ford, Carl "Bubber" 157, 165–66, 167, 169
Ford, Jim 110, 130, 132, 178
Fort Benning, Georgia 43, 59, 76, 80, 84
Fort Benning Bullets 173
Fort Huachuca Military Reservation 35
Fort McClellan, Alabama 144
Fortson, T. F. 80
Foster, Andrew "Rube" 8, 27, 30, 44–45, 46, 49–50, 82, 93, 103
Foster, Police Chief Lon 94
Foster, Willie 44–45, 103, 112, 132
Fourth Street YMCA, Nashville 167
Fowler, John "Bud" 7
Fox, Al 192
Franklin, George "Fireball" 149, 154, 159
Frazier brothers 106
Frederick (Chattanooga pitcher, 1927) 70, 72

Gadsden Chiefs 191
Gadsden-Florida Tigers 190, 191, 192, 193, 195
Gadsden Giants 24
Gadsden Red Sox 195

Gadsdsen Tigers 195
Gaither(s) (Albany infielder, 1926) 66
Garrett, Marshall 8, 24, 26
Gatewood, Bill 51, 54, 57, 62, 65, 73
George, Johnny *11*
Gibson, "Frenchy 32
Gibson, Josh 99, 102, 103, 123, 132, 148
Gigo (Chattanooga pitcher, 1929) 77
Gilkerson Union Giants 70
Gillespie, Murray 83, 86, 90, 93, 96
Gilliam, James "Junior" 147, 155
Gilliam, Ted 51
Gilliard, Luther 122, 124
Gilmore, Quincy J. 49
Gisentaner, Willie 9, 19, 112, 118, 121
Glass, Carl 34, 35, 51
Glass, Jim 117
Glover, Tom 116, 117
Glover, Walter 117
Goins, Walter 163
Gone with the Wind 166
Gonzalez, Winslow 170
Goodgame, Dr. J. W. 54
Grady, Henry 7
Graves, Lawrence "Cannonball" 31
Gray (Birmingham infielder, 1921) 32
Gray, Pete 2, 144
Greason, Bill 172
Green, Carl 117
Green, Vernon 115
Greenberg, Hank 73
Greene (umpire, 1926) 65
Greene, James "Pea" 144
Greenlea, Gus 92, 115, 131, 144, 154
Greensboro Red Birds 199
Greensboro Red Wings 199
Greenville Black Spinners 160
Greenville Delta Giants 195, 197, 199
Greenville Tigers 181, 183
Grey, Milton H. 125
Griffin (Monroe player, 1934) 122, 123, 124
Griffin, G. 32
Griffin, William 41
Griffith, Robert 132
Griggs, Bennie 181
Grimes, Burleigh 73
Gurley (Chattanooga manager, 1929) 77–78
Gurley, James 73, 77, 78

Hadley, Henry "Red" 139, 140, 143
Hailey, Bud 135, 143
Haley (Memphis infielder, 1927) 69
Hall, Jim 37, 38
Hall, Prim 146

Hamilton (Knoxville player, 1922) 39
Hamilton, L. 39
Hampton, Eppie 41, 122, 132, 133
Handy, George 159
Handy, W. C. 87
Hannon, Henry 8, 10, *18*, 19, 33, 49, 51, *53*, 84
Harden, John 145, 151, 153, 154, 157, 167, 169, 178, 179, 180, 185, 189, 193
Hardy, Paul 95, 122, 144
Hardy, Wheeler 83
Harlem Globetrotters 142, 154
Harper, Charles L. 180
Harper, David T. 149, 163, 173
Harper Field 188
Harris (Evansville player, 1927) 69
Harris (Jacksonville shortstop, 1946) 163
Harris (Knoxville pitcher, 1920) 21
Harris (New Orleans outfielder, 1923) 46, 48
Harris, Ben 27
Harris, Chick "Moocha" 116
Harris, Curtis 62
Harris, Hill 199, 200
Harris, R. 10, 23
Harris, Vic 123
Harrison (New Orleans outfielder, 1920) 25
Hart, W. S. 122
Hart Undertaking Parlor 122
Hartwell Field 199
Harvey, B. T. 125, 128, 189, 195, 198, 199
Harvey, Bill 111
Harvey, Bob 177
Harvey, "Son" 111, 113, 121, 132
Haskins, Ovan 189
Hatcher, Joe 50
Hatten, Rufus 155, 157, 163, **168**, 196
Havana La Palomas 175
Hawkins, Charlie 51
Hayes, Thomas H. 44, 94, 151, 155
Haynes, Sammy 159, 166, 170–71, 174
Hefner, Arthur 155, 157, 159, 166, **168**
Heinemann Park 8, 20, 34, 112
Heitzman, Babe 773
Henderson, Charlie **126**
Henderson, Henry 85, 87
Henderson, Joe 117
Henderson, Lenon 93
Henderson, Leonard 87, 132
Henderson, Slim 86–87
Henderson brothers 79, 87
Henry, John 166
Henry, Otis "Red" 122
Hensley (Evansville pitcher, 1927) 73
Hensley, Logan "Eggie" **126**
Herman, Alex 149

Index

Herndon Stadium 188, 192
Heskett, "Red" 73
Hewitt, Joe 73, 94, 118, 121
Hickman (Monroe shortstop, 1933) 107
Hildreth, Dr. 166
Hill (Mobile outfielder, 1921) 32
Hilldale 76
Hogan (Louisville pitcher, 1922) 38
Holland, Floyd 91, 97
Holland, J. T. 85
Holland's Knoxville Giants 91, 97
Holliday (South team player, 1935) 133
Holmes, Leroy "Phillie" 157
Holt, Dr. J. W. 145, 163, 168
Holt, Will 25, 32, 35
Homestead Grays 16, 76, 101, 105, 138, 142, 143, 147, 148, 150, 152, 166, 170, 189, 195, 197
Hopkinsville Athletics 67, 76, 135, 138
Hornet Stadium 161
House of David 122, 124, 196
House of David ball park 152
House of Moses-New York Zulu Cannonball Giants 136
Houston Black Buffaloes 52, 93, 111
Houston race riot 80
Howard (Atlanta player, 1936) 139
Howard, Bill 113, 122, 124, 128, 132, 133, 134
Howard, Herman "Red" 123, 184–85
Howard, William "Bull" 146
Howard University 129
Hubbell, Carl 73
Hubbell, E. S. 107
Hueston, Judge W. C. 76
Hughes, Sammy 122, 132
Humber, Charlie 164
Humphrey, S. M. 80, 136, 137
Huntingburg Athletics 80
Hyatte, C. L. 156, 157, 167

Illinois Giants 69
Impo 173
Indianapolis ABCs 8, 9, 46, 62, 67, 82, 91, 92, 105, 144, 147, 189, 191, 192, 197
Indianapolis Athletics 142
Indianapolis-Atlanta ABCs 199
Indianapolis Cardinals 145, 150, 151
Indianapolis Indians 94, 105
Irvin, Monte 144
Isabella, "Junior" 152

Jackson, Bozo 106, 146
Jackson, C. 114
Jackson, C. E. 116
Jackson, E. G. 167
Jackson, Edgar 127
Jackson, Emory O. 4, 137, 151, 153

Jackson, General 187
Jackson, Dr. Hildreth 189
Jackson, "Jumbo" *11*
Jackson, Mack 133
Jackson, Marion E. 4, 174, 180, 188, 197, 198
Jackson, Matthew 122, 124
Jackson, R. B. 82, 96, 98, 100, 145, 147, 148, 154–55, 156, 164, 165, 167, 178, 189, *190*, 195
Jackson, Major R. R. 142, 143
Jackson, R. T. 49, 76, 77, 80, 82
Jackson Bear Cats 106, 110
Jackson Black Senators 106
Jackson Colored Baseball Association 108
Jackson Cubs (1927, 1928) 67, 76
Jackson Cubs (1951) 199
Jackson Giants 181
Jackson Royal Giants 182, 189, 195
Jacksonville Eagles 151, 156, 157, 162, 163, 167, 173, 185, 197
Jacksonville Red Caps 133, 139, 143, 144, 170
Jacksonville Stars 9
James Keyes Hotel 169
Jaynes, L. 79
Jeff (Gadsden player, 1949) 192
Jeffries, Harry 157, 162, 166
Jeffries, Jim 51, 62, 63, 64
Jemison (New Orleans player, 1926) 58
Jenkins, W. M. 83
Jiminez, Bienvenido 19
Joe Louis-Billy Conn fight 161
John Finner (Evansville pitcher, 1927) 73, 77
Johnson (Albany third baseman, 1926) 66
Johnson (Atlanta third baseman, 1946) 166
Johnson (Royal Ponciana Hotel club player, c. 1920) *53*
Johnson, "Bullet" 160
Johnson, Claude "Hooks" 90, 110, 127, 133
Johnson, Frank 110, 114, 115, 121, 122
Johnson, H. L. 189
Johnson, Oscar "Heavy" *130*
Johnson, P. 155
Johnson, Dr. R. L. 108
Johnson, T. J. 49
Johnson, Victor 174
Johnson, W. J. 51
Jones (Birmingham pitcher, 1934) 122
Jones (Monroe third baseman, 1934) 122
Jones, Dr. A. D. 60
Jones, Arthur "Mutt" 124
Jones, Casey 198
Jones, Ellis 181
Jones, Eugene "Lefty" 171, 173
Jones, Lucius "Melancholy" 4, 95, 116
Jones, Reuben 63, 99, 124, 127, 132, 133

Jones, Scipio A. 107
Jones, Slim 132
Jones Valley Elks Lodge 49
Joseph, W. L. 114, 115, 116
Junior Chamber of Commerce, Atlanta 95
Juran, Eli 27, 35, 36, 45
Juran, John "Bubber" 27, 32, 36, 38, 39, 44, 45, 48

Kansas City Monarchs 8, 46, 62, 76, 78, 82, 96, 102, 114, 117, 118, 122, 142, 143, 159, 180, 183
Keith Simmons Company 83
Kemp, James 143
Kemp, John 13, 23
Kendricks, Leonard 153
Kennedy (Montgomery first baseman, 1946) 166
Kennedy, J. R. 8
Kenney, R. C. 127
Kerr, A. J. 10
Key, Mayor James L. 116, 117
Key, Ludie 114
Kilgo, H. B. 168
Kincaide (Pittsburgh player, 1935) 132
Kincaide, C. J. 145, 147, 157, 167
Kincannon, Henry 132
King, Brennan L. 153, 157, 159, 171
King, C. B. 76
King, Early 183
Kizer (Nashville shortstop, 1949) 192
Knights of Peter Claver band 149
Knoxville City League 97
Knoxville College 9, 161
Knoxville Giants 9, 24, 82, 91, 96, 97, 156, 157, 159, 161, 164, 167
Knoxville Grays 145, 146–147, 149, 157
Knoxville Packers 200
Knoxville Tigers 197
Kranson, Arthur 122, 123
Kritzky, W. N. 49–50
Kuebler, Conrad 73

Labott (New Orleans player, 1934) 122
Lacey, Raymond 175
Ladies Day 55, 61, 79, 106, 107
Ladson, St. Julian 173
Lakeland Tigers 191
Lamar (Jacksonville infielder, 1946) 164
Lanoy, W. H. 114
Laurant, Milt 58, 93, 116, 121, 122, 132, 133
Lautier, Louis R. 8
Lawrence, George 155
Lawrence, Pete 38
Lawson, Babe 154
Lawson, George 163, 165, 166, 171
Lawson, George (band leader) 198
Lawson, "Lefty" 146

Index

Leland, Frank 8
Lewis (Memphis shortstop, 1933) 110
Lewis, "Chief" 10, *11*, 12, 20, 23, 32
Lewis, Clarence "Foots" 85
Lewis, Henry N. 145, 146, 153, 154
Lewis, Joe 147
Lewis, R. A. 41
Lewis, R. C. 56
Lewis, R. S. 44, 49–50
Lewis Athletic Park 54, 64, 69, 87
Lexington Hard Hitters 91, 96, 97
Lexington Hustler 189
Liggon, Rufus 122, 127
Lilly, John 58
Lincoln Giants 76
Little Masonic Temple building 137
Little Rock Black Travelers 82, 83, 85, 92, 96, 145, 150, 151, 152
Little Rock Grays 85, 91
Little Rock Stars 106, 110
Little Rock Travelers 147
Little Sam, "The Wonder Boy" 191
Lloyd, Eff 170
Lockwood, Bill 160
Lockyear (umpire, 1927) 74
London Creole Giants 7
Long, Ernest 160, 165, 171, 172
Longley, Waymon "Red" 122, 123, 127, 129, 132, 133
Looney, Mrs. C. C. 83
Louis, Joe 161, *198*
Louis Reichert construction company 67
Louisiana Stars 126
Louisville All-Stars 196
Louisville Black Caps 77, 80, 91, 92, 93
Louisville Black Colonels 156, 196
Louisville Black Sox 115
Louisville Caps 114, 118
Louisville Congo Zulu Giants 172–73
Louisville Giants 197
Louisville-Nashville Cubs 195, 197
Louisville Red Caps 97, 118
Louisville Red Sox 97
Louisville Stars (1922) 33
Louisville Stars (1951) 197
Louisville White Caps 80
Louisville White Sox 33, 82
Lovinggood, Buster 146
Lowe, William 51, 64, 87
Lutton, Commissioner Luther 94
Lyles, John "The Brute" *126*, 132
Lyons, Granville 87, 196
Lyons, Jimmie 73

Mack (Nashville infielder, 1927) 75
Macon White Sox 24
Madam Butler's Beauty Salon 169
Maddox, Forest (Wing) 2, 9, 12, 13, 15, 17, 25, 28, *29*, 35, 38, 39, 40, 45, 46, 51, 57, 72–3, 129
Madison Kernels 162
Malarcher, Dave 98
Mann, Earl 127, 129
Manning (Montgomery first baseman, 1931) 90
Manning, Felix 145–146, 153, 157, 158, 171
Maple Stars 161
Marcom (New Orleans player, 1934) 122
Marine, W. C. 40, 43
Markham, Willie 89
Marquez, Phil *11*
Martin, Dr. A. B. 114, 115
Martin, Dr. B. B. 24, 106, 114, 115, 119, 121, 125
Martin, Dr. B.M. 83
Martin, D. 99
Martin, Dr. J. B. 24, 44, 49, 106, 110, 114, 115, 118, 119, 121, 122, 125, 131, 135, 178, 179–80
Martin, Dr. M. S. 167, 171
Martin, Dr. R. B. 167
Martin, Dr. W. S. 114, 115, 122, 125, 127, 195, 196, 198
Martin Building 114, 12
Martin Park 106, 128, 131, 181, 182, 183, 197–98
Martinsville Black Cardinals 161
Mason, "Big" *14*, 17, 19, 23, 30, 31, 32, 36
Mason, Jim 110, 122, 123, 124
Matthews (New Orleans player, 1934) 122
Matthews, Clifford 145
Matthews, Dick 93–94
Maxwell, Jiggs 109, 113
Mays, Seth 183
Mays, W. H."Cat" 127, 134, 178, 182
Mays, Willie 1, 127, 134, 158, 178, 181, 182, 183, 185, 187, *187*
Mayweather, Eldridge "Head" 121, 122, 123
McAllister (Memphis infielder, 1933) 90, 110
McAllister, George 30, 36, 48, 63, 93, 122, 127, 133
McCarthy, C. H. 24
McClure, Will 157, 167
McComb, Mississippi, team 27
McCord, Butch 181
McCormick, C. B. "Bob" *14*, 25, 36
McCormick Field *146*, 164, 176
McCrary (Knoxville player, 1922) 39
McCrary, Fred D. 115
McCray, George E. 189
McCullough, A. M. 76
McDaniel, Hattie 166
McDonald (Albany pitcher, 1926) 62, 65
McDonald, Webster 154
McDonough, Louisiana, team 28
McDuffie, Terris 80
McFarland, John 79, 116
McGavock, Hub *14*, 30, 38
McGraw, Virgil 189
McHaskell, J. C. 59
McIntyre (Knoxville infielder, 1921) 28
McKibben, Sam 139
McKinnis, Gready 147
McNeal (McNeil) (Evansville player, 1927, 1929) 69, 77
McNeal (Montgomery outfielder, 1931) 88
McNeil, William 52
McQueen, Pete 127, 132, 133
Means, Lewis 136, 137
Meharry Medical School 191
Memphis Blues 167, 171, 181, 182, 183
Memphis Cardinals 181, 183, 187, 193
Memphis Giants 67
Memphis Red Caps 195, 197, 199
Memphis Red Sox 2, 21, 24, 43, 48, 51, 76, 82, 91, 92, 106, 110, 114, 115, 121, 122, 124, 127, 130, 132, 135, 139, 142, 143, 148, 167, 171, 179, 182, 197–98
Meneese, Ed 135
Meredith, Buford "Geechie" 12, 13, 25, 26, 36, 45, 48, 63, 83, 93
Mexico City Aztecas 99
Meyers (Nashville pitcher, 1920) 19
Meyers, George "Deacon" *14*, 23, 26, 31, 32
Miles (Knoxville third baseman, 1922) 39
Miller (Birmingham outfielder, 1922) 36, 39
Miller (Evansville infielder, 1929) 77
Miller (Knoxville infielder, 1921) 28
Miller, Bob 59
Miller, Charlie 122
Miller, Dempsey 89
Miller, "Dim" 96
Miller, Fred 149
Miller, J. W. 33, 35
Miller, Dr. L. O. 159
Miller, "Parson" 34, 37, 38, 40
Miller, Percy 112, 122
Millon, Herbert 165
Mills, Charles A. 73
Milton & Yost 61
Milwaukee Bears 46, 47
Mimms, Richard "Lefty" 154
Mirabel, Juanello 16, 23
Miro, Pedro 150, 151
Miss Atlanta 128
Miss Zona 118
Missouri Pacific Railroad 85
Mitchell, Alonzo "Fluke" 19, 133
Mitchell, James 153
Mitchell, Joe 63
Mitchell, Otto 69

Index

Mixon, Joey 183
Mobile Black Bears 145, 147, 149, 156, 160, 163, 167, 195, 199
Mobile Black Shippers 145, 147, 199
Mobile Braves 24
Mobile County Training School Band 149
Mobile-Detroit Shippers 191
Mobile Shippers 189, 190
Moffett, Lewis *11*, 20, 32, 35
Moffitt, Muff 116
Monroe, Al 98, 114, 142
Monroe Monarchs 89, 91, 92, 106, 107, 110, 114, 115, 124, 125, 131
Montalvo, Estaban 19
Montgomery, A. G. 49
Montgomery, J. S. 50
Montgomery, John 57
Montgomery Black Sox 24
Montgomery Dodgers 156, 159, 160, 161
Montgomery Giants 191, 197
Montgomery Grey Sox 10, *14*, 18, *18*, 19, 21, 24, 41, 43, 51, 54, 67, 80, 82, 91, 92, 99, 106, 110, 125, 135, 137, 167
Montgomery Greys 192, 193
Montgomery Homestead Grays 191
Montgomery Red Sox 156, 161, 162, 163
Montgomery Tigers 189, 190, 192, 195
Montgomery White Sox 24
Montreal Royals 147
Mooers Field 152
Moore, Bob *168*
Moore, "Bun" 16
Moore, C. L. 145, 152, 155, 157, 160, 164, 165, 166, 167, *168*, 178
Moore, Mrs. Dora 116
Moore, James "Red" 116, 133, 144, 153
Moore, King 180
Moore, Roy "Square" 34, 35, 44
Moore, William 121
Morehouse College 9, 51, 54, 128
Morgan, William "Sack" 166, 171
Morgan State College 180
Morney, Leroy 89, 102, 103, 133
Moro Castle Park 10
Morris, Andrew 29, 33, 37
Morris, Barney 94, 96, 101, 109, 112, 122
Morris, Jim 79
Morris Brown College 8, 51, 54, 116, 128, 137, 192
Mosely, Amos 178
Moss (Birmingham pitcher) 42
Moss, Jim Hugh 42
Moss, Jimmy *14*, 42
Moss, Porter 140
Moultrie (Negro Southeastern League team) 24
Muncie, Indiana 7
Murden, "Suggarty" 51, 59

Murdon (Murden) (Chattanooga shortstop, 1929) 77, 78
Murray, Cowboy 192
Murray, Robert 72
Muse, Clarence 166
Mussolini, Benito 144

Nail, C. W. 115
Nance, J. A. 83, 91, 97, 114
Nash (Birmingham pitcher, 1934) 122
Nash, George 129
Nashville All-Stars 196
Nashville Black Vols 135, 147, 152
Nashville Cubs 156, 160, 161, 163, 164, 167, 169, *169*, 170, *172*, 174, 175, 178, 180–11, 185, 190, 191, 192, 193, 194, 195, 199, 200
Nashville Elite Giants 2, 10, 24, 26, 43, 47, 48, 67, 76, 77, 80, 82, 88, 91, 92, 101, 105, 115, 122, 122, 169
Nashville Pythian Giants 26
Nashville Vols 10
Nashville White Sox 10, 24
Nashville YMCA 114
National Association 144
National Association for the Advancement of Colored People 180–81
National Baseball Hall of Fame and Museum 1, 2, 21, 45, 102
National Benefit Life Insurance Company 76
National Broadcasting System 101
Neal, Charlie 175
Neal, James 175
Neeley, A. C. 161, 162, 163, 165, *168*
Negro American Association 178, 185, 187, 199
Negro American Association All-Stars 185
Negro American League 2, 76, 141, 142, 144, 145, 149, 152, 156, 161, 164, 165, 167, 178, 179, 180, 182, 187, 189, 193, 195, 197
Negro Boy Scouts, Mobile 149
Negro Carolina League 168
Negro Chamber of Commerce, Atlanta 116
Negro Dixie Series 41, 62, 74–75, 84, 88–90, 101, 102, 111, 112
Negro Elks Club, Mobile 149
Negro Industrial School, Birmingham 137
Negro Leagues Researchers and Authors Group 2, 104
Negro National League 2, 7, 8, 46, 48, 49, 59, 62, 67, 69, 73, 76, 77, 80, 82, 91, 92, 94, 105, 106, 113, 114, 115, 117, 121, 130, 131, 133, 143, 144, 145, 147, 150, 156, 165, 167, 170, 187, 189, 195, 197
Negro National League All-Stars 122, 177

Negro Pacific Coast League 192
Negro Southeastern League 24, 41
Negro Southern Association 199
Negro Southern League All-Stars 100, 121, 155, 176, 197–98
Negro Texas League 111, 120, 188, 191
Negro Texas-Louisiana League 88, 92
Negro World Series 101, 102, 111, 112, 142, 195
Neil Park 98
Nelson (New Orleans catcher, 1923) 46
Nelson, Everett 90
Nesbitt (Nashville pitcher, 1921) 32, 38
Nesbitt, Dr. E. E. 80
Nesbitt, "Wild Bill" 26
New Orleans Black Pelicans 8, 10, 52, 64, 67, 77, 80, 82, 101, 111, 126–27, 151, 156, 195
New Orleans Black Sox 28
New Orleans Browns 11
New Orleans Caulfield Ads 5, 9, 10, *11*, 19, 24, 31, 33, 43, 46, 48, 52, 120
New Orleans Creoles 1, 156, 167, 171, 176–177, 178, 180, 181, 183, 185, 187, 188, 191, 192, 196, 197, 198, 199
New Orleans Crescent Stars 10, 34, 41, 106, 111, 114, 115, 116, 118, *119*, 120, 121, 125, 127
New Orleans Eagles 200
New Orleans Giants 47
New Orleans Pelicans 9, 112
New York Black Yankees 16, 101, 142, 155, 157, 162, 187
New York Bushwicks 175
New York Cubans 150, 155, 162, 175
New York Giants 162
New York Lincoln Giants 16
New York Mets 175
New York-Pennsylvania League 73
Newark Eagles 142, 143, 162, 177, 187
Newberry, Jim 144
Newman, Zipp 16
Newsome, Isaiah 182
Newton, Charles 118
Newton, J. A. 33, 37
Newton Park and Community Center 138
Nicklin, Strang 37
Noel, Eddie 26, 31, 32, 34, 37, 40, 52, 55, 65, 79
Norfolk Eagles 152
Norman (Knoxville infielder, 1921) 28
Norman, Garrett 46
North Carolina A&T College 153
North Decatur Street Park 137
North Maryville, Tennessee 97
North-South All-Star Game 122, 131–133, 143, 154–55

Index

Nunley, Beauford 122, 127
Nyassas 173

Oden, Webb 63
Ohio-Indiana League *190*
Ohio-Michigan Negro League 191
Oklahoma Indians 79
Old Gold Cigarettes 181
Olive, Benjamin 122
Oliver (Birmingham player, 1934) 122
Oliver, Martin 93
O'Neil, Buck 144
O'Neill, Charles 19
Only the Ball Was White 2
Opening Day ceremonies 10, 11, 25, 44, 54–55, 69, 78, 80, 83, 93, 94, 95, 107–08, 127, 128, 137–38, 145, 147, 148–149, 159, 160, 168–69, 180–181, 183, 196
Optimist Park 196
Organized Baseball 1, 179–180, 185, 189
Original Zulu Giants 192
Osborne, Coleman 42
Owens, Aubrey 32
Owens, DeWitt 63
Owens, "Dusty" 163
Owens, Jesse 162
Owens, Judge 155
Owens, Nathan 155
Owens, Sylvester 127, 130
Owensboro Boy Scouts 196
Owensboro Braves 196

Pacific Coast League 45
Page, Allen 126, 145, 167, 172, 178, 179, 180, 185, 189, 199
Page, Ted 1, 103
Page Fence Giants 7
Page Hotel 114
Paige, Leroy "Satchel" 1, 4, 51, *51*, 55, 61, 67, 70, 102, 103, 123, 124, 174, 178, 189, 197
Paige's All-Stars 174
Palm, Clarence 133
Paradise Ballroom 169
Parker (Montgomery pitcher, 1921) 30
Parker, "Big Train" 116
Parker, Tom 122, 133
Parker, W. 69
Parks, John 116
Parks, Sam 145, 147, 151
Parkway Field *172*, *184*
Parnell, Roy "Red" 52, *52*, 55, 56, 57, 58, 65, 89, 93, 94, 95, 104, 112, 113, 116, 118, 121, 122, 133
Paseo YMCA 8
Patterson (Dallas pitcher, 1927) 75
Patterson, J. L. 120
Patton (Montgomery assistant manager, 1920) *14*
Patton (umpire, 1946) 164
Pearl Harbor 144
Pelican Stadium 176, 177, 180, 185

Pendleton, James 178, *179*
Pennell, Burgin 168
Pennell, George 159
Penner, R. H. 135
Pensacola Colored Giants 43
Pensacola Giants 10, 24
Pensacola Pepsi-Cola Giants 10
Pensacola Sea Gulls 189, 191, 195
Pensacola Stars 43
Peppers (Philadelphia player, 1935) 133
Perdue, Frank M. 8, 9, 10, 19, 22, 25, 31, 33, 45, 115, 117
Perez (Birmingham infielder, 1920) 19
Perkins (umpire, 1920) 19
Perkins, Bill 61, 115, 117, 124, 132, 144, 145, 147
Perkins, Dr. C. F. 183
Perkins, Miss Freddie 128
Perry (Chattanooga pitcher, 1946) 166
Perry, Alonzo 154, 157, 159
Perry Stadium 94, 99, 105
Peterson (Memphis pitcher, 1933) 110
Peterson, Harvey 117, 122
Peterson, Robert W. 2
Philadelphia Hilldale Giants 154
Philadelphia Stars 132, 133, 142, 157, 175
Phillips, Dewey 198
Phillips, "Hooty" 34, 36, 39
Phillips, Vernon "Butch" 160, 161, 165, *168*
Pickens (Gadsden pitcher, 1921) 26
Pickett Springs 55
Pigler (Montgomery vice president, 1920) *14*
Pine Bluff Black Cats 156
Pine Bluff Boosters 111
Pinkston, Alfred 196
Pipkin, Robert "Black Diamond" 89, 122
Pittman, New Jersey, white team 162
Pittsburgh Crawfords 16, 92, 101, 102, 105, 113, 115, 117, 122, 131–32, 133, 142, 144, 154, 164
Place Grill 168
Platt, B. 26, 32, 34
Playoffs (league) 30–31, 62–64, 88, 131, 176–77; squabbling, rowdiness 19, 39, 63, 64–5, 72, 74, 84, 92, 95, 96, 97, 98, 106, 119, 149, 164; transportation 52, 54, 55, 60, 73, 78, 85, 88, 93, 108, 116, 118, 122, 127, 163, 175, 185, 197; umpire problems 18–19, 38, 64–5, 68, 74
Poindexter, Robert 51, 58, 62, 63, 64, 65, 127
Polo Grounds 162, 173, 175
Ponce de Leon Park 8, 95, 116, 129, 136, 138, 139, 148, 150, 152, 153, 154, 165, 169, 175, 181, 185, 188, 191, 192, 197

Porter, Andrew "Pullman" *92*, 93, 122, 123
Posey, Jeff 127
Powell, Bill 163
Powell, Elvin 90
Powell, Melvin 103
Powell, William 103
Pratt City 27
Preston (Montgomery player, 1920) *14*, 18
Price, J. 155
Pritchett (Evansville player, 1929) 77, 78
Providence Grays 7
Pryor (Memphis pitcher, 1927) 69
Puerto Rican Winter League 185
Purvis (Memphis outfielder, 1931) 90
Pythian Temple, Birmingham 40

Qualls, Sam W. 76, 128

Radcliffe, Ted "Double Duty" 61, *69*, 69–70
Ragsdale, Mayor L. N. 80
Rainbow Division 5
Raleigh Grays 168, 178
Raleigh Tigers 167, 172, 176, 199
Ralton, Frank 107
Ramsey (Chattanooga pitcher, 1948) 187
Ray (Jacksonville shortstop, 1946) 166
Ray, Johnny 34
Rayville, Louisiana, team 94
Redding (Albany pitcher, 1926) 65
Reese, Jim 139
Reeves, A. G. 41
Reeves, Donald 129, 133
Reichert, Louis 67, 74
Reichert, Manson L. 67, 74
Rhodes, Claude "Schoolboy" 85, 87, 143
Richardson (Knoxville pitcher, 1951) 200
Richardson, Jesse 191, 197
Richardson, Johnnie 174
Richardson, Johnny 163
Richmond Cardinals 151–152
Richmond Giants 150
Richmond Tigers *190*
Rickey, Branch 154, 164
Rickwood Field 5, 8, 9, 29, 49–50, 58, 106, 117, 122, 127, 143, 155, 163, 164
Ridley, Jack 75
Riesener, Bob 3
Riley (Louisville pitcher, 1922) 34
Ritz Restaurant 169
Rivers, Ed "Betson" 138, 140, 143
Robe, Billy 191, 192
Roberson (New Orleans player, 1920) *11*
Roberts, Ric 128–129, 132, 136, 138, 139
Robinson (New Orleans player, 1926) 66

Index

Robinson (Royal Ponciana Hotel club player, c. 1920) 53
Robinson, Billy 166
Robinson, Frazier 166
Robinson, Jackie 1, 91, 147, 149, 161, 179–80, 189
Robinson, Sheriff Garner 183
Robinson, William "Bobby" 147
Rockport, Indiana 196
Roddy, Bert M. 49, 54, 56
Roddy, Cashier 41
Roddy, S. R. 38, 57
Rodgers (Chicago outfielder, 1935) 133
Rodriguez, Conrado "Red" 19, 23
Rogan, Wilbur "Bullet" 118
Rogers (Knoxville pitcher, 1922) 38, 39
Rogers, William "Nat" 103, 132, 157, 159, 160
Roggan (Jacksonville pitcher, 1946) 166
Rosella, M. 19
Ross (Albany outfielder, 1926) 66
Roth, Herman "Bobby" *11*, 23
Roussell (New Orleans outfielder, 1923) 46
Roussell (New Orleans outfielder, 1926) 58
Rowe (New Orleans pitcher, 1926) 65
Rowe, "School Boy" 166
Rowell Field 83
Royal Ponciana Hotel team 53
Rubber (umpire, 1922) 39
Rudolph *see* Ash, Rudolph
Runyon, Damon 70
Rush, Joe 43, 45, 46, 49
Russell, Frank 155, 176
Russell, J. H. 30
Russell, T. 46, 48

SABR Negro Leagues Committee 2
Sadler, John 154, 157, 159
St. Louis Browns 2
St. Louis Giants 8, 73
St. Louis Stars 40, 46, 59, 73, 76, 82, 117, 142, 144, 147
Salazar, Santiago 150
Sallee, "Slim" 30, 31, 32
Salmon, Harry "Fish" 19, 27, 35, 45, 48, 58, 62, 63, 64, 65, 83, 84, 88, 90, 93
Sampson (Knoxville pitcher, 1921, 1922) 28, 32, 40
Sampson, Tommy 144, 178, 181, 183
San Francisco Sea Lions 192
San Juan Stars 185
Sanders (Memphis player, 1934) 122
Sanders, Jess 169
Saperstein, Abe 142
Saucier, Sidney 150, 151
Saunders, Bob 101
Savannah, Negro Southeastern League team 24

Savannah Tigers 197
Saylor, Alfred *126*
Scales, Bennie 135
Scales, George "Tubby" *14*, 16, *17*, 25
Schaine, Mike 143
Schell, Barbara 128
Schorling's Park 30
Scott (Evansville first baseman, 1929) 77
Scott, A. F. 115, 119
Scott, Joe 104
Scott, Willie Lee 94
Scott Newspaper Syndicate 139
Seals, Sam 171
Segula, Percy *see* Wilson, Percy "Segula"
Senate Avenue Branch YMCA 142
Sharp, L. C. 56
Shaw, Bishop B. G. 54, 127
Shaw, W. J. 8, 9, 25
Shepherd, Beck 178, 182, 189
Sheppard, Freddie 146, 170, 171, 181
Shreveport Cubs 106, 107, 110
Shreveport Sports 74
Shreveport Tigers 167
Sias (Chicago player, 1933) 113
Sias (New Orleans player, 1934) 122
Silvers, Sylvester "Pie" 146, 149, 160, 163, 165, 187
Simon, Sylvester 73–74
Simpson (Chattanooga pitcher, 1936) 138
Simpson, Harry "Suitcase" 149
Sims (Monroe outfielder, 1934) 122
Sims, F. 107
Sims, Fred 163
Sims, Jay 151
Sioux City Ghosts 124
Slaughter, Dave 189
Sleight, Gilbert 168
Sloan, Bob 88, 89
Slow's Recreation and Billiard Parlor 168
Smiley (Evansville pitcher, 1929) 78
Smith (Atlanta player, 1935) 129
Smith (Claybrook third baseman, 1935) 133
Smith (Knoxville outfielder, 1920) 23
Smith (Memphis player, 1935) 132
Smith, C. 122
Smith, Clarence 51, 58, 63, 64
Smith, H. H. M. 137
Smith, Hilton 1, 101, 102, *102*, 112
Smith, Hulan "Mule" 143
Smith, James H. 53
Smith, Joel W. 152–153, 157, 162, 163, 169, 170–71, 180–81
Smith, Milton "Mighty Blood" 117
Smith, Morris 112

Smith, "Pitcheye" 143
Smith, Robert 121, 122, 123
Smith, Taylor 187
Smith, Teddy 132
Smith, Thelma 137
Smith, Theolic "Fireball" *126*, 131
Smith, Tiny 137
Smith, Tuker 117
Smithson, W. M. 98
Snow, Felton 122, 132, 175, 193
Society for American Baseball Research 2
Solvent Savings Bank 41, 49
South Alabama Negro League 191
Southeastern League 60, 191
Southern All-Star team 162
Southern Association 2, 7, 8, 9, 74, 84, 112, 147, 199
Southern League 7
Southern League of Colored Baseballists 7
Southern Newspaper Syndicate 145, 146, 148
South's Selected All-Stars 163
Southside Park 10, 11
Southwestern Colored League 34
Spartanburg Sluggers 160, 176
Spearman, William 75
Spiller Park 54–55, 60, 78
Spiller, R. J. 78
Spratt, Adolph 72
Stamps, Hulan 51, 65
Staples, John 18, *20*, 26, 30
Staples, T. J. 33
Starling, Earl A. 169
Start, Joe 7
Statham, Cliff 176
Stearns, Norman "Turkey" 1, 21, *21*, 23, 25, 30, 35, 48, 103, 112, 123, 131
Stephens-Lee High School band 168
Stewart, George S. 50
Stewart, Kenneth 191
Stockham team 127
Stone, Toni 1, 191, 196, *198*, 198
Stovall, Fred 92, 93, 102
Stovey, George 7
Stratton, Leroy 26, 33, 34, 36, 40, 52, 71, 75, 79, 83, 89
Strawbridge, H. 80
Streeter, Sam *14*, 15, 16, 17, 23, 32
Stuart, Kenneth 189
Sulphur Dell Park 10, 33, 50, 84, 88, 103, 122, 140, 153, 165, 174, 176, 183, 193, 200
Sunshine Babies 78
Suttles (Settles), J. T. 43, 46, 48
Suttles, George "Mule" 1, 36, 45, 48, 112, *120*, 122, 131

Tabor, R.H. 9, 25
Talley, Sterling 163, 166, 171, 181, 182
Tally (Pensacola pitcher, 1920) 13, 23

Index

Tate, Roosevelt "Bill" *126*, 132
Tatlor, Ben 164
Taylor, C. I. 9, 10
Taylor, "Candy Jim" 92, 94, 115, 132
Taylor, Herman 160–161, 162, 163, 166, *168*
Taylor, Mathews 5, 12
Taylor, Olan "Jelly" 144
Tell City team 80
10th Cavalry Regiment 35
Terrell, S. M. 92
Terrell, Willie Marvin 173
Terry, "Babe" 69
Texas All-Stars 31
Texas All-Stars (1934) 121
Texas League 3, 74
Texas-Louisiana League 80, 81, 82, 84
Texas-Oklahoma-Louisiana League 76, 79
Thomas, Frank *see* Thompson, Frank
Thomas, J. 104
Thomasville Giants 24, 31
Thompson, Clifford 42
Thompson, Eula 42
Thompson, Frank "Groundhog" 148
Thompson, Hank 144
Thompson, James "Sandy" 126
Thompson, Dr. O. M. 8
Thompson, Sammy "Runt" 127
Thompson, Will 153, 164, 173
Thornton, Jack 143
Threakill, Clarence 90
Three-Eye League All-Stars 73
Three-I League 2, 73
Tiant, Luis 123
Tiptonville Tigers 183
Toledo Crawfords 144
Toledo Tigers 46
Trammell, Nat 63, 64, 80
Travelers Field 147
Tremholm, Harper C. 83
Trent, Ted 73–74
Tri-State League (1935) 126
Tri-State League (1948) 181, 183
Trouppe, Quincy 178
Tubbs, "Black Babe Ruth" 36
Turgison (Gadsden pitcher, 1949) 192
Turner, Addeerly 166
Turner, Joe 106
Tuskegee Army Air Field Warhawks 154
Tuskegee Institute 19
25th Infantry team 35, 173
24th Infantry team 43, 64, 76, 80, 173
Tyler, John 27
Tyler, William "Steel Arm" 56, 59, 62, 63, 65

United Negro College Fund 161
United States Baseball League 154–55, 164
Unity Insurance Company 40
Universal Life 122
University of Leon 191

Vance, Columbus 80, 122, 123
Van Dyke Colored House of David 127
Vaughn, Joe 82
Veale, Robert, Sr. 83
Veeck, Bill 107
Vero Beach Pelicans 152
Vincennes, Indiana 71

Walden, Col. A. T. 116
Walker, Alfreda "Freddo" 137
Walker, Andrew M. 135, 137, 142
Walker, Charles 119
Walker, J. C. 76
Walker, Moses Fleetwood 7
Walker, Weldy 7
Walls, Greeney 44, 121
Ward, C. "Pinky" 51, 55, 59
Ward, "Wu Fang" 124
Warner, Jack 73–74
Warren (Knoxville pitcher, 1922) 40
Warren, Jesse 182
Washington (Jacksonville outfielder, 1946) 163
Washington, Peter 51
Washington Black Senators 143
Washington Black Yankees 157
Washington Elite Giants 142
Watson, A. 36, 38
Watson, Amos 187
Watson, Tom 36
Waverly, Tennessee team 196
WEAS radio station 180–181
Welch, Winfield *11*, 162
Wellmaker, Roy "Snook" 136, 138, 139, 140, 144
Wells, Willie 73, 122, 132
Wesley, Charles "Two-Sides" *14*, 16, 23, 45, 48, 51, 63, 82
Wesley, Edgar 48
West (Nashville player, 1935) 132, 133
West, Billy 50
West, Jim 93, 96, 122
West, Sammy 58
West Palm Beach Rockets 189
West Tennessee Valley Lodge No. 1152 160
Westmoreland (Nashville catcher, 1926) 61
W. H. Avery Shooting Gallery 169
Whatley, David 140, 144
Whatley, John 157, 159
WHBQ radio station 198
White (Montgomery pitcher, 1931) 88
White, Clarence 65
White, Dr. *168*
White, J. W. 8
White, Ladd 183
White, William Edward 7
White patronage 8–9, 25, 47, 61, 65, 87, 93, 95, 98, 107, 108, 112, 116, 127, 159, 168, 193
Wichita, Kansas, baseball tournament 131
Wiggins, Joe 96
Wilder, W. A. "Pete" 178
Wiley, Joe 150
Wilkes, Jimmy 177
Wilkes, Ulysses 163, 165, 166, 171
Wilkinson, J. L. 114, 142
Williams (Atlanta player, 1926) 64
Williams (Montgomery outfielder) 166
Williams (Thomasville pitcher, 1921) 31
Williams, Bo 133
Williams, C. 166
Williams, Carl 149
Williams, Chester 132
Williams, Elbert 93, 94, 95, 101, 102, 108, 109, 112, 113, 122, 133
Williams, Ennis 146, 163, 171
Williams, Fendall 80
Williams, Georgia Mae 1, 152
Williams, Godfrey 8
Williams, Harry 171
Williams, Jim 167
Williams, "Lefty" 78
Williams, Percy 136, 143
Williams, Poindexter *14*, 23, 45, 48, 51, 63, 64, 82, 93, 117, 127
Williams, T. 155
Williams, Thomas 166
Williams, Vinicius "Nish" 51, 59, 79, 122, 197, 198
Willis, Jim "Smokey" 58, 59, 63, 64, 78, 79, 83, 88, 103, 112, 122, 123
Wilson, Artie 144, 163
Wilson, Dan *126*
Wilson, Emmett *126*
Wilson, Fabiola 1, *184*, 185
Wilson, J. W. 107
Wilson, Percy "Segula" *11*, 12, 20, 23, 26
Wilson, T. T. 115
Wilson, Thomas T. 10, 26, 33, 35, 38, 52, 80, 82, 87, 88, 89, 101, 103, 105, 114, 115, 132, 135, 143, 148, 165–166, 167, 170, 172, 178
Wilson Park 88, 135
Wilson's Barber Shop 168
Wingfield, David 20
Wingo, "Doc" 150
Winston, Charles *53*
Winston-Salem Grays 156
Winston-Salem Pond Giants 163
Winters, Clarence 107
Wissell, Leo *190*
Woods, Parnell 183
Workman, Dr. L. D. 54
World War I 9, 191
World War II 1, 2, 141, 144, 145, 149, 174, 183
"World's Pecan Center" 60
Worthy, Fred 159, 161, *168*

Wright (Nashville player, 1935) 133
Wright, George *53*
Wright, Henry "Red" 78, 88–89, 122
Wright, Maceo 139
Wright, Zollie 89, 102, 116, 121, 122
Wyatt, Bud 166
Wyatt, Leon 166, 171, 173

Wyrick, Silas 167
Yancey, Bill "Skipper" 157
Yankee Stadium 162
Young (Birmingham pitcher, 1922) 34, 37
Young (Nashville pitcher, 1922) 38
Young, Ernest 171
Young, "Slow Time" 140

Young, Frank 30
Young, Monroe D. 8, 22
Young, William 114
Young, Willie 174, 183, 187–88, 193

Zaharias, Didrikson, Babe 124
Zapp, James 191
Zeigler, Gordon 15, 16, 19, 26, 48
Zulu Giants 193

www.ingramcontent.com/pod-product-compliance
Lightning Source LLC
Chambersburg PA
CBHW081546300426
44116CB00015B/2777